Between States and Markets

Between States and Markets

THE VOLUNTARY SECTOR IN COMPARATIVE PERSPECTIVE

Robert Wuthnow, Editor

CONTRIBUTORS

Helmut K. Anheier	*James A. Beckford*
John Boli	*Helen Hardacre*
Eliezer D. Jaffe	*Michèle Lamont*
Ted Perlmutter	*Jack Veugelers*
David Harrington Watt	*Robert Wuthnow*

PRINCETON UNIVERSITY PRESS

PRINCETON, NEW JERSEY

Copyright © 1991 by Princeton University Press
Published by Princeton University Press, 41 William Street,
Princeton, New Jersey 08540
In the United Kingdom: Princeton University Press, Oxford

Library of Congress Cataloging-in-Publication Data

Between states and markets : the voluntary sector in comparative perspective /
Robert Wuthnow, editor : contributors, James A. Beckford . . . [et al.].
p. cm.
Includes index.
1. Voluntarism—Congresses. 2. Associations, institutions, etc.—Congresses.
3. Corporations, Nonprofit—Congresses. 4. Social ethics—Congresses.
I. Wuthnow, Robert. II. Beckford, James A.
HN49.V64B48 1991
302'.14—dc20 91-11510 CIP

ISBN 0-691-09462-4 (alk. paper) — ISBN 0-691-02861-3
(pbk. : alk. paper)

Publication of this book has been aided by a grant from the
Lilly Endowment

This book has been composed in Linotron Times Roman

Princeton University Press books are printed on acid-free paper,
and meet the guidelines for permanence and durability of the
Committee on Production Guidelines for Book Longevity of the
Council on Library Resources

Printed in the United States of America

10 9 8 7 6 5 4 3 2 1
10 9 8 7 6 5 4 3 2 1
(Pbk.)

Contents

Acknowledgments

THIS VOLUME was made possible by a generous grant from the Lilly Endowment. We wish to thank Robert Wood Lynn, then Vice President for Religion at the Lilly Endowment, for his encouragement in initiating the project, and Craig Dykstra, his successor, for his continuing support. The grant made it possible to bring a group of scholars together at Princeton University in 1987 to discuss the theoretical issues that might be addressed in a comparative study of states, markets, and the voluntary sector. Participating in that conference were Jeffrey Alexander, Randall Collins, James Douglas, Paul DiMaggio, Lester Kurtz, Jane Mansbridge, John Meyer, and Paul Starr. A second conference was held in 1988 to identify the particular countries on which the volume would focus and to sketch the main issues to be addressed for each country. In addition to the present contributors, this conference was attended by Edward Freeland, Virginia Hodgkinson, Estelle James, Robert Liebman, Richard Rogers, John Sutton, John F. Wilson, and Julian Wolpert. David Jacobson and Kevin Hartzell helped us put together a preliminary bibliography, and Clara Kim compiled an array of statistics. Jack Veugelers and Michèle Lamont wish to thank Martine Barthélemy, Frank Dobbin, Benjamin Gregg, Jean Leca, Wolfgang Seibel, and Robert Wuthnow for their helpful suggestions. Jack Veugelers acknowledges the assistance of the Social Sciences and Humanities Research Council of Canada. We are also grateful to the Lilly Endowment for making it possible for each of the authors to spend a period of time in the country he or she studied, collecting materials not available in the United States. Dick Boscarino provided the drawings that appear in chapter 1. Jane Lincoln Taylor copyedited the manuscript. We also wish to thank Gail Ullman and Walter Lippincott at Princeton University Press for their cooperation and personal interest in the project.

Between States and Markets

The Voluntary Sector: Legacy of the Past, Hope for the Future?

Robert Wuthnow

ON HIS VISIT to the United States in the 1830s, Alexis de Tocqueville ([1835] 1945) noted with special interest the prominent place of voluntary associations in American society. Impressed by their diversity and the seriousness with which their members took them, he returned repeatedly in his journals to the subject of churches, community groups, fraternal associations, and civil organizations. Americans, he wrote, did for themselves through these voluntary efforts what people in other societies expected governments and elites to do for them. When some tragedy befell them, or when some project needed to be organized, people simply banded together to get the job done. The result, he felt, was a stronger, more vibrant democratic society.

Generations of scholars have followed Tocqueville in emphasizing the importance of the voluntary sector. Taking their cue from Tocqueville's interest in the sources of American democracy, many have stressed the connection between voluntary associations and political participation, arguing that the voluntary sector helps mobilize an informed electorate. Others have paid heed to Tocqueville's warning that needs unmet by voluntary efforts provide an excuse for government to intervene, and with intervention comes control, and with control comes totalitarianism.[1]

But Tocqueville was interested in voluntary associations for more reasons than simply their role in augmenting and restricting the political system. Whether or not voluntary associations mediated in some way between the average citizen and the government, they were important to society in their own right. They were important, above all, because they expressed the nation's values; in expressing these values, they sustained them and permitted them to be examined, reshaped, and applied. The nation's religious organizations provided both a crucible in which spiritual convictions could be tested and a public witness to the nation's spiritual values. By supplying assistance to the disadvantaged, voluntary organizations dramatized to the entire community that caring and helping were values worthy of public attention. The numerous fra-

---

[1] For some of the arguments inspired by Tocqueville about the relations among voluntary associations, political participation, and democracy, see Olson (1972), Hansen et al. (1976), Shapiro (1983), Poulantzas (1978), Carnoy (1984:112–21), Bellah et al. (1985:221).

ternal associations, guilds, and self-help groups, Tocqueville argued, sustained not only the stated objectives of those groups but also reinforced the value of community itself and, within each community, the diversity of individual talents and interests. In short, Tocqueville recognized that voluntary associations make an important contribution to the *cultural health* of a nation.

Tocqueville's method was observational, interpretive, impressionistic. Like many of his contemporaries he was intrigued with the new nation that had arisen on the western shores of the Atlantic, wondering if this brave experiment would contribute a brighter vision of modern civilization or if its institutions were in some way fundamentally flawed. Although his method was not systematically comparative in the same sense that cross-national studies have since tried to be, it was rooted in the implicit comparisons he was able to make between the United States and the European societies with which he was most familiar, principally France. These implicit comparisons strengthened his analysis by focusing his attention on large societal questions and by providing him with fresh insights about the peculiarities of the American experience. They were also in many respects problematic and have remained a perplexing feature of our understanding of the ways in which our nation's history is different from—or similar to—that of other nations in the Western world.

More than a century and a half after Tocqueville's visit, the questions he raised about the social role of voluntary associations remain as timely and as problematic as ever. In recent years growing attention has been paid to the voluntary sector as a result of fiscal crises in government budgets, which have forced an increasing share of the burden for social-welfare services to be shifted to this sector. But, in keeping with the short-term, service-oriented nature of this demand, much of the resulting scholarship has been preoccupied with the managerial and administrative questions of fund-raising, recruitment of volunteers, coordination of efforts among nonprofit agencies, relations with government programs, and the like. On a somewhat broader level, social commentators and politicians still, for the most part, espouse the Tocquevillean conviction that voluntary efforts contribute vitally to the health of American society. Whether this contribution is indeed a distinctly American characteristic, or whether the role of voluntary associations is similar in other societies, however, are questions for which little evidence has been available.

Most at issue is the question of whether voluntarism itself is viable. The demand for voluntary services is great. But on every side rules and regulations, constraints and competitors impinge on the functioning of these agencies. Market forces make it hard for people to give time and money to voluntary organizations, and these forces increasingly try to draw profitable services into the orbit of the market economy. Government agencies and political parties expand continuously, leaving less and less room for voluntary initiatives to play a truly independent role. In many cases the social needs of the disadvantaged are met—up to a point. But the cultural costs remain uncalculated. How, Tocqueville would ask, can the virtues of individual freedom, of community responsibility, of compassion, of altruism, be maintained against the growing influence of market-oriented efficiency and state-oriented bureaucracy?

In the chapters that follow, descriptions of the voluntary sector in the United States and in other advanced democratic societies—including a discussion of how the voluntary sector has been affected by changes in the state and the marketplace, where religious activities fit into the broader range of voluntary associations, and how these associations have contributed to the expression of public values—are presented. Our intent is to provide both a descriptive overview of the way in which the voluntary sector is constructed in the various societies and a basis for addressing the comparative questions that have been present in discussions of voluntary associations since Tocqueville, particularly the question of whether a strong, independent voluntary sector is a necessary component of a vibrant public sphere in which collective values can be articulated. To that end, we have examined a similar array of issues in each of the substantive chapters, paying special attention to common patterns of development in the state and the marketplace that may be altering the quality of public discourse, but also emphasizing the distinctive characteristics of each society—features that indeed raise questions about the applicability of Tocqueville's framework itself. In the concluding chapter we draw these observations together in order to consider the role of the voluntary sector in advanced industrial societies generally and, with added perspective, the special role this sector appears to play in the United States. Before turning to these discussions, though, there are a number of conceptual issues (as even these brief remarks make evident) that must be addressed.

THE THREE-SECTOR MODEL

Implicit in Tocqueville's discussion is the idea that society can be divided into various zones or regions of activity—what will here be called sectors. In contrasting the activities of government with the voluntary efforts of its citizens, Tocqueville is invoking a crude distinction between two such sectors. Elsewhere in his discussion of American society he draws an additional distinction between those activities done without respect for remuneration or compensation and those performed in the context of economic relationships. Thus there is at least the rough outline of a three-sector model, the components of which are the voluntary sector, the state, and the market (see fig. 1).

How, more precisely, are the three sectors distinguished from one another? In the most general terms (which will be useful here because of the substantive differences among the societies to be considered), the state can be defined as the range of activities organized and legitimated by formalized (and in modern societies, centrally coordinated) coercive powers; and the market, as the range

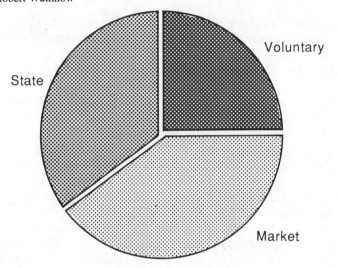

Figure 1.1 Three-Sector Model

of activities involving the exchange of goods and services for profit, based on a pricing mechanism linked to relative levels of supply and demand.[2]

Seen in this way, the state is more than simply a body of elected officials or the agencies through which these officials govern. It is also distinguished less by the actual presence of coercion than by the fact that it reserves for itself the right to enforce compliance. Behind any directive of the state lies the compulsory authority of the courts, police, jails, and the military. Even when this authority is delegated or applied to other spheres of action—for example, when business become the agents of the state in collecting sales taxes—it is still the state's monopoly over the right of coercion that is at work. Organizations whose primary objective is to gain access to the coercive powers of the state—namely, political parties—must also be included within this broad sectoral definition of the state.

The market, in comparison, operates on a principle of noncoercion. Customers are not compelled to buy from a particular vendor under free-market conditions. Transactions are instead based on a pricing mechanism that presumably allows parties to estimate the relative utilities of various options. (In

[2] I emphasize "formal" and "central" as characteristics of the *modern* state that while not always present, help distinguish the state from other authorities that may resort to coercion; for example, a parent might "coerce" a child to clean his or her room, but this authority is not formalized in any legal or constitutional document or part of the hierarchy of central administration in a society. Were the parent's action challenged in court, however, the court's action in ruling for the parent or the child—even if decided by common law—would represent an application of the formal and central powers of coercion held by the state.

modern societies these estimates are generally based on monetary calculations.) An orientation toward profitability is generally present as well, and this orientation often provides a basis for distinguishing between for-profit and nonprofit organizations, because the former are expected to distribute surplus revenues among owners, while the latter are legally prevented from doing so. The more important feature of the market sector, however, is the price-supply-demand mechanism itself—meaning that markets are not simply an accretion of the profit motives of individual entrepreneurs, but complex systems that regulate the pricing and exchange of goods and services.

The voluntary sector—or "third" sector—can thus be defined residually as those activities in which neither formal coercion nor the profit-oriented exchange of goods and services is the dominant principle. Framed less negatively, the voluntary sector consists of activities that are indeed voluntary in the dual sense of being free of coercion and being free of the economic constraints of profitability and the distribution of profits.

It should be evident that this way of conceptualizing sectors corresponds roughly with distinctions that are common in American law and in the activities of organizations. For example, the various bureaus, agencies, and activities of which the state consists are mandated by law, do not operate to produce profits, and can generally engage in a variety of coercive activities, ranging from military conscription to taxation to the issuance of subpoenas. For-profit firms, in contrast, are prohibited from engaging in the same kinds of coercive practices, hold certain immunities from government interference, and operate only as long as these firms are able to compete successfully in the marketplace. Nonprofit organizations and other, more informal voluntary associations often enjoy a special legal status, are prohibited from coercing their members to provide donations of time or energy against their will, and do not attempt to sell goods or services in the marketplace.[3]

At the same time, it should be clear that the three-sector model draws attention to a somewhat different set of issues and distinctions than those on which many other conceptions of modern society have been based, and it will be helpful in thinking about sectors if these differences are kept clearly in mind. In the social sciences, for example, it has been particularly common to distinguish the basic elements of societies in terms of major functions and the dominant institutions attending to these functions: the polity thus becomes an institutional domain concerned with setting the overall goals or policies for a society; the economy, an institutional realm oriented toward adapting social relations to the physical environment; the family, an institution concerned with nurturing children, passing along basic values, and providing for inti-

[3] The idea that voluntary associations compose a special realm—also sometimes referred to as an "independent sector" or "third sector"—has become well established, especially in literature on the United States, but also in some comparative studies. See, for example, Sumariwalla (1983), Kramer (1984), Gamwell (1984), and Van Til (1988).

macy and community; and so on. Other institutions sometimes regarded as having sufficiently distinct purposes to be distinguished from others include religion, education, health, communications, and entertainment.[4] The sectoral model, by contrast, recognizes that these various functions may well be provided by organizations in several different sectors. In the United States, for instance, education is provided partly by the governmental sector and partly by the voluntary sector. Religious organizations in the United States fall within the voluntary sector because of the constitutional separation between church and state, whereas in other societies (Great Britain, for instance) the existence of a state church places much of the religious function within the governmental sector. By implication, then, the use of a sectoral model suggests that it makes a difference not only that a function such as religion or health or education is provided but also *how* (in which sector) that function is provided. The difference it makes may have more to do with the values that are expressed and dramatized than with the services actually rendered.

A different way of conceiving of social activities that has become prominent in many recent discussions—and that overlaps with some of the present concerns—emphasizes the distinction between public and private. In this conception, "public" usually corresponds loosely to activities performed by government or at public expense, and "private" refers to those activities not performed at public expense but voluntarily or for profit by individuals or organizations. This distinction also has other connotations, of course, as when we say that someone appeared in public or that people keep their private lives shielded from public view. We shall find it necessary on occasion to resort to this language, but in general we will try to avoid using the terms "public" and "private" in this way because "private" then refers both to the market and to the voluntary sectors.

Depending on the nature of the task at hand, there is value to these alternative conceptions. But for present purposes it is imperative to bracket these alternatives, not only to focus attention on the voluntary sector as such, but also simply to avoid confusion. It will be helpful, therefore, to emphasize the distinctions among the state, the marketplace, and the voluntary sector as primary categories of analysis, and to separate these categories from the others just mentioned in the following ways. "Sector" refers to kinds of activities distinguished by their dominant principles of association: coercion, in the sense of applied or potential application of force, even if this force is legitimated as normal authority; profitability, as a guiding economic principle, whether or not realized in practice; and voluntarism, as a principle involving freedom of association for purposes of mutuality, camaraderie, or services rendered free of obligation or remuneration. Institutional distinctions, by con-

---

[4] This way of thinking about social institutions will of course be identified with the work of Talcott Parsons (e.g., 1951), but has been widely influential throughout the social sciences.

trast, are based largely on a concept of the major goals (or functions) that need to be accomplished in order for a society to sustain itself. But these goals need to be distinguished from the activities in various sectors that may contribute to their attainment. For example, we may wish to think of the economic institution as a set of activities oriented toward adaptation to the physical environment, but some of these activities may be accomplished within the market sector (by for-profit firms), some may be accomplished within the state (for example, the disposal of radioactive waste), and some may be accomplished by voluntary organizations (environmental watchdog groups, for instance). It will also be particularly important in the context of the present discussion to see that the setting of major societal goals and values is not simply the domain of the state. Certainly firms within the marketplace set societal goals and values as well, not simply by lobbying for governmental action, but directly (and increasingly so) through advertising and corporate training. By the same token, it should be recognized that the voluntary sector can at least potentially contribute directly to the shaping of societal goals and values. In short, all three of the major sectors of interest here should be understood as having the capacity to accomplish or contribute to a variety of social (institutional) functions, from setting goals to influencing the physical environment to promoting interaction and solidarity. Our central concern is not with all these possible functions, but with the shaping of collective values.

The relation between a sectoral model and the language of public-private distinctions is also potentially confusing, but it is clarified somewhat more easily. As noted, ''public'' often refers to governmental activities and for this reason corresponds closely to the state sector; ''private,'' by contrast, tends to subsume both the market and the voluntary sectors. In the following chapters we shall sometimes find it necessary to use the terms ''public'' and ''private'' in these ways, either in drawing on literature rooted in this distinction or because of cultural differences not adequately captured by the sectoral model. Apart from these exceptions, we will employ the three-sector distinctions because of our concern with separating the nonprofit and for-profit components.

The other usage of ''public'' and ''private'' (as in ''public space'' and ''private lives'') is more helpful for our present purposes. In this sense, all three sectors include some activities that focus on the private lives of individuals and some that involve the public life of the society at large. Activities of the state range from certifying marriages (private) to negotiating arms agreements with foreign powers (public); the marketplace produces commodities such as bed linens and toothpaste, which are consumed in private, but also trades its shares of stock publicly and uses the public airwaves for advertising; and the voluntary sector provides many private services to the individual, such as comfort for the bereaved or companionship for the lonely, but also engages in public-awareness campaigns aimed at influencing larger values and priorities. We might distinguish between the relatively more private and the relatively more public of these activities in figure 1.1 by locating the former closer to the center of the circle and the latter closer to the periphery. As the term "public discourse" suggests, we will be more concerned with the public contribution of the voluntary sector than with its private activities.

Having dealt with some of these alternative concepts, we can now return to the central questions raised by the idea of a three-sector model. Chief among these questions are the relative sizes of the various sectors ant their respective relations with each of the other sectors.

In figure 1.1 the voluntary sector makes up 25 percent of the pie, the state 35 percent, and the market 40 percent. Such figures are of course hypothetical. No precise measures exist for any set of societies that would permit, say, the proportionate contribution to the gross national product to be determined with such accuracy. Nevertheless, societies do differ in the degree to which the various sectors contribute to the economy—or to the provision of certain services, or, for that matter, to the consumption of wealth, time, and other resources. In some, the voluntary sector is quite significant to the way in which collective activities are organized; in other societies, a voluntary sector is quite significant to the way in which collective activities are organized; in still other societies, a voluntary sector as such scarcely exists. What a chart like figure 1.1 does is sensitize us to these differences.

Figure 1.1 also suggests that certain trade-offs among the three sectors are likely to be present. Assuming a fixed stock of resources, for example, a large state sector may mean a smaller voluntary sector, or the same might be the case for the relations between the voluntary sector and the market: growth in one might mean shrinkage of the other. In comparing societies, we must also keep the possibility in mind, however, that the size of the whole pie may vary. Were changes in the voluntary sector measured over time, for example, it might appear in a particular society that decline had occurred relative to the other two sectors, but in absolute terms all three of the sectors might have grown.

Where an image like figure 1.1 proves inadequate is in depicting the complex relations among the various sectors. In theory these relations may appear as sharp conceptual distinctions, but in practice the line between any pair of sectors is not sharp. The distinction between the state and the market sector, for example, has been blurred in recent decades by joint ventures between government and business in science and technology and by the numerous ways in which government intervenes in the marketplace (regulation, tax incentives, bailouts, etc.). Similarly, the line between the state and the voluntary sector is often blurred as a result of cooperative programs between the two, government chartering of voluntary associations, and government financing. The boundary between voluntary and market sectors is sometimes vague as well, especially in instances of complex organizational schemes that bring for-profit and nonprofit activities under the same administrative umbrella. It would thus be better to think of each of the three sectors overlapping the other sectors, rather than their being separated by a firm line. Indeed, one of the significant variations we shall see from society to society is the degree to which the various sectors overlap.

Whether the degree of overlap is substantial or only slight, each of the three sectors is related to the others. Figure 1.2 depicts the three sectors differently in order to highlight these relationships. Rather than each sector merely being separated from the other two by a conceptual boundary, as in figure 1.1, the sectors here are shown with double lines running between each pair, emphasizing the point that various transactions characterize their relationships. These relationships include competition and cooperation, the exchange of various resources, and a variety of symbolic transactions.

Examples of competition are most common when similar services are being provided by organizations in more than one sector and where their sectoral location makes some difference in their access to the resources needed to provide these services. In the town where I live, for instance, a for-profit spa and fitness club has brought suit against the local YMCA, claiming that the latter is able to engage in unfair competition because of tax-exemption privileges. Examples of cooperation often receive less publicity, but are particularly common when diverse resources have to be merged in order to address major social problems. For instance, a program to provide meals to the elderly depends in many cities on cooperation among all three sectors: government provides funding to pay for the food, for-profit firms (restaurants and bakeries) are paid to prepare the meals, and nonprofit organizations coordinate these efforts and provide volunteers to deliver the meals.

This example illustrates some of the exchanges of resources among the various sectors. Other exchanges include organizational and managerial expertise, facilities, legal protection, and publicity, all of which may represent

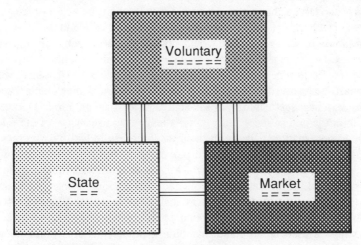

Figure 1.2 Relationships among Sectors

flows into the voluntary sector, and reciprocal flows of resources from this sector to the others, such as public relations, votes, monies raised voluntarily to support political candidates or social programs favored by particular officials, solutions to the ill-effects of business cycles, or means of curbing government programs and therefore tax increases. At issue in many of these exchanges are important questions of symbolism, including the very identity of the various sectors, their ability to make claims on public resources, and the legitimacy of the values they espouse.

SECTORAL DYNAMICS IN ADVANCED INDUSTRIAL SOCIETIES

Well after Tocqueville's visit to the United States in the 1830s, the voluntary sector continued to grow, not only in North America but throughout Europe as well. Even in societies that developed strong working-class movements, socialist parties, and early forms of the welfare state, the growth of commerce and industry—and with it the rise of the middle class—resulted in an enormous proliferation of voluntary associations of all kinds. Youth organizations, reading clubs, informal societies to promote business and agriculture, community-improvement leagues, temperance societies, immigrant associations, cycling clubs, benevolent associations, missionary groups, and poor-relief and charity associations all developed in profusion.

But Tocqueville had also warned of a different tendency in modern societies. The time was coming, he predicted, when the state would take over more and more of the functions of voluntary associations. The public would then become apathetic, he feared, and totalitarian tendencies would increase.

Other social observers in the nineteenth century also made predictions that suggested a diminishing role for the voluntary sector. Karl Marx and Friedrich Engels viewed it as a temporary solution to the growing contradictions of industrial capitalism. For a time, the bourgeoisie might be able to placate the working class with mutual-aid societies and singing clubs. But the misery and exploitation of the proletariat would continue and deepen, encompassing larger and larger segments of the population, until a mass political movement would rise up in rebellion. The contradictions of industrial capitalism would eventually be resolved, Marx and Engels predicted, not by the voluntary sector but by a radical restructuring of the state and the market. Emile Durkheim, writing at the end of the century, took a less pessimistic view of the role of voluntary associations, seeing in them (as Tocqueville had) possibilities for sustaining more democratic forms of governance. But he also worried about the rising cult of the individual—which he associated with the expansion of the state—and the limitations of voluntary associations in mass societies to guard against alienation, normlessness, and the arbitrary use of power. Others, including Max Weber and Robert Michels, examined the extent to which various kinds of association could maintain community and a commitment to common values in modern societies, but observed a powerful tendency, particularly within the state, but also within the voluntary sector itself, toward a stifling growth of bureaucracy.[5]

It is somewhat surprising that, given their prominence of place in the classic theoretical literature, voluntary forms of associations have in recent decades been examined with quite different questions in mind. Empirical questions have focused largely on readily measurable issues such as membership rates, finances, lobbying patterns, and organizational styles. Indeed, microscopic approaches treating the voluntary sector as a function largely of individual psychology and organizational muscle have far outweighed approaches concerned with the macroscopic or societal questions raised by Tocqueville, Marx, Durkheim, Weber, and others.[6]

There has, however, been a continuous stream of theoretical inquiry concerned with the dynamics of advanced industrial societies. This literature has focused primarily on the other two sectors: questions (largely of Weberian origin) about the effects of growing bureaucratization within the contemporary welfare state, and questions (often of Marxist origin) about the changing dynamics of advanced industrial capitalism itself. Many times this literature has simply taken the predictions of nineteenth-century theorists concerning the diminishing importance of the voluntary sector at face value, and for this reason, has dismissed the voluntary sector as being relatively inconsequential compared with the enormous power of the modern welfare state, on the one hand, and the vast economic resources and imperatives of the capitalist marketplace, on the other. Nevertheless, these lines of inquiry, especially to the extent that they have raised questions about the effects of changes in the state and the marketplace on other realms of private and public life, have provided a valuable context in which to reopen and reconsider the scope and functioning of the voluntary sector.[7]

Of the work by recent social theorists, that of German sociologist Jürgen

[5] The writings of the classical theorists on voluntary associations are scattered throughout their work, often consisting of mere fragments presented in the context of other discussions concerning topics such as the bourgeoisie, guilds, secondary associations, civil morals, authority, the family, and bureaucracy. See especially Marx and Engels ([1848] 1967), Alford and Friedland (1985), Gorz (1967), Van Til (1988:59–67), Durkheim ([1911] 1957), Michels ([1915] 1962), Orum (1978), and Weber ([1911–1920] 1978:1195–99).

[6] Studies of the economic, organizational, and psychological dimensions of the voluntary sector and bibliographic guides to this literature include Powell (1986), Weisbrod (1988), Hodgkinson (1990), Oleck (1980), and Knoke and Wood (1981). Sills (1968) remains a remarkably useful overview of the main sociological aspects of voluntary associations, but, with the exception of some brief observations at the end about the functions of these associations for societies, focuses entirely on their internal dynamics. Comparing Sills with more recent overviews indicates that comparative, historical, and societal levels of analysis are becoming more important.

[7] Theoretical discussions that provide useful background for the present volume include Habermas ([1962] 1989, 1985), Hohendahl (1979), Gilbert (1983), Poulantzas (1978), and Bell (1973, 1976).

Habermas ([1962] 1989, 1976, 1985) has perhaps been most influential in bringing together a variety of observations about the ways in which public discourse may be changing as a result of master tendencies in advanced industrial societies. Habermas has been consistently concerned with the character of public discourse, although his particular conceptions of its essential features have undergone considerable change over the years. It is nevertheless possible to state, without oversimplifying his views, that Habermas conceives of communication about collective values as the most vital challenge facing modern societies, that "communicative rationality," as he calls it, is to be sharply distinguished from the more technical and instrumental forms of rationality that dominate much of modern thought, and that something called a "public sphere" needs to be present either as a place or as a process in which communication about collective values can take place.

Habermas has also paid much attention to the theoretical implications for his notion of a public sphere of political and economic developments in advanced industrial societies. Two distinct kinds of implication, which arise at different theoretical levels of analysis, can be identified. At one level, the importance of the public sphere has been magnified in advanced industrial societies because of an increasing interpenetration between the political and economic sectors. Free markets that operate within a strict conception of laissez-faire no longer exist, in Habermas's view, because of various competitive pressures that require intervention and regulation. As a result, the state becomes a major actor in the economic arena itself. But this role involves the state in certain normative contradictions, such as that between serving special interests and advancing the common good. Advanced industrial societies are thus faced with a "legitimation crisis" that raises questions not only about the proper bases on which the state should govern but also about conceptions of the common good itself. Some form of public discourse about the common good—discourse that presumably cannot be orchestrated by the state alone—is, therefore, essential. But societies may also simply try to duck the issue of what constitutes the common good by letting technical and procedural considerations determine the shape of collective values.

The latter possibility brings us to Habermas's second level of theoretical interpretation of the problems facing advanced industrial societies. Both the state and the marketplace expand the scope of their activities and functions. Quite apart from the question of how much they interpenetrate, they become increasingly important in determining the fate of modern societies. Here, Habermas has borrowed the idea of "life-world" to indicate the social space in which people live and to designate some residual category into which the state and the market expand. The life-world, he suggests, is increasingly becoming colonized by the state and the market. In what way? Principally through the broader extension of norms dominant in these spheres of activity. The dominant norms of the state include bureaucratization, and those of the market include instrumentality and technical efficiency. Both tendencies seem to increase, penetrating the life-worlds in which people reside and shaping the way they think about collective values. In reaction, various countercultural movements, rebellions, uprisings, and forms of withdrawal have developed. But Habermas questions whether any of these "protests" can adequately address or reverse the larger cultural processes he identifies.

Habermas in thus concerned with questions not dissimilar from those of Tocqueville. The essential differences are that Habermas, writing from the perspective of a much more economically advanced social milieu, envisions the effects of political expansion in a more systemic way than Tocqueville did, believes there is greater conflict between capitalist norms and collective values, and is less concerned about the role of voluntary associations as such. Indeed, Habermas's very conception of society springs more from Hegel than from Tocqueville and raises questions (as we shall see) about the contemporary applicability of Tocqueville's model for societies that operate more on the basis of Hegelian distinctions between the state and civil society than on a Tocquevillian conception of societal sectors. Habermas's perspective, pitched as it is at such a high level of theoretical generality, also raises questions about how clearly such generalizations may be evident in concrete societies. While it may be the case that instrumental rationality is a pervasive tendency influencing the public sphere everywhere, we would want to know whether specific changes in the role of the state and the market make a discernible difference in the way the public sphere is constructed. Habermas has clearly paid more attention to master cultural tendencies than to the variations in social arrangements among advanced industrial societies. For that reason, and because of other assumptions (for example, about consensus and rationality) inherent in his analysis, his perspective appears more useful as a sensitizing or orienting device than as a set of empirically testable hypotheses. We shall thus not attempt in the following chapters to "test" Habermas's ideas from country to country. Nevertheless, it is possible to follow Habermas's lead in identifying tendencies within the state and the marketplace, albeit at a lower level of theoretical abstraction, that may be particularly consequential for the voluntary sector and for the articulation of collective values.

Over roughly the past half century, if the end of World War II can be taken as a kind of historical dividing line, the role of centralized state agencies and state-mandated programs has increased significantly in virtually all advanced industrial societies. Military obligations in many of these societies expanded dramatically during the cold war, giving central governments more effective means of enforcing their agendas and placing them at the center of a vast complex of bureaucratic, economic, and technological activities. With the development of nuclear weapons, and with greater reliance on technological innovation for the improvement of conventional weapons, state agencies found themselves supporting broad programs of scientific research and development, attempting to standardize and upgrade public education, and coordinating wide networks of government labs and for-profit firms devoted to the production of military supplies. In addition, the social-welfare policies that had begun to be implemented in most Western democracies during the half century preceding World War II now expanded as labor unions and business leaders alike sought to avoid a return of the catastrophic social conditions of the Great Depression. Government agencies were created to administer huge programs for old-age and retirement insurance, public health, and housing, and these were gradually expanded to include entitlement plans for the disabled, the disadvantaged, racial and ethnic minorities, and a variety of other groups. With the creation of new entitlements and wider constituencies for government programs, the role of political parties has also greatly expanded. While formally and organizationally distinct from the state in most cases, these parties are often so concerned with electoral politics and with legislation that their operative norms are scarcely distinguishable from those of official state bureaucracies.

Government programs also emerged to promote and regulate business, and as economies grew, so did states' commitment to the activities of fiscal planning, underwriting the cost of transportation and communications networks, negotiating trade arrangements with other countries, and monitoring the health and safety of the public. As a result, the budgets of central governments have multiplied at least several times in most democratic societies during the past half century, the role of public expenditures has risen sharply as a proportion of the gross national product, and a larger share of the overall labor force is employed in the government sector.[8]

The period since World War II has also witnessed dramatic growth within the market sector—the central sphere of advanced industrial capitalism itself. In both absolute and per capita terms, the GNP of advanced industrial societies has shown strong growth during most of the period since World War II. Corporate profits have risen and the scale of corporate activities has expanded, while the range of smaller for-profit firms has also been enlarged.

The specific character of advanced industrial economies has also undergone considerable change. For example, domestic and foreign markets have become integrated across a wider range of product lines and geographic locales, resulting in more intense international competition and larger-scale efforts to penetrate, distribute to, and coordinate national and international networks of trade. In the process, consumer goods have become the mainstays of advanced industrial capitalism, linking larger and larger shares of disposable income, as well as time, to the price-demand-supply mechanism. Principally through the inclusion of women, larger proportions of the adult population have been in-

---

[8] Specific evidence on increases in government revenues and expenditures, as well as broader economic patterns, is presented in each of the following chapters.

corporated into the labor market. Heavy industry and unskilled work has been exported to less-developed countries. And a greater share of the economic activity of advanced industrial societies has been concentrated in the professions, in service industries, in occupations dependent on high technology, and in the communications and information-processing industries.

From one perspective, both the developments within the bureaucratic welfare state and the developments within advanced industrial capitalism pose serious threats to the viability of the voluntary sector. Government agencies concerned with social-welfare programs have sometimes taken over the activities once performed by voluntary organizations, supplying services to the needy as a basic right or entitlement, rather than encouraging the various moral obligations that once bound recipients to the voluntary sector, and doing so at public expense, instead of having to raise money by soliciting voluntary donations. Besides direct competition to provide services, the gradual rise of the bureaucratic welfare state has also posed an alternative way of thinking about public responsibility itself. Rather than feeling personally responsible for their neighbors and their communities, individuals could turn increasingly to central agencies, and to the professionals employed by these agencies, as a more effective means of addressing the complex problems of contemporary society. From the same perspective, the changes occurring in the market sector also carry negative implications for the spirit of voluntarism. In particular, the extension of market principles into the service industries means a larger and larger share of these activities being performed by paid professionals rather than by volunteers. The incorporation of women into the work force means fewer people with available time to devote to voluntary organizations. Greater emphasis on technical education, scientific research, and specialization may diminish the likelihood of people having the opportunity to opt for training with a focus on wider human values. And the intensification of competition among large firms and among the industrial nations themselves heightens the likelihood that norms of efficiency, instrumentality, rationality, and effectiveness will erode such values as community and caring that have long been the focus of voluntary associations.

But the various threats to the voluntary sector that have been envisioned in some analyses cannot be taken as the only or even the most compelling predictions. Other arguments suggest that the voluntary sector will continue at familiar, if not higher, levels of activity. The bureaucratic welfare state has mandated that services be provided in a wider arena of public and private life, even expanding the definition of basic rights through its entitlement programs. But it has not always been capable of delivering these services through its own agencies. Considerable sums of money, raised as taxes, have thus been transferred to voluntary organizations charged with the dissemination of government-mandated services to the needy. The expansion of industrial capitalism has not only increased the burdens facing the average worker but has also created leisure time and an enlarged middle class with discretionary income. Time and money that can at least conceivably be devoted to the work of voluntary associations have thus been made available.

Even those who have taken a more critical perspective on the changing role of governments and firms in advanced industrial societies have suggested that these changes may not be entirely negative for the voluntary sector. After an initial period of optimism that saw government agencies being able to shoulder responsibility for all the ill-effects generated as by-products of advanced capitalism, recent years have witnessed a more sober assessment of these possibilities. The competitive pressures to which all capitalist societies are subject inevitably limit the degree to which government agencies can intervene on behalf of social needs. Intervention requires larger government budgets, and larger government budgets can be sustained only through deficit spending or by raising taxes, neither of which has proven healthy for the competitive position of capitalist societies in international markets. Deficit spending promotes inflation, which leads to negative export-import balances, and high rates of taxation produce similar effects by raising wage levels or reducing domestic consumption. Government programs are likely to face economic limitations, therefore, at the same time that competitive pressures within the economy itself continue to produce the social side effects these programs were designed to address—unemployment, homelessness, rising health-care costs, urban decay, and environmental hazards. The solution most likely to be favored by government and industry alike is thus a program of voluntary action. Encouraging citizens to donate their own time and money to efforts concerned with social problems gives political and business leaders a way to acknowledge the importance of these concerns without burdening the staffs of government bureaus or taxing the marketplace.

It is, therefore, a matter of some importance to examine empirically what the effect of various developments in the state and market sectors of advanced industrial societies on the voluntary sector has been. One possibility is that the voluntary sector has in fact been squeezed by the growth taking place in the other two sectors. Even if the constraints facing government and business leaders force them to seek the assistance of voluntary agencies, this squeeze would be suggested by the fact that these same constraints place limits on the resources likely to be available to the voluntary sector. A second possibility is that the voluntary sector has grown or at least maintained its historic position relative to that of the other two sectors. This possibility is suggested not only by arguments about the ways in which growth in the other two sectors may have inadvertently strengthened voluntary associations but also by arguments stressing the importance of historical precedent and inertia. According to the latter, participation in voluntary activities may be such a natural expression of basic needs for meaning and belonging that these activities, once established as part of the traditions of a society, simply do not die easily. A third possibility, however, is that voluntary associations may neither diminish nor grow with changes in the wider society but may instead be transformed in character. In some societies they may continue but be subsumed largely within the dominant welfare-state bureaucracy itself; in others, they may also continue, but turn to advertising and other entrepreneurial activities that distinguish them less clearly from the for-profit sector.

As soon as comparative questions of this kind are raised, however, we are confronted again with the historical particularities of each advanced industrial society. Generalizations about the effects of state expansion or economic growth on the voluntary sector become, as we shall see, extremely tenuous because long-standing differences already exist in the ways in which activities are allocated to the various sectors and in understandings of the relationships among sectors. It remains possible, of course, to determine whether similar effects may be present despite these historical differences. It also remains possible to compare countries having similar histories with other countries to determine whether recent societal changes may generate effects of a more serious nature under some conditions than under others.

Although limiting to the social scientist in pursuit of theoretical generalizations, this last possibility provides a valuable opportunity for those especially concerned with the present and future shape of the voluntary sector in particular societies. Returning momentarily to Tocqueville's sense of the exceptionality of the American case, for example, we can see with the greater clarity provided by these comparisons whether a strong voluntary sector is indeed essential for the articulation of democratic values, whether the expansion of centralized welfare provisions necessarily erodes those values, or whether the answer to these questions in fact varies markedly with historical and cultural precedents.

THE SPECIAL SIGNIFICANCE OF RELIGION

For the sake of convenience, I have thus far referred to the voluntary sector as if it were an undifferentiated whole—one activity, value, or organization simply being substitutable for all the others. That, of course, is not the case. The voluntary sector is merely a statistical and conceptual aggregation of hundreds—and in most societies, thousands—of diverse organizations, some scarcely organized at all, except for the caring activities of a few like-minded individuals, others existing at a variety of levels, ranging from local neighborhoods and communities, to counties and regions, to states and nations.

Both for historical and for contemporary reasons, the distinction between religion and other, more secular components of the voluntary sector is particularly important. The historical reasons are twofold: religious values and the struggles of religious communities, it appears, often provided the ground from which voluntary associations of other kinds arose in the first place; and the historical pattern of conflicts between religion and other social institutions, particularly the state, appears to have played a decisive role in shaping the voluntary sector in particular societies as well as in influencing its internal composition and, indeed, the degree to which it exists as a sharply differentiated sphere of activity at all. The contemporary reasons are simply extensions of these historical factors. Understanding how recent changes in the state and the marketplace may affect the voluntary sector requires knowledge of the special issues embedded in controversies involving religious and political leaders, the constitutional and legal relations between church and state, and the positioning of religious institutions in relation to economic discussions, particularly the discussions of labor-oriented, leftist, or culturally critical intellectuals.

Although the history of relations between religious institutions and the voluntary sector has not yet been traced systematically, it appears that what are now popularly conceived of as voluntary associations evolved gradually from the struggles during the early modern period, if not earlier, waged by religious leaders to impose limitations on the powers of monarchs and representative officials.[9] Religious reformers associated with the various dissenting bodies and free-church traditions were especially important in these struggles. In the process of challenging the alliances between established religions and political authorities, these reformers sometimes forced other religious leaders into an even closer relationship with the state. It should thus not be assumed that religious leaders were always on the side of curtailing the powers of the state. Nevertheless, the debates that ensued—and to a greater extent, the period of intense religious strife that engulfed much of Europe during the seventeenth century, which served as the immediate backdrop for the founding of the American colonies—encouraged political leaders themselves to define a public space in which religious values could be debated apart from strict political controls.

The long period of religious strife that preceded the various democratic revolutions of the eighteenth and nineteenth centuries also prompted the drawing of an important distinction between religious institutions and newly emerging associations devoted to other kinds of activities. The scientific and literary academies that appeared in increasing numbers at the beginning of the eighteenth century, for example, largely eschewed the discussion of religious topics and saw in their own commitment to enlightened philosophy a way of advancing beyond the religious controversies of the preceding century. These academies, salons, reading clubs, and improvement societies became the basis of both an intellectual tradition that would radically challenge the authority of religious institutions and a secular voluntary sector composed of free associa-

---

[9] The arguments of Max Weber, James Luther Adams, and others about the role of religion in giving rise to voluntary associations are summarized briefly in Stackhouse (1990).

tions formed without religious sanction, sometimes for purposes explicitly competitive with those of religious organizations.[10]

Much of the variation in the scope and functions of the voluntary sector in contemporary advanced industrial societies can be traced to the historical patterns that were established during the Enlightenment, and later, during the republican revolutions and social-democratic upheavals of the nineteenth century. In societies that developed a relatively pluralistic tradition of competing religious organizations, all restricted from making special claims in the name of political authority, a significant voluntary sector emerged that was also decidedly pluralistic, in which religious agencies competed actively with secular organizations. In contrast, societies that institutionalized close relationships between a single established church and the political sector generally followed a different course, variously incorporating more of the activities associated elsewhere with voluntary associations into the religiopolitical bureaucracy itself, or, in responding to the criticisms of minority parties or working-class movements, attempting to foster these activities through an expanded welfare state, through labor unions and socialist parties, or through the critical debates encouraged within the universities and by the secular intelligentsia.

The place of religion in the voluntary sector is thus an important clue to historical variations in the development of this sector, and these variations in turn provide the necessary background for understanding why this sector may appear relatively strong in some cases and virtually absent in others. But even in the former the place of religion within the voluntary sector has not been examined as fully as might be expected. For reasons no more significant than disciplinary specialties and programmatic concerns, recent studies of the voluntary sector have often focused on secular nonprofit organizations rather than paying attention to the full range of churches, synagogues, and parareligious associations that also make up this sector. Yet the few studies that have been reported, as well as evidence easily pieced together from studies of religious organizations themselves, indicate that a very substantial number of voluntary services in some societies are in fact provided by religious organizations, and in other societies religious values may be related to voluntary activities in significant ways.

If religion is an important, yet neglected, dimension of the voluntary sector both historically and at present, then its role merits special attention, at least to the extent that it continues to provide a foundation for the voluntary activities present in some societies. To that extent, we must also be mindful of the distinctive ways in which social and cultural changes may be relevant to the religious dimension. Much of the activity associated with the bureaucratic

---

[10] On the relations among religious struggles, the state, and other factors contributing to the development of a public sphere in which voluntary associations played a prominent role in Western Europe, see Wuthnow (1989).

welfare state and with advanced industrial capitalism, for example, has been decidedly secular. New welfare programs and new consumer products are typically legitimated in terms of utilitarian criteria rather than religious value or divine mandate. The growth that has taken place in these two sectors therefore may have more serious consequences for the religious component of the voluntary sector than for secular nonprofit agencies. Furthermore, in countries such as the United States in which constitutional barriers separate the religious from the political sector, this component may find itself at a distinct disadvantage in competing with secular nonprofit agencies. The changing role of religion can thus provide an important key to the ways in which the voluntary sector more broadly may be undergoing a transformation in composition and orientation.

THE SHAPING OF PUBLIC DISCOURSE

As these comments suggest, the voluntary sector is vitally concerned with the provision of social services, and its relations with the state and market sectors are most likely to be defined by the manner in which various services are allocated among the three sectors. But the sheer provision of social services does not exhaust the contemporary significance of the voluntary sector. The voluntary sector is too important to be left entirely to economists whose primary concern is the provision of social services by nonprofit organizations. Important as these services may be to their recipients, it is Tocqueville's own question of how the voluntary sector contributes to the shaping of public discourse with which we are most concerned.

Public discourse, which we define simply as the process of arriving at collective values, has become popularly associated with political debate and the shaping of political debate by the mass media and various lobbying organizations. That it has taken on this connotation is itself, if attributable to some extent to Tocqueville, testimony to the expanding role of the state in modern societies. But all three sectors clearly contribute to the shaping of collective values—meaning that public discourse must be thought of in terms broader than those of political debate alone. Its essential concern is with the collective, not necessarily in the sense of the entire society, but with the relationships among individuals, between individuals and communities, and among communities. Public discourse—or what is often referred to as the public sphere— is thus the arena of questions about the desirable in social conduct: How shall we live as a people? What do we hold as priorities? To what ends shall we allocate our time, our energy, our collective resources? Where do we locate hope? How do we envision the good?

Sometimes we debate these questions directly; more often, they are the underlying premises on which the more practical debates that do in fact dominate politics or advertisements or educational programs depend. Even with infinite resources we could neither evoke all such assumptions nor hope to arrive at consensus about them; that is why public discourse is a continuing process. But the question Tocqueville asked remains vital, even if it cannot be answered definitively.

Tocqueville's question is whether the shape of public discourse depends in some important way on the vitality of the voluntary sector. Put differently, does it make any difference at all to the collective values we articulate and espouse—to the way we frame our assumptions about the desirable—if there is a viable and active voluntary sector or if public discourse is shaped largely (exclusively?) by the state and the marketplace?

Because of the prominence the voluntary sector has enjoyed in American culture, it is perhaps easy for those living in the United States to assume, with Tocqueville, that the vitality of this sector does in fact make a difference to the shape of our collective values. When public officials proclaim the importance of doing volunteer work, or expound on the ennobling qualities of such activities, or suggest that this involvement is what keeps hope alive, we in fact are given visible testimony that voluntarism is still connected in some way to the higher values we hold dear as a society. But what are these values? Would they be diminished were the voluntary sector to erode? Are they absent in societies without a distinct voluntary sector?

Let me offer an example that will seem trite but for that reason alone illustrates well the complexity of these questions. Freedom is generally regarded as one of the values that Americans hold dearest. It is also a value we sometimes associate with our voluntary sector: we tell ourselves, for example, that it is better to provide day-care centers through voluntary associations than through government because the voluntary sector gives parents more freedom to choose among a variety of alternatives. We might suppose therefore that the strength of our voluntary sector may contribute importantly to the high place we give freedom among our collective values. But it is in fact the rhetoric of a Republican president who presides over the largest government bureaucracy in history from which this specific example is taken. Indeed, it is perhaps more common to hear the rhetoric of freedom from the state and the marketplace than from the voluntary sector itself. Politicians tell us our freedom depends on huge military expenditures to fight communism. Business leaders argue that free markets are essential to a free society and point out how capitalism gives us all the freedom to choose. Proponents of a stronger voluntary sector, in contrast, may well argue that the value we attach to individual freedom gets in the way of our willingness to help others less fortunate than ourselves.

Were the point of this example only to raise the question of whether a strong voluntary sector increases the value we place on freedom, the answer could easily be found by surveying individuals to see whether the two went hand in hand, either in the same country or across a number of countries. But public discourse is, as I have emphasized, a process. Because of the historical differences among societies we could examine variations in opinion surveys and still not learn much about *how* the voluntary sector contributes to the shaping of collective values. A preferable approach is to go beyond aggregate comparisons of opinions, economic indices, and the like, to see how the various sectors relate to one another and to see how the dynamics of these relationships may affect the character of the public sphere.

It is in the process of shaping public debates that the precarious and changing relations among the three sectors should be most evident. Returning momentarily to the illustration of rhetoric about day-care centers, for example, it may in fact be significant that the possibility of nonprofit centers provides a political leader with an alternative to government programs, rather than the only alternative being for-profit centers. Were that the case, we might imagine the arguments hinging primarily on criteria of efficiency. Surely it is significant that we prefer a voluntary program to some other program that might actually be more efficient. Yet we can also imagine that the great expansion of government and the marketplace over the past half century has made us more likely than in the past to elevate norms of efficiency to a status above many other values. For instance, we find few proponents in the society at large of turning the public schools over to voluntary associations in hopes of teaching children to be more relaxed or caring or appreciative of a spring day. Instead, we hear relentless talk about making the public schools ever more efficient, presumably to heighten our competitiveness in world markets, at the expense (we may sometimes wonder) of childhood itself.

The fear that public discourse about collective values may be undergoing a significant transformation is thus a concern that focuses not only on the sheer size of each of the three sectors but on the operating norms and assumptions governing all three. In the United States it has generally been assumed that the voluntary sector has somewhat greater latitude in articulating alternative norms and assumptions than the state or the marketplace. By virtue of the fact that the state operates at public expense and depends on achieving assent from a sizable majority of the public to legitimate its programs, the state is necessarily concerned with efficiency and effectiveness, with validating its decisions according to rational procedures, and with appealing to those values assumed to be shared by nearly everyone or beneficial to everyone, such as national security and economic prosperity. It might be possible for the state to assert tolerance toward other values, but certainly it would be hard for the state actually to champion the values of, say, a secessionist ethnic minority, a religious commune promoting profligate generosity and indulgence, or an artist proclaiming the virtues of irrationality. Much the same would have to be said about the marketplace. Its very logic requires emphasis not only on efficiency and rationality, but also on profitability and competitiveness. Business leaders might argue that a prosperous market system can foot the bill for the pursuit of other values. But they would be unlikely to argue that the marketplace itself should be organized around such value-laden activities as daydreaming, pursuing mystical enlightenment, or giving one's possessions away in order to feed the poor.

Whether the voluntary sector is capable of sustaining itself, both as an arena of activities and as an example of alternative norms and values, against the growing prevalence of the state and the marketplace, therefore, is the underlying question toward which this volume is directed. We shall not of course be able to answer this question, for it raises issues that go well beyond the scope of any single empirical study. What we can provide, however, is comparative evidence that will help us know whether the question itself is a good one. To think of the voluntary sector as an endangered zone, like a treasure trove of our most cherished possessions, surrounded by the marauding forces of state bureaucracy and rampant capitalism, is after all a distinctly American way of thinking about the problem. In other societies the dangers are understood quite differently, despite the fact that similar economic and political trends are at work. To see ourselves more clearly, therefore, we need to begin by understanding that ours is not the only way of seeing.

A LOOK AHEAD

The chapters that follow originated as part of a collaborative project, the first phase of which was to bring together a group of scholars from a variety of disciplines to discuss the conceptual and theoretical questions raised by the idea of the voluntary sector. It was from those discussions that many of the issues I have just outlined grew. Given the emphasis that emerged on broad macroscopic issues of the relations among sectors and the role of sectors in shaping collective values, an early decision that also grew out of this process was the decision to focus on a number of societies. Although our primary aim was a better understanding of the role of the voluntary sector, religion, and public discourse in the United States, and not the discovery of mere generalizations that might apply to all societies, we recognized that we could only investigate the distinctive features of the United States by comparing it with other societies.

The next step in the process involved bringing together a group of scholars with expertise on particular countries to discuss in a preliminary way what the relevant substantive questions might be and what the range of variation on these topics might look like. These discussions not only sharpened our earlier conceptual and theoretical ideas; they also called some of these ideas into question. From the beginning, for example, it seemed clear that a three-sector model, which worked conveniently for the United States, ran afoul of the way in which cultural distinctions functioned in certain other societies. That, we decided, was how it should be, for if we could tease out those points of conceptual incongruity, we would know better what was in fact unique about the

United States. Rather than simply abandoning all conceptual frameworks (were that possible) or opting for something at an extremely abstract level of generality, we decided to retain the sectoral model as a guiding metaphor, but to let ourselves be instructed about its shortcomings and the limits of its genererality.

This stage of the process also resulted in our present choice of countries for inclusion. We decided to limit our primary attention to a relatively small number of countries in order to provide a reasonably thorough treatment of all the relevant issues for each one. For that reason we also decided to focus our attention on countries having certain basic similarities in political and economic systems. All of us, for example, acknowledged the value at some point of knowing how the questions we were addressing might look in the context of, say, Latin America, the Middle East, or for that matter, Eastern Europe.[11] But we also agreed those broader comparisons were beyond the scope of the present volume.

Having focused our attention on advanced industrial societies with democratic governments, we then restricted our inquiries further to particular countries among the nearly two dozen that might qualify by various definitions of those criteria. In part our selections were based on being able to find scholars with knowledge of the relevant countries, languages, and issues. As it happens, each of the contributors not only has the relevant theoretical background and language skills but also has lived both in the country on which he or she has written and in the United States, thus enhancing his or her ability to think about comparative issues. Our selections were also based on the sense that grew out of our preliminary discussions and reading of the literature that the social role of the voluntary sector was likely to differ considerably among advanced industrial democracies with different political, religious, and cultural traditions.

The following chapters consider the changing relations among states, markets, religion, the voluntary sector, and the public sphere in the United Kingdom, West Germany, Sweden, France, Italy, Israel, Japan and the United States.[12] All of these societies are linked with one another culturally and eco-

---

[11] In the initial phase of our project we devoted considerable attention to Poland, but despite the fascinating developments that were already becoming evident in that society, we concluded that the rapidity of change in Poland, its low level of economic development, and its nondemocratic system of government made it too different from any of the other societies for us to handle it adequately.

[12] Although comparative studies of the voluntary sector and studies of particular societies other than the United States are relatively rare, some significant work has begun to appear in the past few years; see especially Kramer (1984), James (1987, 1989), Wolch (1990), Wolfe (1989), and Anheier and Seibel (1990). These studies for the most part are more concerned with organizational matters and economic concerns than with the cultural issues raised here, but they provide useful information, especially on some of the societies (the Netherlands, for example) that we were not able to examine.

nomically; they share democratic forms of government; and their economies are among the most industrially advanced in the world. Each of these societies has experienced much growth in the governmental sector since World War II and has sustained both growth and restructuring in the economic sector during the same period. But these societies also vary considerably, for historical and contemporary reasons, in the way public discourse—a public sphere—is constituted, in the relations between religion and the other two sectors, and in the scope, functioning, and even identity of the voluntary sector. These variations permit us to defamiliarize ourselves with familiar ways of thinking about the problems of public discourse in the United States. Indeed, they raise questions about many of the assumptions prominent in our own society about the voluntary sector and the cultural space it occupies in relation to the state and the marketplace. They suggest alternative ways of thinking about the public sphere and they show that voluntary associations can sometimes function effectively even in much closer cooperation with the state than they do in the United States. To the extent that all these societies have moved further toward a welfare-state conception of society, these comparisons also permit us to rethink some of our assumptions about the relations between voluntarism and the collective good.

References

Alford, Robert R., and Roger Friedland. 1985. *Powers of Theory*. Cambridge: Cambridge University Press.

Anheier, Helmut K., and Wolfgang Seibel. 1990. *The Third Sector: Comparative Studies of Nonprofit Organizations*. Berlin: De Gruyter.

Bell, Daniel. 1973. *The Coming of Post-Industrial Society*. New York: Basic Books.

———. 1976. *The Cultural Contradictions of Capitalism*. New York: Basic Books.

Bellah, Robert N., et al. 1985. *Habits of the Heart: Individualism and Commitment in American Life*. Berkeley and Los Angeles: University of California Press.

Carnoy, Martin. 1984. *The State and Political Theory*. Princeton: Princeton University Press.

Durkheim, Emile. [1911] 1957. *Professional Ethics and Civic Morals*. London: Routledge and Kegan Paul.

Gamwell, Franklin I. 1984. *Beyond Preference: Liberal Theories of Independent Association*. Chicago: University of Chicago Press.

Gilbert, Neil. 1983. *Capitalism and the Welfare State: Dilemmas of Social Benevolence*. New Haven: Yale University Press.

Gorz, André. 1967. *Strategy for Labor*. Boston: Beacon Press.

Habermas, Jürgen. [1962] 1989. *The Structural Transformation of the Public Sphere: An Inquiry into a Category of Bourgeois Society*. Translated by Thomas McCarthy. Cambridge, Mass: MIT Press.

———. 1976. *Legitimation Crisis*. Translated by Thomas McCarthy. Boston: Beacon Press.

———. 1985. *The Theory of Communicative Action*. Translated by Thomas McCarthy. 2 vols. Boston: Beacon Press.

Hansen, Susan, Linda Franz, and Margeret Netemeyer-Mays. 1976. "Women's Political Participation and Policy Preferences," *Social Science Quarterly* 56:101–10.

Hodgkinson, Virginia A. 1990. *Motivation for Volunteering: A Bibliography*. New York: Foundation Center.

Hohendahl, Peter Uwe. 1979. "Critical Theory, Public Sphere, and Culture." *New German Critique* 16:89–118.

James, Estelle. 1987. "The Nonprofit Sector in Comparative Perspective." In *The Nonprofit Sector: A Research Handbook*, edited by Walter W. Powell, pp. 397–415. New Haven: Yale University Press.

———, ed. 1989. *The Nonprofit Sector in International Perspective: Studies of Comparative Culture and Policy*. Oxford: Oxford University Press.

Knoke, David, and James R. Wood. 1981 *Organized for Action: Commitment in Voluntary Associations*. New Brunswick, N.J.: Rutgers University Press.

Kramer, Ralph M. 1984. *Voluntary Agencies in the Welfare State*. Berkeley and Los Angeles: University of California Press.

Marx, Karl, and Friedrich Engels. [1848] 1967. *The Communist Manifesto*. Baltimore: Penguin.

Michels, Robert. [1915] 1962. *Political Parties: A Sociological Study of the Oligarchical Tendencies of Modern Democracy.* New York: Free Press.

Oleck, Howard L. *Nonprofit Corporations, Organizations, and Associations.* 3d ed. Englewood Cliffs, N.J.: Prentice-Hall.

Olson, Marvin. 1972. "Social Participation and Voting Turnout: A Multivariate Analysis," *American Sociological Review* 37:317–32.

Orum, Anthony M. 1978. *An Introduction to Political Sociology.* Englewood Cliffs, N.J.: Prentice-Hall.

Parsons, Talcott. 1951. *The Social System.* New York: Free Press.

Poulantzas, Nicos, 1978. *State, Power, Socialism.* London: New Left Books.

Powell, Walter, ed. 1986. *The Nonprofit Sector: A Research Handbook.* New Haven: Yale University Press.

Shipiro, Virginia. 1983. *The Political Integration of Women.* Urbana: University of Illinois Press.

Sills, David L. 1968. "Voluntary Associations: Sociological Aspects," In *International Encyclopedia of the Social Sciences*, edited by David L. Sills, pp. 362–79. New York: Free Press.

Stackhouse, Max. 1990. "Religion and the Social Space for Voluntary Institutions." In *Faith and Philanthropy in America: Exploring the Role of Religion in America's Voluntary Sector*, edited by Robert Wuthnow and Virginia A. Hodgkinson, chap. 2. San Francisco: Jossey-Bass.

Sumariwalla, Russy D. 1983. "Preliminary Observations on Scope, Size, and Classification of the Sector." In *Working Papers for the Spring Research Forum: Since the Filer Commission*, pp. 433–49. Washington, D.C.: Independent Sector.

Tocqueville, Alexis de. [1835] 1945. *Democracy in America.* 2 vols. New York: Vintage.

Van Til, Jon. 1988. *Mapping the Third Sector: Voluntarism in a Changing Social Economy.* New York: Foundation Center.

Weber, Max [1911–1920] 1978. *Economy and Society.* Berkeley and Los Angeles: University of California Press.

Weisbrod, Burton A. 1988. *The Nonprofit Economy.* Cambridge, Mass.: Harvard University Press.

Wolch, Jennifer R. 1990. *The Shadow State: Government and Voluntary Sector in Transition.* New York: Foundation Center.

Wolfe, Alan. 1989. *Whose Keeper?* Berkeley and Los Angeles: University of California Press.

Wuthnow, Robert, 1989. *Communities of Discourse: Ideology and Social Structure in the Reformation, the Enlightenment, and European Socialism.* Cambridge, Mass.: Harvard University Press.

CHAPTER TWO

Great Britain: Voluntarism and Sectional Interests

James A. Beckford

THE UNITED KINGDOM's social structure, historical development, cultural patterns, and present constitutional system conspire to make the notion of an independent, public, or third sector at best elusive, and even problematic. The ambiguous nature of charities, the unclear status of religious organizations, and the increasingly corporatist relationships between the British welfare state and voluntary organizations are all associated with the difficulty of conceptualizing an independent public sector. In order to substantiate this argument I will sketch some of the features of the United Kingdom's social structure before going on to discuss the country's economy, welfare state, voluntary and informal sectors, charities, and religion. The conclusion will draw together the difficulties associated with the concept of an autonomous public sphere in the United Kingdom.

AN OVERVIEW OF U.K. SOCIETY

As in the United States, the lion's share of public debate in the United Kingdom occurs in the political realm. But the way in which political parties function adds a special dimension. The major political parties in the United Kingdom have powerful organizations at national, regional, and local levels. Candidates are carefully selected to represent their parties in contests for the single seat available in each constituency. At the level of administrative counties and districts, a proportion of seats is renewed in rotation. But in general elections, all seats in the House of Commons are contested at the same time. Elections are decided on the basis of a simple majority of the single, nontransferable votes cast for each candidate. As a result, governments and local councils can take office with a minority of the total vote. It also follows that fairly lengthy periods of relative stability in policy and legislation alternate with brief periods of sudden change. In these circumstances, the chances for bipartisan politics are negligible. This means that, from one point of view, there may be a need for an autonomous sphere of public debate. But it also means that the prospects for such a sphere are not good.

Despite the existence of the national welfare state and nationally effective political parties, the 1980s saw the growth of a further social division in U.K. society: the increasingly wide gap between, on the one hand, the deindustrialized regions of the North, Scotland, Wales, and Northern Ireland and, on the other, the reindustrializing South. The historical gradient of relative prosperity and security has always favored the South, but the disparities have recently become much greater.

But these domestic considerations must be located in a wider context because, as international competition for trade has increased, so the state has expanded and intervened more and more directly in economic affairs. This intervention includes the regulation of finance, business, and the provision of collective services (prisons, roads, schools, health facilities, armed forces, police) that are considered necessary for increasing national competitiveness and security. The expansion of the British state in modern times has, therefore, been inseparable from the changing position of British interests in changing world-systems. But agencies of the state can only operate effectively if they are financed by taxes generated, in the main, by the economic activity of private individuals and companies. The struggle to find a balance between the imperatives of national competitiveness and private freedom from state intervention has been a leading theme in British politics since the 1950s.

A very distinctive phase of development began in 1979 when Mrs. Thatcher's first Conservative government came into office. Her explicit policy from that point on was to reduce the size of the state apparatus and to withdraw it from certain spheres of activity to which, she argued, "privatized" arrangements were more appropriate. This process of "re-commodification" (Offe 1984) went to work in some of the former nationalized industries and utilities as well as in certain parts of the welfare and education services. At the same time, economic exigencies also disposed the government to pursue a policy of retrenchment.

As a proportion of gross domestic product (GDP), general government expenditure has been declining since 1980. The public sector (central and local government) also employs a decreasing proportion of the work force. Still, the state continues to consume about 40 percent of GDP or 20 percent of private income, despite the fact that expenditure on its goods and services represents a shrinking part of its budget. This corresponds with the claim that the government is cutting back the services supplied by the state while continuing to maintain a huge state apparatus. Each stage of state "withdrawal" has been accompanied by measures that have had the effect of increasing the state's centralized control over activities and services that had previously been regulated by local or regional organizations. This places limits on the development of a truly independent sector in the United Kingdom.

Further aspects of state hegemony in the United Kingdom concern the lack of a Bill of Rights and the government's heavy-handed commitment to the highly restrictive laws on official secrets. The growth of massive bureaucracies to monitor and regulate ever-widening areas of private and collective life has, in the absence of anything approaching a Freedom of Information Act, enabled agents of the state to operate with virtual impunity. The Recent attempts by the government to impose injunctions on newspapers, books, and television programs in order to suppress alleged breaches of national security have made it even more difficult to monitor state activity. For this and other reasons, there is considerable anxiety about the dangers of the Leviathan becoming even less accountable to citizens in the future. The largely unwritten constitution of the United Kingdom seems to allow any government with a large majority in the House of Commons to adapt and enlarge the state apparatus with impunity.[1]

Nevertheless, the importance of the voluntary sector was frequently acknowledged by Mrs. Thatcher's government, but the ideological reasons advanced were far removed from those of the eighteenth-century liberal advocates of civil society. Rather, the thrust has been toward radical ways of increasing the United Kingdom's productivity and competitiveness in the capitalist world-system by reducing taxation and state expenditure in order to maximize the potential for private capital investment and profit. "Rolling back the boundaries of the state" in the United Kingdom has little to do with a pluralist doctrine of democracy and much to do with creating opportunities for private profit in the apparent belief that practically all aspects of life would benefit from the competitive spirit of the marketplace. The government, therefore, implemented numerous schemes for training young people in vocational skills and giving them work experience, and for retraining older people in order, paradoxically, to boost the private sector's contribution to national economic performance.

In sum, it is doubtful whether modern British society has enjoyed a buoyant third sector of Tocquevillean character in the recent past. The history of the major educational, cultural, religious, and philanthropic institutions has tended to link them with the state either by royal charter and patronage or by the network of elite kinship. The notion of an Establishment in this sense is quite inclusive insofar as it has successfully incorporated to varying degrees all the major public institutions of what might be termed "civil society." Only radical political groups, some minority religions, and some labor unions have maintained effective independence from the state, but they could hardly be described as "mediating structures."

---

[1] According to Johnson (1987), the adversarial style of politics in the United Kingdom since the 1960s, in combination with the tendency for governments to intervene in all areas of life, has undermined the authority and the public respect for political institutions. It has also fostered an unrealistically "providential" view of the government's capacity to cope with all major problems. Consequently, "the people expected too much of governments and, at the same time, appeared to endorse practices which made it virtually certain that any government would lack the authority to act" (Johnson 1987:148).

ECONOMIC DECLINE

Current thinking about the performance of the British economy in the twentieth century is that the process of secular decline relative to some other Western European countries, Japan, and the Unites States had its origins in the failure to plan adequately for the efficient exploitation of new markets and new resources in the late nineteenth century. The results of a rather rigid adherence to laissez-faire doctrines were evident even before World War I in a relative slowness to appreciate the importance of technical and scientific education, training, business studies, and labor relations. The experience of mass warfare, mass mobilization, worldwide economic depression, rearmament, and increasing competition from more recently industrialized nations did little to modify the essentially conservative and noninterventionist policies of successive British governments prior to World War II. It was only in the 1940s that the Treasury began to involve itself extensively in planning and forecasting the shape and performance of the national economy.

At present, the United Kingdom's weakness in industrial productivity is largely responsible for a serious decline in the country's living standards in comparison with those of other advanced industrial societies. Even the improvements registered recently in rates of inflation, unemployment, and productivity may merely reflect the very low levels to which the country's economy had sunk since the early 1970s. It is also questionable whether the current fashion for encouraging entrepreneurship, small business, and philanthropy will compensate for the relative lack of long-term investment in research, education, and social infrastructure. For example, the proportion of young adults enrolled in universities and polytechnics in courses leading to degrees was virtually the same in 1984–1985 (13.7 percent) as it had been in 1970–1971 (13.8 percent).[2] This is in marked contrast to the situation in most other advanced industrial societies, where a much greater proportion of young people participates in higher education. University and polytechnic students represent only 1.79 percent of the U.K. population. This compares very unfavorably with the figures for the United States (5.14 percent), the Netherlands (2.7 percent), West Germany (2.54 percent), France (2.36 percent), and Japan (2 percent). Similarly, public expenditures on education in the United Kingdom accounted for 6.7 percent of GNP in 1975 but dropped to 5.7 percent in 1980 and to 5.2 percent in 1984.

The medium-term outlook also gives cause for concern because the exhaustion of North Sea oil and gas reserves early in the twenty-first century and the

[2] The figures represent the ratio of new students under twenty-one years of age to the average of the U. K. population aged eighteen and nineteen.

disposal of nationalized industries will probably have hampered continuing economic competitiveness and growth.

Additionally, the prospect for a significant improvement in the United Kingdom's balance of international payments situation appears uncertain because of the country's heavy dependence on both exports and imports. In 1985 the export of goods and services amounted to 29.1 percent of GDP, and imports amounted to 27.6 percent. Roughly 36 percent of food and raw materials for industry were imported. The state of the economy is therefore peculiarly susceptible to fluctuations in the world economy and is consequently to a large degree beyond the direct control of British authorities. The United Kingdom's share of world exports of manufactures declined dramatically from 20.41 percent in 1954, through 11.9 percent in 1967, to 9 percent in 1983.

It is immensely difficult to assess fully the impact of recent economic changes in the United Kingdom on the country's prospects for a buoyant public sphere. But evidence from sophisticated studies of relatively high rates of unemployment, loss of skills, and the decline of manufacturing industries (Gershuny 1983; Pahl 1984) indicates that a process of polarization is progressively dividing the typically employed, qualified, prosperous Southeasterners from their less fortunate fellow Britons in the North and on the Celtic fringes of the country. Regional disparities in opportunity have always been a feature of British life, but the divisions are now probably deeper than they have ever been in modern times. Even the availability of a truly national press and broadcasting industry has been unable to overcome this divisiveness. In these circumstances, the prospects for the health of an independent public sphere are not good. Yet the need for voluntary services is persistently strong. The weakness of the traditionally tolerant and liberal centers of public opinion is reflected in the growth of "welfare pluralism" and in the relative decline of the mainstream religious organizations. The voluntary organizations in social welfare also find themselves increasingly in demand but swamped with problems and deprived of the resources necessary for the accomplishment of their tasks. This is the point at which to turn to a more detailed consideration of the significance of the welfare state for public discourse in the United Kingdom.

THE STATE AND SOCIAL WELFARE

In order to understand the distinctive position of the voluntary sector in the United Kingdom, it is essential to realize that the British welfare state has three main roots: the Poor Law, mutual aid, and philanthropy.

The provision of social welfare was an integral, though not outstanding, feature of many medieval European societies. The Roman Catholic church was especially active in cultivating and applying the Christian duty to "help thy neighbor" through a kind of ecclesiastical Poor Law and through schemes that enabled wealthy donors to support the church's own charitable activities.

But by the mid-seventeenth century the old system had collapsed in Britain, partly as a consequence of the English church's separation from Rome and partly because the manorial economy was being disturbed by a revolution in agriculture and by the increasing power of town-based trading companies. An urban proletariat and bourgeoisie were asserting themselves in ways that threatened to break the molds of the feudal institutions.

With the church in decline, donations to secular charities (especially in education and poor relief) increased dramatically in the sixteenth century. The Tudor state also became more actively involved in the control and management of vagrants and beggars, culminating in a statute of 1572 that empowered parishes to levy "poor rates" for the maintenance of workhouses, houses of correction, and almshouses. Legal changes also rationalized the status of charities and established the administrative apparatus for monitoring them.

The paternalism that characterized Tudor attitudes toward charity eventually gave way in the eighteenth century to a more laissez-faire approach, which permitted the quality of the Poor Law institutions and of the charitable trusts to deteriorate. The overriding aim of early nineteenth century legislation appeared to be to make a sharp distinction between workers and paupers, and to coerce the latter into employment. Paupers were deprived of many rights and were subjected to humiliating conditions in the workhouses. Civil unrest in the poorest parts of London in the 1860s and 1870s, amply publicized by moral reformers and especially by the findings of Charles Booth's empirical surveys of poverty, eventually persuaded the authorities that the Poor Law had to be replaced by a more humane and universally equitable system for relieving poverty, which could not be a charge on local residents alone. The earliest measures included a rudimentary income maintenance scheme (1905), state retirement pensions (1908), labor exchanges (1909), and compulsory subscription to national insurance sickness and unemployment (1911).

The accelerating pace of industrialization and migration from rural to urban areas in the mid-nineteenth century created the conditions in which various forms of mutual aid among predominantly working-class people became popular. The common feature of this type of mutual aid was insurance against potentially disastrous episodes of sickness or unemployment. Friendly and cooperative societies were the most popular forms of mutual aid and they were subsequently imitated by trade unions. These mutual-aid charities still enjoy a special legal status and fall under the general supervision of the Registrar of Friendly Societies. Many of the associations formed in the nineteenth century are still in operation, although they primarily function nowadays as savings clubs, building societies (savings and loans), or supplements to statutory benefits.

The tradition of philanthropy is ancient and has taken many different forms, some of which are still evident among today's registered charities. Philanthropy tended originally to take the form of grants of money or land donated by relatively wealthy people for the improvement of the living conditions of specific classes of relatively poor, underprivileged, or disabled people. These bequests were exempt from taxation and from governmental interference provided that they were made in due form and correctly administered by independent trustees. The number of philanthropic charities began to increase in number and scale around the middle of the nineteenth century, largely in association with the evangelical revival and with religiously inspired schemes for the moral "uplift" of the urban "masses." Many of the United Kingdom's most respected and powerful charities date from this period.[3]

Long before the end of the nineteenth century it had become apparent that the haphazard and inefficient provision of social welfare by both the overburdened Poor Law Boards and the mutual-aid and philanthropic associations was inadequate. Piecemeal reforms were instituted by successive governments, but the prevailing opinion was that, with the exception of education, it was still advisable for the state to do no more than plug the gaps left by voluntary organizations.[4] Statutory and voluntary bodies were kept rigidly separate except in the field of education until 1914, when state funds were made available for the first time to voluntary organizations in various fields of welfare. The progressively closer relationships between the statutory and voluntary bodies were cemented by mass mobilization in World War I, with its attendant problems, and by the subsequent years of economic depression.

The consolidation of the British welfare state in the mid-1940s was partly an extension of the all-pervasive powers assumed by the state in World War II and partly a response to moderate socialist thinking. In particular, there were ideological objections to the notion of patronizing, top-down charity and to its particularism. There were strong calls, instead, for universal entitlement, progressive taxation, and minimally acceptable standards of service. The balance of responsibility therefore shifted away from the voluntary sector and onto the state as the main provider of a basic level of welfare in health, education, housing, unemployment benefits, and personal social services. Welfare pluralism is the ideological justification for the resulting mixture of statutory and voluntary provisions. The welfare state was, from its beginnings, a national institution, but control and delivery of many services have always been in the hands of local government and health-authority agencies. The justification for this division of labor between the national and regional or local levels of the state is that it helps attenuate feelings of alienation from the massive bureau-

---

[3] For example, the Royal National Institute for the Blind (1868), Dr. Barnado's orphanages (1870), the Royal National Lifeboat Institution (1854), the Young Men's Christian Association (1844), the National Society for the Prevention of Cruelty to Children (1884), and the Howard League for Penal Reform (1868) were all established during this period.

[4] The Education Act of 1870 had provided free schooling at the elementary level alongside schools run by churches on a fee-paying basis.

cracies of government ministries and to increase the sense of participation in the management of services that affect clients directly.

The most important pieces of legislation framing the welfare state included the Education Act (1944), the Family Allowance Act (1945), the National Insurance Act (1946), the National Health Service Act (1946), and the National Assistant Act (1948). The welfare state was also central to the 1945–1951 Labour government's program for nationalizing the key industries of British society. Without central ownership and control of the main industries and utilities, the socialists argued, there could be no hope of redistributing wealth, raising minimum standards of living, and achieving greater equality of opportunity.

Public-opinion surveys consistently show that a majority of Britons still approve in general of the welfare state and are especially attached to the National Health Service. But the cutbacks in funding for many welfare services, beginning in the early 1970s, have caused a crisis in some areas, and criticism of services is widespread. The future of the welfare state is, therefore, at the very center of British politics today. The Labour party has committed itself to protecting and improving the delivery of welfare and educational services, while the Conservatives have pursued a policy of making the services more efficient and cost-effective. No other issue currently comes closer to an ideological debate about the nature of British society. But the statutory services are increasingly hard to separate from the voluntary and informal sectors.

THE VOLUNTARY AND INFORMAL SECTORS

The centrality of the welfare state to virtually all aspects of life in British society creates some difficulties for conceptualizations of the public sphere. Special attention must be paid to the way in which the British categorize agencies in the field of social welfare, since this is an area where the interface between state and society takes on unusual significance. The post-World War II consolidation of the welfare state might have been expected to displace the voluntary organizations that had previously been the major supplier of most social-welfare services. But the voluntary organizations continued to function and even to grow alongside the statutory agencies. Indeed, evidence suggests that the existence of statutory services actually encouraged a demand for still more services and that the voluntary organizations expanded to meet the new demands.

In any case, the shortage of government funds meant that the statutory services were simply unable to replace the voluntary organizations entirely. It is not surprising, therefore, that three successive official investigations of (i) charitable trusts (the Nathan Report, 1952), (ii) social workers in local authority health and welfare services (the Younghusband Report, 1959), and (iii) local authority and allied personal social services (the Seebohm Report, 1969) all concluded that there was a vital role for the voluntary sector to play in the fields of social and personal welfare despite the fact that it had been superseded by the state in many respects. There was general agreement that, among their other functions, the voluntary organizations could usefully catalyze interest in public-welfare issues and encourage people to monitor the standards of care being provided by the government and local authorities.

The most authoritative public review of the role of the voluntary sector in the United Kingdom to date, the Wolfenden Report of 1978, concluded that "the voluntary system . . . can now best be seen in terms of the ways in which it complements, supplements, extends and influences the informal and statutory systems" (Wolfenden Committee 1978:26). The expectation was that the voluntary system would *extend* the scope of statutory services by identifying new needs and pioneering new methods; *supplement* the state's services by providing alternatives and by attracting the help of volunteers who would not be attracted to work in the statutory sector; and *influence* the public sector by showing how improvements would be made and by criticizing statutory arrangements. But the Wolfenden Committee's view of the matter seriously underestimated the importance of voluntary initiatives (mainly at the local level), which remain the sole provider of certain services (for example, marriage guidance, citizens advice bureaus, emergency help telephone lines, lifeboats, animal welfare, and first aid in public places).

The timing of Wolfenden's inquiry was fortunate in that the collection of information was still in progress when the present phase of austerity and selective cutbacks in government spending began to affect the voluntary and statutory sectors of welfare. The inquiry's timing also meant that it was able to take account of some significant changes in the character of voluntary organizations that had begun to gather momentum under the Labour government of the mid-1970s. In particular, there had been a proliferation of groups engaged in advising claimants about their statutory entitlements to benefits in an increasingly complex welfare state, raising awareness of outstanding problems, lobbying legislators for improved services, organizing volunteers, and stimulating a bewildering variety of self-help initiatives. In many cases, these highly active and well-informed groups were based on American models of community or neighborhood organizations. Many of them quickly gained nationwide membership and forms of organizations. Their relatively rapid achievement of power, resources, and influence has been attributed partly to the roles that some well-placed agents of the welfare state had played in the groups' early stages and partly to their ability to "slipstream" the emergent consumer protection movement in the United Kingdom (Hatch 1980). There are good grounds for thinking that the experiences gained in the course of various feminist campaigns and struggles also fed directly into these new movements.

An equally important factor in the success of the "new-style" voluntary

organizations of the 1970s was the massive increase in government funding of
the *statutory* social services between 1965 and 1972 (Webb 1980). This, coupled with appropriate legislation, enabled the state agencies to enter into contractual arrangements with the voluntary organizations. According to Brenton
(1985:43), "Local authority social services department subsidies to voluntary
organizations grew from £2.5 million in 1972/73 to nearly £8 million by 1975/
76." A symbol of the new relationship between the statutory and voluntary
sectors of welfare was the Conservative government's establishment in 1973
of the Voluntary Services Unit as a means of stimulating and coordinating
closer cooperation between the sectors. Tangible consequences of the partnership that Wolfenden advocated are difficult to find, however.

In the present context it is worth drawing attention to the vocabulary used
by the Wolfenden Committee, which is still widely used in discussions of the
British welfare state. Categorical distinctions are drawn between the statutory,
the voluntary, and the informal sectors of U.K. society. The first consists of
agencies established by law, functioning within the framework of the state and
staffed by employees of the state. The second consists of initiatives pursued
by organized and formally established groups of citizens acting voluntarily.
The initiative may, of course, be administered by a mixture of paid staff and
unpaid volunteers. The third sector is confined to initiatives by private citizens
acting without formal rules and independent of any organization. It includes
caring activities conducted within the household or neighborhood either by
unpaid relatives or by neighbors and friends.

This tripartite scheme cuts across the categories of public, private, and nonprofit, for some nonprofit organizations operate in the public realm, and others
in the private. The most glaring difference from American usage concerns
"private." For-profit (commercial) activity tends to be conceptualized in the
United Kingdom as part of the *public* realm (which overlaps with the state)
and has rarely been taken into consideration in connection with the welfare
state. "Private," in the British sense, tends to refer either to the individual
person or to the domestic sphere of life. The situation is changing, however,
in the wake of government plans to facilitate the commercial provision of services in health care, nursing, and leisure. If the Wolfenden Committee were
at work today it would have to take these "commercial" concerns more fully
into account.

Since there has historically been very little competition between commercial and nonprofit organizations in the United Kingdom (except perhaps in
education), the vocabulary of social analysis is more sensitive to the importance of the distinction between statutory and voluntary sectors. The former
consists of agencies and services that are required by law, while the latter
depends on the initiative of groups or individuals. Between these two categories fall the for-profit organizations that may act as subcontractors to statutory
or voluntary agencies. The further distinction between voluntary organizations

and informal networks of care became more important in the 1980s because many voluntary organizations increasingly operated as clients of the state. The greater independence of the informal networks from state funding and contracting is felt to warrant a separate category. Good Neighbor and Neighborhood Watch schemes represent hybrid types of informal-cum-voluntary organizations.

The main finding of a recent study of the effects of government grant aid to voluntary organizations in the United Kingdom (Leat 1986) was that the benefits to client organizations outweighed the costs. A three-stage multiplier effect was identified:

1. The higher the level of government aid, the higher the levels of paid staff, volunteers, *and* nongovernmental funding.
2. The higher the levels of staff and funding, the greater the output of effort, services, and achievements.
3. The higher the levels of achievements and public profile, the stronger the public interest in most areas of voluntary activity (especially when intermediary bodies such as volunteer bureaus are involved).

The costs were far from inconsiderable, however. The two principal costs of being an agent under contract to the government were, first, a higher degree of uncertainty about future funding, and, second, a certain loss of independence. The character of the government/agent relationship was also said to be changing. Informal relations of trust were giving way to more formal, contractual relations based on explicit objectives and clear criteria of accountability. As a result, there is a distinct danger that the much-vaunted flexibility and innovativeness of the voluntary organizations might be compromised. Success is increasingly measured in terms of growth in budgets and objective indicators of activity.

The evidence from the United Kingdom seems to confirm James's (1987) conclusion of her comparative study of the nonprofit sector:

The subsidies [from government] facilitate private and private-sector growth, but they also enable the government to extract concessions in return, in the form of regulations over inputs, outputs, and other characteristics that satisfy diverse constituencies. The subsidies, and the regulations and market forces that accompany them, have the effect of raising costs. . . . Thus, the very factors that originally created the demand for a private sector also set in motion forces making the private sector more like the public; as the private sector grows, with government funding and regulating, it becomes quasi-governmental. (James 1987:413)

It is very difficult, however, to assess the impact of the increasingly contractual relationship between statutory and voluntary sectors. Part of the difficulty arises from the paucity of reliable and comprehensive information in the United Kingdom (but see Leat 1988). There are wide discrepancies among estimates of even the most basic and elementary statistics about voluntary organizations. There are numerous guides to voluntary organizations (for example, *The Voluntary Agencies Directory*) and an increasingly sophisticated compilation of annual statistics about the levels of charitable giving among large companies, local and central governments, and charitable trusts or foundations (*Charity Trends*). In addition, numerous compilations of grant-awarding bodies in specific fields of activity are available.

It is impossible, however, to obtain good evidence about the precise extent of voluntary activity in the aggregate (but see Prochaska 1988:9–11). This is surprising in view of the fact that most charitable organizations appear on the Charity Commission's register, and most of them are required to file annual accounts. Yet according to the evidence given by the Chief Charity Commissioner to the House of Commons Committee of Public Accounts in 1988,[5] only 23 percent of registered charities had actually submitted accounts in the previous five years. The committee reported that it had been "disturbed" by this finding, and it found the fact that only 4 percent of accounts were monitored each year entirely unsatisfactory. In other words, there is little prospect of obtaining reliable information about charitable activity in the absence of adequate machinery for simply recording it. Nor is this particular situation likely to change if the government's proposals for relevant legislation are implemented,[6] for the recommendation is merely to put a mark in the charity register against the entries of charities that fail to submit annual accounts.

Two further considerations must be borne in mind. First, many voluntary organizations are not registered charities and do not, consequently, appear in any official statistics. Second, religious charities are exempt from the requirement to submit their accounts. In these circumstances, sample surveys are the only realistic method of collecting information, but the lack of a comprehensive sampling frame makes even this method problematic.

The most authoritative estimate of the percentage of adults engaged in unpaid work of service to others in 1981 was 23 percent, with a slightly higher proportion of women than men. These findings from a sample survey of the British population conceal what more restricted surveys have found: namely, that women who are not in paid employment outside the home are much more likely to commit a lot of their time to voluntary activities. But the national sample did discover that, for both men and women, people in the professional class were more than three times as likely to be volunteers than were unskilled workers. Subsequent surveys have discovered higher rates of volunteering. Definitional differences make comparisons hazardous, but 44 percent of respondents to the survey conducted by the Charities Aid foundation in 1987

[5] The Sixteenth Report from the Committee of Public Accounts, Session 1987–1988: "Monitoring and Control of Charities in England and Wales."
[6] *Charities* (1989).

reported that they had taken part in voluntary activities in the month preceding the survey. This contrasts sharply with Hatch's (1980) finding that only 5.2 percent of the respondents to his survey in 1978 had acted as volunteers.

Information about the finances of voluntary organizations is no less problematic, but a study of a sample of groups involved in personal social services found that, between 1970 and 1976, the proportion of their income from fees and charges increased by about 7 percent, whereas all other sources of income declined. Nevertheless, voluntary giving still amounted to about half of the total income (Unell, 1979). By 1985, however, Posnett (1987) estimated that fees and receipts from sales of goods represented 60.7 percent of charities' income and that, as a proportion of their total income, fees had more than doubled their significance. Yet there were wide variations between types of charitable organization. Fees amounted to 41.3 percent of income in education, 35 percent in arts and culture, and 20 percent in housing, but only 3.1 percent in special interest groups, and 0.6 percent in social welfare. Smaller charities appear to rely more than larger ones on fee income.

Other studies have also detected a proportionate decline in the volume of private donations to voluntary organizations, but the decline has been compensated for by increases in fees, charges, and income from sales and royalties. At the same time, income from local and central governments in the form of either grants or payments for contracted services probably increased substantially from the early 1970s to the mid 1980s before going into decline, albeit with wide variations between regions and organizations. But once again, information about the voluntary sector as a whole is scarce and difficult to interpret.

The annual surveys conducted by the Charities Aid Foundation show that there is considerable volatility in the distribution of charitable giving to the largest fund-raising charities. Table 2.1 shows changes in the levels and sources of income of the top two hundred fund-raising charities in the period from 1983 to 1987.

Yet the balance between voluntary and other sources of income has been remarkably stable in this period. On average, 55 percent comes from voluntary donations, and 45 percent comes from other sources. On the other hand, the annual rate of increase in both sources of income has fluctuated considerably, although it has been generally declining since 1984–1985. The levels of expenditure have followed the same trend.

Table 2.2 show the distribution of voluntary income across the major sectors of voluntary activity.

Information about the extent of donations to voluntary organizations on the part of large companies is among the most reliable because it is based on replies to sophisticated questionnaires. The Charities Aid Foundation's analysis of this information indicates that the top four-hundred corporate donors gave cash donations of £72.5 million, which represents, on average, 0.19 percent

TABLE 2.1
Income of the Top Two Hundred Fund-Raising Charities, 1983–1987

	1983–1984	1984–1985	1985–1986	1986–1987
Voluntary income				
Covenants	7.0%	5.0%	5.0%	7.0%
Legacies	33.0%	28.0%	33.0%	36.0%
Other gifts	60.0%	67.0%	62.0%	47.0%
Voluntary fund-raising	—	—	—	10.0%
Total voluntary income (£)	526,521	697,734	721,364	770,182
Other income				
Trading	7.0%	8.0%	6.0%	2.0%
Sales of goods and services	—	—	—	24.0%
Central government	17.0%	17.0%	17.0%	—
Local government fees	22.0%	19.0%	20.0%	—
Local government grants	1.5%	1.0%	1.0%	—
Combined government fees	—	—	—	22.0%
Combined government grants	—	—	—	19.0%
Rents, investments, etc.	21.0%	21.0%	20.0%	18.0%
General	31.5%	34.0%	36.0%	15.0%
Total other income (£)	430,179	525,251	596,864	692,664
Total income (£)	956,700	1,222,000	1,318,000	1,462,000
Proportion of income				
Voluntary	55.0%	57.0%	55.0%	53.0%
Other	45.0%	43.0%	45.0%	47.0%
Annual change in real terms				
Total voluntary income	+13.0%	+25.0%	+0.4%	+2.0%
Total other income	+10.0%	+15.0%	+10.0%	+11.0%
Total income	+11.0%	+21.0%	+5.0%	+7.0%

Source: Adapted from Charity Trends, no. 11 (1988), p. 114.

of their annual profits in 1986–1987. This also amounts to £13.22 for each of their employees. But a separate study of the total community involvement of the 110 largest companies showed that their cash donations account for only 32 percent of their voluntary expenditures (compared with a rate of roughly 80 percent for the United States). Other expenditures included secondment of personnel to voluntary organizations, sponsorship of communal activities, employment schemes, and use of premises.

These findings may be a helpful indication of the general pattern of the

TABLE 2.2
Voluntary Income of the Top Two Hundred Charities, by
Major Sector

Sector	Proportion of Voluntary Income (%)
Medicine and health	32.6
General welfare	27.6
International aid	21.2
Animal protection	6.8
Religious mission	5.6
Preservation of history	5.1
Arts and youth	1.0

Source: Social Trends, vol. 19 (1989).

community involvement of large companies, but further research is required to discover whether this pattern can be generalized to smaller companies and whether it is in process of changing significantly. A Guide to Company Giving (1986–87) estimated, on the basis of the National Income and Expenditure Survey, that the 1.5 million companies registered in the United Kingdom contributed a total of about £200 million to charitable purposes in 1985. The 1988 Finance Act allegedly made it easier for companies to make charitable donations, and the growth of umbrella bodies such as the Per Cent Club and the Council for Charitable Support is also expected to augment the volume of company giving in the future.

Similarly, recent changes in the law relating to the income tax recoverable on charitable donations made by private individuals are expected to increase the contributions from Britain's 21.7 million households. The Charity Household Survey of a random sample of 963 households in 1987 discovered that the mean monthly contribution to charity was £8.60, or approximately $13, with 40 percent giving less than £1 and 5 percent giving more than £30. Allowing for sampling variation, the total value of household donations to charity on a national scale was estimated to lie between £1,800 million and £2,700 million. The median value of £2 per household represents .24 percent of the median total gross household income for the United Kingdom. This is substantially lower than the 2.05 percent of personal incomes that Americans donated to voluntary organizations, according to Weber (1988).

The mean figures conceal significant differences between income groups. The government's Family Household Survey discovered a consistently strong and positive connection between net income and the incidence of charitable giving in 1984. But with reference to the average size of donation, the connection was less clear. The connection between the occupation of the head of household and the size of the average donation as a percentage of net income was also quite variable. Table 2.3 shows this inconsistency.

It is too early to know whether the new tax-free payroll deduction scheme will seriously affect the frequency and volume of individuals' charitable giving. In the first year of its operation the plan netted about one million pounds, but the expectation was that, with improved publicity and greater experience, it would raise at least ten times as much in its second year. Regardless of its degree of success, this scheme represents a perfect example of the increasingly intricate relationships among the central government, employers, employees, and the voluntary sector.

At the level of regional, county, and district governments, relations with voluntary organizations are even more complex and intense. The Charities Aid Foundation's survey of regional and district health authorities, for example, showed that the overall level of grant making has continued to rise to £25.2 million despite the financial problems of the National Health Service. Variations between authorities were quite marked, however, and the average value of grants barely exceeded ten thousand pounds. Projects dealing with addiction and mental health were the most numerous recipients of grants from health authorities in 1986–1987, but in terms of the average value of grants, hospices and projects concerned with children and child abuse headed the list. The present government's policy of deinstitutionalizing the mentally ill and the elderly seems likely to stimulate even closer relationships between health authorities and voluntary organizations.

Local authorities, other than health councils, paid a total of £402 million in grants and fees to voluntary organizations in 1986–1987. This represents a slight decline in comparison with the levels of funding in the previous two years. Central government policies of imposing limits on local government

TABLE 2.3
Donations to Charity, by Occupation of Head of Household, 1984

	Average Donation Per Week (£)	Donation as Proportion of Income (%)
Professional/technical	2.60	1.16
Administrative/managerial	1.31	0.65
Teaching	1.55	0.96
Clerical	0.99	0.48
Shop assistants	0.88	0.70
Skilled manual	1.63	1.61
Semiskilled manual	1.40	0.84
Unskilled manual	1.20	1.76
Average	1.46	0.95

Source: Adapted from Charity Trends, no. 11 (1988), p. 42, based on Family Expenditure Survey.

expenditure and of abolishing the Greater London Council and the other metropolitan counties have created considerable turbulence in expenditure levels and destinations. Spending on social services consumes the highest percentage of grants and fees (33.2 percent), but this represents a 5 percent decline over the previous year's level. Spending on housing also declined relative to other areas. But the proportion of spending on education, leisure, recreation, and the arts increased slightly. These changes imposed particularly difficult conditions on the already hard-pressed voluntary organizations in inner-city areas.

Central government grants to voluntary organizations amounted to £279.5 million in 1986–1987. This represents an increase of 4.31 percent (in real terms, only 1.1 percent) over the level of support provided in the previous financial year and is indicative of the uneven rate of growth in central-government support for voluntary organizations. Table 2.4 shows the fluctuations that have occurred in this area. In addition to these grants, the central government gave £1,048 million to housing associations and societies in 1986–1987. The Inland Revenue estimated that the value of tax concessions to voluntary organizations in the same year amounted to about £600 million. Finally, a large number of nondepartmental public bodies (quangos) also made grants exceeding £1,649 million.

This brings the total of public-sector support for the voluntary sector to £4,147 million for 1986–1987—a decrease in real terms of .45 percent over the previous year. Yet, according to Prochaska (1988:4), "In its various guises the government . . . is now the largest single contributor to philanthropic causes." But Pinker (1986:117) persists with the view that numerous foundations and voluntary agencies continue to attach a high value to "their autonomy and constitutional independence from the government, despite their increasing dependence . . . on financial grants from both central and local government." In fact, the fall in the level of central and local government support has almost been matched by the sharp increase in funding from health authorities and in the size of tax concessions to the voluntary sector following the 1986 Finance Act. These changes in the relative weight of the major funding sources correspond to the government's express policy of reducing the level of direct grants from the central state; strengthening the contractual relationship between statutory agencies and voluntary organizations; and providing tax incentives for corporate and household charity.

CHARITIES

The term "voluntary sector" includes practically all the organizations that are registered as charities in the United Kingdom. But as the legal status of charities is different from that of many other voluntary organizations, it is necessary to specify more carefully their position in relation to the rest of the voluntary sector. Charities are also under considerable pressure to conform with the state's view of how they should conduct their affairs. This is primarily

TABLE 2.4

Central Government Support to Voluntary Organizations, 1980–1986 (thousands of pounds)

	1980	1981	1982	1983	1984	1985	1986
Agriculture, fisheries,							
food	70	93	91	99	103	118	172
Defense	2,004	2,673	2,361	2,644	3,285	3,544	4,826
Education and science	11,454	12,381	11,175	14,318	16,583	18,089	16,230
Employment	21,391	23,207	26,380	27,720	29,180	30,316	33,294
Energy	—	91	134	91	344	865	1,118
Environment							
Direct grants	683	763	976	1,220	2,178	2,566	3,612
Urban Programme	22,000	27,000	37,500	46,500	54,000	76,300	76,011
Foreign and							
Commonwealth	523	584	—	748	813	823	881
Health and social							
security	12,247	13,775	15,462	23,123	30,068	32,046	35,076
Home Office	14,466	15,396	15,559	16,890	17,088	18,300	19,541
Industry	501	479	660	—	—	—	—
Lord Chancellor	469	529	583	—	669	692	727
N. Ireland							
Department	16,885	20,398	9,480	12,091	13,711	16,801	14,975
Overseas							
Development							
Administration	5,709	6,393	9,030	10,772	24,027	31,233	26,823
Scottish Office							
Direct grants	4,741	5,515	6,500	6,824	7,413	8,247	8,970
Urban Programme	1,007	3,189	4,897	6,750	10,200	11,700	16,600
Trade and industry	4,063	4,965	5,600	6,221	7,370	8,063	8,689
Transport	423	451	440	509	564	605	636
Welsh Office							
Direct grants	1,929	2,448	3,280	3,281	4,615	5,094	8,468
Urban Programme	244	690	862	1,325	2,200	2,375	2,850
Totals	120,000	140,000	150,000	182,000	224,000	267,000	279,000

Source: Adapted from Charity Trends, no. 11 (1988), p. 32.

because charities enjoy relief from various taxes and because they are entrusted with the right to raise funds by appeal to the public. The Charity Commission does not actually grant tax exemptions, but the Inland Revenue usually accepts the fact of registration as confirmation of charitable purpose. Charitable status therefore confers major benefits on voluntary organizations; this is why they occupy a distinctive and noteworthy position in the voluntary sector of U. K. society.[7]

[7] The special status of charities in England and Wales has attracted favorable attention in the

The notions of "trust" and charitable "use" arose in the fourteenth century and were formalized by statute in 1601, but the modern history of charities in England and Wales (Scotland and Northern Ireland have different arrangements) began with the establishment of the Charity Commissioners, by Act of Parliament, in 1853. So many charitable organizations had found themselves in financial trouble in the mid-nineteenth century that it was considered necessary to regulate their affairs to some extent. The Commissioners regulated, by registration, only those charities that had an endowment and that therefore depended on the active management of their assets. In order to offer a measure of political independence to the Commissioners, of whom there are now three with a staff of several hundred, their appointments have always been for an indefinite period. Moreover, they are only attached to the Home Office for administrative convenience. Their reports go directly to Parliament each year and are not, therefore, a product of the government of the day. The cost of the Charity Commission in 1989 was in excess of seven million pounds.

The number of registered charities grew steadily throughout the Victorian age, but the rate of increase accelerated in the mid-twentieth century and indirectly led to the Charities Acts of 1960 and 1985. These statutes introduced some badly needed order into the administration of the charities and enabled the Commissioners for the first time to register charities that were actively involved in fund-raising. They also created the Charities Official Investment Fund in which any charity may invest its funds in unit trusts under the Official Custodian. Far from being relegated to a peripheral position by the advent of the welfare state, British charities have continued to increase in number since World War II. The rate of increase has actually accelerated, as table 2.5 indicates, with the result that about one-third of all registered charities have been founded since 1960.

By 1985, the total number of registered charities had reached 154,135. But a note of caution is required at this point. The charity "professionals" are confident that the reported rate of increase in the growth of charitable activity is genuine, but it must be added that the increasing scope and efficiency of the Charity Commission have also helped induce this growth. It is difficult to separate the effect of improved monitoring of charities from their real rate of growth. This is an ironic instance of the state's growing influence in shaping social activity that, by definition, is expected to be relatively free from such influence.

Following the creation of the full-fledged welfare state in the United Kingdom after World War II, the Charity Commissioners played an active role in rationalizing the local distribution of charities. They took the initiative in ad-

United States. One of the Research Reports prepared for the Commission on Private Philanthropy and Public Needs (1973–1975) specifically recommended that the United States should selectively borrow features from the British arrangements for administering charities (Spuehler 1977).

TABLE 2.5
Annual Registration of Charities, 1971–1985

	Newly Registered	Newly Founded
1971	1,967	769
1972	2,219	1,006
1973	2,527	1,165
1974	3,110	1,412
1975	2,859	1,386
1976	2,988	1,549
1977	3,598	1,830
1978	3,560	1,743
1979	3,299	1,736
1980	3,955	2,147
1981	3,425	1,822
1982	4,057	2,105
1983	3,804	1,990
1984	3,837	2,270
1985	3,942	3,790

Source: Charity Commission, *Reports of the Charity Commissioners for England and Wales.*

vising local authorities on ways of minimizing overlaps between charities, and between charities and statutory services. This was in recognition of the welfare state's coming to provide services that had previously been the preserve of charitable organizations alone. Many small charities were thereby amalgamated or coordinated, and their collective income was considerably increased.

A more intrusive role for the Charity Commissioners was also apparent in their request that the National Council of Social Service (NCSS),[8] a charity that had mediated between government and local social-service organizations since 1919, should investigate charitable fund-raising, accounting procedures, advertising, and cooperation. The Charity Commissioners were trying to maintain the independence of charitable organizations but at the same time to make them more accountable in ways that suited the state's own accounting practices. It may be significant, then, that an American specialist on charities described the Charity Commission as a "government-paid adviser to trustees" (Spuehler 1977). This description captures the close association between the state and voluntary sectors quite well. There is more than a hint of corporatism in this association.

The modus vivendi that has been worked out among charities, the Charity Commission, and the Inland Revenue owes much to the work of the Charities Aid Foundation (CAF), which has raised funds and has campaigned on behalf

[8] The name was changed to the National Council for Voluntary Organizations (NCVO) in 1980.

of charities in general. Replacing the Charities Aid Fund in 1974, the CAF undertook to mediate between donors (corporate or private) and charities. In addition to acting as a clearinghouse for donations and giving advice and practical help on the intricacies of legal covenants, the CAF is now much more aggressive in its schemes for eliciting donations from companies and for lobbying politicians on the need for new legislation. Its most recent innovations include a plan for investing charities' funds in the equivalent of a bank deposit (CAFCASH) and, more controversially, an arrangement whereby employers can be authorized to deduct charitable donations from salary payments (give-as-you-earn). With the explicit aim of imitating the American model, CAF has also been the driving force behind the Community Trust Development Unit, which was established in 1986 with government funds to stimulate local community trusts. Fifteen community trusts are already in operation, and a further sixty-four are in the process of being developed. The Charities Aid Foundation's annual publication, *Charity Statistics* (since 1988, *Charity Trends*), is the best source of information about the major trends and issues.

Although the law does not define "charity," it has always been understood that, for an organization to be charitable in law, it must exist for one or more of the following purposes: relief of poverty, advancement of education, advancement of religion, or to benefit the community. It is noticeable that the Commissioner's annual reports since World War II have been preoccupied with the problems of organizations that become involved in the causes with which their work is concerned—especially those that function as lobbies, pressure groups, or action groups. The Commissioners' practice has been to refuse registration to organizations that try to achieve political goals, and to warn those already registered that they run the risk of being removed from the Register of Charities if they substitute advocacy or lobbying for the direct pursuit of their lawful objective. For example, the middle-of-the-road Student Christian Movement was rebuked for donating three hundred pounds to a left-wing political group. And the Students Union of Sussex University was prevented from financially supporting the international aid agency War on Want. About one thousand complaints alleging abuse of charitable status were received in 1984.

The Charity Commissioners have the power to accept or reject applications for registration or reregistration as charities. But, as became clear in the protracted and ultimately abortive campaign to have the charitable status of two wings of the highly controversial Unification Church revoked in the early 1980s, the Commissioners do not have the power to remove charities from the Register. This is a matter for the High Court and is sometimes pursued by the Inland Revenue Department. Even in cases where the Commissioners have strong evidence of fraud or other wrongdoing, the most they can do is to bring a legal action for breach of public trust. They cannot revoke the registration of a charity in any other way. They can, however, prosecute trustees for failing to submit annual accounts, for failing to see that the charitable objectives are pursued, or for failing to make effective use of property and trust funds.

There is wide variation in the financial strength of registered charities. It was estimated in the early 1970s, for example, that well over half of all charities had incomes of less than one hundred pounds per annum, and only about 6 percent had more than five thousand pounds (this latter percentage rises to 90 percent, however, if the calculation is confined to relatively *new* charities, according to Gallagher 1975). But it is apparent that the wealthiest charities are becoming less and less representative of the whole charitable sector. The large charities with national or international outreach and effective fund-raising machinery are increasing their incomes at a much higher rate than are their smaller competitors. In 1985, for example, the income of the top two hundred charities increased by 21 percent their 1983–1984 levels. Their income from voluntary sources grew by 25 percent, and from other sources by 15 percent. The fastest-growing charities are actually those that specialize in overseas welfare. Their income grew by 16 percent in 1983–1984 and by a spectacular 110 percent in 1984–1985. By comparison, domestic charities were beginning to show signs of decline in 1985, with organizations in the fields of medicine and health registering a gain in real terms of only 2 percent over the previous year. The increase among general-welfare organizations was 6 percent. Nevertheless, Posnett (1987) estimated that the income of charities amounted to about 3.7 percent of GNP in 1985.

The current vogue for partnership between the state and the voluntary sector runs into severe problems in connection with charity law. The conditions of registration may be vague and ambiguous, but there is no doubt that they conspire to exclude organizations with the explicit aim of changing the political or social order in the United Kingdom. The relevant legislation still reflects the ancient belief that benefactors are separate from beneficiaries—the former are assumed to be wealthy and to have charitable obligations; the latter are presumed to be poor and to owe duties to their benefactors. But politically oriented activity and self-help groups are generally denied the fiscal benefits of charitable status. As these activities and groups were characteristic of the new wave of voluntarism in the 1970s, criticism of the convoluted laws and procedures governing charitable status has grown more intense but, as yet, without achieving tangible success. There is a widespread suspicion among activists of the new type of voluntary group that current legislation is biased in favor of middle-class objectives such as private schools, colleges, and professional associations but against working-class objectives such as changes in the law relating to entitlement to welfare benefits. As a result, the current arrangements are unhelpful to many voluntary organizations and they make no contribution toward reshaping the relationship between the state and the voluntary sector. On the contrary, they can be considered an obstacle to change because they disqualify many potential agents of social change from the kinds of fiscal benefits that might make them more successful.

The proposals published by the government in its White Paper of May 1989 (*Charities: A Framework for the Future*) for revising the law on charities in the light of the findings of two official reports[9] show a greater concern with the technicalities of the registration and monitoring of charitable organizations than with fundamental questions about the definition of charitable purposes in an advanced industrial society. Indeed, this was apparent in the White Paper's summary of its proposals: "[They] are designed to produce a stronger and a more modern framework of supervision which will equip the Charity Commission for a more active role, narrow the scope for abuse, encourage trustees to shoulder their responsibilities, and ensure continuing public confidence in the sector" (*Charities* 1989:4). The Home Secretary will propose legislation designed mainly to modernize the administration and effectiveness of the Charity Commission, to improve the monitoring of charities, to introduce charges for the Commission's services, to harmonize the laws relating to commercial and charitable companies, to regulate new agencies and forms of fundraising, and eventually to bring the administration of charities in Scotland and Northern Ireland into line with the practice in England and Wales.

Although registered charities have long played an important role in the public sphere of British society, it is questionable whether the current restrictions on their aims and procedures really allow charities to act as an independent sector between the state and the market. They purchase their fiscal privileges at a price that effectively stifles their capacity to criticize the status quo or to challenge statutory arrangements. On the other hand, the failure of successive governments to rationalize the laws relating to charity arouses suspicions about the abuse of charitable status, and this, in turn, further weakens the potential for charities to serve as a medium for creative debate and innovation. In short, the extent to which charitable organizations can actually contribute to the strengthening of the democratic social order is limited in the United Kingdom.

RELIGION

Misapprehensions about the place of religion in the British public sphere are widespread but understandable. The constitutional marriage of church and state and the (until recently) relatively low level of religious diversity may engender the inference that formal Christian organizations play a prominent role in public life. Yet the reality is quite different. The mainstream religious organizations are marginal to many public forums and issues.

---

[9] "Efficiency Scrutiny of the Supervision of Charities" (1987), known as the Woodfield Report, and the Public Accounts Committee's "Monitoring and Control of Charities" (1988).

The United Kingdom has two established churches (the Church of England and the Church of Scotland), of which the sovereign is the titular head. Parliament is technically responsible for the relevant legislation governing the Church of England's broad organization and forms of worship, and the prime minister's office recommends to the monarch candidates for the position of bishop and archbishop. The shortlist of candidates is nowadays heavily influenced by the church. In this respect and others, the Anglican church thoroughly penetrates the upper echelons of the political, legal, educational, cultural, and philanthropic institutions of the United Kingdom, but the religious situation is also pluralistic. Anglicanism remains probably the most salient religious confession in the country, and its cultural importance has been unquestionable. Yet active participants in the church's activities make up a small minority of the adult population, and the church is increasingly challenged by both Christian and non-Christian competitors.

There have occasionally been moves toward disestablishment, and controversy has on occasion surrounded particular episcopal appointments. But the fact that the twenty-four senior bishops and the two archbishops (all of whom have seats in the House of Lords) seem to keep ecclesiastical politics out of parliamentary politics much of the time[10] means that the church's internal disputes rarely cause more than small ripples in public life. The bishop of Durham, however, has been at the center of considerable theological and political controversy in recent years for his radical views on Christology and for his attacks on the government's social and economic policies. The church's leading cleric, the archbishop of Canterbury, has also been heavily criticized by conservatives for preaching reconciliation instead of celebrating victory after the Falklands War against Argentina and for allegedly sitting on the fence in various theological and moral controversies.

In view of the interweaving of state and religion in the United Kingdom, it is not surprising that the editor of a recent collection of papers on politics and religion concluded that "the boundaries between governmental and non-governmental, between public institutions and private institutions, and even between partisan and non-partisan bodies are often very difficult to locate. Not least is this the case with the Church of England" (Moyser 1985:10). The fact that the church has commissioned four separate reports on church-state relations in the twentieth century (1917, 1935, 1952, 1970) also indicates the sensitivity of the issue (see Dyson 1985). It is at least clear, however, that the established churches can claim with some justification to be *national* churches and therefore to act as a forum for public debates about matters of general interest. In fact, recent debates in the General Synod of the Church of England

---

[10] But heated controversies have arisen in recent years over the House of Commons' refusal to sanction the church's proposals for revisions of liturgy and for amendment of the rule excluding divorced men from ordination.

and in the General Assembly of the Church of Scotland have made a significant contribution toward clarifying several important public issues. The public impact of these debates varies mainly with the extent to which the mass media report them.

The Roman Catholic church in the United Kingdom contained, until quite recently, two main constituencies. On the one hand was a group of relatively wealthy descendants of the recusant families that had survived the Reformation and its aftermath without abandoning their Catholicism. On the other was a much larger group of people descended mainly from indigent migrants from Ireland, Poland, and southern Europe. They were concentrated in London and cities in the North and Scotland. With gradual assimilation into the British way of life and with upward social mobility, however, the cultural distinctiveness and the restricted social privileges of these lower-class Catholics have been eroded. The research of Hornsby-Smith (1987) has shown that the gap between the "old" Catholics and the "new" has narrowed and that Catholics, as a category representing abut 8 percent of the British population, now have virtually the same opportunities as their fellow Britons. The Roman Catholic vote still tends to be left of center, however, and Catholic participation in labor unions is believed to be disproportionately strong.

The pattern of assimilation and upward social mobility among Jews in the United Kingdom parallels that of the Roman Catholics in some respects. Extensive migration into the country from eastern Europe at the end of the nineteenth century created dense concentrations of underprivileged Jews in many cities, but as a group, Jews have subsequently enjoyed disproportionately high rates of both social and geographical mobility (Alderman 1980). On the other hand, there are still several Orthodox communities in London, Leeds, Manchester, and Newcastle in which the degree of assimilation into British society is strikingly low. Theological and political differences are marked between Jewish organizations, but one of their underlying strengths is commitment to Jewish charities. This has been singled out as a distinctive feature of Jewish identity among even those Jews who are most strongly assimilated in other respects. The charitable aspects of Jewish life would probably conform with Tocqueville's criteria for assessing whether voluntary organizations would contribute to a healthy public sphere.

The Methodist, Baptist, Presbyterian, and United Reform Churches are the largest Protestant denominations and are distributed evenly across the United Kingdom. In addition, Scotland, Wales, and Northern Ireland have some variants of, or secessions from, these major denominations. Smaller denominations (for example, Quakers, Christian Spiritualists, Unitarians, Elim Pentecostals, and the Salvation Army) are also widely, but thinly, distributed across the country. None of these denominations is even managing to keep pace with the slow growth of the population; some are shrinking fast. Older sectarian organizations such as Christian Science, the Brethren, and Christadelphians are also declining rapidly in the number of participants and local groups. By contrast, the Jehovah's Witnesses, the Mormons, the Seventh-Day Adventists, and many small Pentecostal sects have continued to expand since the 1950s. In the case of the Adventists and the Pentecostals, most of their support comes from the families of black immigrants from the Caribbean region. Unlike the older sects, the Adventists and the Pentecostal groups serve as a focal point for many inner-city communities of Afro-Caribbean minorities. Yet it is doubtful whether these sectarian groups are interested in contributing directly to the well-being of a public sphere or an independent sector of British society. This is not to say, of course, that the example of their exclusiveness does not have any indirect influence on public life.

Two overlapping groups of predominantly white, conservative Protestants have grown in number and influence since the early 1970s: charismatic "fellowships" and house-churches. The charismatics are found, of course, in several mainline churches, but there has been a growing tendency for them also to gravitate toward relatively separate fellowships, healing circles, Bible study groups, and prayer meetings. Links with older Pentecostal traditions in the United Kingdom are weak, however, and it seems unlikely that charismatic phenomena alone will serve as a basis for complete separation from parent churches.

On the other hand, the house-church movement (which includes some charismatic phenomena) has recently given rise to separate organizations in some cases—much to the chagrin of some mainline clergy. Patterns of communal living, shared resources, and an authoritarian style of leadership in particular have aroused considerable anxiety, but Walker's (1985) authoritative account of the movement emphasizes its haphazard character. In any case, the overall number of participants is still small. Despite their importance as religious innovations, neither the charismatics nor the house-church groups have had a significant impact on British public life. They are unquestionably conservative in theology and morals, but, like most religious groups in the United Kingdom, they have made very few attempts to translate their ideas into political programs.

This is not to deny that the British churches, separately or in combination, are not concerned with political issues. It is merely to underscore the fact that, outside Northern Ireland and excluding calls for Muslim separatism, it is rare nowadays for explicitly political ideas to be made public in the name of religion. Indeed, given the strength and rigidity of the party political system in the United Kingdom, it is difficult for any religious organization to obtain a public hearing outside the framework of an established political party. As a result, there is a reluctance among religious leaders outside Northern Ireland to make directly political pronouncements. They prefer to confine themselves to clarifying the religious values that might have a bearing on any particular political question. In any case, if they made explicitly political pronouncements in the context of a registered charity they would run the risk of being investigated by the Charity Commission for breach of charitable objectives. It is a matter of speculation whether religion would play a more salient role in British public life if the law on charities were less restrictive. The American notion of a nonprofit association appears to offer greater scope for religious groups to involve themselves in politics without jeopardizing their tax-exempt status.

The investment of British religious organizations in programs of social action and political activity is negligible in comparison with that of their American counterparts. Not only have even the most liberal churches in the United Kingdom lacked the recent experience of political struggles in, for example, the civil-rights movement, the anti–Vietnam War campaign, or the sanctuary movement, but it would also be virtually inconceivable that any religious organization would allow candidates for political office to address their gatherings. What is more, religion has very low visibility in public life. Televangelism has had little impact, political campaigns along the lines of the Moral Majority barely exist, and the divisions separating liberal and conservative persuasions have only rarely erupted in public conflict. The "cults" are generally regarded with suspicion, but in most other respects religion in the United Kingdom has shown no signs of becoming more controversial or even newsworthy.

Even in the case of social and moral controversies that lack clear articulation with party political matters, the voice of religious professionals is not especially loud in the United Kingdom. The history of controversies surrounding, for example, birth control, pacifism, nuclear weapons, ecology, human rights, abortion, and euthanasia shows that British religious leaders tend to respond to matters of public concern after the event and largely in nonreligious language. Exceptions include the Roman Catholic church's outspoken opposition to artificial means of birth control and the Quakers' consistent line of reasoning against warfare and weapons of all kinds. On most other issues of public concern, however, it is difficult to hear any original or distinctively religious statements of principle outside the closed communities of sectlike organizations.

Finally, it is still difficult to see clearly how the increasingly numerous and geographically dispersed communities of Muslims (mainly from Pakistan and Bangladesh), Sikhs, and Hindus (mainly from India and East Africa) will fit into British society. They are represented, for example, on local councils for racial equality, culture, and community development. In many cases, they have also entered into relations with interfaith organizations. But the tendency is still strong for them to represent their communal interests in a fairly exclusive fashion in such things as separate schools, youth associations, political groups, and leisure activities. Muslim, Sikh, and Hindu religious leaders are prominent in many of these initiatives. The furor over the publication of Salman Rushdie's novel, *The Satanic Verses*, seems to be reinforcing these separatist tendencies at the time of this writing. Interfaith councils strive to overcome the tensions between religious communities, but they have not yet managed to canalize religious differences into constructive forms of public dialogue.

Thus, while these Middle Eastern and Asian communities of faith have already developed extensive and dynamic forms of community development and mutual aid, there are very few signs of integration into the wider nonprofit sector. What is more likely to happen is that a form of societal pillarization (the development of separate cradle-to-grave institutions for fellow religionists) will take place in those neighborhoods where ethnic and religious communities represent substantial majorities of the population. The notions of a melting pot and of cultural pluralism have so far met with relatively little enthusiasm. Tocqueville's vision of a liberal, open democracy of public debate makes no sense of these ethnic enclaves within British society.

RELIGION AND THE INDEPENDENT SECTOR

The established churches of England and Scotland inherited the parish structure and universalist outreach of their Roman Catholic predecessor. They have been central to many of the arrangements for the relief of poverty and other social problems, and many of their charitable services have survived into the modern era. Yet, like the Roman Catholic church, they were slow to adapt to the conditions of rapid urbanization and progressive depopulation of rural areas in the nineteenth century. The midcentury evangelical revival and the growth of an Anglo-Catholic wing of the Church of England both inspired extensive programs for building churches, schools, and social-welfare organizations. Similar developments took place, albeit on a much smaller scale, in other denominations. The Salvation Army was particularly distinctive for the high priority it accorded to the improvement of material conditions in the slums and skid row districts.

Unlike the situation in many other European countries and in the United States, the provision by British religious organizations of social welfare, education, and health-care services in the nineteenth century was matched almost immediately by statutory provisions. In fact, the state was quick to monitor and, in some cases, to take over services that had been instigated by religious organizations (Yeo 1976). Consequently, with the possible exception of Catholic agencies, the provision of collective goods has never been strongly "pillarized" on the basis of religion, politics, or linguistic differences. There are as a result relatively few paradenominational organizations. Moreover, the rapid expansion of the British state apparatus in the early twentieth century had the effect of quickly outstripping the growth of religious contributions to public welfare. Denominational schools, colleges, hospitals, orphanages, nursing homes, shelters, and the like today form a significant but relatively small complement to the welfare state. What is perhaps more important for present purposes is that the state now purchases, funds, or subsidizes many of these services.

In the presence of established churches and in the absence of a constitutional check on the state's entanglement with any religious organization, it has been easy for cooperation to develop between the statutory sector and the religious wing of the nonprofit sector. This is more apparent, despite some early controversies (Cruickshank 1963; Hastings 1986), in the field of education where there are no restrictions on the extent to which religious schools and colleges may collaborate with the state. The relationship may be closer or distant: religious status, in itself, makes no difference. This kind of unfettered collaboration may be evidence of corporatism. But it also points to a deep-seated presumption that the United Kingdom is a Christian society that only tolerates other expressions of religion.

In the words of Mrs. Thatcher's address to the Assembly of the Church of Scotland in May 1988, for example: "The Christian religion . . . is a fundamental part of our national heritage. I believe it is the wish of the overwhelming majority of people that this heritage should be preserved and fostered. For centuries it has been our very lifeblood. Indeed we are a nation whose ideals are founded on the Bible." But in view of the special status of Christianity and of the established churches in the United Kingdom, it was historically inaccurate and slightly disingenuous of Mrs. Thatcher to add that "people with other faiths and cultures have always been welcomed in our land, assured of equality under the law, of proper respect and of open friendship. There is absolutely nothing incompatible between this and our desire to maintain the essence of our own identity. There is no place for racial or religious intolerance in our creed." Two issues that currently expose the gap between the government's rhetoric and the realities of a culture and legal system favoring one particular religion are (a) the presumption that the law against blasphemy refers only to the deities of Christianity, and (b) the Ministry of Education's reluctance to give the same kind of assistance to Muslim schools that it gives to Christian and Jewish schools. In short, tolerance does not necessarily imply evenhandedness, let alone equality. The discrimination in favor of Christianity is an obstacle to the creation of a genuinely public sphere in the United Kingdom.

In sum, religious organizations have been central to the nonprofit sector of British society for centuries without necessarily being separated from the state. It is a mistake to think that the state has impinged on nonprofit activities only in the twentieth century. There has, in fact, been close cooperation between these two sectors since medieval times. The history of the established churches is a clear case in point.

CONCLUSION

There is no easy way to understand the significance and functioning of the public sphere in British society. This is partly because, as my analysis of the British economy, polity, and welfare state indicated, the apparatus of the state affects virtually every aspect of life and, consequently, leaves very little room for public activity that is genuinely independent of the state or the market. The evolution of the welfare state since the 1940s provides a particularly clear picture of the various ways in which voluntary organizations have been progressively drawn into client relationships with the state and with for-profit businesses. In these circumstances, the United Kingdom bears little resemblance to Tocqueville's vision of a democracy based on the cross-cutting ties of independent voluntary associations.

But the United Kingdom does resemble Habermas's (1976:54) depiction of the public sphere in the "social welfare state mass democracy" as a "field for the competition of interests, competitions which assume the form of violent conflict." Nowhere is this better illustrated than in recent conflicts in the United Kingdom over the policing of ethnic and industrial unrest. The highly contested laws relating to the definition of British nationality and the limits of legal strike activity have not evolved from any kind of moral consensus in the public sphere. They reflect the compromise struck between ruling interests in government, politics, law enforcement, and business. Once in place, such laws can then function to circumscribe, if not actually suppress, open and honest debate about the matters they regulate. This is a further instance of the interpenetration of the state and society that virtually precludes the possibility of a public sphere of the type envisaged in liberal political philosophies of the eighteenth century. In addition, Heclo's (1974) study of the involvement of senior civil servants in framing social policies and the associated laws in Britain is a useful reminder that these agents of a modern welfare state are also active, but largely invisible, in shaping British society somewhat independently from the forms of political accountability.

This does not mean, however, that the public function of debating and challenging collective values cannot be fulfilled in the United Kingdom. Political parties, social-movement organizations, labor unions, professional associations, and some churches, for example, are constantly engaged in precisely this function. But these organizations are far from being independent from, or neutral toward, interest groups. In fact, they are allied, to varying degrees, with some social classes and status groups. Their participation in the public sphere is not therefore disinterested; it is actually part of a struggle to promote and to protect sectional interests. Looked at from this point of view, the public sphere is the site of struggles for power and influence that take place through the medium of political, ideological, ethical, and religious discourse. There is no special field of concerns peculiar to the public sphere. Nor does it have a distinctive form of discourse. Rather, it represents the point at which struggles for collective power take place in the form of discourse about collective values.

But the terms of the struggles are not equal. Some parties have more power than others to set the agenda, to police the forum, and to make their voices heard. Agents of the state also make it possible for certain interests to be more prominently represented than others. The very bureaucratic procedures of government and civil service tend to select for the responses of some organizations rather than those of others. Moreover, laws relating, for example, to the limits of charitable activity, to the protection of official secrets, and to the public expression of protest all have a bearing on the likelihood that any given contribution to debates in the public sphere will be able to reach its intended audience. Ownership and control of the media of mass communication are therefore crucial to the outcome of struggles for power and influence.

The close connections that exist in the United Kingdom between the owners of the mass-circulation mass media, the so-called captains of industry and finance, and conservative political causes mean that access to the public sphere reflects social-class interests. It also means that the exigencies of the capitalist market shape the form and influence the content of the mass media, making them especially susceptible to the fluctuations of consumer demand. As a result, it makes very little sense to think of the public sphere as a neutral territory where an exchange of informed opinion takes place between private individuals in a reasoned manner. A more accurate picture of the situation in the United Kingdom would emphasize the fact that the state presumes to hold a monopoly over all public activity and to permit certain activities mainly by concession. The notion of individual rights is correspondingly weak, but privileges are common.

The privileges historically enjoyed by the established churches in Britain and the intimate connection between strongly centralized political parties and cabinet government have combined to reduce the scope for more religious organizations to play a prominent role in the public sphere. The nonestablished religious organizations (with the possible exception of some Muslim, Sikh, and Hindu organizations) are simply unable to compete effectively in the struggle to structure the political consciousness of their adherents and sympathizers. Those political parties and labor unions that *are* efficiently adapted to the British state's structures and procedures tend to relegate religious organizations to the margins of the public sphere. In other words, the nature of the politico-constitutional system is not normally responsive to religiously informed argument unless the latter is conveyed through the "regular" political channels. Analogously, the long-standing campaigns for environmental protection began to achieve success in the United Kingdom only when they were mediated by political parties.

British society is structured primarily by social class, ethnicity, and gender.

The undeniably vigorous activity of hundreds of thousands of voluntary associations tends to conform loosely with these structural contour lines. Paradoxically, the increasingly intrusive activity of the central and local state goes some way toward creating national forums that transcend these structural divisions. At the same time, however, voluntary associations that enter into collaborative or client relationships with the state run the risk of compromising their presumed autonomy. The combination of structural divisions and an intrusive state is not currently conducive to the kind of open and rational discussion of collective values, identity, and purpose that is integral to the notion of a public sphere.

On the other hand, as numerous studies of British society have confirmed, this combination of characteristics does not necessarily mean that the United Kingdom is seriously deficient in cohesion. The social fabric is resilient but it now draws its strength less from consensus than from "instrumental collectivism based on sectional self-interest" (Marshall 1988:7). This implies that "particular groups are more likely to look after their own interests than to consider their possible common cause with those who happen to share the same class position" (Marshall 1988:6). There may even be a note of fatalism in this outlook insofar as people consider that perceived social problems and inequities exceed their capacity to remedy them. The most significant implication of these views and of the foregoing analyses of the public sphere in the United Kingdom is that the voluntary sector of British society undoubtedly plays a major role in catalyzing collective values but that these values represent sectional rather than societal interests. The public sphere is therefore a process of contest and struggle at least as much as it is a catalyst of consensus.

References

Alderman, G. 1980. "The Jewish Vote in Great Britain since 1945." *Studies in Public Policy*, no. 72.

Brenton, M. 1985. *The Voluntary Sector in British Social Services*. London: Longman.

Charities: A Framework for the Future. 1989. London: HMSO.

Charity Commission. 1988. *Reports of the Charity Commissioners*. London: HMSO.

Cruickshank, M. 1963. *Church and State in English Education*. London: Macmillan.

Department of Health and Social Security. 1969. *Report of the Committee on Local Authority and Allied Personal Social Services* (Seebohm Report). London: HMSO.

Dyson, A. 1985. " 'Little Else but the Name'—Reflections on Four Church and State Reports." In *Church and Politics Today: The Role of the Church of England in Contemporary Politics*, edited by G. Moyser, pp. 282–312. Edinburgh: T. and T. Clark.

Gallagher, J. P. 1975. *The Price of Charity*. London: Robert Hale.

Gershuny, J. 1983. *Social Innovation and the Division of Labour*. Oxford: Clarendon Press.

Habermas, J. 1976. *Legitimation Crisis*. Translated by Thomas McCarthy. Boston: Beacon Press.

Hastings, A. 1986. *A History of English Christianity, 1920–1985*. London: Collins.

Hatch, S. 1980. *Outside the State*. London: Croom Helm.

Heclo, H. 1974. *Modern Social Politics in Britain and Sweden*. New Haven: Yale University Press.

Hornsby-Smith, M. 1987. *Roman Catholics in England*. Cambridge: Cambridge University Press.

James, E. 1987. "The Nonprofit Sector in Comparative Perspective." In *The Nonprofit Sector: A Research Handbook*, edited by W. W. Powell, pp. 397–415. New Haven: Yale University Press.

Johnson, N. 1987. "The Break-up of Consensus: Competitive Politics in a Declining Economy." In *The State or the Market*, edited by M. Loney et al., pp. 144–60. London: Sage.

Leat, D., et al. 1986. *A Price Worth Paying? A Study of the Effects of Government Grant Aid to Voluntary Organizations*. London: Policy Studies Institute.

———— 1988. "Identifying Public-Private Partnerships." University of Warwick, England.

Marshall, G., et al. 1988 *Social Class in Modern Britain*. London: Unwin Hyman.

Ministry of Health. 1959. *Report of the Working Party on Social Workers in Local Authority Health and Welfare Services* (Younghusband Report). London: HMSO.

Moyser, G., ed. 1985. *Church and Politics Today: The Role of the Church of England in Contemporary Politics*. Edinburgh: T. and T. Clark.

Offe, C. 1984. *Contradictions of the Welfare State*. London: Hutchinson.

Pahl, R. 1984. *Division of Labour*. Oxford: Blackwell.

Pinker, R. 1986. "Social Welfare in Japan and Britain: Formal and Informal Aspects of Welfare." In *Comparing Welfare States and Their Futures*, edited by E. Oyen, pp. 114–28. Aldershot, England: Gower.

Posnett, J. 1987. "Trends in the Income of Registered Charities, 1980–85." In *Charity Trends 1986/87*, pp. 6–8. Tonbridge, England: Charities Aid Foundation.

Prochaska, F. 1988. *The Voluntary Impulse*. London: Faber and Faber.

Report of the Committee on the Law and Practice Relating to Charitable Trusts (Nathan Report). 1952. London: HMSO.

Spuehler, D. R. 1977. "The System for Regulation and Assistance of Charity in England and Wales, with Recommendations on the Establishment of a National Commission on Philanthropy in the United States." In *Research Papers*, Commission on Private Philanthropy and Public Needs 5:3145–87. Washington, D.C.: U.S. Government Printing Office.

Unell, J. 1979. *Voluntary Social Services: Financial Resources*. London: Bedford Square Press.

Walker, A. 1985. *Restoring the Kingdom: The Radical Christianity of the House-Church Movement*. London: Hodder and Stoughton.

Webb, A 1980. "The Personal Social Services." In *Labour and Equality*, edited by N. Bosanquet and P. Townsend, pp. 279–95. London: Heinemann.

Weber, N., ed. 1988. *Giving USA: The Annual Report on Philanthropy for the Year 1987*. Washington, D.C.: American Association of Fund-Raising, Counsel Trust for Philanthropy.

Wolfenden Committee, 1978. *The Future of Voluntary Organizations*. London: Croom Helm.

Yeo, S. 1976. *Religion and Voluntary Organizations in Crisis*. London: Croom Helm.

CHAPTER THREE

West Germany: The Ambiguities of Peak Associations

Helmut K. Anheier

THIS CHAPTER examines the relation between the public sphere and the voluntary sector in West Germany.[1] The public sphere has been described as a mediator between the state and the private world of its citizens. The voluntary sector represents the universe of organizations between market and political institutions. At the intersection of the public sphere and the voluntary sector are such private, nonprofit organizations as foundations, religious and voluntary associations, academies, civic societies, political groups, and interest associations, as well as many hybrid forms such as quasi-nongovernmental organizations, public-law corporations, public foundations, and civil-law associations with statutory governance functions.

THE PUBLIC SPHERE

In Germany, as in most other developed countries, the public sphere represents a complex functional arena of many specialized audiences. By concentrating on institutional and organizational factors, we can identify the unique characteristic of the public sphere in West Germany: it is institutionally embedded between state and society. The public sphere is located between the *decentralized public sector* and the *centralizing tendencies within civic society*. That the public sphere is embedded between two opposite "movements" is indicative of its ambiguous function in modern Germany. This ambiguity is related to the two functions the public sphere serves for the civil society and the state.

Certainly, the public sphere is larger than the area where it intersects with the voluntary or third sector. In focusing on institutional and organizational aspects, this chapter will necessarily neglect other aspects of the public sphere. The media, for example, are part of the public sphere, but they fall largely outside the voluntary sector: the print media are primarily for-profit corporations, with the great majority of newspapers being published on a for-profit basis. Until recently, few for-profit television corporations existed, and commercial private nonprofit television (the "public" stations in the United

---

[1] This chapter, written prior to the economic and political unification of West and East Germany, will focus on West Germany; however, in a postscript I will briefly consider some of the implications of unification for the relation between the public sphere and the voluntary sector.

States) do not exist in West Germany. However, the overall role played by the media is not much different in West Germany than in other European countries.

The role of intellectuals, too, is important for the constitution of the public sphere. The role of intellectuals in West Germany has by and large become similar to that of intellectuals in other European societies. However, the traumatic experiences of the Nazi period, with its deep and far-reaching disruption of the public sphere, influenced the academic, literary, and cultural life of the Federal Republic for several decades (Bering 1978). The sum of the many individual experiences of exile, imprisonment, and violence, exemplified by the biographies of Thomas Mann, Berthold Brecht, Erich Mühsam, Theodor W. Adorno, and thousands of other, lesser-known intellectuals, overshadowed the relation between intellectuals and the state and left it uneasy and strained (see, for example, Weyrauch 1960; Jaspers 1966; Enzensberger 1967). On the other side, West German intellectuals have passed through periods similar to those experienced by their European counterparts, whereby the "restoration" of the 1950s was followed by the "progressive era" of the late 1960s, to be followed by the "conservative shift" a decade later.

The Ambiguity of the Public Sphere

The first function fulfilled by the public sphere goes back to its bourgeois roots. In bourgeois society the public sphere served as both the source of and the arena for social and political innovation. Opinions, ideologies, convictions, and policies were created, formulated, discussed, and disseminated independent of the absolutist state. Here, individuals participated in public debate as citizens and not primarily from the vantage point of their occupations or social status.[2]

The second function of the public sphere is potentially opposed to the first: to foster the interests of special economic, social, and political groups. Institutionalization rather than deinstitutionalization accompanies this function—a process to which Habermas (1962) referred as the refeudalization of the public sphere. The public sphere becomes politicized, redirected at the state, and refocused on political power. According to Habermas (1985:151), the politicized public sphere lacks the critical and innovative potential associated with the liberal model; it changes to a public sphere that negotiates rather than creates policies, that seeks to influence rather than initiate public debate, that accommodates rather than experiments with new positions, and that reinforces the parameters of political power rather than offers an arena for political discourse free of established political interests.

---

[2] For Luhmann (1971), this deinstitutionalization of differentiated role structures is essential to the constitution of the public sphere.

For Habermas (1973, 1985), the liberal, bourgeois public sphere has increasingly become included under the umbrella of political power. However, at least in the German case, it remains an open question whether the liberal model of the public sphere has ever fully existed. In this case, the liberal model might contain normative, even romantic elements that others project into the Marxist notion of a proletarian public sphere (Negt and Kluge 1972). In any case, the important point in Habermas's (1962, 1973) critique is that political power by itself appears ill-equipped to bring about ideological and policy innovations.

The functional ambiguity of the public sphere in advanced industrial societies results from the concurrent processes of deinstitutionalization and (re)institutionalization (Habermas 1985). In Germany, the functional ambiguity of the public sphere derives from its relationship with a *decentralized state* and a *centralized, state-oriented civic society*. The voluntary sector and the public sphere intersect where the centralizing institutional tendencies of civic society and the decentralizing tendencies of the public sector and political administration overlap. In Germany, the voluntary sector acts as major "institutionalizer" and "centralizer" of the public sphere.

Öffentlichkeit and Gegenöffentlichkeit

The German version of the relation between the public sphere (*Öffentlichkeit*) and the voluntary sector encourages incremental, planned, almost "rehearsed" changes and political discourse rather than spontaneous, unplanned, voluntary participation. Decentralized public authorities and centralized private-interest institutions operate and negotiate in a formal, regulatory environment that, at the same time, commands and encourages cooperation as well as compromise. As Katzenstein (1987) and Seibel and Anheier (1990) point out, in West Germany's decentralized state and centralized civic society, the government and large parts of the voluntary sector are "walking hand in hand," neither quickly nor dynamically, but smoothly and without excitement. The price society pays for this neocorporatist arrangement is potential immobility and inflexibility.

The liberal democratic image of a public sphere and the emergence of values, conflicts, and new subjects of public discourse do not take place in the "official" public sphere (*Öffentlichkeit*) but in the *Gegenöffentlichkeiten* ("counterpublic spheres" or "alternative spheres"). New social movements such as the student movement of the 1960s, the environmental movement of the 1970s, and the peace movement of the early 1980s did not emerge in the public sphere, but as *Gegenöffentlichkeiten*. Only once the public sphere had been challenged did voluntary-sector institutions follow the strategy of incorporating the acceptable claims of the counterpublic sphere. The "official" public sphere accommodated parts of the counterpublic, which then led to incremental policy changes and later resulted in general changes in values, as happened in the cases of the environmental movement and the peace movement.

This chapter examines the public sphere from an organizational point of view. It adds a new perspective to the study of the public sphere by focusing on the voluntary sector. However, sociological discourse on the public sphere in Germany is certainly not new. In fact, the fruitful period of sociological reasoning in Germany between 1900 and 1930 saw the concept of *Öffentlichkeit* emerging as a central variable.[3] The German discussion of the public sphere shared neither the voluntaristic elements that have sometimes become associated with interpretations of the Tocquevillean model, nor those of the Jacobinian ideology, which discouraged the existence of an intermediate sphere between the state and its citizens. However, there is no "German model" of the public sphere, neither an "autocratic model" based on the Prussian system of state administration, nor a model based on the localized and often fragmented political landscape that characterized the pre-March era (1815–1848) and the Weimar Republic (1919–1933). Ever since its emergence in feudal society during a period ranging from the Enlightenment and the French Revolution to the Vienna Congress in 1815, the public sphere has changed continuously—sometimes very abruptly.

Major Political and Social Characteristics

The Federal Republic of Germany, a country of about ninety-six thousand square miles (roughly the size of Oregon) and a population of sixty-two million, came into existence in 1949. Although not the first democratic country on German soil, it has by far been the most successful one in political and economic terms. The present political system in West Germany contains many corporatist elements—a result of continuous conflict accommodation and discontinuous conflict resolution. It is beyond the scope of this chapter to review all the relevant events and factors that have influenced the development of the public sphere and the voluntary sector; I will restrict myself to the most important ones.

A Brief History

In the latter part of the eighteenth century, elements of a bourgeois public sphere began to develop in Germany, which was at that time a loosely structured confederation of numerous smaller kingdoms, principalities, and city-states. The emergent public sphere was not yet the forum for political move-

---

[3] Examples are Tönnies (1922); Simmel (1908); Weber (1917); Hilferding (1924); and Schmitt (1932), to be followed up again in the 1950s and 1960s by scholars like Habermas (1962, 1973) and Luhmann (1971).

ment toward the nation-state. Rather, it was part of a development throughout Europe characteristic of the late Enlightenment era. In Germany, such activities took the institutional form of reform universities, political journals, reading societies, clubs, and associations (see Wehler 1987:317–31). The ideology of the new political, university-oriented public sphere found its clearest expression in the *Gelehrtenrepublik*, an imaginary *republique des lettres* of reason, humanism, and progress, where social origin, nationality, and religion no longer mattered. In general, the public sphere of the late absolutist era, in conflict with both the religious and the secular powers, was largely restricted to the elite and the upper echelons of the bourgeoisie (*Bürgertum*).

The Napoleonic Wars brought the dissolution of the empire and a wide-ranging secularization. Consequently, the voluntary sector, still almost exclusively church-oriented, diminished substantially. Unlike in England and France, no broad democratic and revolutionary tradition had taken root in Germany by the mid-nineteenth century; what little had developed was reversed by the "restoration" that followed the revolution of 1848. The restoration had a strong impact on the public sphere, and the voluntary sector was considerably reduced in size. The dissolution of the reading societies is a good example. Reading societies were founded between 1750 and 1840 to provide a public forum for literary discussions and political debate. Their growth paralleled the development of the publishing industry and book trade: in 1800 about 430 reading societies existed, and by around 1830 their number had grown to about 600; however, all but a few had disappeared by midcentury (Wehler 1987:320).

It is important to note that both the underdevelopment and the discontinuation of the democratic movements in Germany shaped the way the public sphere and the voluntary sector developed in the late nineteenth century. Unlike the French Loi de Chapelier of 1791 or the British General Combination Act of 1799, no legislation attacked the remains of late medieval society. In particular the status groups (estates, *Stände*) and associations of commerce and crafts remained unchallenged. With general political representation lacking, status groups changed to *Verbände* (associations). They became influential economic and political instruments in the period of rapid economic development between 1850 and 1900. The extensive system of associations (*Verbandswesen*) has become characteristic of the German voluntary sector.

The state, however, was not a passive recipient of associational interests. To the extent that the associations learned the ways of politics, the state intervened in associational affairs, supported the hierarchical arrangement into "peak" associations (discussed below), and when politically necessary also created some associations, most notably in the field of social policy. Throughout the periods of the Empire, the Weimar Republic, and the Federal Republic, the state has maintained its characteristic policy of creating relatively independent public-law associations. Prominent recent examples are in the fields of

AIDS prevention (German AIDS Foundation), antiabortion policy and assistance to single mothers (Foundation for Mothers and Children), German reunification (Foundation of Germany), and science and research (German Research Association).

In other areas, however, conflict characterized the relationship between the state and its voluntary sector. The increased emergence of Prussian hegemony from the Vienna Congress to the proclamation of the Second Empire in 1871 culminated in the *Kulturkampf*. This conflict between Bismarck and the Catholic church, including politically related groups and organizations, lasted from 1871 to 1891. To a large extent, it was a political struggle between secular and religious powers over influence and responsibility in the areas of education, culture, and welfare: the central issues of this political struggle were who controls and who has access to institutions that prepare citizens for participation in the public sphere.

Likewise, when Bismarck laid the foundation for a relatively comprehensive welfare system he did so for political reasons and against the opposition of established religions. Social insurance and welfare was used as a tool of social and political control (Rimlinger 1971:114; Sachse and Tennstedt 1986); social rights to welfare were granted, in part, to prevent the transfer of greater political rights.

The major lines of conflict in German society, already visible in the late nineteenth century, culminated in the tumultuous years between 1918 and 1923: Catholics versus Protestants; nationalist versus regional and separatist movements; working-class associations and parties versus bourgeois groups; agrarian status groups versus the new urban-based industrialists; political opponents of the republic versus monarchists and democrats; and Communists versus Fascists. None of these conflicts was fully settled in the brief democratic interlude, which lasted until 1933.

The Weimar Republic witnessed an expansion of the voluntary sector, especially in the areas of politically oriented associations, economic-interest organizations, and the welfare system. Industry, commerce, and the voluntary sector succeeded in revitalizing and expanding a complex system of associations (*Verbände*) that became major proponents of corporatist tendencies in the early 1930s. The legal authorities assumed a more passive role, and laws restricting the creation of voluntary associations were liberalized.[4] The discrimination against religious (particularly Catholic) organizations, and the antisocialist policy of the Empire, were replaced by more accommodationist policies.

---

[4] For example, the Weimar Constitution of 1919 (section 124.II.2) changed section 61.II. BGB (1900) ("'The administrative authority can reject registration if, according to the Code of Association [*Vereinsrecht*], the association is illegal, or may be declared illegal, *or follow political, socio-political, or religious objectives*"'), and dropped the part of the sentence shown here in italics.

More than other parties of disloyal opposition and antirepublican political movements of the Weimar Republic, national socialism linked many different segments of society. The strategic position of many party members, with their multiple ties to other parts of the community and to local as well as regional and national organizations, multiplied their influence and helped spread national socialist ideology to a cross section of society. This structural position of the national socialist movement became one of its major strengths and advantages in exploiting the public sphere to further political ends.

For Mommsen (1990), the "organizational opportunism" of securing local power bases in the "conquest of bourgeois infrastructure" represents an important factor among the social structural preconditions of national socialism's success.[5] Lepsius (1978:39) argues that the democratic potential of the Weimar Republic "rested on the coherence and integrative capabilities of its intermediary organizations." Many of these intermediary. voluntary organizations originated in the Bismarckian and Wilhelmine era when they achieved great influence, in part because political interests could not translate into political parties. Much of the corporatist and technocratic-political influence of intermediary organizations carried over into the 1920s. In the fragmented political landscape of the Weimar Republic, this part of the political economy and the public sphere provided the safeguard for the democratic core of society, yet it was also increasingly eroded by national socialism.

The Third Reich from 1933 to 1945 was not only a period of voluntary-sector contraction but also a period of far-reaching leveling of the organizational landscape. Foundation matters were extremely restricted. The free-welfare associations were first regrouped under a single (national socialist-controlled) umbrella organization, and soon, with the exception of the Red Cross, were reorganized as the National Socialist People's Welfare. Thousands of intellectuals and academics were forced to emigrate and to see their organizations banned and their work dishonored; others disappeared in concentration camps. The public sphere was reduced to a propaganda machine.

In 1945, many previous conflicts, while never resolved or settled, no longer

---

[5] Reviewing a number of regional studies on the development of national socialism in Germany, Jaschke (1982) suggests—besides the extensive use of political propaganda—two aspects that are central in order to understand its success: (1) the translation of class conflicts into local social and community activism and participation (e.g., the social-welfare activities); and (2) the infiltration of the local associational system (*Vereinswesen*) and the cooptation of other social and political protest movements. In a study of party members in Marburg, Koshar (1987) examines interpersonal linkages among members and concludes that much of the party's local success can be attributed to its ability to integrate the bourgeois public (*bürgerliche Oeffentlichkeit*) by establishing personal ties between different segments of society. Unlike other extremist political parties and groups, members of the National Soziale Demokratie Arbeiters Partie (NSDAP) were "joiners," linking many different strata and segments of society, thereby reaching a wider cross section of society.

"existed." Regional differences and separatist tendencies became much less manifest, and no regional party has been represented in parliament since 1957. The weakened agrarian groups were incorporated into the Christian parties, which in turn made attempts to avoid confessional politics. Combined with the allied licensing system for associations and parties between 1945 and 1949, the overall result was a far-reaching "depoliticization" and "deideologizing" of the organizational landscape. By 1950, Germany was a more homogeneous country than ever before in its history.

The history of postwar Germany is first the history of economic reconstruction and political reorientation to the West; it is, second, the history of relative economic success combined with political restraint by pursuit of strongly integrationist policies, both domestically and abroad (e.g., toward the European community).

After the 1950s, West Germany developed into a society of organizations and associations where little "association-free" terrain remains (Beyme 1987). Business, professional, political, and religious interests have all become organized, incorporated interests, represented in several thousand major associations. These associations tend to be associations of associations (not individual membership associations as such); they represent the "associational system" (*Verbandswesen*) and constitute a major aspect of the public sphere. The extensive character of the "associational system" is demonstrated by the fact that even "antiestablishment" parties such as the Greens and political movements such as the environmentalists organize their interests in the form of a political party, a nonprofit bank, and a foundation (in the case of the Greens), or as a "Federal Association of Citizen Initiatives—Environment" with hundreds of member organizations.

Religion

Although the important role of religion in modern German history is readily apparent, it is useful to highlight some aspects of its relatively privileged position in the Federal Republic. The two most salient aspects of this are the legal status and the tax status of the churches. "Church tax" is a portion of the income tax levied by the state for the churches' benefit; the churches, in turn, pay an administration fee for tax collection. The church tax is a central reason West Germany has been home to some of the richest and best-endowed Catholic and Protestant churches. The tax enables churches to take on many social-welfare activities and to engage in long-range institutional planning.

Ecclesiastical law is constitutionally equivalent to public administrative law. Churches are established not under civil law but under public law, and they form *Körperschaften des öffentlichen Rechts* (corporations of public law). As public-law corporations, they are by definition exempt from many forms of taxation and public control. This legal privilege applies only to the member churches of the Rat der Evangelischen Kirchen Deutschlands (the Council of Protestant Churches in Germany, whose congregations make up 41.5 percent of the population) and the Roman Catholic church (43.3 percent of the population). Other religious communities, in particular the numerous "free religious associations" and the close to two million Muslims, form civil-law organizations.

The reasons for the special treatment of the two state churches are historically as complex as they are politically controversial. The principle of subsidiarity (Isensee 1966) is important to understand the development of the state-church relationship in the Federal Republic (see Bauer and Diessenbacher 1984). The principle originated in Jesuit thinking and was first formulated by Pope Pius XI in the 1931 encyclical *Quadragesimo anno*. In essence, subsidiarity means that the larger social unit (the state) should only assist the smaller unit (the church or community) if the latter can no longer rely on its own resources. The principle served as the basis for the division of labor between state and church in the field of social welfare as it developed in the 1950s, when church-state relations were particularly cordial. The principle of subsidiarity is one of the major reasons for the prominent role of the churches in social welfare. The principle has also been introduced into welfare economics, where it plays a central role in the foundation of the social market economy.

The Public Sphere and the Voluntary Sector

In this section I will focus on the contemporary relation between the public sphere and the voluntary sector in two major areas of German society; politics and the economy. Several general features of West Germany's political system are important for understanding this relationship.

Federalism

West Germany is a federal republic in which the eleven individual states (*Länder*) enjoy a relatively high degree of political power. This is particularly so in the fields of education and culture, the "traditional" domains of the voluntary sector, which are almost exclusively a *Länder* matter. In recent years, some *Länder* have even opened offices in Brussels to represent their interests at the level of the European community.

The chancellor is in a weaker position than the French president or the British prime minister. Moreover, unlike in the United States and the United Kingdom, there is no institution equivalent to the Government Printing Office or Her Majesty's Stationery Office by which the federal government disseminates information. The Federal Press and Information Office manages primarily news and information from the chancellery and the cabinet, whereas the individual ministries operate their own public information offices.

The system of political administration is designed in such a way that federal and state governments, federal, state, and local administrations, and the semiautonomous parapublic institutions must cooperate. This is achieved by a process of political negotiation that stresses compromise and accommodation rather than open conflict and central directives.

The federal government does not possess the personnel resources to carry out policies without support by the *Länder*. Federal ministries are relatively small, with fewer than seventeen hundred top-level administrators. The politically highly important Ministry of Inner-German Affairs has a staff of only about three hundred. The largest, the Ministry of Finance, has about two thousand employees. Moreover, policy making within the federal government's structure itself is relatively decentralized and remains a matter of ministries (individual *Resorts*) rather than of the cabinet (Mayntz 1984). Thus, even if the federal government decided to follow a political course contrary to that of the *Länder*, the federal government's action would be extremely limited since it relies on the *Länder* administrations for policy implementation. In turn, the *Länder* must cooperate with the federal government for constitutional and fiscal reasons. Similar principles apply to the relations between *Länder* and local administrations.

Like the state-church relationship, the decentralized political system is based on the principle of subsidiarity (Isensee 1966). Thus, ideally, the *Länder* should take on only functions and activities left by the municipal and regional administrations, and the federal government should assume those tasks that cannot be met by the *Länder* themselves.

The high degree of decentralization is evident if we compare the number of employees working at the federal, state, and local levels. Only about 8.2 percent of all civil servants work for the federal government, whereas 40.1 percent work for the *Länder*, and about one-fourth (24.9 percent) at the county or municipal level. About one in four civil servants (or 26.8 percent) works for one of the numerous institutions under public law. These institutions include the Bundesbank (Federal Reserve Bank), the Federal Employment Office, the Federal Archives, the Federal Statistical Office, the Federal Health Association, the Federal Agency for the Environment, and the Federal Criminal Office. Many of the public-law institutions find their equivalents at the state level.

Although the number of federal employees has almost doubled since the founding of the Federal Republic in 1949, the majority of this increase occurred in the 1950s and can be attributed to the introduction of the federal army. Ranging between 13 percent and 15 percent, the proportion of civil servants among the economically active population has remained relatively stable since 1950. Beyme (1984:45f.) points out that with 64 civil servants for every 1,000 inhabitants, the Federal Republic ranks well below the Scandinavian welfare states (Sweden has 156); it also ranks below the United Kingdom (96) and the United States (78), countries of antietatist traditions whose policies have long emphasized deregulation.

Complex Legal System

While civil law regulates the relations among individuals and legal entities, public law regulates the relations among state and public entities, and between the public and the private. The distinction between civil law (*ius privatum*) and public law (*ius publicum*) is anything but clear and, combined with the ideology of codification and legal abstraction, has generated a legal landscape of the utmost complexity. Moreover, many civil-code stipulations find public-law equivalents. For example, the code of associations (*Vereinsrecht*) is public law and regulates legal entities established under civil law in their relation to the state.

In line with the German tradition of positive law, the judiciary is organized uniformly in all states with four levels (district, county, and superior courts, and the federal Supreme Court as the final court of appeals). Ordinary civil and criminal jurisdiction rests with these courts. There is no separate *Land* and federal judicial system, as there is in the United States. However, there are additional judicial hierarchies vested with such legal specialities as labor law, fiscal and taxation matters, administrative law, and social law.

The federal Constitutional Court, whose judges are elected by the Bundestag and the Bundesrat, fulfills several other functions, too. In the last four decades the court has been called upon in more than sixty-five thousand cases. Its introduction did not only assist in protecting the constitution via judicial review; most importantly, the judiciary and legislative were opened to the public, which brought both systems closer to the public sphere. As was the case with the United States Supreme Court, its German counterpart has increasingly become more influential in deciding on politicized issues from foreign policy and university administration to abortion.

Political Parties

The prominent role of political parties must be seen in the context of two factors: the complex and ambiguous public-private character of political parties in legal and political terms, and their role in the country's decentralized political system. In fact, political parties constitute an arena "where a decentralized public and a centralized private sector converge in the formulation of public policy" (Katzenstein 1987:35). Thus, political parties are a major force in both decentralization and centralization.

More so than the government itself, parties tend to behave in the tradition of etatism by assuming responsibility for many aspects of civil society. Occupying a prominent position in the political landscape, political parties have often been accused of blurring the separation of party, government, and administration. The state becomes a "party-run state" in which parties extend into more and more areas of civil society and the public sphere (Beyme 1979). Today's political parties have grown into large organizations with a seemingly insatiable demand for finance.

Party finance continues to present the most controversial political issue. During the 1960s, parties received relatively generous public subsidies, which were distributed with minimal public control. Then the federal Constitutional Court declared public contributions exceeding 50 percent of the party's income unconstitutional. After this decision, a dual system of public and private financing emerged (Beyme 1984), which encourages private donations through preferential tax treatment and dispenses public funds proportionate to the parties' votes received in elections.

Nevertheless, despite the legal limitations and publicity requirements attached to large donations, the system was open to abuse—as in the party scandals of the early 1980s, when industrial corporations were accused of trading preferential tax treatment for party contributions. It was also discovered that several nonprofit organizations, officially set up as *staatsbürgerliche Vereinigungen* (civic societies), were largely concerned with laundering funds for political parties. Although legal provisions regarding party financing have since then introduced stricter controls and greater publicity requirements for large contributions, these scandals and accusations did much to harm the image of the established parties. The word *Parteiverdrossenheit* ("party weariness") was coined to capture popular opinion of the party system (Ellwein 1989).

In the first three decades after the creation of the Federal Republic, the party system experienced a far-reaching concentration process in which many smaller parties either dissolved or declined into insignificance (Beyme 1987). Although numerous smaller parties continue to exist, a de facto three-party system has emerged because, among other factors, a 5 percent share of all votes cast is required for parliamentary representation (to avoid a repetition of the extreme party fragmentation of the Weimar Republic).[6]

[6] Three political parties have dominated West German politics for over four decades:

1. The Christian Democratic Union (CDU) had about 716,000 members in 1987–1988 and received 34.5 percent of all votes cast in the 1987 federal elections; its Bavarian sister party, the Christian Social Union (CSU), had about 184,000 members and received 9.2 percent of the votes cast. Both are center-right parties that for many years managed to integrate various conservative, Catholic, and Protestant groups.

2. The Social Democratic Party (SPD) had about 910,000 members and received 37 percent of the votes cast during the 1987 federal elections.

3. The Free Democratic Party (FDP), which represents the tradition of economic liberalism, is largely located on the center-right. The party had about 65,000 members and received 9.1 percent of the votes cast in 1987.

The Party Foundations

All the major parties operate party foundations. Besides the social-democratic Friedrich-Ebert Foundation (created in 1925), party foundations are a product of the 1950s, when the British and American powers tried to encourage the development of democratic parties and trade unions. The party foundations maintain some legal, financial, and even political distance from the parent parties; they are nevertheless organizations largely financed through public funds, usually in the form of government subsidies.

The party foundations are multipurpose organizations: they operate as ideological think tanks that put party programs to continuous testing vis-à-vis new political ideas and emergent political problems; they monitor both the counterpublic and the public sphere by detecting new social problems, seeking out new themes, and anticipating possible solutions and programmatic steps; they carry out party-related research, maintain historical archives, and support research projects at universities in Germany and aboard; they operate seminar series, workshops, and lectures for party members and a diverse "external" audience; and they work in international relations and are active in development aid.

The Economic Sector

Much has been written in Germany (Abelshauser 1983; Beyme 1979, 1987; Ellwein 1989, among others) and abroad (Grosser 1988; Katzenstein 1987) about the successful performance of the West German economy. In addition to the favorable economic climate of the 1950s, generous American support (the Marshall Plan), and a skilled labor force (57 percent of the total work force have undergone formal vocational training), there are three characteristics that contributed to Germany's economic success: the organization of trade and industry, the autonomy of employers and employees in industrial and trade negotiations, and the policy of "supportive nonplanning" by the state.

The organization of trade and industry is one of the major aspects of Germany's centralized society. All firms are represented by three types of associations: industrial business associations, employers' associations, and chambers of commerce and industry. A key characteristic of the West German landscape of economic organizations is the grouping of decentralized constituencies into more central units to form "peak associations."

The creation of economic-interest associations among firms in the same trade or industry has a long history in Germany. The guildlike craft associations go back to medieval times and are better preserved in Germany than in other European countries. Together, economic associations (*Wirtschaftsverbände*) provide perhaps the prototypical example of liberal corporatism. Compared to other groups, they enjoy privileged treatment in the legislative process. The *Verbände* are represented on parliamentary committees (usually linked to the relevant department or ministry). In the course of the legislative process, committees must schedule hearings at which the *Verbände* can present their cases.

In political influence, they surpass all other institutions in the voluntary sector, including foundations and welfare associations. The business-state orientation constitutes one of the major characteristics of the German voluntary sector where the for-profit sector organizes common interests in the form of nonprofit organizations. The for-profit sector uses the voluntary sector to further its political interests in the public sector. As Beyme (1987) remarked, the economic emphasis coexists with a relative paucity of political voluntary-sector organizations outside the organizational compass of the political parties.

Several examples demonstrate the encompassing nature of business associations. Businesses in the crafts sector, which include many small-scale industries, form 1 federal peak association, 41 regional peak associations, and 6,202 other formal interest organizations representing 492,000 businesses. Parallel to the general representation, they are also organized into 66 federal peak associations, 331 regional ones, and 6,176 other associations by branches as well as by product and service types. Agriculture is organized into one federal peak association, 56 regional ones, and 305 special-interest associations to represent 750,000 farms. The trade sector has 10 peak associations, 74 regional ones, and 336 special-interest associations to represent 570,000 firms. About 100,000 import-export businesses form 1 federal peak association, 12 regional ones, and 42 special-interest associations.

For most firms, joining business and interest groups is both necessary and useful. The size distribution of West German industries shows that the great majority have between 2 and 20 employees. Only 891 of 360,463 manufacturing firms have more than 1,000 employees, and about 1,200 employ between 500 and 999 people. Moreover, while there are only about 2,000 stock corporations, there are more than 340,000 limited-liability companies. These companies, many family-run, enjoy virtually no publicity requirements. At the same time, they were by themselves in a weak bargaining position vis-à-vis political bodies unless they joined with other businesses, which would also allow for economies of scale in union negotiations, information management, and staff training—hence the relatively high incentive of West Germany's many small and medium-sized firms to form powerful peak associations.

There are three major peak associations for business and industry. They are represented, together with fifteen other business and industry associations, in the Gemeinschaftsausschuss der Deutschen Gewerblichen Wirtschaft (Joint Committee of Trade and Industry). This committee serves as a forum in which economic and social policies are formulated and discussed.

The Federal Association of German Industry (Bundesverband der Deutschen Industrie, or BDI) consists of thirty-nine consortiums, which themselves divide into some six hundred associations to represent about one hundred thousand member organizations. Peak associations, as the representatives of local, regional, and special (cross-cutting) interests, negotiate with political bodies at the state and the federal level. The BDI pursues "the economic policy interest of German industry in a constant dialogue with the Federal Parliament, the Government and the Opposition, the trade unions and other social groups, the bodies of the European Communities as well as numerous other national and international institutions" (BDI:1981).

Next to the BDI are the employers' associations, which represent all businesses in the areas of social policy, wages and salaries, and collective bargaining. The peak association of the employers' associations is the Bundesvereinigung der Deutschen Arbeitgeberverbände (BDA), a confederation of eleven *Länder* associations and forty-six special-industry associations.

The third type of business association is the chamber of industry and commerce. Whereas the BDI and BDA are voluntary associations established under private law, the chambers are public-law associations with comprehensive and compulsory membership. They represent the overall interests of trade and industry vis-à-vis all public institutions within their local and regional constituencies. The sixty-nine chambers of industry and commerce are grouped into seven regional peak associations at the *Länder* level, and at the federal level, the Deutscher Industrie- und Handelstag e.V. (Association of German Chambers of Industry and Commerce).

The importance of the economic peak associations derives also from their high participation rate. Weber (1977) reports that 90 percent of all industrial establishments are membrs of the BDI. It is estimated that 80 percent of all eligible employers are members of the BDA.

The existence of three types of peak business associations at the federal level has several advantages. First, joint actions can be developed whereby one peak association engages in strong lobbying activities, whereas the others negotiate along more moderate paths in related policy fields. Second, the tripartite organizational structure of business representation makes it virtually impossible for the government to pursue policies without the early involvement of the three peak associations. Third, their encompassing structure gives the peak associations a strategic advantage in terms of information. Often, the government relies on economic peak associations for the provision of up-to-date information and the preparation of policy initiatives.

The unitary trade union is the second characteristic of the organization of the German economy. In this respect, "unitary" means foremost that the union represents all blue-collar and white-collar workers in an industry. For the unions, this type of collective bargaining reduces conflict among employees within and between firms. For employers, it avoids negotiations with several, perhaps even competing, unions. The second meaning of "unitary" implies that unions are politically neutral, although they have traditionally been closer to the SPD than to other parties, just as the employers' associations bear a closer affinity to the FDP and the CDU.

Like their counterparts, the employers' and business associations, the unions are grouped into peak organizations. The most influential of these is the Federation of German Trade Unions (Deutscher Gewerkschaftsbund, or DGB) with about 7.7 million members representing 34.5 percent of all private and public-sector employees. The DGB consists of nine regional associations and seventeen separate unions, with the metal-industry union being the most influential and powerful.

As is the case with the BDI and the BDA, the purpose and task of the DGB goes well beyond collective bargaining. The DGB constitution states that "workers' interests have to be represented not only vis-à-vis employers, but also vis-à-vis parliaments, administrations, and other institutions in society since these, too, take major decisions affecting the living and working conditions of the dependently employed" (DGB 1981:14). The most visible example of DGB participation in general policies and political coordination was the neocorporatist "concerted action," when government, employers' associations, and the DGB sat at the same table to negotiate political steps in response to the economic crises of the late 1960s and early 1970s.

The third characteristic of German business and industry is that its peak organizations are a firm part of governmental "policy of nonplanning." Relatively independent of political ideology, all governments since 1949 have operated with a minimum of state planning (Beyme 1987:188; Mayntz and Scharpf 1975:16). The ideology of a social market economy survived in few other countries as well as it did in West Germany, despite the strong welfare component in social security and in the public provision of social services. The unspoken policy of nonplanning, which leaves many policy initiatives and their implementation to independent public organizations, *Länder* agencies, employers' associations, and unions, has in part remained influential because any direct state planning and intervention was thoroughly politically discredited by both national socialism and the cold-war experience with East German communism.

THE ORGANIZATION OF THE PUBLIC SPHERE

This section examines organizations concerned with the constitution of the public sphere in several areas: education and research, culture, the media, religion, politics, the economy, and social welfare. Table 3.1 presents an overview of the number of establishments and employees in central areas of the public sphere. Table 3.1, based on the result of the 1987 census of workplaces (Statistisches Bundesamt 1989), shows that the for-profit sector, the voluntary sector, and the state sector are to varying degrees involved in the constitution of the public sphere. In some areas, such as education, research,

TABLE 3.1
The Public Sphere: For-Profit, Voluntary, and State Organizations

	For-Profit Sector		Voluntary Sector		State Sector	
	Establishments	Employees	Establishments	Employees	Establishments	Employees
Education and research						
Universities	21	495	90	2,307	2,662	19,240
Libraries and archives	49	439	56	441	246	860
Scientific institutions	526	37,456	384	17,405	468	2,460
Schools	407	10,955	1,101	38,115	23,929	58,036
Vocational schools	1,877	35,791	1,738	43,546	2,489	12,561
Adult education			657	9,559		
Culture						
Theaters and operas	269	7,227	62	1,414	184	2,961
Orchestras, choirs, and ballets	976	4,231	60	652	30	122
Museums, zoos, and gardens	650	3,352	187	1,604	899	1,534
General libraries	6,461	18,083	176	821	1,779	1,655
Media						
Television and radio			391	30,530		
Book publishers	2,852	27,142				
Journal publishers	2,067	29,610				
Newspaper publishers	1,760	76,070				
Independent journalists	3,443	4,610				
Religion and ideology						
Religious and ideological associations			25,005	162,367		

Educational and cultural institutions			1,861	23,971		
Political parties			2,772	16,876		
Economy						
Unions			1,497	12,178		
Local and regional peak associations			111	3,449		
Employers' associations			354	3,762		
Business associations			2,924	31,431		
Public-law professional associations			1,329	32,775		
Social welfare						
Free-welfare associations	3,126	51,376	6,438	93,501	3,814	56,291
Social-welfare homes	84	1,071	8,991	243,033	56	1,100
Reform and correctional schools	422	1,576	271	6,964		
Kindergartens			14,577	97,076	7,549	57,229

Source: Statistisches Bundesamt (1989).

and social welfare, all three are represented. In other fields one sector dominates, notably in media, religion, and the economy.

In *education* and *research*, the state sector dominates universities, scientific libraries, and archives. With very few exceptions (for example, the Catholic University in Eichstätt or recently established private universities), universities are public institutions, although the churches maintain influence in theological seminaries. Private, for-profit universities remain politically controversial and have been able to establish themselves primarily in the area of business administration. Scientific research institutions are more evenly distributed among the three sectors, although voluntary-sector research institutes are only half as numerous as for-profit organizations in this area. However, prestigious research organizations such as the sixty Max Planck Institutes and the Fraunhofer Gesellschaft are registered private associations, although they rely almost completely on public funds. Primary and secondary schools are largely in the public system. Private schools, predominantly Catholic, educate 6.6 percent of all students up to the university level. Vocational training shows considerable input by both for-profit and voluntary-sector organizations. In contrast to the predominance of the state sector in primary and secondary education, adult education is basically carried out within the voluntary sector in the form of nonprofit, open-enrollment community colleges with 4.8 million students.

Prominent actors in the public sphere are the numerous private, nonprofit academies and institutes for adult education (*Bildungsstätten*), which organize seminars dealing with a wide range of topics, from religious, and ecumenical issues, environmental policies, corporate culture, and vocational training to development aid, AIDS, sports, language and literature, death, the media, feminism, and human rights. These *Bildungsstätten* are organized into three strata and peak associations: The Council of Catholic Academies, with over 20 member organizations; the Council of Evangelical Academies, having 13 member academies; and the Working Council of German Bildungsstätten, which includes secular, nonpolitical academies with over 140 members. The larger academies, in particular the Catholic and Protestant institutions, typically organize between one hundred and five hundred seminars and conferences each year. Like the political foundations, the academies act as both a monitoring device and a forum for the public sphere.

In the area of *culture*, all three sectors are represented. For theaters, operas, orchestras, ballets, choirs, museums, zoos, and gardens, as well as general libraries, the voluntary sector is least significant in terms of the number of establishments and employees. However, the statistics reported in table 3.1 include only those establishments with at least one paid employee, which excludes, for example, all informal cultural associations.

The general organizational principle of the intersection of the voluntary sector and the public sphere is also present in the cultural field, for example in the case of the German Cultural Council (Deutscher Kulturrat). The Kulturrat is a peak association of about 170 member organizations (some of which are peak associations themselves), and is divided into eight sections: the German Music Council, the Council for the Performing Arts, the Working Committee on Literature, the Arts Council, the Architectural Arts Council, the German Designer Council, the Section on Film and Audiovision, and the Council of Socioculture. Together, the Kulturrat and its constituent organizations represent about six million individual members. The Kulturrat, which seeks to improve the general conditions for art and culture, carries out broad lobbying activities. Besides general information campaigns about social, political, financial, and other salient matters pertaining to the arts and culture, the council focuses particularly on the areas of media, taxation, copyright law, and cultural policies, and also addresses international issues.

The media are essentially in the for-profit sector, with the exception of the television and radio stations, which are public-law associations. We have already seen how the value-rationality of television is partially avoided by ensuring broad participation of different social, political, and economic interests. The Deutsche Presserat (German Press Council) is a good example of the self-regulating function the voluntary sector performs in the public sphere. Set up by publishers' associations, the association of journalists, and the relevant union (IG-Druck), it aims at guarding press freedom by identifying any predicaments in news reporting and access to information and by acting as a court of appeals for any complaint about unfair, biased, unethical, or prejudiced reporting in the media. In 1988, the Presserat was called upon in 246 cases, 66 of which were subject to formal deliberations. In about two-thirds of the cases, the council decided in favor of the complainant.

Although I have already described aspects of *religion* and the *political system*, it is useful to add three examples that demonstrate the encompassing nature of peak associations in this area. The first one relates to the Ring Politischer Jugend (Circle of Political Youth), an umbrella organization for the politically active between the ages of eighteen and about thirty. The Ring was founded in 1950 to combat "antidemocratic influences on the young generation and to thwart any efforts to abuse and misuse youths for political ends"— a clear reference to the incorporation of youths into the Nazi regime. It has four member organizations, each of which is in fact the youth organization of one of the three leading parties (the CDU-CSU, the SPD and the FDP), in addition to the Young Democrats who left the FDP party organizations in 1982 to form an independent youth wing. Although the direct political influence of the Ring is limited, and it rarely features prominently in public debate (in contrast to its member organizations), it nevertheless serves an important integrative function in elite recruitment: it offers a forum for future party leaders to meet, have discussions, and form elaborate alliances and networks within and across political party lines.

In organizational and political terms, the Humanistische Union (Humanist Union) represents the counterpart to the elite orientation of the political establishment of the Ring. The union was founded in 1961 to "oppose the conservative restoration and increasing inertia of the late Adenauer era" and to safeguard civil rights for and from "a still not democratic people." (The specific occasion was the ban of a performance of The Marriage of Figaro in 1961 by the Catholic Church on the grounds of obscenity.) Since then the union has developed into the German equivalent of the American Civil Liberties Union, largely concerned with the protection of the constitution and civil rights: "Even the best constitution cannot defend itself—we want to do it" serves as a guiding principle of its work. The union, which includes members from all political parties, has played a prominent role in numerous cases relating to civil liberties, social justice, and human rights.

The Deutsche Frauenrat (German Women's Council) is a peak association that represents the interests of women vis-à-vis the parliament, political parties, and other associations. In particular, legislative activities that either directly or indirectly pertain to the status and role of women fall within the compass of the council. The council occupies an influential position in policy making and public debate. However, because of its politically encompassing membership, which includes segments of all major political parties, the council has found it difficult to take issue with such politically highly sensitive and controversial topics as abortion. The reason for the strength as well as the potential political paralysis of the council is found in its organizational structure: it is a peak association with a membership of forty-three associations (four of which are peak associations themselves) and numerous, often organizationally weak, regional groups with a total of about ten million individual members.

In the areas of *social services* and *welfare*, the "free-welfare associations" in West Germany are a prime example of the close relationship between corporatist arrangements of peak associations in the welfare state and the value-rationality of the voluntary sector. Organized in a peak association as the Federal Consortium of Free Welfare, they run 60,517 institutions in the areas of health care and youth and family services, as well as services for the handicapped, elderly, and poor. They provide 70 percent of all family services, 60 percent of all services for the elderly, 40 percent of all hospital beds, and 90 percent of all employment for the handicapped. The free-welfare associations employ nearly 500,000 full-time and about 175,000 part-time staff members. Operating independently but organizationally linked to its 60,517 institutions are 22,120 self-help groups, clubs, and local voluntary associations. Caritas alone employs more people than the industrial conglomerate Siemens, one of the largest employers in the Federal Republic.

Each of the free-welfare associations represents an institutional response to a basic dilemma (Bauer 1978; Bauer and Diessenbacher 1984; Heinze and Olk

1981). The Diakonisches Werk (Protestant), founded as the Innere Mission (Inner Mission) in 1848–1849, developed outside the official Protestant church structures. It began as a welfare-oriented evangelical movement, often in conflict with the secular political world. In contrast, Caritas ideologically grounded in Catholic social ethics and the principle of subsidiarity, developed within the Catholic church and is integrated into the religious hierarchy. The Arbeiterwohlfahrt (Workers' Welfare, secular), founded in 1919, has historically been linked to the Social Democratic Party. For the Social Democrats, who advocated public rather than private welfare provision, the creation of the Arbeiterwohlfahrt was a result of a "reconciliation of workers and the capitalist state" (Bauer 1978). The Zentralwohlfahrtsstelle der Juden in Deutschland (Jewish) was created in 1917. The Deutscher Paritätischer Wohlfahrtsverband, founded in 1920, is a consortium of nondenominational, nonpartisan private welfare organizations. Like Jewish welfare associations, the Deutscher Paritätischer Wohlfahrtsverband was in part an organizational response to the expansion of denominational and partisan welfare. Finally, the Red Cross, international and humanistic in orientation, is perhaps the most autonomous of the welfare organizations.

The relationship between the free-welfare associations and the state is complex and goes well beyond monetary transfers. In the immediate post–World War II era, the Allies favored and supported the rapid reestablishment of free-welfare associations, which they regarded as politically less suspect than public welfare organizations. During the Christian Democratic administrations of the 1950s and 1960s, the free-welfare associations were able to gain much ground vis-à-vis the state. The Christian Democrats institutionalized the principle of subsidiarity. Today, the free-welfare associations occupy a quasi-monopolistic position: for example, since 1961 municipalities or other potential suppliers are barred from establishing child-care and youth institutions if the free-welfare associations are planning to do so. Alternative suppliers need the consent of the free-welfare associations.

While the welfare associations may develop and protect local monopolies, they have also established a cartel at the federal level. For example, foreign workers are assigned to different associations that, while leaving the individuals little choice, are then exclusively responsible for their well-being. Workers from the predominantly Catholic countries of Italy, Spain, and Portugal are assigned to the Catholic Caritas, as are Catholic Croatians from predominantly non-Catholic Yugoslavia. Non-Croatian Yugoslavs, Turks, Moroccans, and Tunisians (in other words, those from predominantly Islamic countries) are domain of the secular Arbeiterwohlfahrt (Workers' Welfare). The Protestant Diakonisches Hilfs werk serves all the Greeks living in the Federal Republic.

In terms of services and finances, the state and the free-welfare associations are closely interrelated. The Arbeiterwohlfahrt had a total operating budget of about one hundred million deutsche marks in 1984. According to the (balanced) budget, it spent 40 percent on "participation in public tasks of the federal government" and received about 45 percent in public subsidies. Similarly, 25 to 30 percent of Diakonisches Hilfswerk funds come from public subsidies, while the figures for Caritas are 25 to 40 percent.

While acknowledging the immense importance of the free-welfare organizations, critics such as Thränhardt (1983) argue that their historical development, which today leaves hardly any aspect of the average citizen's life untouched, is not the result of purposeful collective decisions to provide welfare and to cater to the public good. Most of these peak associations originated primarily for political reasons; the legal and social-policy rationales of the system were introduced later.

The examples presented in this section and in table 3.1 relate to formal associations with at least one paid employee only. Official reporting systems exclude all associations that run only on a voluntary basis. The number of tax-exempt organizations is estimated at two hundred thousand (Bundesministerium der Finanzen 1988:32), only few of which employ staff. Thus, little and inconclusive data are available on volunteering. The Red Cross (2.5 million members) has 398,053 volunteers; other, similar voluntary associations such as the Malteser Hilfsdient, the Arbeiter-Samariter, and the Johanniter-Hilfsdienst gather between 20,000 and 30,000 volunteers each. Nine hundred thousand people volunteer in the local fire brigades, and the free-welfare associations claim one and a half to two million volunteers. Braun and Röhrig (1986) report that in the mid-1970s, 6 percent of the population volunteered once a week, and 27 percent less than once a month. A 1979 survey found that 42 percent of the adult population had volunteered at least once during the previous two years (Institut für Demoskopie 1979). A survey in medium-sized cities by Braun and Röhrig (1986) reached similar conclusions for the mid-1980s.

In terms of membership, some data are available from a recent General Social Survey (ALLBUS 1986), which included several questions on personal membership in different types of voluntary associations. Three-quarters of all respondents in the nationally representative sample claimed not to be members of any union or professional association—which implies that about one in four adults in the Federal Republic participates by membership in the economic part of the public sphere. About 15 percent said that they were members of unions; 2 percent were members of civil-servant associations; 5 percent belonged to professional associations. More than half (52.7 percent) of the adult population belong to sports clubs, choirs, or other leisure-time associations. Six percent are members of church-related organizations; in addition to being church members, 3.3 percent are members of a political party.

Few data are available on the counterpublic sphere, the *Gegenöffentlichkeit*. As already mentioned above, the counterpublic sphere emerged from the student movement and the extraparliamentary opposition of the 1960s. A central aspect of the counterpublic sphere in the 1970s and 1980s was the citizens' initiatives (*Bürgerinitiativen*), usually largely informal associations organized at the local level. The initiatives emerged at a time when Willy Brandt's declaration in parliament "to dare more democracy" coincided with widespread disenchantment with the "party state" (party weariness). Brandt's plea for more democracy was welcomed by the populace, but was implemented largely outside the formal, established public sphere of political parties. The draft of the Orientation Paper of the federation of citizens' initiatives in the area of environmental protection (BBU; see below) stated in 1977 that "citizens feel that social developments or state planning measures are encroaching upon their elementary rights. The experience of being helpless in the face of superior economic and political interests induces them to get together with like-minded people to protect their rights" (Hauff 1980:343; citing the translation in Schweitzer et al. 1984:246). The same document attributes the success of citizens' groups to their nonpartisan and decentralized organizational structure; they are spontaneously formed, local groups.

The great majority of citizens' initiatives of the 1970s and 1980s were ad hoc, informal associations of individuals who shared concerns, be they decisions taken by local authorities, nuclear-waste disposal, or regional traffic projects that affected the people's well-being (Guggenberger 1980). Only 4 percent of the initiatives had more than one thousand members, with three-quarters having less than one hundred (Kodolitsch 1975). These data underline the essentially local character of the initiatives. About 60 percent of the initiatives were largely concerned with environmental protection, followed by education, child care, housing, and urban planning (Kodolitsch 1975). Moreover, the environmental groups were also the first to organize coordinating mechanisms between initiatives. The emerging extended network of citizens' initiatives and coordinating groups became a great source of political mobilization, which culminated in the founding of the Green Party in 1980, the first environmentalist political party in the Western world. The extended network of local groups also benefited the social movements of the 1980s, in particular the peace and antinuclear movements, which were able to call demonstrations with over three hundred thousand participants.

The most visible of the new peak organizations is the Federal Association of Citizens' Initiatives—Environment (Bundesverband Bürgerinitiativen Umweltschutz, or BBU), which grew from fifteen member organizations in 1972 to more than one thousand in the mid-1980s, representing a total membership between three hundred thousand and five hundred thousand. The BBU functions as the major peak association for environmental matters, and has become an important player in all policy issues in this area. In addition, more than a thousand environmental groups are registered with the Federal Agency for the Environment.

The citizens' initiative movement introduced new elements into the public sphere. The citizens' groups emerged from the extraparliamentary opposition and began as informal, local associations. Meeting at least with partial success (which about half of all initiatives in one survey felt they did [Müller 1983]), they became an accepted part of the German political landscape. Yet in some ways they are incorporated into the elaborate system of interorganizational structures and peak associations. Thus, they tend to replicate the essential characteristic of voluntary-sector organizations in West Germany, the centralization of decentralized organizations and constituencies.

CONCLUSION

This chapter has developed several themes on the public sphere and the voluntary sector in West Germany. It has shown the ambivalent character of the public sphere, which has become institutionalized largely in the form of voluntary-sector organizations. It has gone beyond Habermas's argument about the functional ambivalence of the public sphere in advanced industrial societies and taken explicit account of how the public sphere is institutionally embedded. I argued that in West Germany the public sphere is located between the decentralized public sector and the centralizing tendencies of society.

In particular the areas of the economy and the polity, as well as other aspects of religious, social, and cultural life, show how the public sphere is embedded in an institutional environment shaped by a decentralized state and a centralized, state-oriented civic society. This is at one and the same time the major strength and the major weakness of the public sphere in Germany. The system of peak associations is the most significant aspect of Germany's centralized civic society. Peak associations form a comprehensive, centralized organizational system that represents special economic, political, and social interests. The associations are highly encompassing and exist in all major areas of society, polity, and the economy—employers' associations, unions, professions, social welfare, culture, religion, and agriculture.

Institutions of the public sphere have increasingly become aware of their limitations in basic policy alternatives and innovation. They have learned to monitor the relevant *Gegenöffentlichkeiten*. The political foundations in particular, as well as business and political think-tank organizations, act as detecting devices to search out the emergent topics, ideas, formations, and developments in the counterpublic spheres. Aspects of these emergent trends are then analyzed, "translated," and incorporated into official political and policy strategies. In terms of value changes and policy innovations, the public sphere tends to nurture itself from the counterpublic sphere.

POSTSCRIPT

With the adoption of West Germany's currency and economic system, East Germany is undertaking far-reaching measures for political, economic, and social reform. At present, the voluntary sector in East Germany is rapidly expanding in areas left vacant by the retreating public-sector economy and the disintegrating state apparatus. Not surprisingly, precise data are lacking; however, if the many notices and reports announcing the founding of new associations in daily newspapers are any indication, the voluntary sector in East Germany must be undergoing dramatic growth. This surge (and, in some instances, renaissance) of voluntary-sector activity is in part the result of newly emerging local and economic interests, but in many aspects is also a delayed expression of civic society in a centralized, state-dominated country.

Dilemmas and Challenges

I hypothesize that the East German voluntary sector faces two main challenges. Each challenge presents itself in the form of a dilemma.

The first challenge is a domestic one: in the likely situation of economic difficulties and increased unemployment, nonprofit organizations will have to help provide some of the social services no longer provided by the state. Moreover, they will have to strengthen their contribution to civil society by encouraging citizen participation in the new social order if the political transformation of East German society is to succeed. Thus, the voluntary sector will have to contribute to the legitimacy of the new political and economic entity it helped bring into being. At the same time, the voluntary sector has to meet an increased demand for social services left unmet by the retreating state. This dual role of service provider and legitimacy provider contains a dilemma: even if the overall transformation of East German society is relatively successful, the voluntary sector may not be able to fulfill both functions equally, and one may come at the expense of the other.

This dilemma is most pronounced for the churches and the civic associations that emerged under religious auspices and protection in the 1980s. The churches became the institutional harbor for opposition groups and social movements: the peace movement ("swords into plowshares"), the environmental movement, and many groups expressing local concerns that could not be addressed within the official party and state structures. The church became a major advocate of change, and both an arena for and an actor in the public sphere.

The second challenge refers to the possible impact of the West German voluntary sector. To what extent will the West German sector expand into East Germany and occupy organizational space and functional arenas of the public sphere left by the defunct socialist bureaucracy? The dilemma for East German nonprofit organizations is that a significant reliance on West German funds and management skills may create irreversible dependency effects that could undermine organizational autonomy, and may even reduce local legitimacy.

These challenges become more acute if we consider the strikingly different social, legal, and economic environments in which the nonprofit sector operates in both parts of the country. West Germany is characterized by a decen-

90 · Helmut K. Anheier

tralized political system and a relatively centralized society, whereas East Germany had a highly centralized political and economic system and has recently shown increasingly decentralized tendencies in society, in large part due to the loss of legitimacy of many social institutions associated with the socialist system. In both cases, the voluntary sector plays a major role: it has traditionally tended to strengthen centralizing tendencies in West Germany, and it has contributed to decentralizing tendencies in the East.

References

Abelshauser, W. 1983. *Wirtschaftsgeschichte der Bundesrepublik Deutschland, 1945–1980*. Frankfurt: Suhrkamp.

ALLBUS. 1986. *Allgemeine Bevölkerungsumfrage*. Cologne: Zentralarchiv für empirische Sozialforschung der Universität zu Köln.

Bauer, R. 1978. *Wohlfahrtsverbände in der Bundesrepublik*. Weinheim and Basel: Beltz.

———. 1987. "Intermediäre Hilfesysteme personenbezogener Dienstleitungen in zehn Ländern—Eine Einführung." In *Verbandliche Wohlfahrtspflege im internationalen Vergleich*, edited by R. Bauer and A. M. Thränhardt, pp. 9–30. Opladen: Westdeutscher Verlag.

Bauer, R., and H. Diessenbacher, eds. 1984. *Organisierte Nächstenliebe: Wohlfahrtsverbände und Selbsthilfe in der Krise des Sozialstaats*. Opladen: Westdeutscher Verlag.

Bering, D. 1978. *Die Interlektuellen: Geschichte eines Schimpfwortes*. Stuttgart: Metzler-Poeschel.

Beyme, K. von. 1979. "Der Neo-Korporatismus und die Politik des begrenzten Pluralismus in der Bundesrepublik." In *Stichworte zur geistigen Situation der Zeit*, edited by J. Habermas. Vol. 1, *Nation und Politik*, pp. 229–62. Frankfurt: Suhrkamp.

———. 1984. *Parteien in westlichen Demokratien*. Munich: Piper.

———. 1987. *Das Politische System der Bundesrepublik Deutschland*. Munich: Piper.

Braun, J. and P. Röhrig. 1986. "Umfang und Unterstützung ehrenamtlicher Mitarbeit und Selbsthilfe im kommunalen Sozial- und Gesundheitsbereich." In *Freiwilliges soziales Engagement und Weiterbildung*, edited by Bundesminister für Bilding und Wissenschaft. Bonn: Bundesminister für Bilding und Wissenschaft.

Bundesarbeitsgemeinschaft der Freien Wohlfahrtspflege. 1985. *Gesamtstatistik 1984*. Bonn: Bundesarbeitgemeinschaft der Freien Wohlfahrtspflege.

Bundesministerium der Finanzen. 1988. *Gutachten der unabhaengigen Sachverstaendigenkommission zur Pruefung des Gemeinnuetzigkeits-und Spendenrechtes*. Schriftenreihe Heft 40. Bonn: Bundesministerium der Finanzen.

Bundesverband der Deutschen Industrie (BDI). 1981. *The Federation of German Industries*. Cologne: BDI.

Deutscher Gewerkschaftsbund (DGB). 1981. *The German Trade Union Federation*. Cologne: DGB.

Ellwein, T. 1989. *Krisen und Reformen: Die Bundesrepublik seit den sechziger Jahren*. Munich: DTV.

Enzensberger, M. 1967. *Deutschland, Deutschland unter anderem: Äusserungen zur Politik*. Frankfurt: Suhrkamp.

Grosser, A. 1988. *La RFA*. Paris: Presses Universitaires de France.

Guggenberger, B. 1980. *Bürgerinitiativen in der Parteiendemokratie: Von der Ökologiebewegung zur Umweltpartei*. Stuttgart: Metzler-Poeschel.

Habermas, J. 1962. *Strukturwandel der Öffentlichkeit*. Frankfurt: Suhrkamp.

―――. 1973. *Legitimationsprobleme im Spätkapitalismus*. Frankfurt: Suhrkamp.

―――. 1985. "Die neue Unübersichtlichkeit: Die Krise des Wohlfahrtsstaates und die Erschöpfung utopischer Energien." *Merkur* 39 (1): 1–14.

Hauff, V., ed. 1980. *Bürgerinitiativen in der Gesellschaft*. Bonn: Villingen.

Heinze, R. G., and T. Olk. 1981. "Die Wohlfahrtsverbände im System sozialer Dienstleistungspoduktion: Zur Entstehung und Struktur der bundesrepublikanischen Verbändewohlfahrt." *Kölner Zeitschrift für Soziolige und Sozialpsychologie* 1.

Hilferding, R. 1924. "Probleme der Zeit." *Die Gesellschaft: Internationale Revue für Sozialismus und Politik* 1:1–17.

Institut der Deutschen Wirtschaft. 1988. *International Economic Indicators*. Cologne: Institut der Deutschen Wirtschaft.

Institut für Demoskopie. 1979. *Die Stellung der freien Wohlfahrtsverbände*. Allensbach: Institut für Demoskopie.

Isensee, J. 1966. *Subsidiaritätsprinzip und Verfassungsrecht*. Berlin.

Jaschke, Hans-Gerd. 1982. *Soziale Basis und soziale Funktion des Nationalsozialismus: Studien zur Bonapartismustheorie*. Opladen: Westdeutscher Verlag.

Jaspers, K. 1966. *Wohin treibt die Bundesrepublik?* Munich: Piper.

Katzenstein, P. J. 1987. *Policy and Politics in West Germany: The Growth of a Semisovereign State*. Philadelphia: Temple University Press.

Kodolitsch, P. von. 1975. "Gemeindeverwaltungen und Bürgerinitiativen: Ergebnisse einer Umfrage." *Archiv für Kommunalwissenschaften* 3:39–54.

―――. 1980. "Effizienzsteigerung oder Systenüberwindung—Zur empirischen Erfolgbilanz der Bürgerinitiativen." In *Bürgerinitiativen und repräsentatives System*, edited by B. Guggenberger and U. Kempf, pp. 318–32. Opladen: Westseutscher Verlag.

Koshar, R. 1987. "From Stammtisch to Party: Nazi Joiners and the Contradictions of Grass-Roots Fascism in Weimar Germany." *Journal of Modern History* 59:1–24.

Lepsius, R. M. 1978. "From Fragmented Party Democracy to Government by Emergency Decree and National Socialist Takeover: Germany." In *The Breakdown of Democratic Regimes: Europe*, edited by Juan J. Linz and Alfred Stepan, pp. 34–79. Baltimore: Johns Hopkins University Press.

Luhmann, N. 1971. *Politische Planung*. Opladen: Westdeutscher Verlag.

Mayntz, R. 1984. "German Federal Bureaucrats: A Functional Elite between Politics and Administration." In *Bureaucrats and Policy Making: A Comparative Overview*, edited by E. N. Suleiman, pp. 174–205. New York: Holmes and Meier.

Mayntz, R., and F. W. Scharpf. 1975. *Policy Making in the German Federal Bureaucracy*. Amsterdam: Elsevier.

Mommsen, Hans. 1990. *Die verspielte Freiheit: Der Weg der Weimarer Republic in den Untergang 1918 bis 1933*. Frankfurt: Propyläen.

Müller, M. 1983. "Bürgerinitiativen in der politischen Willensbildung." *Aus Politik und Zeitgeschichte* 11 (19 March): 17–28.

Negt, O., and A. Kluge. 1972. *Öffentlichkeit und Erfahrung: Zur Organisationsanalyse bürgerlicher und proletarischer Öffentlichkeit*. Frankfurt: Suhrkamp.

Rimlinger, G. 1971. *Welfare Policy and Industrialization in Europe, America, and Russia*. New York: Wiley.

Sachse, C., and F. Tennstedt, eds. 1986. *Soziale Sicherheit und soziale Disziplinierung*. Frankfurt: Suhrkamp.

Schmitt, C. 1932. *Der Begriff des Politischen*. Leipzig: Duncker and Humboldt.

Schweitzer, C. C., et al., eds. 1984. *Politics and Government in the Federal Republic of Germany: Basic Documents*. Leamington Spa: Berg.

Seibel, W., and H. K. Anheier. 1990. "Sociological and Political Science Approaches to the Third Sector." In *The Third Sector: Comparative Studies of Non-Profit Organizations*, edited by H. K. Anheier and W. Seibel, pp. 1–36. Berlin and New York: De Gruyter.

Simmel, G. 1908. *Soziologie*. Berlin: Dunker and Humboldt.

Statistisches Bundesamt. 1987. *Statistisches Jahrbuch für die Bundesrepublik Deutschland*. Stuttgart: Metzler-Poeschel.

———. 1988. *Statistisches Jahrbuch für die Bundesrepublik Deutschland*. Stuttgart: Metzler-Poeschel.

———. 1989. *Unternehmen und Arbeitstätten*. 2d ed. Stuttgart: Metzler-Poeschel.

Thränhardt, D. 1983. "Ausländer im Dickicht der Verbände: Ein Beispiel verbandsgerechter Klientelselektion und korporatistischer Politkformulierung." In *Sozialarbeit und Ausländerpolitik*, edited by F. Hamburger et al., pp. 97–111. Neuwied and Darmstadt: Luchterhand.

Tönnies, F. 1922. *Kritik der öffentlichen Meinung*. Berlin: Springer.

Weber, J. 1977. *Die Interessengruppen im politischen System der Bundesrepublik Deutschland*. Stuttgart: Kohlhammer.

Weber, M. 1917. *Gesammelte Politische Schriften*. Tübingen: Mohr.

Wehler, H. U. 1987. *Deutsche Gesellschaftsgeschichte, 1700–1815*. Munich: Beck.

Weyrauch, W. ed. 1960. *Ich lebe in der Bundesrepublik*. Munich: Piper.

CHAPTER FOUR

Sweden: Is There a Viable Third Sector?

John Boli

IN DISCUSSIONS of societal corporatism over the past decade, Sweden has always stood out as an exemplary case. The "iron triangle" of business, labor, and government is depicted as operating in collusion to negotiate economic and social policy in a sort of "grand compromise" among elite figures in each sector. Everybody knows everybody else; everyone has roughly the same goals; hostility and confrontational attitudes are generally absent. Ordinary folk—employees, union members, voters—are effectively excluded from the high-level bargaining process through a multilevel representative democracy system that shields elite groups from the bother of public opinion.

The neocorporatist view of Swedish politics and policy formation is strongly favored by foreign observers of the Swedish scene (Schmitter and Lehmbruch 1979; Katzenstein 1985; for a particularly condemnatory analysis see Huntford 1972). Swedish scholars sometimes agree (Torstendahl 1985), but more often they argue to the contrary. The counterargument runs something like this. *Of course* the Trade Union Confederacy (Landsorganisationen, or LO) is closely allied with the Social Democratic party. The one is the economic arm of the workers' movement, the other the political arm. Through effective, democratic mass mobilization, the Social Democratic party has dominated the state throughout most of the twentieth century. LO and the Social Democrats have thus worked together to hold capitalism's exploitative and inegalitarian tendencies in check. Capitalist enterprise, as represented by the Swedish Employers' Association and other organizations, was convinced early on by the militant labor movement that capital's interests could best be served through industrial peace and social reforms that made the labor force better educated, more adaptable, and more productive. Thus Swedish policy formation and industrial relations, though based on the underlying class conflict between workers and capitalists, is essentially harmonious because everyone's interests are served by this "middle way." In the absence of democratic institutions, however, effective checks on capitalism could never have been instituted (see Korpi 1983; Esping-Anderson 1985; Rothstein 1987).

The debate regarding corporatism seems quite impervious to resolution. However, it can serve as a useful starting point from which to analyze the Swedish third sector, which we conceive in this volume as consisting of all those voluntary associations that stand outside the iron triangle of labor, capital, and the parties/state complex. My analysis will show that the same sort of ambiguity that has emerged regarding explicitly economic and political organizations—that they are so highly integrated into the public-policy process as to be only weakly bounded, if at all, by the state—is present regarding the third sector.

To begin, a few remarks on the concept of the state are in order. My point of departure is the observation that the state should not be equated with the formal organizational structures that are conventionally identified as its constituent organs. Just as the "workers' movement" is a broader and more elusive entity than its organizational expressions, such as LO and the Social Democratic party, so too is the state a broader and more elusive entity than its organizational expressions, such as parliament and governmental bureaucracies. I conceive the state as the *central authority structure* and the *locus of ultimate authority* in society. In this broad conception, *any* organizational structure that exercises central authority and acts as a "court of last resort" regarding social behavior should be characterized as, at the least, "statelike."[1]

This conception makes it possible to inquire as to the "stateness" of all sorts of organizations that are usually considered entirely private. Consider, for example, the Swedish temperance movement. Throughout the twentieth century the temperance societies have been highly overrepresented in the Riksdag (parliament), constituting a special caucus that meets regularly to discuss alcohol policy. Until the 1950s, most municipal governments (*kommuner*) had temperance boards overseeing alcohol-related municipal policy. The temperance societies were strongly represented on these boards as well. Further, whenever a state commission has been established to prepare a proposal for a change in national alcohol policy, the temperance movement has had representatives on the investigatory committee. In short, in both the formulation and the execution of governmental policy, the temperance organizations have acted as *authorized components of the central authority structure* of society. They have been seen as representatives of an important segment of the population and therefore "entitled to" a significant role in formal state operations.

In what follows I will apply this broad conception of the state to the third sector in Sweden. As my title indicates, my main concern is how much sense it makes to claim that a Swedish third sector exists at all. As the literature on corporatism suggests regarding the labor-capital complex, Swedish central authority has expanded so much that whether *any* organized activity remains outside the state is singularly problematic. Yet the matter is complex, and I

---

[1] Nothing is said here about a "monopoly on the legitimate use of force," which Weber and many others following him have seen as a key characteristic of the state. In my view, a central authority structure is statelike if it rests on an institutionalized claim to legitimacy and can apply sanctions to enforce its authority. Such sanctions need not include force or violence. As Weber emphasized, though, all modern states claim to have the sole authority to use force.

will risk disappointing the reader already by saying that I cannot answer the question in my title definitively. In Sweden, the state is highly expanded; central authority is ubiquitous; politicization has been taken very far. Yet the integration of society into the state is not complete, questions are often raised about the desirability of *étatisation*, and there are signs that the process may have peaked.

THE THIRD SECTOR: A CHARACTERIZATION

With a total Swedish population of 8.3 million, in 1985 memberships in Swedish *föreningar* (voluntary organizations) and *folkrörelser* (popular movements) were estimated at 31 million (SOU 1987b). Most memberships were in cooperative organizations of producers and consumers, followed by sports and recreation groups, labor unions, parties and other political organizations, cultural and adult education bodies, and religious or "worldview" associations (table 4.1). The overall participation rate of nearly four memberships per capita is often described as the highest in the world, the nearest competitor being the United States. By subtracting multiple memberships, table 4.2 shows the proportions of the adult population (ages sixteen to seventy-four) belonging to various types of organizations in 1980. Survey results indicate that between 80 and 90 percent of the population belong to at least one association (Westerståhl and Johansson 1981; Vestlund 1981).

Several points should be made about tables 4.1 and 4.2. First, noticeably lacking is a category of "charitable organizations." Such organizations are certainly present in Sweden—the Salvation Army goes back to the turn of the century, for example—but in no analysis of voluntary organizations have I encountered the category of charities. Most such organizations are assigned in table 4.1 to the "International" category—the Save the Children Fund, Swedish UNICEF, the Red Cross, church-related charities such as Luther Help, and so on. Hence, the second point is that charitable activities are generally oriented outward. Domestic social welfare is the responsibility of the state; individual compassion is directed toward the third world. Third, membership in the national Lutheran church is not included because such membership is automatic, not voluntary. I will return to this point later in the chapter.

How active are individuals in these organizations? Swedish researchers have approached this issue in several ways. Individuals are asked to characterize their participation as active or inactive, or to state the number of meetings they have attended in the past year, or to describe their participation in such activities as attending meetings, leafletting, or helping with a newsletter. Table 4.3 presents, for a number of types of organizations, several activity measures for the entire adult population (ages sixteen to seventy-four), and table 4.4 offers a commonly used activity measure, the proportion of individuals who describe themselves as active or say they have attended at least ten meetings in the past year.

TABLE 4.1
Membership in Organizations, 1985

Type of Organization	Local Affiliates (thousands)	Memberships (thousands)
Animal-related	1.3	358
Automobile, traffic safety	0.6	293
Child and youth[a]	3.4	238
Civil defense	6.7	796
Cooperative	6.9	9,384
Cultural, adult education	10.1	1,410
Disabled and patient	1.7	414
Family and relations	0.1	24
Health	0.3	46
Hobby and craft	2.2	154
Housing[b]	1.0	530
Immigrant	0.8	165
International	7.6	933
Labor union	12.9	3,714
Nature and environmental	0.8	207
Political	14.1	2,022
Religious, worldview	11.8	1,412
Retiree	2.7	529
School-related	2.2	358
Sports and recreation	52.3	6,381
Temperance, antidrug	5.3	1,306
Other	0.5	318
Total	145.8	31,060

Source: SOU 1987b, p. 22.

[a] Most child and youth organizations are included with their adult affiliates.

[b] Housing cooperatives are included with Cooperative organizations.

Table 4.3 is based on a large survey from 1978, which found that 85 percent of the adult population belonged to at least one organization (SCB 1982b). Nearly 40 percent of the population claimed active participation, fully 23 percent had an official position within an organization, and over 60 percent had attended at least one meeting during the previous year. Although nearly 20 percent said, on the contrary, that they had never attended any organization meeting of any sort, these figures indicate quite active participation. As table 4.4 shows, however, there is much variation among organization types. Members of consumer organizations are as a rule highly inactive, as are members of tenant and labor unions. The most active members are found in local interest and action groups, which are mostly short-lived associations mobilized around a particular local issue such as parking, pollution from a specific factory, or preservation of a historical landmark. Members of sports and immigrant organizations are also relatively active. Comparing activity figures with those of memberships, we find a generally inverse relationship—activity rates are higher the smaller the proportion of the population involved (Spearman's rho = − .44). The only strong exception is sports organizations, as one might expect.

The general picture that emerges in these tables is one of a population highly given to joining organizations (even if we exclude labor unions as not being "third-sector" in nature) and quite active within them. As with large organizations everywhere, the bulk of the membership is not actively engaged in day-to-day operations, but virtually every organization is structured on open, democratic principles, and most make a considerable effort to encourage member participation. Particularly noteworthy is the high proportion of members in official positions. On the other hand, if we assume that most such individuals describe themselves as active members, the proportion of self-described active members *not* holding office is quite low—only 10 to 15 percent.

In the literature the high participation rates of the Swedish population are invariably described in positive terms. The ubiquitous view is that a plethora of organizations and multiple memberships by much of the population are crucial for the health of Swedish democracy. Yet concern is often expressed that the organizations have become too big, too bureaucratic, too "established," and even, in the view of some analysts, too dependent on the state. There is not much room for individual members to "make a difference," and many organizations have tended to become little more than service units with no "movement" character at all (Vestlund 1981; SSU 1975).

Another concern, which first surfaced in the early 1970s, is that many of

TABLE 4.2
Adult (16–74) Membership in Organizations, 1980

Type of Organization	Members (thousands)	Proportion of Population (%)
Labor union	3040	51.6
Cooperative, consumer	1750	29.7
Sports and recreation	1550	26.3
Tenant, homeowner	1350	22.9
Political	800	13.6
Parenting	780	13.2
Local action, environmental	500	8.5
Farming, industrial	290	4.9
Retiree	280	4.8
Temperance	150	2.5
Immigrant	60	1.0

Source: Referensgruppen för folkrörelsefrågor (1980:14).

TABLE 4.3
Adult (16–74) Participation in Organizations

Level of Participation	Proportion of Adult Population
Member of at least one organization	85.0
Member of four or more organizations	15.9
Attended at least one meeting in previous year	61.5
Have ever spoken at a meeting	51.6
Participate actively in an organization	38.3
Hold official position in an organization	23.2
Attended twelve or more meetings in previous year	14.6
Never attended an organization meeting	19.7

Source: SCB (1982b); survey conducted 1978.

TABLE 4.4
Active Participation in Organizations

Type of Organization	Active Participants (% of Membership)
Local action, environmental	61
Sports and recreation	51
Immigrant	50
Retiree	43
Temperance	42
Political	38
Parenting	34
Farming, industrial	34
Labor union	21
Tenant, homeowner	18
Cooperative, consumer	7

Source: Vestlund (1981:42); survey conducted 1976.
Note: Respondents were asked if they "participate actively" or attended at least ten meetings in the previous year.

the functions once served by the voluntary organizations have been taken over by state and local governments. This was the central point of the 1974 manifesto produced by the Social Democratic Youth League, "Together for an Idea" (SSU 1975; see also Isling 1978; Lindholm 1983). This document helped convince the state to convene a conference on the *folkrörelser* in April 1975. In attendance were representatives of twenty-five prominent organizations, particularly those explicitly or indirectly affliated with the Social Democratic party, and several members of the government.

The 1975 conference sparked a major debate over the next few months about the role of the *folkrörelser* in society. While there was little disagreement on several basic issues—that the organizations were important, that they needed revitalization, that "democracy must be deepened" (Isling 1978) both within the organizations and, through them, in society as a whole—a rancorous dispute arose about the goals of the *folkrörelser* and, in consequence, their relationship to the state. SSU's manifesto, which set the tone for the debate, envisioned a society in which the organizations would essentially meld with the state, taking over a wide range of activities that had become governmental functions but doing so under state guidance and by means of state monies. The ultimate goal was a kind of populist socialism that would eventually squeeze out all forms of private enterprise (capitalism) and yield a totally collectivized but individual-based and democratic society. Predictably, critics of this proposal came mainly from the liberal and conservative segments of the political spectrum. Some critics complained that the Social Democrats were attempting to co-opt the organizations as political instruments, while others argued on a more principled basis that a healthy democracy requires independent, autonomous citizen organizations, and hence a self-conscious distancing from the state.

The primary outcomes of the debate were typical of the Swedish system. The government had already asked in its 1975 budget proposal for the establishment of a delegation to conduct research on the *folkrörelser*. The new Committee for Research on the Popular Movements soon set to work, undertaking some twenty-five major projects by 1985 (Forskningsrådsnämnden 1985). In 1977 a separate research group known as the Committee on Local Government Democracy was established, and in the next few years it produced a wide range of reports that touched on third-sector issues. A number of additional state commissions were established in succeeding years: the Committee on Cooperatives, the Committee on Popular Rule, the Study of Voluntary Contributions, and, as a culmination, the 1986 Study of the Folkrörelser (see References below, under SOU). In short, the state undertook to study the issue to death.

The second major outcome of the *folkrörelser* debate was that state and local government agencies enormously expanded their support for the organizations. This outcome will be discussed below.

SWEDISH VOLUNTARY ORGANIZATIONS AND THE STATE

A terminological discussion is in order. I have employed the term "organizations" rather than "voluntary associations" to translate *folkrörelser* and *föreningar*. An important distinction is at stake here. *Folkrörelser*, literally "popular movements," is applied primarily to the three early social movements that emerged in the latter part of the nineteenth century: the free-church, temperance, and labor union movements. Less commonly, it is also used to designate all voluntary associations. *Folk* designates "people" in the sense of "nation." The term thus indicates that the associations were from the outset conceived as expressions of nationally collective social action, not as simply local, independent groupings; *folkrörelser* contains a sense of the entire polity in movement.

Förening (singular form), a more recent and more frequently employed term, means "a uniting" or "combination" (like a "compound" in chemistry). It carries a sense of "joining together," of two or more entities that become one. For both terms the connotative emphasis lies more on the collectivity than on the individuals who join together to form it—on the Hobbesian rather than the Lockean version of the social contract, one might say. For this reason I am hesitant to use the term "voluntary association" to express these designations. This latter term attributes more substance to the individuals who join than is appropriate in the Swedish context, suggesting that they merely associate rather than become "one."

In what follows I will employ *föreningar* rather than "voluntary associations." My hope is that this term will keep readers in mind of the Swedish conception of these organizations. This should facilitate a better understanding of the cultural logic that has led to the present close relationship between *föreningar* and central-authority structures.

A second terminological matter requiring discussion is the Swedish usage of the terms *stat* (state) and *samhälle* (society). In English, these terms are clearly distinct: society is something other than the state; it "contains" the state or is "governed" by the state. In Swedish, however, the two terms are often used synonymously, and not solely by socialist (or Social Democratic) polemicists. Where an American debater might write "The state has a responsibility to provide health care to the poor," a Swedish debater is likely to say "*Society* has a responsibility to provide health care," it being understood that *samhälle* means *stat*, that is, central and local government.

Hence, in the 1960s when the term "welfare state" became common coinage, Swedish analysts began to speak of *det starka samhället*, the "strong society," to designate the highly expanded public sector that ensures the rights and material well-being of the population. "Society should be strong enough to act as a counterweight to the market economy jungle by distributing services according to need and not according to the thickness of one's wallet," runs the argument (Lindholm 1983:30). Here society and state are equated and placed in opposition to the market economy, which is barely accorded a place in "society" at all.

Both of these terminological peculiarities are symptomatic of the theory of social organization that dominates Swedish culture. We cannot speak of voluntary associations in Sweden, even though the *föreningar* are voluntary and associational, for these organizations are unifying, national, politywide, and absorbing (approximately 75 percent of all *föreningar* are formally affiliated with national organizations; only 25 percent are purely local; SOU 1987b). The flip side of this observation is that the boundary between state and society is nebulous, not only empirically but also conceptually. It is therefore revealing that an equivalent to the term "third sector" is entirely lacking in Swedish. One can speak of *folkrörelser*, of *föreningar*, and at times of *organisationer* (organizations), but the Anglo-Saxon concept of the political sector, the economic sector, and the third sector that is neither of these is not directly applicable to Swedish social organization.

A passage from the report of the Study of the Folkrörelser (SOU 1987b:26) states the matter succinctly: "In most other countries the preferred term is 'voluntary organizations and associations.' The choice of terms depends not only on linguistic differences but also on political differences. In Sweden our *föreningar* usually participate in popular rule in a totally different way from that of other countries." My task is thus to investigate this "totally different way" that Swedish *föreningar* are involved with central social authority. I will begin by developing an overview of the context in which the *föreningar* have developed during the past few decades.

Etatisation and Politicization

By 1985 total government spending had reached about 67 percent of GNP, government consumption was over 30 percent of GNP, and government employment had reached 38 percent of the labor force (Rodriguez 1980; SCB 1985; Furåker 1987). All of these figures were the highest in the non-Communist world. As elsewhere, the two periods of greatest state expansion were the 1930s, when the foundations of the welfare state were laid, and the ebullient 1960s. Until the latter decade the public sector's shares of consumption and employment were at about the mean for the countries belonging to the Organization for Economic and Cultural Development (OECD) (SOU 1987a). Since then the Swedish state has risen to a class all its own, though a few other countries (notably the Netherlands and Denmark) are only slightly behind (Furåker 1987).

Note, however, that this extraordinary expansion of central authority structures has *not* involved the *étatisation* of private enterprise. The state has never controlled more than about 10 percent of industry and related production enterprises. It is indeed a welfare state in the pure sense of the term, devoted more to redistribution (transfer payments) than socialization of the private economy. On the other hand, of course, the high figures for government employment and consumption indicate the creation of a large socialized segment of the economy. Carlsson (1987) reports that 49 percent of all paid-labor hours (as opposed to employment positions) in 1983 were in the public sector; if paid hours in state-owned industry are added, the figure rises to 56 percent.

It should also be noted that this expansion combines state and local government growth. In recent decades the county councils (which are responsible for most health care and some public transportation) and municipalities have grown faster than the central state. County expenditures rose from 2 percent to 12 percent of GNP between 1960 and 1984, while municipal expenditures jumped from 12 percent to 25 percent of GNP, implying a growth for the central state from 17 percent to about 30 percent (SOU 1987a). The central state's share of public employment fell from 38 percent in 1970 to 28 percent in 1984, while the county share rose from 18 percent to 26 percent and the municipal share went from 42 percent to 44 percent (Furåker 1987).

At first sight the increasing role of local government at the expense of the central state may seem surprising, but it is largely consistent with the Swedish model of government. A tradition of local self-government reaches back at least to the seventeenth century, when the local village and parish meetings that were only marginally supervised by the state became important authority structures. Since the mid-nineteenth century, local autonomy has been progressively circumscribed by the increasingly intrusive central state, which has imposed new or expanded responsibilities on the municipalities while providing funds to a variable extent. Many new governmental programs initiated in the 1930s and 1940s were administered directly by the central state (retirement pensions, work accident insurance, housing construction subsidies, children allowances), but a clamoring for decentralization and a restoration of municipal self-direction from the late 1960s onward reversed this trend. Most state programs today are formulated through so-called framework laws that specify goals and objectives but leave day-to-day details of program implementation to lower governmental units. Yet the state's supervisory control over municipal operations has continued to increase—something like 80 percent of municipal budgets, and 90 percent of county council budgets, consist of programs mandated by law (Andersson, Melbourn, and Skogö 1978; Birgersson and Westerståhl 1987). A sometimes uneasy partnership between central and local authorities has thus emerged.

The rapid expansion of central authority's role in society has been accompanied by comprehensive party politicization. Parties first became the dominant vehicles for political action early in this century, but what is now known as "block politics" crystallized only in the 1970s (Ruin 1985). More than ever before, the five-party system has come to be defined as consisting of two opposed camps—the "socialist" camp of the Left-Party Communists (VPK) and Social Democrats, and the "bourgeois" camp of the Center party (formerly the Farmers' party), the Liberal party (Folkpartiet), and the Moderate party (formerly the "Right" or Conservative party). Prior to the 1970s the party system had been more fluid, especially in the middle, with the Farmers' party often helping keep the Social Democrats in power and only the Conservative party being continually in opposition.

Party politicization has been especially marked at the local level. This development is often attributed to the municipal government consolidation process undertaken in the 1950s and 1960s that reduced the number of municipalities from about 2,500 in 1952 to only 277 in 1974 (Birgersson and Westerståhl 1987). Justified by the perceived need for more populous municipal units with a larger tax base and greater technical expertise to deal with the municipalities' expanding responsibilities, this reform cut the number of local elective positions from between one hundred fifty thousand and two hundred thousand in the 1950s to forty-two thousand in 1974. It also stimulated a rapid bureaucratization and technocratization of local government (SOU 1975a; Strömberg and Norell 1982).[2]

In counterpoint, for the first time party politics entered the local arena in force. Until the 1970s most municipalities operated on a nonparty basis (and, before the 1950s, through general town meetings in which anyone could participate), but by the 1980s municipal elections were completely organized around distinct party lists, and the composition of municipal councils was determined in accordance with principles of strict proportional representation. The various parties began to write local political programs; mass-media coverage of municipal elections increased dramatically (Asp 1987). Committee and administrative-board chairmanships are now commonly appointed by the majority party or coalition, and most municipalities allocate one to three paid positions for local party leaders acting as municipal councilors. Understandably enough, open conflicts in the decision-making process have become much more common (Birgersson and Westerståhl 1987; SOU 1975b).

Party politicization is thus very much in evidence, particularly at the local level. Even more significant, perhaps, is the increasing politicization outside the party system, a development the parties view with great alarm. Beginning in the 1960s with the political activism generated by the movement against American war making in Vietnam, extraparty activity became an established feature of Swedish political life in the 1970s. For example, in 1971 some 90 municipalities reported the presence of local opinion or pressure groups; by 1974 the figure was over 150 (SOU 1975b). Studies of local political activity suggest that the proportion of individuals initiating direct contact with local politicians or administrators to deal with their problems more than doubled from the 1960s to the 1980s. The result is that the citizenry is now more likely to join local action groups or contact officials directly than to participate in party activities (Westerståhl and Johansson 1981).

It is also worth mentioning that voting rates are exceptionally high in Sweden. About 80 percent of eligible voters cast ballots in the 1950s, 87 percent

[2] The median number of full-time administrators per municipality rose from 118 in 1965 to 288 in 1979, while specialized educational requirements became increasingly obligatory for aspirants to administrative and technical positions in local government (Strömberg and Norell 1982).

in the 1960s, and over 90 percent in the 1970s and 1980s. For this key rite of formal political participation, the saturation point has been reached.

Implications for the Folkrörelser and Föreningar

The twin trends of *étatisation* and politicization are thus very much in evidence. As the scope and complexity of central authority have grown, individuals have become more involved in politics (particularly outside the party structure), local government has become more techno-bureaucratic, and local politics have been party-politicized. In light of such changes, it should astonish no one to find that the links between government bodies and the *föreningar* have greatly multiplied. Important developments include the following:

1. Public support of the *föreningar* has increased enormously.
2. *Förening* participation in central-authority operations has expanded.
3. The *föreningar* have come to be seen as agents of central authority to a considerable degree.
4. To some extent, many *föreningar* are as much creations of the central authority structure as voluntary initiatives of individuals.

1. Public support of the *föreningar*. Public-money support for the *föreningar* began in the 1930s, when some youth organizations, political-party affiliates, and adult-education groups were targeted for subsidies. Until the 1960s, however, subsidies were few in number and involved relatively small sums (SOU 1988a). The first major form of support was that given to the political parties, a practice that originated in the concern about the epidemic of newspaper deaths in the 1950s and 1960s (Hadenius and Weibull 1985). Because about 80 percent of all newspapers are owned by or explicitly affiliated with the parties, the argument was advanced that a numerous and diverse press was a necessary condition for a healthy democracy and, therefore, that state subsidies were not only appropriate but imperative. As the debate about press subsidies raged, in 1965 a Center party proposal for direct party subsidies resulted in the establishment of (what else?) a state commission to study the issue. The result was both press support *and* direct party subsidies (Bäck 1980).

A 1969 law gave county and municipal government units the right to grant party subsidies as well, a practice that greatly stimulated the party politicization of local politics (Gidlund 1988). By 1986 total subsidies amounted to 161 million crowns from municipalities, 100 million crowns from county councils, and 95 million crowns from the central state. Nearly 70 percent of all national-level party revenues come from the state; at the local and regional levels, dependence on public monies varies from 40 percent to 70 percent for the different parties. It is not uncommon to find local party organizations obtaining over

90 percent of their revenues from public funds (Gidlund 1988; Birgersson and Westerståhl 1987; SOU 1988b).

The establishment of party subsidies opened the floodgates, and from the 1970s onward public subsidies to *föreningar* have flowed increasingly freely. A recent study (Riksrevisionsverket 1987) found that sixty-six state administrative agencies (of about one hundred total agencies in the various ministries) were involved, dispensing a total of almost 5 billion crowns in budget year 1985–1986. County council subsidies totaled over 200 million crowns; direct municipal subsidies about 900 million crowns; indirect municipal subsidies, such as the provision of meeting and athletic facilities, amounted to an additional 2.7 billion crowns (SOU 1987b). Altogether, public subsidies to *föreningar* thus equaled almost 9 billion crowns—roughly 1,100 crowns per capita, or 300 crowns for each of the 31 million memberships in *föreningar*.

Which *föreningar* are the happy recipients of this remarkable public largesse? The most comprehensive estimate available suggests that they include some thirty thousand organizations, ranging from the largest national bodies to local theater-arts groups of half a dozen performers (Riksrevisionsverket 1986, 1987). National *föreningar* often act as subsidy allocators, spreading most of their grants among their member organizations. For example, the Swedish Sports Federation channels subsidies to dozens of national bodies for individual sports, the Swedish Free-Church Council distributes money to numerous denominations and their youth affiliates, and the Central Committee of the Federation of Disabled Persons supports activities by many specialized groups.

As might be expected, no comprehensive figures are available regarding the extent of *förening* dependence on public subsidies. A few examples will have to suffice. In 1986–1987 the adult-education associations derived 70 percent of their revenues, and the Red Cross derived 46 percent of its cash revenues, from public subsidies (Skolöverstyrelsen 1988; Jansson 1986). The comparable figure for the fifty-five sports organizations making up the Swedish Sports Federation was 55 percent in 1979–1980; for county-level sports federations it was 69 percent (Halldén 1985). At the local level, a 1980 survey of six municipalities found that public subsidies accounted for 29 percent of the budgets of sports organizations, 43 percent for scouting groups, 51 percent for temperance societies, and 25 percent for religious groups—a mean of 30 percent (Statens ungdomsråd 1980). On the other hand, most small *föreningar* receive no subsidies at all; the total number of *föreningar* is estimated at over one hundred fifty thousand.

Though public subsidies have developed haphazardly and come to constitute an extremely complex web of government/*förening* relationships, they should not be seen as undirected by explicit policy. On the contrary, at least twenty-seven state commissions and reports have considered policy in this area, beginning with the 1920 Adult Education Commission. Their recommendations have almost invariably supported further central authority support of the *föreningar* (SOU 1988a). In many reports the dangers of increased dependence of the *föreningar* on the state have been pointed out, but the contrary argument—that government has a responsibility to promote the *föreningar* because of the many benefits they bring to society—has always won the day.

2. *Förening* participation in central-authority operations. The *freningar* are not simply passive recipients of public support. They have become active participants in the formulation and execution of public policy as well. It is in this dimension that we begin to see how indeterminate the line between central authority and the third sector really is. Such participation is taken for granted in Sweden, to the point that most of what I will discuss in this section receives little attention in the public forum.

I will begin with the state commissions, whose reports, I should note, have been indispensable for the writing of this chapter. Commissions can be appointed by the government (cabinet) as a whole, by individual ministers, or by the Riksdag.[3] Members of the commissions are drawn from four principal sources: Riksdag delegates, high-level state administrators, independent experts, and representatives of organizations likely to be affected by policy changes in the area under study. Most members are state administrators—another sign of the techno-bureaucratization of the state, as this is a recent development—while organizational representatives make up only about 10 percent of commission members (Birgersson and Westerståhl 1987).

However, the organizations themselves view state commissions as their most important means of influencing policy (Elvander 1966), not so much by virtue of their participation on the commissions as through the round-robin process whereby commission work is conducted. Typically, commissions prepare preliminary reports and working documents at several stages of the study process, each time circulating the reports to interested organizations (which can be very numerous—the just-completed proposal for a sweeping reform of the secondary schools is being circulated to 387 organizations and governmental bodies) for commentary and evaluation. In this way, the final product generally reflects a compromise between government desires, the weight of organizational opinion, the politically possible, and the administratively feasible. Government desires tend to have the upper hand, in the view of Heclo and Madsen (1987), but it is not unusual for proposals to be greatly modified and even, at times, completely abandoned if the commentaries indicate widespread opposition.

The organizations that produce the most numerous commentaries on state reports are the labor unions, industry and employer associations, and the as-

---

[3] At any one time, some three hundred commissions and studies are concurrently being conducted, involving up to four thousand individuals. They produce about a hundred official policy reports a year and another hundred internal ministerial reports dealing with organizational and interpretive issues.

sociations of county councils and municipal governments (Andersson, Melbourn, and Skogö 1978), but a wide range of *föreningar* are also involved. The practice of circulating reports and proposals to *föreningar* and other organizations at the *municipal* level is less well studied, but one report (SOU 1975a) found that, in 1974, 51 percent of all municipalities formally employed such procedures. This figure has almost certainly increased since then.

A second formal channel for *förening* participation in central-authority structures is provided by the "lay supervisory boards" (*lekmannastyrelser*) that are attached to nearly all state administrative agencies. These boards consist of politicians, administrators from other state agencies, representatives of employees within the agency in question, and representatives of associations and interest groups. The latter composed about 35 percent of all board members in 1978. The Advisory Delegation for the National Traffic Safety Office, for instance, includes representatives from the Transport Workers' Union, the Automobile Transport Employers' Association, the Home and School Association (PTA), the Abstaining Motorists' Association, and the Federation of Swedish Farmers, among a total of fifteen organizations (Andersson, Melbourn, and Skogö 1978). As usual, employer associations and labor unions are most prominently represented, but again we find a vast number of other *föreningar*, including many of the traditional *folkrörelser*, with places on the boards.

In theory the lay supervisory boards are charged with helping to determine long-term policy and planning for their respective agencies. Studies of the boards' actual practices suggest, however, that their relationship to the agencies they are supposed to supervise is problematic. Critics hold that board members tend to be absorbed by the agencies—they lack the time and expertise needed to understand the agencies' operations well, so they are generally steered by upper-level administrators within the agencies and tend to become mere advocates of the agencies in budget discussions and public debate. Others hold that administrators and technical experts tend to take board views into account even before decisions are made—during the preparatory process when proposals are being formulated (SOU 1985; Andersson, Melbourn, and Skogö 1978; Brunsson and Jönsson 1979). Hence, even if proposals for change are often presented in take-it-or-leave-it form, outside influence—from the *föreningar* and other sources—is still considerable. Whatever the case may be, the lay boards clearly strengthen the links between *föreningar* and the central authority.

A third form of *förening* inclusion within the ambit of state authority is in some respects the most extreme. Beginning with the labor court in 1929, a number of specialized courts have been established to deal with civil cases in particular social sectors. The labor court mainly handles disputes regarding collective bargaining agreements. It consists of a panel of six legally trained judges and sixteen other members, of which four are nominated by the Swedish Employers' Association, six by the major labor confederations, and one each by the state, county, and municipality employers' associations. Another specialized court is the market court from 1971, which has two judges plus three representatives each from consumer and labor organizations, on the one hand, and business associations, on the other. It can levy fines for violations of marketing laws, monopolistic practices, contractual violations, and so on. A third is the housing court from 1975, with three judges, a technical expert, and twelve other members. The latter may (but need not) be candidates nominated by relevant interest groups, but half of the lay members must "be knowledgeable about" the situation and problems of tenants, while the other half must be knowledgeable about the landlords' situation. All three courts have final jurisdiction.

Thus, in the Swedish system *föreningar* are brought into the very heart of the authority structure—in several sectors they are empowered to act in the capacity of judges (or, at least, permanent jurors) whose decisions cannot be appealed.[4] That the labor court was established so early is a good indicator of the much greater degree to which unions and employer organizations are constituent parts of the state (in my expanded sense of the term) than other *föreningar*, but the fact that consumer and tenant associations entered the judicial arena in the 1970s, the period when public subsidies to *föreningar* took on serious proportions, is an equally good indicator of the nebulousness of the boundary between public and private for associations that are less purely economic in nature.

At the local level we find a fourth form of *förening* incorporation into central authority, in a cobweb of formal and informal links to the municipalities. A 1977 survey (Kommundepartementet 1978; Referensgruppen för folkrörelsefrågor 1980) found that 85 percent of the municipalities maintain association registers (lists of *föreningar* active within the municipality) and 80 percent have some sort of permanent liaison offices to manage municipality/*föreningar* relationships. Nearly 90 percent of the municipalities have an Advisory Council for Disabled Persons, and 90 percent have an Advisory Council for Pensioners. Such councils always include representatives from the relevant associations. Other, less-common links include an Advisory Council for *Föreningar* (17 percent of municipalities) and an Advisory Council for Immigrants (13 percent). In addition, a third of all municipalities regularly sponsor association conferences at which *förening* representatives can talk over their problems and needs with municipal officials.

The 1977 survey also asked the municipalities to describe the mix of municipal and *förening* responsibility for meeting facilities. Nearly half (47 per-

---

[4] The municipal courts (*tingsrätter*) also bring *föreningar* into the administration of justice in that the permanent jurors, known as *nämndemän* or boardmen, are appointed by the political parties, usually in proportion to the parties' shares of the vote in local elections.

cent) of the municipalities reported that the *föreningar* usually owned the buildings, but 43 percent said that the municipality owned most of the facilities while the *föreningar* were responsible for the activities carried on within them. With respect to after-school recreation programs, 52 percent of the municipalities owned the facilities and conducted most of the programs themselves, but in 13 percent of the cases the *föreningar* conducted half or more of the programs in municipally owned buildings. In 18 percent of the cases *föreningar* owned the buildings and conducted programs without municipal participation.

If we consider solely interest-group associations (see below), we find that, as with the special courts, they are often absorbed into the political structure directly. Tenants' unions routinely negotiate rent levels for most rental housing with the corresponding landlord associations, which include municipalities as prominent members (some 38 percent of all rental units are publicly or quasi-publicly owned; SCB 1982a). The Federation of Disabled Persons or its local affiliates are regularly consulted when major construction projects are being planned. In Helsingborg, where I presently live, the local bowling club was intimately involved in the planning process for a new municipal bowling hall. And so it goes: *föreningar* are brought into the central authority decision process in a wide variety of ways and very much as a matter of course (cf. Gidlund et al. 1982; SCB 1987).

It is also worth mentioning that *förening* representation in local and state authority structures is informally increased by virtue of the simple fact that politicians and bureaucratic administrators are themselves active members of associations—more active than the population as a whole (Strömberg and Norell 1982; Holmberg and Esaiasson 1988). The degree to which their affiliations affect their daily work is a little-studied question, but Holmberg and Esaiasson show that members of the Riksdag often see themselves as representing *föreningar* to which they belong, though they rarely say that such affiliational loyalties are the primary factor guiding their parliamentary activities.

3. *Föreningar* as agents of central authority. In most cases, public support of the *föreningar* is supplied with few formal strings attached. However, an attitude one often encounters in studies of the *föreningar*, especially studies sponsored by the state, is that the *föreningar* are important to democracy not only as channels for input to the political system but also as vehicles for the implementation of state policy and programs. For example, the participation of *föreningar* on the Advisory Delegation of the National Traffic Safety Office is seen as a plus because a number of these *föreningar* faithfully participate in safety campaigns initiated by the agency.

This sort of *förening* execution of public policy is widespread. Some additional examples: the Swedish International Development Agency channels much of its foreign development assistance through a large number of *fören-*

ingar that organize development projects and disaster relief in poor countries. The National Social Welfare Board grants money to some three dozen *föreningar* (only a few of which are temperance organizations) to enlist them in its campaigns against alcohol and drug abuse. The Environmental Protection Agency heavily subsidizes the monthly magazines produced by two major conservation associations in order to encourage the dissemination of information on environmental issues (Riksrevisionsverket 1986). Public support is thus not merely for the direct benefit of the *föreningar* and the indirect benefit of Swedish democracy. It is also used to bring central authority directly into society.

Furthermore, the impression given in a number of analyses is that program initiatives are seen as lying with the central authority structure, not with the *föreningar* or the individuals who compose them (Referensgruppen för folk-rörelsefrågor 1980; Statens ungdomsråd 1980; Lindholm 1983). Some critics express the concern that the *föreningar* are too much at the beck and call of the state, urging greater independence and a critical attitude toward government. In everyday life, though, my experience is that Swedes consider it quite natural that central authority be diffused to every nook and cranny of society. Central authority was highly expanded through the state church, especially from the mid-seventeenth century onward; now it is highly expanded through state and local government. What could be more banal?

4. *Föreningar* as creations of central authority. The final and most extreme form of confusion between the state and society, or central authority and independent social groups, occurs when the groups themselves are created by the state. This is one of the key features of pure corporatism, of course, and in explicit form it is as much lacking in Sweden as it is in the United States. But we also know that politicization and *étatisation* are important elements conditioning the rise of state-oriented social movements (Ramirez 1987), so that the expansion of central authority in Sweden can be seen as a general cause of the expansion of *föreningar*. Here I will try to make this argument more specific.

At this point it will be useful to bring in Engberg's (1986) findings in his analysis of four categories of "popular movements in the welfare society." His categories are idea movements, the labor movement, leisure and recreational associations (referred to below as the personal-development movement), and pressure and interest-group associations. The idea movements comprise the original *folkrörelser* (the free-church and temperance movements), which he depicts as associations based on broad, sweeping ideological visions of the proper structure and development of society. They are the only *föreningar* that have not grown dramatically in the twentieth century.

Leaving aside the labor movement as being outside the third sector, the other two types of movements are relatively recent phenomena. The personal-development category is a broad construct, including *föreningar* for everything from sports to adult education to chess to rabbit racing to the promotion of space exploration. Such *föreningar* are in my view essentially rationalized elaborations of individualism, the individual being parceled out and formally organized as a series of different identities embedded in wider collective structures.

The final category, pressure and interest-group associations, are mostly of postwar origin. They include such *föreningar* as tenant unions, homeowners' associations, consumer organizations, women's associations, and organizations of immigrants, the disabled, and retirees. What is distinctive about them is that they have arisen with the explicit goal of influencing central-authority policy and programs; they are inherently political.

It is hardly coincidental that the idea movements have lost ground while the interest-group associations have expanded explosively in the twentieth century. Both developments can reasonably be linked to the expansion of central-authority structures. The temperance and free-church movements have been undermined by the welfare state's emergence as the general managerial apparatus of society. The state has become the vehicle for the pursuit of the perfect society; in a sense, the "ideas" (ideals) of the idea movements have been institutionalized as elements of the bureaucratized pursuit of heaven on earth. This techno-bureaucratization of societal development runs directly counter to the all-encompassing ideological approach adopted by the original popular movements, and they have not adapted to it; hence their decline. From this perspective it is significant that the most successful segment of the idea movement in recent decades is the Abstaining Motorists' Association, a specialized body clearly linked to one aspect of technical development.

The interest-group associations, on the other hand, are encouraged by the expansion of central authority. State entry into a social domain prepares the soil for collective movements: when the state promotes reforms favoring women, the elderly, the disabled, apartment tenants, immigrants, or abused children, the categories of individuals affected are stimulated into action. A concrete example is provided by Persson (1975), former Information Secretary for the Central Committee of the Federation of Disabled Persons: "An important cause [of the growth of the movement for the disabled] is the establishment of municipal advisory councils for the disabled. When [this occurred], . . . courses, conferences, study circles increased rapidly. . . . A heightened sense of solidarity among the disabled persons' groups began to develop. In countless places around the country, coordination committees were established among the *föreningar*."

While little work has been done regarding the extent to which interest-group associations have been activated by central authority, it seems likely that the experience of the disabled is more typical than exceptional. One clear example is the many immigrant associations that were formed in the late 1970s. The National Immigration Board decided in the mid-1970s that immigrant groups needed *föreningar* to help them "maintain their cultural integrity." The board, accordingly, began offering subsidies for immigrant *föreningar*. Suddenly the Serbians and Turks and Macedonians and Greeks became avid *förening*-founders. Andersson (1980:253) similarly argues that the adult-education associations, which are among the largest and most active of all, were not simply the result of spontaneous grass-roots action: "The timing of the establishment of the associations reveals the directive effects of state subsidies. To a not insignificant extent, the subsidies determined the scale of associational activity in the area of adult education." In other words, subsidies began to be offered and new associations sprang into existence. How much they grew was at least partially a function of the size of the subsidies available.

This perhaps unduly detailed review of *förening* links to state, county, and local government entities establishes, I hope, the very real problem of locating the boundary between the state and the voluntary sector in Swedish organizational culture. During the twentieth century the private sphere has been reduced to a highly confined arena of space and time, the individual (or the family in the household) engaged in leisure activities. Particularly since the 1960s, even this limited arena has been gradually absorbed into the public realm. At the practical level this means that the individual has difficulty engaging in voluntary activities without joining an association and turning his or her "idle pursuits" into publicly accountable, rationalized action.

Let me give a couple of close-to-home examples. When I moved to Sweden I was interested in playing basketball—not on a team, not in formal competition, but just some good ol' freelance pick-up basketball. This proved almost impossible. Pick-up basketball (or soccer, or ice hockey, or bowling) is virtually nonexistent—if you want to play, you have to join a team. The team I joined, like many others, almost never practiced, which meant that all my basketball time was spent in uniform with the clock running and a referee puffing beside me with a whistle around his neck. Of course, the local basketball association is heavily subsidized by the city and state.

Another example came up in relation to a friend who is the musical director of a large theater company in a nearby town. Year after year the future of the company is in doubt, despite the widely acknowledged excellence of its productions and the many sacrifices its members make to keep it going. In the final reckoning, there is only one way the company can make it: it must continually try to wrangle money out of no fewer than six local government bodies. Without these subsidies, the company would fold.

This second example illustrates a key contrast between the Swedish model of social organization and its American counterpart, the latter lying, one might say, at the opposite end of the Western public/private axis. In the United States, the theater company would likely turn to "private enterprise" for support, the result being ads in the company's programs, a corporate sponsor's name in its publicity releases, and so on. In Sweden, private industry plays a much less prominent sponsorship role (though it has expanded in the 1980s). "Society" runs through the public realm, the broadly conceived state; society and state are to a large extent coextensive. Thus, while the American saying goes "If you want a job done, you have to do it yourself!" the Swedish version would be "If you want a job done, you have to get plugged in!" This means that direct hostility to the state, or government more generally, is quite unusual, and there is virtually no organized opposition of the "taxpayer revolt" sort. Central public authority is a necessity rather than an evil, whereas in a more individualistic theory of society, central authority is more evil than necessary.

RELIGIOUS ORGANIZATIONS AND RELIGIOUS VOLUNTARISM

To this point I have said little about religious organizations. My reticence is due to the very limited role organized religion plays in Swedish society, in sharp contrast to the situation in more individualistic Protestant countries like the United States, England, and the Netherlands.

The Swedish Lutheran church, founded in the 1520s as one of the earliest national reformed churches, is still the established state church under the authority of the Riksdag. Some 93 percent of the population belongs to the church, and all children born to church members are automatically members. Membership is thus only marginally voluntary—one can resign, but few Swedes do. Financially the church is supported by an obligatory tax amounting to about 1 percent of taxable income. In structural terms, then, the state church dominates the religious scene.

The free churches have their spiritual roots in the early eighteenth-century reformist strivings of Pietists and Moravians. Their organizational roots lie in the 1850s, when the Baptists first began to form separate denominations. After a period of expansion to about 1940, total free-church membership has stagnated in recent decades. Membership in several churches, particularly the Methodist and Baptist churches, has declined, while some new denominations, above all the Pentecostalists (who now constitute the largest single denomination) but also Jehovah's Witnesses and the Mormons, have expanded considerably. Total free-church membership (including the Evangelical Fatherland Foundation, the reform movement within the state church) was only about 4.1 percent of the population in 1930, 4.8 percent in 1960, and 4.0 percent in 1978. Most free-church members are also members of the state church.

As these membership figures suggest, religious renewal has not characterized contemporary Sweden. In the 1970s the "new spiritualism" that was so evident elsewhere was much more subdued in Sweden. One report from 1979 found that such movements as the Unification Church, Hare Krishna, the Divine Light Mission, and so on, had less than five hundred members in all in

Sweden. Rather, as Gustafsson (1981) and Dahlgren (1985) have documented, religiosity is on the whole quite weak. By 1979 only 2 percent of the population attended state church services on an average Sunday, as compared to approximately 17 percent in the 1890s and 6 percent in the 1920s. Attendance at free-church services typically involves another 2 or 3 percent. In 1968 only 42 percent of the adult population said they attended church as often as several times a year, and by 1980 only 50 percent claimed to believe in God, a precipitous decline from the 83 percent figure in 1947. Free-church members are much more pious—in a survey from 1979, over 80 percent of them said they prayed daily or almost daily (compared to 18 percent of the entire population), and over 70 percent attended church at least once a week—but they are few and far between.

Declining religious faith does not, however, imply that church rites have disappeared from daily life. In 1978, 76 percent of all children under the age of one were baptized in the church, 60 percent of all weddings took place in the church, and 94 percent of all funeral services were conducted in the church. As the Swedes themselves are wont to put it, no one believes in heaven any longer, but everyone takes out a church insurance policy anyway.

The high degree to which voluntary associations are incorporated into the central authority structure might lead one to expect that Swedish religious organizations would be strongly politicized. Such is not the case. When free-church members were asked in 1978 to pick the two concerns they considered of greatest importance for their congregations in the future, "political consciousness" came in next to last of eleven items. The other items with political import—international peace efforts, awareness of social injustice, and aid to less-developed countries—were all considered far less important than evangelization, personal faith, revitalization of church services, and the like. Yet free-church members belong to more nonreligious *föreningar* than other Swedes and are much more likely to be members of political parties (Lundkvist 1979). Similarly, when Riksdag delegates were asked in 1985 to say how much they thought each of nine factors affected voters' electoral choices, "religious and moral conceptions" came in dead last (Holmberg and Esaiasson 1988). A wide chasm thus separates religion and politics. The religious is private, spiritual, individual; the political is public, temporal, and collective. To an extreme degree, the twain do not meet.

On a more qualitative basis, religiosity is markedly absent from Swedish public life. Politicians never invoke God in their speeches or debate articles. Invocational prayers are almost unknown. Religious groups are not visible politically, and the only explicitly religious political party, the Christian Democratic Assembly, is unable to garner enough votes to win entry to the Riksdag (4 percent of the total vote is required). Religious viewpoints or arguments are extremely rare in debates regarding such issues as abortion, the definition of death, AIDS, science education, or homosexuality. Nothing even remotely resembling the Moral Majority has developed. One might argue that the burgeoning environmental movement is at least partially religious in nature, but I have yet to see an environmentalist argue that pollution and environmental degradation are offenses to God's creation.

In my view, the depoliticization of religion in Sweden is largely due to the state's replacement of the church as the backbone of the polity. A long process was involved, beginning, indeed, with the Reformation itself, when the king dispossessed the church and used its wealth to strengthen the monarchy. After 1686, when the revised church law brought the church firmly under state control, parish priests gradually became as much secular as spiritual authorities. By the nineteenth century the state had emerged as the dominant central-authority structure in society while religion had been thoroughly spiritualized and privatized. The compartmentalization of Swedish culture that was then established—the spiritual and the temporal are radically disjoint spheres—has lasted to this day. The result is a population that in traditional terms is largely nonreligious but still belongs to the state church as a symbol of Swedishness, and a small but devout free-church sector that accepts the welfare state as the worldly caretaker and puts most of its energy into preparing the souls of its members for the world to come.

As *föreningar* rather than congregations, on the other hand, Swedish religious bodies are in much the same position as other organizations. The free churches receive substantial state subsidies, they participate in state commissions and review commission proposals relevant to their activities, and they serve as conduits for state development assistance to the outside world. On the whole they lead quiet but comfortably established existences, staying out of politics and never themselves becoming the object of public concern. The state church too stays away from the public forum. I suspect, in fact, that a strong political statement by the archbishop—on any issue at all—would be greeted with incredulity and condemnation. The state manages organized life in the here and now. Religion is limited to private morality and the hereafter.

VITALITY OF THE THIRD SECTOR: SOME COUNTERVAILING TRENDS

Though the third sector in Sweden has been extensively incorporated into central authority, there is some evidence that the pendulum has begun to swing the other way. One indicator is the increasing penchant of individual citizens for rejecting established political channels in their efforts to influence policy decisions. I have earlier mentioned the survey finding that individuals are now more likely to contact local politicians and administrators directly than to press their claims through the political parties. Individuals have also become more willing to form autonomous action groups to lobby, demonstrate, and propagandize regarding specific local issues. Even though action groups usually focus on government policy rather than attempt to generate independent solutions to the problems that activate them, this type of agitation reflects a sharper separation of society from the state. Organizational structures happily wedded to the state are sidestepped in favor of more voluntaristic structures.

Another indicator is the increasing liberation of voters from strict party loyalty. Three trends are apparent. One, voters are increasingly likely to change party preference from one election to another. Between the 1954 and 1956 elections only 7 percent of the voting electorate changed party preference. From about 1960 this proportion rose quickly, to 16 percent between 1968 and 1970 and nearly 20 percent in the 1979–1982 interval. Two, voters are increasingly inclined to vote a split ticket. In 1970 only 6 percent of the voters chose a different party at the national level than at the local level, but this figure had risen to 16 percent by the 1985 election (Holmberg and Gilljam 1987). Younger voters and better-educated voters split their tickets more than the elderly and the less-schooled (Johansson 1987), indicating that the trend may continue. Three, voting is decreasingly a function of social class and increasingly a function of political views. Holmberg and Gilljam (1987) show that class identification had a much greater impact than political views on voting preferences in the 1950s and early 1960s, but since 1970 political views have become a good deal more important than social class.

If party and class loyalties are on the wane, so too is general voter support of the political system. In 1968 about 65 percent of those casting ballots described themselves as loyal to one of the parties, but by 1985 only 53 percent were willing to apply this description to themselves. Holmberg and Gilljam also report that the proportion of the electorate expressing a general lack of confidence in the parties and politicians has risen steeply since 1968, with most of the increase coming in the 1970s. This growing lack of trust is widespread—neither sex, age, class, nor party preference is related to political distrust.

While rising political disaffection is often described by commentators as a sign of illness in the body politic, it can also be seen as a healthy trend. A central authority structure that absorbs an ever-larger proportion of all social activity tends to inject a thick layer of formalistic organizational molasses between the individual and the loci of decision making. Individuals cannot easily wade through this goo, but if they recognize its absorptive properties and react against it—by opting for unconventional political activity and a critical attitude toward the established political system—autonomously generated efforts toward democratic revitalization may be strengthened.[5]

[5] From this perspective the unwillingness of American citizens to vote in elections is not necessarily lamentable, for it indicates that the reach of central authority is relatively weak and the arena for autonomous self-assertion relatively broad. On the other hand (and this is the argument often given in Sweden), if people do not participate in politics then the important decisions are left to elite minorities. The question that then arises is whether universal participation in formal political activities diminishes elite domination. In the Swedish representative parliamentary sys-

Two major political events of the past fifteen years support this view. The first was the anti-nuclear power movement of the 1970s, a locally generated and highly energetic movement that led, with a little help from a place in the United States called Three Mile Island, to a referendum on the issue in 1980. Given that referendums are exceedingly rare in Sweden (the nuclear-power vote was only the fourth of this century), the fact that grass-roots campaigning was able to force a plebiscite indicates that the incorporative tendencies of central-authority structures are much less than omnipotent.

The second event was the Green party's entry into the Riksdag in 1988. For the first time in over sixty years, a new political party—and a party that, while not in principle opposed to a highly expanded central-authority structure, has strongly criticized established political procedures and priorities—gained enough electoral clout through autonomous organizing to disturb the extremely stable party structure. The long-term effects of these developments are difficult to predict, for the nuclear-power vote produced only a nonbinding decision to decommission all nuclear power plants by 2010, and the Greens' prospects of surviving the hard and dulling labor of day-to-day parliamentary drudgery are hardly certain. That both of these events reflect a relatively high degree of independence from prevailing structures and methods, however, seems abundantly clear.

Further signs of political autonomy are evident within the mass media, particularly the press. Though readers' inclination to choose newspapers matching their own party preferences has declined only modestly, within the journalism profession a strong ethic of impartiality and independence from party influence has emerged since the 1950s. Journalists are highly critical of party ownership of newspapers, their political sympathies are increasingly likely to be at odds with those of the newspapers that employ them, and the journalistic corps has gained greater influence over editorial policies (Hadenius and Weibull 1985). A modest trend toward more investigative and authority-challenging journalism, particularly since the murder of Olof Palme, is also apparent. By American standards Swedish reporters are still inordinately tame and obsequious, but the trend is unmistakable—with the inevitable result that those who come under scrutiny increasingly attempt to blame the press when the molehills of questionable practices they have tried to shield from view suddenly are made to look like mountains of unrestrained abuse of power. Holmberg and Esaiasson (1988) report, accordingly, that Riksdag members see the press as the primary culprit behind political disaffection.

The *legal* situation of the *föreningar* certainly offers few obstacles to autonomous voluntarism. Freedom of association was included as one of the fun-

tem, where formal channels allow for little more than a ritualistic trienniel plebiscite, and semicorporatist cooperation among political, business, and *förening* elites is legion, the answer to this question appears to be negative. Whether the Swedish political system is more elite-dominated than those of other countries of comparable size and complexity is, however, an open question.

damental pillars of the new constitution promulgated in 1973, and today there is still no specific legislation regulating *förening* activity as such. Neither are nonprofit *föreningar* (so-called idealistic associations) subject to income taxes, a remarkable fact in light of the ubiquity of taxes of all sorts in Sweden. What is more, the Riksdag and various state commissions have demonstrated a clear unwillingness to initiate state regulation of the *föreningar*. Numerous legislative proposals have consistently been rejected over the years, and a study of *föreningar* fund-raising activities in 1977 concluded that legislative action regarding fund-raising would be both inappropriate and unnecessary because it would interfere too much with *förening* activities that were already being conducted in a satisfactory manner (SOU 1977). Hence the gate is wide and voluntary passage is open to all.

At a more general level, I am tempted to argue that the incorporation of *föreningar* into the public-policy process has contributed positively to what I regard as a quite lively and extensive public forum for political debate and repartee in Sweden. This forum is well institutionalized in the form of "debate articles" that regularly appear in many newspapers. A large proportion of debate article authors write as representatives of one or another *förening*, and their analyses are almost always well informed and knowledgeable. The high quality of their efforts is due in no small part to the fact that many of these authors are full-time experts employed by *föreningar* for just this purpose— they do research on the relevant issues, they may well publish in academic journals, and they often are backed by sizable staffs. The *föreningar* also sponsor a wide array of public debates, information and mobilization meetings, study circles on social issues, and publications promoting their views. When a major issue emerges, such as the nuclear-power debate of the 1970s, tens of thousands of study circles and debate forums may be conducted. In short, public debate seems very much alive and well.

Yet the ambiguity remains. As I have mentioned, one of the recurring issues in the public forum over the past fifteen years has been the situation and role of the *föreningar* themselves and how structural conditions of the political system might be altered to improve democracy-through-*föreningar*. Many voices have expressed concern: the *föreningar* are sclerotic, corporatism is a danger, internal *förening* democracy is on the wane, participation is far too often passive rather than active. Yet the solutions proposed are usually either governmental intiatives or expanded "private" claims against state and local authorities. Truly independent solutions—the *föreningar* taking autonomous action in accordance with a "hands off!" attitude toward central authority— are rare. Hence, it still remains the case that less than 1 percent of primary schooling is privately organized, fewer than two hundred of the many thousands of day-care centers are operated by parent cooperatives or other associations, and barely 1 percent of all hospital beds are maintained by associations (SOU 1987b). What is more, most of the "private" initiatives in this area are at least partly subsidized by public funds.

It can be difficult to evaluate the impact of several prominent trends in governmental policy in light of this fundamental ambiguity regarding voluntarism. What are we to make of a deliberate state decentralization program that moves major administrative departments from Stockholm to smaller cities if the agencies' agendas continue to expand? Of government efforts to streamline administrative processes and dump boatloads of red tape into the Baltic (to give the bureaucracy a "human face" and shorten the distance between decision-makers and citizens) if citizens are simultaneously further incorporated into the state through ever more numerous social programs? Of subsidies intended to relieve financial pressures on the *föreningar* and improve their chances of actively engaging their members if the *föreningar* are thereby tied more closely to the central authority through fiscal dependence? Of state deregulation of the economy (regarding air traffic, telecommunications, agriculture, capital flows) when government revenue as a proportion of GNP continues to increase and a wide range of areas—schooling, health care, social charity, child care—are formally or informally off-limits to *förening* initiative?

I should say straight out that I am not here advocating the American voluntaristic model as an ideal to which Sweden should aspire. The relative lack of autonomy of Swedish society vis-à-vis the state may greatly reduce alternatives and restrict freedom of choice, but it also carries the appreciable advantages of a relatively even distribution of life's necessities, the virtual absence of poverty, and greatly reduced commercialism and faddish consumerism. To an American the ubiquity of central authority and the weakness of independent voluntarism can seem oppressive and stifling. To a Swede, born and raised in a political culture in which collective organizational forms are deemed not only normal but also proper, rational, and just, sink-or-swim individualistic voluntarism smells of chaos, irresponsibility, and hardhearted indifference to the plight of the poor. In any case, that the Swedish third sector is part and parcel of the central-authority structure of society is no barrier to democratic policy formulation and lively political debate. It does imply, however, that solutions to social problems are likely to be sought in collective and obligatory bureaucratic programs, not in local autonomous efforts. Freedom is thereby greatly reduced, but the excesses and inequities that untrammeled individualism often entails are also greatly attenuated.

References

Andersson, Bo. 1980. *Folkbildning i perspektiv* (Adult Education in Perspective). Stockholm: Liber.

Andersson, Simon, Anders Melbourn, and Ingemar Skogö. 1978. *Myndigheten i samhället* (Public Agencies in Society). Stockholm: Liber.

Asp, Kent. 1987. "Rikspolitik och kommunalpolitik—Valrörelsernas utrymme i svensk dagspress, 1956–85" (National Politics and Local Politics—Coverage of Election Campaigns in Swedish Dailies, 1956–85). In SOU 1987a, pp. 353–70.

Asp, Kent, Stig Hadenius et al. 1982. *Väljare Partier Massmedia: Empiriska studier i svensk demokrati* (Voters, Parties, the Mass Media: Empirical Studies in Swedish Democracy). Stockholm: Liber.

Bäck, Mats. 1980. *Partier och organisationer i Sverige* (Parties and Organizations in Sweden). Stockholm: Liber.

Birgersson, Bengt Owe, and Jörgen Westerståhl. 1987. *Den svenska folk-styrelsen* (The Swedish System of Popular Rule). Stockholm: Liber.

Brunsson, Nils, and Sten Jönsson. 1979. *Beslut och handling: Om politikers inflytande på politiken* (Decisions and Implementation: On Politicians' Influence on Politics). Stockholm: Liber.

Carlsson, Bo. 1987. "Hur stor är egentligen den offentliga sektorn?" (How Big Is the Public Sector?). Stockholm: Bratt.

Dahlgren, Curt. 1985. "Sverige" (Sweden). In *Religiös förändring i Norden, 1930–1980* (Religious Change in Scandinavia, 1930–1980), edited by Göran Gustafsson, pp. 196–237. Malmö: Liber.

Elvander, Nils. 1966. *Intresseorganisationerna i dagens Sverige* (Interest Organizations in Contemporary Sweden). Lund: Gleerup.

Engberg, Jan. 1986. *Folkrörelserna i välfärdssamhället* (Popular Movements in the Welfare Society). Ph.D. diss., Umeå University.

Esping-Anderson, Gösta. 1985. *Politics against Markets: The Social Democratic Road to Power*. Princeton: Princeton University Press.

Folkstyrelsekommittén, ed. 1985. *Makten från folket* (Power from the People). Stockholm: Liber.

Forskningsrådsnämnden. 1985. *Forskning om folkrörelser* (Research on Popular Movements). Report 85:5. Stockholm: Forskningsrådsnämnden.

Furåker, Bengt. 1987. *Stat och offentlig sektor* (State and Public Sector). Stockholm: Rabén and Sjögren.

Gidlund, Gullan. 1988. "Tendenser i svensk partifinansiering" (Trends in Swedish Party Financing). In SOU 1988b, pp. 115–38.

Gidlund, Janerik, Jan Engberg, Ulla-Britt Hallin, and Anders Lidström. 1982. *Folkrörelser och kommunalpolitik* (Popular Movements and Municipal Politics). Report 12 from the Research Group on Municipal Democracy. Stockholm: Kommundepartementet.

122 · John Boli

Gustafsson, Göran. 1981. *Religionen i Sverige* (Religion in Sweden). Stockholm: Esselte.

Hadenius, Stig, and Lennart Weibull. 1985. *Mass medier: En bok om press, radio & tv* (Mass Media: A Book on the Press, Radio, and TV). Stockholm: Bonniers.

Halldén, Olle. 1985. "Idrottsrörelsen i samhället" (Sports Organizations in Society). In Forskningsrådsnämnden 1985, pp. 35–40.

Heclo, Hugh, and Henrik Madsen. 1987. *Policy and Politics in Sweden: Principled Pragmatism*. Philadelphia: Temple University Press.

Hermansson, Jörgen, Urban Laurin, Lennart Nordfors, and Anders Westholm. 1985. *Riksdagen och de organiserade intressena* (The Riksdag and Organized Interests). Project description. Uppsala University: Department of Political Science.

Holmberg, Claes-Göran, Ingemar Oscarsson, and Per Rydén. 1983. *En svensk presshistoria* (A Swedish History of the Press). Stockholm: Esselte.

Holmberg, Sören, and Peter Esaiasson. 1988. *De folkvalda: En bok om riksdagsledamöterna och den representativa demokratin i Sverige* (The People's Choice: A Book on the Members of the Riksdag and Representative Democracy in Sweden). Stockholm: Bonnier.

Holmberg, Sören, and Mikael Gilljam. 1987. *Väljare och val i Sverige* (Voters and Elections in Sweden). Stockholm: Bonnier.

Huntford, Roland. 1972. *The New Totalitarians*. New York: Stein and Day.

Isling, Åke. 1978. *Folkrörelserna i ny roll?* (The Popular Movements in a New Role?). Stockholm: Sober.

Jansson, Malte. 1986. *Om Röda korset: Insamling och kassan* (On the Red Cross: Fund-Raising and Finances). N.p.: Röda korset.

Johansson, Folke. 1987. "Delad röstning" (Split-ticket Voting). In SOU 1987a, pp. 323–41.

Katzenstein, Peter. 1985. *Small States and World Markets*. Ithaca: Cornell University Press.

Kommundepartementet. 1978. "Kommunerna och föreningslivet: redovisning av en enkätundersökning" (The Municipalities and the Voluntary Organizations: Presentation of a Questionnaire Survey). Stockholm: Kommundepartementet.

Korpi, Walter. 1983. *The Democratic Class Struggle*. London: Routledge and Kegan Paul.

Lindholm, Berndt. 1983. *Rörelsen och folkhemmet: Välfärdsstaten, den kommunala demokratin och medborgarmedverkan* (The Movement and the People's Home: The Welfare State, Local Democracy, and Citizen Participation). Stockholm: Rabén and Sjögren.

Lundkvist, Sven. 1979. "Demografiska och socio-ekonomiska data" (Demografic and socio-economic data). In *Frikyrkosverige—en livstilsstudie* (Free-Church Sweden: A Lifestyle Study), edited by Hans Zetterberg, Sven Lundkvist, Torbjörn Freij, and Thorvald Källstad, pp. 73–88. Stockholm: Ansvar.

Nilsson, Macke. 1968. *Ombuds-Sverige* (Officialdom-Sweden). Stockholm: Prisma.

Persson, Margareta. 1975. "Folkrörelserna kan delta i samhällsarbetet utan att passiveras—se på handikapprörelsen!" (The Popular Movements Can Participate in the Policy Process Without Becoming Passive—Look at the Movement for the Disabled!). In Isling 1975, pp. 70–73.

Ramirez, Francisco O. 1987. "Comparative Social Movements." In *Institutional Structure: Constituting State, Society, and the Individual*, edited by George Thomas, John Meyer, Francisco Ramirez, and John Boli, pp. 281–96. Beverly Hills: Sage, 1987.

Referensgruppen för folkrörelserfrågor. 1980. *Folkrörelserna och demokratin* (The Popular Movements and Democarcy). Stockholm: Kommundepartementet.

Riksrevisionsverket. 1986. *Det statliga stödet till folkrörelserna—en kartläggning* (Public Subsidies to the Popular Movements—A Survey). No. 1986:554. Stockholm: Riksrevisionsverket.

———. 1987. *Det statliga stödet till folkrörelserna* (Public Subsidies to the Popular Movements). Stockholm: Civiltryck.

Rodriguez, Enrique. 1980. *Offentlig inkomstexpansion* (The Expansion of Public Revenues). Ph.D. diss., University of Uppsala. Lund: Gleerup.

Rothstein, Bo. 1987. "Corporatism and Reformism: The Social Democratic Institutionalization of Class Conflict." English Series Report no. 5. Uppsala University: Department of Government.

Ruin, Olof. 1985. "Tvåpartisystem, samlingsregering eller vad?" (Two-Party System, Coalition Government, or What?). In Folkstyrelsekommittén 1985, pp. 59–72.

SCB (Statistiska Centralbyrån; Central Bureau of Statistics). 1982a. *Perspectives on Swedish Welfare in 1982*. Living Conditions Report no. 33. Stockholm: SCB.

———. 1982b. *Politiska resurser, 1978* (Political Resources, 1978). Report no. 31. Stockholm: SCB.

———. 1985. *Offentliga sektorn: Utveckling och nuläge* (The Public Sector: Development and Current Status). Stockholm: SCB.

———. 1987. *Föreningslivets engagemang inom offentlig verksamhet* (Association Involvement in Government Activity). Dnr 378/87. Stockholm: SCB.

Schmitter, Philippe C., and Gerhard Lehmbruch, eds. 1979. *Trends toward Corporatist Intermediation*. Beverly Hills: Sage.

Skolöverstyrelsen. 1988. *Studieförbunden inför 90-talet* (The Adult Education Associations Face the 1990s). R 88:31. Stockholm: Skolöverstyrelsen.

SOU (Statens Offentliga Utredningar; Public State Reports). 1975a. *Kommunal demokrati* (Municipal Democracy). No. 41. Stockholm: Kommundepartementet.

———. 1975b. *Kommunal organisation och information* (Municipal Organization and Information). No. 46. Stockholm: Kommundepartementet.

———. 1977. *Måste insamlare kontrolleras?* (Should Fund-Raisers Be Regulated?). No. 95. Stockholm: Handelsdepartementet.

———. 1985. *Regeringen, myndigheterna, och myndigheternas ledning* (The Government, State Administrative Agencies, and the Management of State Administration). No. 40. Stockholm: Civildepartementet.

———. 1987a. *Folkstyrelsens villkor* (Conditions for Popular Government). No. 6. Stockholm: Justitiedepartementet.

———. 1987b. *Ju mer vi är tillsammans (del 1)* (The More We Are Together, Part 1). No. 33. Stockholm: Civildepartementet.

———. 1987c. *Ju mer vi är tillsammans (del 3)* (The More We Are Together, Part 3). No. 35. Stockholm: Civildepartementet.

———. 1988a. *Mål och resultat—nya principer för det statliga stödet till förenings-*

livet (Goals and Results—New Principles for State Subsidization of Voluntary Organizations). No. 39. Stockholm: Civildepartementet.

————. 1988b. *Kommunalt stöd till de politiska partierna* (Municipal Subsidies for the Political Parties). No. 47. Stockholm: Civildepartementet.

SSU (Swedish Social Democratic Youth League). 1975. "Tillsammans för en idé" (Together for an Idea). In Utblick no. 36, "Fakta om folkrörelserna." Johannishov: Frihets Förlag.

Statens ungdomsråd. 1980. *Massor i rörelse: Föreningarna i Sverige* (Masses in Movement: The Associations in Sweden). Stockholm: Liber.

Strömberg, Lars, and Per-Owe Norell. 1982. *Kommunalförvaltningen* (Municipal Administration). Report 15 of the Research Group on Municipal Democracy. Stockholm: Kommundepartmentet.

Torstendahl, Rolf. 1985. "Byråkratisering och folkstyre" (Bureaucratization and Popular Rule). In Folkstyrelsekommittén 1985, pp. 113–39.

Vestlund, Gösta. 1981. *Hur vårdar vi vår demokrati? (How Do We Preserve Our Democracy?)*. Research on Education Report 43. Stockholm: Skolöverstyrelsen and Liber.

Westerståhl, Jörgen, and Folke Johansson. 1981. *Medborgarna och kommunen: Studier av medborgerlig aktivitet och representativ folkstyrelse* (Citizens and the Municipality: Studies of Citizen Activity and Representative Popular Government). Report 5 of the Research Group on Municipal Democracy. Stockholm: Kommundepartmentet.

CHAPTER FIVE

France: Alternative Locations for Public Debate

Jack Veugelers and Michèle Lamont

THIS CHAPTER asks how selected institutions have contributed to the making of the public sphere in postwar France. It also examines the extent to which the discourse produced by these institutions is critical-rational in nature and the product of open and democratic participation. It further asks how one area involved in the public sphere, the voluntary sector, has been shaped by the state and the market. Finally, the actual functioning of the public sphere is explored by considering the societywide debate currently taking place in France about the issues of immigration and nationality.

We chart the influence of the institutional areas that are most important in defining the French public sphere. We find that historically rooted relationships between the state and civil society are important in determining which institutions have the power to set political and social agendas, and the legitimacy to speak on behalf of the collectivity. We argue that in the French case, politics provides the predominant frame of reference for the public sphere largely because the state is present in so many aspects of society.

Building on Habermas (1989) and Hohendahl (1979), we take the concept of the public sphere as referring to a type of communication characterized by open participation in critical-rational public discourse. In order to analyze the extent to which political parties, the mass media, organized religion, and voluntary associations contribute to the public sphere, we assess whether they present the following features of communication: open accessibility, with no regard for differences in social status; active two-way communication among participants who are thus both audience and discussants; and a coercion-free situation in which the rational scrutiny of opinions takes place.

Our findings do not support Habermas's argument that the modern public sphere has become impoverished, with the masses duped and lulled by manipulative mass media while ruling elites benefit (see Habermas 1989). Instead we find in France vital institutions that facilitate the discussion and diffusion of critical social agendas. However, rarely in these institutions do we simultaneously find all the features associated with the public sphere: open accessibility, active participation, and critical-rationality. Consequently, it is necessary to study the independent variation between these separate features, both within and across institutional areas.

In the first section of this chapter, we map the influence of four institutional areas that today are prominent in the making of France's public sphere: political parties, the mass media, organized religion, and voluntary associations. We discuss institutions both as arenas within which public discourse is produced (the intrainstitutional level), and as actors themselves participating in broad societal discussions (the interinstitutional level). In each case, special attention is given to the relative importance of open accessibility, active participation, and critical-rational discourse. In the second section we focus on how the voluntary sector's involvement in the public sphere is shaped by the state and the market. The last section makes our argument concrete using the case of the recent societywide debates surrounding immigration and nationality. As we briefly address some extraordinarily complex questions, our goal is less to offer definitive answers than to indicate paths for future research.

INSTITUTIONAL DOMAINS OF THE PUBLIC SPHERE

Four areas of French society play the greatest roles in that country's public sphere: political parties, the mass media, organized religion, and voluntary associations. None of these domains clearly stands out in terms of overall importance for the public sphere. This is the case whether we consider the intrainstitutional level, and treat institutions as milieus in which public discourse takes place, or instead view them at the interinstitutional level, and see them as actors themselves participating in broad public discussions.

Political Parties

By mediating the left-right split that characterizes French ideological debates, political parties have played a major role in narrowing and defining the agenda of France's public sphere; however, they also provide members and activists with opportunities to participate in discussions pertaining to issues of broad societal importance. Furthermore, they serve as channels for the diffusion of the ideas of leaders and new social movements.

In contrast with the American case, French political parties generally seek to articulate and defend identifiable ideological positions. Postwar French politics have thus been strongly divided between the Left and the Right, and the transition from the Fourth to the Fifth Republic in the late 1950s and early 1960s reinforced this split. Until domestic conflict over the handling of the Algerian crisis left the government paralyzed in 1958, parliament had become factionalized as parties multiplied and poor party discipline left the narrow partisanship of deputies unchecked. Though large stabilizing coalitions were at times achieved, political rhetoric always remained diverse as the parties played up their ideological differences in the competition for votes. Under the constitution of the Fifth Republic, no single party has been able to win more than half the vote alone, and hence party alliances have become necessary. In the process, smaller parties have either merged with others or disappeared. This has affected access and discourse in the public sphere because the result has been a clearer splitting of French politics into left and right alliances and programs (Wright 1983; Hanley 1986).

While reinforcing left and right party identification, the Fifth Republic's majority vote system has also diminished the diversity of legislators' positions. Much more than their American counterparts, French politicians who aspire to national office are dependent on the party for sponsorship and funding. Those who challenge party discipline may be penalized through the withdrawal of influence and resources. The watering down of legislators' autonomy under the Fifth Republic has given France a more stable political regime, but there is now a fear that the national assembly is no longer a forum capable of generating serious discussion and new ideas for running the country (Wilson 1988).

The politicization of the central state bureaucracy has also affected the vitality of political discussion. Because the president enjoys broad powers of appointment, greater even than in the United States, French bureaucrats with high ambitions must take political sides. Whether the Left or the Right has been in power, interpenetration at the upper levels of French politics and administration has been a constant of the Fifth Republic, and has led to a situation where top civil servants make policy. This has contributed to an impoverishment of political discourse, since close relations between political parties and bureaucrats reduce the range of issues open to critical scrutiny, and thus limit political agendas.

To some extent, intraparty factions have counteracted pressures toward ideological conformity, especially within the Socialist party. During the 1970s, socialist groups promoted competing opinions on national industrial policy, and the party embraced major New Left issues—worker self-management, feminism, anti–nuclear energy, protection of the environment—as it absorbed the many activists who found themselves politically homeless after 1968. Since coming to power, the Socialist party has disappointed many of these inner groups, but they continue to support it, trying to work from within (Ladrech 1989).[1] Sustained and open discussion among competing viewpoints remains more difficult to find inside the other parties: policy coalitions do not form as easily within the major parties of the Right, and the leaders of the Communist party and the National Front (a party of the far right) leave little room for dissenting opinion. Recently, however, there have been signs of debate and renewal within the moderate Right, mainly because the National Front is stealing its voters.

[1] A recent French report on voluntary associations found that "most 'activist' associations experienced a significant drop in memberships, especially among youths, between 1978 and 1986. This was particularly true of parents' associations, and ecological and feminist associations. . . . Only political parties have escaped this decline" (*Le Monde* 1989).

The influence of political parties in the public sphere nonetheless remains strong. Despite pressures toward conformity, the parties continue to uphold their distinctiveness: government and opposition are tied to "well-developed party ideologies that offer radically different visions of society" (Wilson 1988:15).[2] Parties offer activists and politicians significant opportunities to participate in broad policy discussions. However, discourse is confined within the boundaries of the enduring left-right opposition, and strategic concerns limit the extent to which parties will incorporate the innovative ideas of social movements like feminism and ecology. At the societal level, parties are influential in transmitting the ideas of selected leaders and issue groups.

The Mass Media

The mass media also play a central role in France's public sphere, mainly by diffusing alternative agendas and positions. These media further provide an arena in which high-profile intellectuals are able publicly to formulate their views of the collective good. However, some mass media reach a wider public than others. Radio and television audiences grew tremendously in the postwar period, and are now considerably larger than the newspaper readership. On the other hand, radio and television have enjoyed less autonomy from the state than has the press. They therefore generally cover a narrower range of opinion, and in the area of politics their news programs have been less likely to adopt the critical stance characteristic of the public sphere. Some state-supported radio and television stations, especially France-Musique and France-Culture, nonetheless place great emphasis on social and cultural criticism. As for participation, mass communication plays only a minor role in the public sphere, since it engages the majority of the population only as an audience.[3]

Prior to the 1980s the state held a near-monopoly over radio and television stations, but after the Left came to power in 1981 it tried to open up these media through deregulation. Private television stations relying on advertising soon began broadcasting, and local radio stations flourished. These reforms undoubtedly expanded the range of broadcasts available to the French. Radio

[2] The electoral system's tendency to split party politics along the left-right seam places serious limits on any foreseeable "Americanization" of French politics. Also, the rise of the National Front does not suggest that the nation's party system is moving toward consensus and compromise.

[3] Television and radio programming devote proportionately less space than the press to critical-rational discourse; this stems not only from marketing pressures and strategies, but also from problems of content and reception inherent in these media wherever they are found. Radio offers mainly music; television, like the press, offers a broader package of items, but like the radio leaves the viewer with no control over the order and speed at which messages are received, unless recording equipment is used. As everywhere, the rapid pace characteristic of most television programming has not made it a medium conducive to sustained rational discourse (McQuail 1987).

stations in particular now offer noncommercial programs to local audiences that may compensate for the weakness of the local press. The new television channels, however, depend on commercial films, sports, and music videos for their revenue, and leave little room for sociopolitical debate (Guéhenno 1987).

This contrasts with the press, which plays a more active role in the diffusion of critical discourse. Between 1880 and 1914 France had the highest rate of press readership in Europe, and French newspapers representing a multitude of competing positions played a key role in animating political debate, especially during the Dreyfus affair. Thereafter the French press lost much of its dynamism due to wartime censorship, steep rises in production costs, and widespread disenchantment with the opinion press (Albert 1983:130–39).

Trends toward industry concentration and reduced diversity continued during the postwar period, and thus although 206 dailies were published in 1939, there are only 88 today. The attendant homogenization of the press, combined with especially steep rises in newsstand prices and competition from television, appears to have left the public disaffected. While France's population has grown by eighteen million since 1946, the circulation of dailies has dropped from nine to seven million copies; in 1967, 60 percent of the French read a daily regularly, while today only 47 percent do so (Albert 1983, table 2). In 1984 estimated newspaper circulation per thousand inhabitants for France was 212, compared with 268 for the United States, 350 for West Germany, 414 for the United Kingdom, and 521 for Sweden (United Nations 1987, table 7.19).

Even if French press circulation rates are no longer so impressive as they once were, newspapers still contribute to the pluralism of voices found in France's public sphere. This is in part because of the number and diversity of Parisian newspapers—twelve dailies offering a greater diversity of political programs and tendencies than any other of the world's major cities. New York, by comparison, now has only three dailies (Albert 1983:89; Le Net 1988:146).

There are many reasons why the French press embraces a broader and more varied political spectrum than can be found in the United States. The state plays a major role through regulation, and it provides the press industry with larger subsidies than are offered in any other Western nation except Italy (Albert 1983:57). A significant number of middle-sized newspapers have thus been able to survive alongside giants like the dailies of the Hersant group, which owns almost 30 percent of the daily press. In 1986 the right-wing government attempted to change the laws regulating newspaper ownership, but its proposals were declared unconstitutional because of the loopholes they contained. The ruling was significant because it upheld the state's duty actively to promote pluralism of thought (Porter 1989:18). Through its subsidies and regulations, the postwar state continues to promote the Jacobin ideal that "all opinions have an equal chance of coming to the attention of readers'' (Miège 1989:176–77).

The tradition of a highly politicized press is still very lively, as exemplified by the growing popularity of the daily *Libération* at the expense of established and more-neutral newspapers like *Le Monde*. During the postwar period most newspapers broke their direct ties with political parties, but even so-called independent newspapers still make their political sympathies clear, especially since the Left's victory in 1981 (Albert 1983:89). A comparison with American journalism generally reflects favorably on the French, which tends toward more comprehensive coverage of domestic and international politics, and also devotes greater attention to broad cultural and literary affairs (Clark 1987:219). Newspapers, however, are having trouble gaining new readers among the young, and there is concern that the press is losing its capacity to generate news independently of the government and business organizations, which feed it news releases, the results of opinion polls, and controlled news leaks (Miège 1989:144–49).

Despite the press's very active role in the dissemination of critical-rational discourse, its elitist dimension should not be neglected. As with radio and television, the participants in journalistic discussion are mainly politicians, intellectuals, and editorialists who often know one another. Certainly their debates contribute to the public sphere, but without actively involving the majority. Under a democratic conception of the public sphere, participation is valued not merely because it stimulates the exchange of opinion, but also because it is seen as intrinsic to the political education of citizens. As Aristotle had it, the very act of public discussion teaches civic-mindedness.[4]

As is the case in many Latin societies, in France it is possible for intellectuals to become media stars.[5] The attention many intellectuals receive through the other mass media, and the role they play in public debates, is remarkable in comparison with the United States. French intellectuals were already prominent in their nation's political discussions at the turn of the century, maintain-

---

[4] A recent development in France offers the technical potential for two-way communication via a mass medium. This is the videotex, known in France as Minitel. All telephone subscribers in France now have the option of accepting, at no extra cost, a screen and terminal that connect with an extensive computer network. The system is interactive and gives the user access to a number of services such as data banks, personal bank accounts, and admissions lists for university registrations. However, apart from consulting the telephone directory, there is a fee for using Minitel. It is becoming increasingly clear that business use of the system will predominate in the long run, and there is thus no reason to believe that computer mail will alter France's public sphere (Miège 1989:35).

[5] Most intellectuals write books, and books sell well in France. The number of titles published tripled between 1955 and 1985, and during the latter year 40 percent of the nearly thirty-eight thousand books published dealt with religion, the social sciences, or politics (UNESCO 1987, tables 7.7 and 7.11). In 1987, four hundred book publishers were in business, with forty-four of them responsible for 76 percent of total sales (Miège 1989:172).

ing a heritage with roots in the Enlightenment and the overthrow of the ancien régime. During the Dreyfus affair, for instance, it was the example of Emile Zola and others who opposed anti-Semitism that proved that the pen—the manifesto and the petition—could affect political outcomes (Reader 1987:2–4). Dialogue between intellectuals and politicians has been facilitated by their concentration in Paris, and by the fact that political elites and intellectuals have often attended the same schools and worked side by side in political parties. This geographic concentration, however, has tended to marginalize viewpoints and concerns rooted outside Paris.

Jean-Paul Sartre epitomizes the high-profile French intellectual of the post-war period. His role in the Resistance, opposition to the Algerian War, and refusal of the Nobel Prize lent moral legitimacy to his later denunciation of the war in Vietnam, his reservations toward the Communist party, and his sympathies with Maoism. Through their books and articles, such intellectuals as Sartre, Raymond Aron, Albert Camus, Maurice Merleau-Ponty, and Simone de Beauvoir became public figures whose political positions served as reference points in postwar discussions, particularly those of the well educated. Often defining the parameters of French ideological debates about collective orientations, their influence was considerable (Hughes 1968).

Ferry and Renaut (1985) have argued that the postwar generation of intellectuals was distinguished by a concern with the public weal that was grounded in Enlightenment ideals of human emancipation and perfectibility. They see the events of May 1968 as a watershed in the recent history of French intellectuals. At the time the revolt seemed mainly a protest against the sacrifice of individuality to the impersonal authority of bureaucracy. When student protestors adopted such slogans as "It is forbidden to forbid," "Power to the imagination," and "Freedom is participation," they had not only the university in mind; the French Communist party itself was perceived as a bureaucratic apparatus that had confirmed its betrayal of the revolution by standing silent during the Soviet invasion of Czechoslovakia that spring. As an affirmation of individuality against the norms of "the system," the spirit of May 1968 constituted a type of humanism, but it nonetheless differed from the position of a Camus or a Sartre because it reoriented political discourse toward private concerns. The logical conclusion of May 1968 has been the narcissism of what Gilles Lipovetsky (1983) calls well-informed hedonism: a lack of interest in public matters accompanied by a preoccupation with self-liberation—the French equivalent to the ideology of America's "me generation." It is in this context that the Solzhenitsyn-inspired "new philosophers" of the late 1970s jumped into the scene. Denouncing Enlightenment thought as a mask for oppression, and seeing in all states the reflection of Stalinism, this handful of young intellectuals quickly rose to public prominence in a well-managed media coup.

The fame of public intellectuals is typically authenticated by a publication, then sealed through discussions and interviews in the media (Debray 1979). High-profile intellectuals are assured an audience because in France intellectual fashions and debates provide the upper-middle class with political rhetoric, values, and cultural practices that mark their status (Lamont 1987). France, then, is a country where the mass media play an important gatekeeping function, introducing the public to the ideas of thinkers such as André Glucksmann, Jacques Derrida, Michel Foucault, Bernard-Henri Lévy, and Jean Baudrillard, and in turn helping to ensure the commercial success of these thinkers' works.

France's mass media contribute to the public sphere mainly by diffusing critical discourse and by providing a forum for the opinions of a minority of the population, especially intellectuals and politicians. For this minority, the mass media provide significant opportunities for active participation in public discourse. Aided by strong state support and the diversity of the press, the mass media ensure a wide diffusion of what from this side of the Atlantic appear to be lively cultural and political debates. However, though these exchanges undoubtedly enrich critical public opinion, they engage most people only as bystanders.

Religion

As an institution with a significant degree of autonomy from the state, the Catholic church played a central role in shaping public opinion, both under the ancien régime and as a major opponent of Republicanism in the nineteenth century. Yet until recently, the church did not provide a strong institutional context for critical-rational public deliberation. With some exceptions, it tended to speak as a single voice in public forums, and was more interested in shaping opinion than in fostering discussion. However, recent growth in religious pluralism and changes in religious practice appear to be enhancing participation and diversity in France's public sphere.

The Jacobin tradition has always opposed the church, viewing it as a force aspiring to spiritual and intellectual primacy over the nation. The resulting tension has been a constant of French political life that periodically erupts into open confrontation. In the aftermath of the Dreyfus affair, during which the Assumptionist Order aroused antagonism between Catholics and anticlerics by publishing anti-Semitic polemics in its journal, the state dissolved over one hundred religious congregations (Cobban 1961:240–47). Later, with the formal separation of church and state in 1905, the state removed the clergy from its payroll, and turned churches and parish buildings over to local governments and "cultural associations" (Coutrot and Dreyfus 1965:31–41). Although Catholic sermons and newspapers supported the national effort during World War I, in the early 1950s one could still find that "in the current vocabulary of many of the French provinces, the word 'Catholic' is quite naturally contrasted not with the word 'Protestant' or 'Freethinker' but with the word 'Republican' " (Goguel 1952:163). On many occasions, the conflict between Catholics and Republicans undoubtedly has tempered the public voice of religion. Nonetheless, through much of this century groups of left-leaning Catholic intellectuals have contributed to Parisian intellectual debates, through the journal *Esprit*, for instance.

Religion used to be an ascriptive characteristic for the French in that sects were few, changes in religious affiliation were extremely rare, and religious groups rarely competed for new converts as they do in America. However, religion in France has undergone a number of major changes since the 1960s, and these in turn have affected the role of religion in the public sphere. Catholicism is no longer the religion of virtually everyone, as it still was in 1961 when 99 percent of the population identified itself as Catholic (Michel 1985:546).[6] Above all, immigration from North Africa has made Islam the second major religion, so that the country is now closer to religious pluralism than at any time since the Huguenots flourished during the seventeenth century. By the 1980s the proportion of French people identifying themselves as Catholic had fallen to 79 percent (Donegani 1984:212).[7]

More than a statistical fact, France's growing religious pluralism has added new voices to the process of public deliberation. The pages of major magazines and daily newspapers, for example, often carry the opinions of Muslim, Jewish, or Protestant religious leaders alongside those of Catholic bishops. The Protestant churches are generally more liberal on issues such as nuclear arms, sexual relations, and the ordination of women. This liberalism, combined with a greater tolerance toward internal discussion and the defense of a lay educational system, often places Protestants in opposition to the Catholic church, and of late official dialogue between the two communities has been described as "blocked" (Flower 1987:174–75). French bishops have also been slow to join their European counterparts in opposing nuclear weapons (Mantrant 1984:94). However, religious leaders from all the major denomi-

---

[6] While higher education has been exclusively public since the Revolution, primary and secondary education are partly privatized. Yet in 1982–1983 only 16 percent of schoolchildren attended private (mostly Roman Catholic) schools (Ambler 1988:10).

[7] The two and a half to three million Muslims, who represent about 5 percent of the nation's population, are nearly all Sunnis. Protestants, who number about one million (over 1.8 percent of the population), are mainly Calvinists and Lutherans. In the late 1950s and early 1960s immigration from North Africa brought around three hundred thousand Sephardic Jews to France; today there are about six hundred thousand Jews, who with only 1 percent of the total population constitute the fourth largest Jewish community in the world after those of the United States, Israel, and the Soviet Union (Borne 1988:163; *Handbook of Nations* 1987). There are also four hundred thousand people who belong to the Armenian and Orthodox churches, six hundred thousand in the "assorted" category, and eight million (15 percent of the population) who are unaffiliated with any religious group (Borne 1988:162; Cholvy and Hilaire 1988:490; Kepel 1987:13).

nations have helped bring questions of racism and civil rights into recent public discussions.

A number of indicators testify to the changing social role of religion. The proportion of Catholics attending Sunday mass weekly dropped from 25 to 10 percent between 1961 and 1984, and today only 15 percent of Protestants attend services once or twice a month, while 61 percent say they never attend (Donegani 1984:209; Michel 1985:548). Sharp declines in traditional religious practices such as praying, Koranic study, and observance of Ramadan have also been noted within the Islamic population (Kepel 1987).[8] However, it would be a mistake to interpret these changes as straightforward signs that religion is losing its influence entirely. Most French people today believe, for example, that it is possible to be a practicing Catholic without attending mass. The most striking feature within French Catholicism today is less a decline in religiosity than a new heterogeneity of practices. The church is not only in competition with other systems; it now contains within itself competing opinions and models of behavior (Donegani 1984:213–16).

This is illustrated by a recent study of the diocese of Bordeaux between 1950 and 1980, which found that the church gradually eased its doctrinal rigidity as it lost control over communication. Because of resource shortages, many parishes were forced to cut back or discontinue auxiliary services such as religious education, or else give laypeople greater responsibility. Simultaneously, officially sponsored groups such as the Action catholique movement became unexpectedly critical and evolved in directions the church hierarchy had never anticipated. The Bordeaux church eventually adapted to these facts by putting less emphasis on orthodoxy and recognizing the right to a plurality of theological positions and religious practices. It thereby abandoned its long-standing refusal to acknowledge any distinction between public and private matters. While the Bordeaux church has lost its claim to a monopoly over religious interpretation, it now fosters public discourse through the groups attached to it (Bertrand 1989). The changes that took place in Bordeaux have happened across the nation, and individual participation in church-affiliated groups or voluntary associations appears to be a new form of Catholic religiosity. Between 1977 and 1989, membership in one national volunteer group, Le secours catholique, jumped from twenty-four thousand to sixty-four thousand people.[9]

[8] Further, atheism is common in France. Fully 29 percent of the French professionals, managers, and businesspeople interviewed in a survey from the early 1980s declared themselves to be atheists, as opposed to 2 percent for the same categories of Americans. (French data from the 1981 European Values survey; U.S. data collected by Gallup in 1981 for the Center for Applied Research in the Apostolate [CARA]. For the French survey, N = 1,199, with 256 respondents included in the above occupational categories; for the U.S. data, N = 1,729, with 192 respondents in these categories.)

[9] Communication from the Service Documentation, Centre National du Volontariat, Paris, 28 July 1990.

The pressures of fund-raising have altered the church's role as an actor in societywide communication, for they have led to greater use of the mass media. During the 1980s the diocese of Grenoble launched a series of fund-raising campaigns that made use of posters, billboards, direct mail, radio commercials, and newspapers ads. However, the use of mass-communication techniques by religious organizations reached its limit in 1988, when a national regulatory commission prohibited church commercials on public-television channels (Miège 1989:161–62).

The church in postwar France has moved away from its old concern with orthodoxy, and now provides a context for public deliberation. It apparently contains a number of newer organizations that involve participants in face-to-face discussions about society's orientations, and its clergy are ready to communicate their opinions on national issues to a wider, nonsectarian public. France's newfound religious pluralism has expanded the diversity of voices heard in the public sphere. However, interdenominational dialogue is impeded by the deep differences that separate liberal Protestants, Catholic traditionalists, and Islamic fundamentalists, and on the whole, religious organizations possess only limited access to the mass-media resources needed for a high profile in the nation's public sphere.

Voluntary Associations

Though not extensively studied in the past, France's voluntary associations play a number of important roles in the public sphere, particularly in helping organize social movements, channeling citizens' demands toward the state, and providing open forums for discussion. Many French people see associations as preeminently democratic institutions that provide valuable opportunities for participation and the promotion of collective values. Indeed, a recent national survey found that when respondents were given a list of organizations including unions, political parties, churches, public authorities, and associations, and asked which one gave the greatest expression to democracy, associations were mentioned most frequently (*La Croix* 1989:17). However, participation in voluntary associations varies quite dramatically across the population. In addition, associations often lack autonomy from the state and party politics, and they have experienced difficulty bringing their message to the wider public. Many associations are also organized around leisure-time activities, which have little impact on broader sociopolitical debates.

Some empirical work in the mid-1950s indicated that on the whole participation in voluntary associations was not much lower in France than in the United States (Rose 1954). However, during the postwar period most observers have differed from this view, observing that French associations are weak and have a low impact on public life (Hoffmann 1963; Crozier 1964; Wylie 1973). For example, France's social clubs and fraternal organizations are relatively insignificant due to factors that encourage sociability outside organizations: low geographic mobility, strong neighborhood cohesion (thanks in part to cafes), and family stability (one out of six marriages ends in divorce, compared to one in three in the United States).[10]

We should note, however, that firm generalizations about the importance of France's voluntary associations are difficult to make because research on them has lagged far behind similar work in the United States (Roudet 1988:26–27). Hence, the number of associations that contribute to the public sphere in some tangible way is unknown. Authorities keep records of new associations, but not of those that have become defunct, and furthermore the number of unregistered associations is uncertain. Estimates are therefore vague, putting the number of associations in France somewhere between three hundred thousand and six hundred thousand (Archambault 1984:8–9). Over one-third of the population belongs to associations, which provide employment for more than seven hundred thousand people (CNVA 1989:22).[11]

Figures such as these obviously conceal a tremendous amount of diversity in terms of voluntary associations' size and their contribution to the public sphere. We do know that during the early 1980s the number of religious, youth, veterans', and sports associations leveled off, while there were increases in the number of associations concerned with trade, feminism, ecology, neighborhoods, the elderly, and social welfare (Service aux associations 1987; Poujol 1988:110). Current data show rates of association membership to be consistently higher in North America than in France, especially for charities and churches; differences in membership are weakest for consumer associations. Compared with North Americans, the French are more likely to volunteer for labor unions, but proportionately fewer volunteer for groups such as charities, churches, and professional associations.[12] Some unions are

[10] Further, while clubs in the United States like the Lions and Rotary encourage the community-minded, in France they belong to an exclusive network that includes the Jockey-Club, the Automobile-Club, and the Cercle du Bois-de-Boulogne (Birnbaum et al. 1978:176). In this sense, a number of French social clubs and fraternal organizations appear to belong more to the private than to the public realm.

[11] Official statistics on the number and types of new associations officially registered indicate a rise in the number of associations created each year: the rate of association creation per one hundred thousand adults was 30.8 in 1937, 38.6 in 1960, 85.1 in 1977, and 103.9 in 1982 (Archambault 1984:4). However, the progression has known its ups and downs, and the greatest increase over the previous year, both in relative and in absolute terms, occurred back in 1977. In any case, these data provide only a crude indication of ongoing participation in associations because very little is known about a number of relevant factors: (a) the size of associations, both at birth and as they mature; (b) the life span of associations; (c) the extent to which membership implies a share in decision making, rather than simple access to an association's services; and (d) the tendency for individuals to belong to more than one association at a time (Forsé 1984).

[12] Data from European Values Survey, 1981, and CARA Values Survey, Gallup Research, 1981. A recent study found that the need to volunteer and to work toward social change are the two major motivations for belonging to associations in France (CNVA 1989:37–38). The scale of

very vocal, particularly those which are close to a political party, like the Conféderation générale du travail (CGT). The CGT, which has links with the Communist party, has tried to play a role in the political mobilization of both its own membership and the wider population.[13]

Voluntary associations typically play a key role in social movements. They organize activists, raise funds, and communicate with the public. Associations pressing for social change recently have included neighborhood associations and antinuclear, antiracist, feminist, and consumer organizations. However, on the whole, new social movements have been weaker in France than in other advanced industrialized countries such as Japan, West Germany, and the United States (Mueller-Rommel 1982). The main exception was the ethnic/regionalist movement of the mid-1970s (Beer 1980). As we saw when looking at the role of political parties, many of the more-organized groups such as the women's movement have now been absorbed into party structures (Jenson 1982).[14]

A number of factors limit the impact voluntary associations have on the public sphere. First, membership in a voluntary association does not necessarily imply active participation and accessibility. The active few who run associations are predominantly male, well educated, and likely to hold similar responsibilities in a number of associations. For instance, a study carried out in Grenoble found that because of multiple memberships a handful of people held nearly half of the directors' seats in the city's associations (Archambault 1984:15, table 8, Roudet 1984:40).

Voluntary associations' impact on the public sphere is also limited by their

---

volunteering in France is unclear. One estimate places the number of volunteers between one million and four million, out of a total population of fifty-six million, while recent data suggest that the base figure of one million is implausibly low, since one million volunteers work in sports associations alone (*Lettre d'information de la Fonda* 1989). Given that the average volunteer in France contributes two hours per week, the total for volunteer work in France would at most equal the full-time work of 1 percent of the active population, as opposed to 2 percent in Canada and 3 percent in the United States (Archambault 1984, table 8, 25–27). Volunteers tend to live in urban centers, and belong to the middle or upper-middle classes (Le Net and Werquin 1985:19).

[13] While the French working class has a long tradition of militancy, today only 10 percent of the active population belongs to labor unions, down from 20 percent in 1963 (Mouriaux 1988, *Le Monde* 1989). The Force ouvrière is a self-proclaimed apolitical union that is surviving the current crisis of French unionism much better than its major counterparts (Wilson 1987:82). The other major union is the Confédération française démocratique du travail, which was originally Catholic but is now closer to the Socialist party, and promotes self-management and decentralization. French unions have supported the peace movement and a subculture of activist groups such as neighborhood associations (Rand Smith 1987).

[14] Teachers constitute 20 percent to 45 percent of the membership in European countercultural groups such as the ecologists and regionalists, and in several cases the proportion of health and welfare professionals is also high (Pinard and Hamilton, forthcoming). This would suggest that the French state, as the main supporter of the education, culture, health, and welfare sectors, maintains a broad institutional environment that sustains and possibly promotes countercultural values.

strong dependence on local governments. Association agendas are shaped by the complicity that typically unites politicians and association leaders (Mendras 1988:176). One study of local government-association relations found that officials exploited associations' financial dependency by treating subsidies as political favors. The flow of patronage was fairly obvious, since among the councillors in the municipalities studied, most had previously been association officials, and half remained so. Because associations in France must often make their political preferences obvious, an unfortunate local election may spell the end of an association (Garraud 1985). French associations' vulnerability to the instabilities of local political life is the major reason they fail to develop into enduring institutions enjoying autonomy in the public sphere (Grémion 1978:19).

Local authorities, for their part, have found that associations maintain a degree of discipline among the citizenry that makes demands less diffuse and therefore easier to manage. Further, giving associations funding and responsibilities creates political capital for local officials while allowing governments to distance themselves from unavoidable but politically risky services. For the leaders of many local associations, closer relations with municipal governments now promise benefits (financing, facilities, employment subsidies, legitimacy) that national organizations seem less and less capable of providing. Combined with dropping grants for national-level leadership posts, the upshot of voluntary associations' greater orientation toward local affairs has been an inability to mobilize on larger issues such as environmental protection (Palard 1988).

This suggests that associations can be seen as mediating bodies in French society, relaying to public authorities the desires and concerns that filter up through their hierarchies, and relaying back to civil society the unwritten rules of the political game. As one observer puts it, new associations are "pilot fish" for the state: through them the state seeks out new areas for intervention. This was true of educational associations in the Third Republic, and of ecological, feminist, leisure, local democracy, and consumer-rights groups a hundred years later under the Socialists (Martin 1988; Conan 1978:41). While articulating demands, however, associations are placed in a precarious position between the state and civil society that limits their autonomy as actors in societal discussions.

Beyond their intraorganizational role as arenas for public discourse, French voluntary associations are themselves fairly active as voices in the public debate. However, their public messages usually aim less at questioning social arrangements than at drawing attention to collective problems like cancer, alcoholism, dangerous driving, or AIDS. These messages, mostly slogans carried by the mass media, contribute little to the reasoned argument associated with the public sphere. In any case, French voluntary associations are less influential in public communication than those in the United States, partly because they lack information about how the mass media work and often tailor their messages to narrow audiences (Théry 1986:9).[15]

Although critical discussion plays a widely varying role in France's different types of voluntary associations, on the whole these organizations make an important contribution to the public sphere because they offer a large number of people their best opportunity for democratic participation. In spite of this, it must be noted that factors such as gender, educational achievement, and political ties affect individual chances for participation. Furthermore, the ability of associations to function as autonomous voices in societal debates is limited by their dependence on the state and the demands of local and party politics. Finally, associations have had difficulty contributing to societywide discussion via the mass media.

Examination of the principal institutional areas involved in France's public sphere does not support the position advanced by Habermas in *The Structural Transformation of the Public Sphere* (1989), where he describes a contemporary public sphere in which the critical function has been lost to a mass culture that trivializes public discourse. We find instead that a number of institutions are involved in the public sphere, and that these institutions display significant variations in levels of participation, accessibility, and critical-rationality. For instance, political parties provide members with significant opportunities to discuss collective values, and they help spread the critical opinions of leaders and affiliated interest groups such as social movements and unions. The mass media—particularly the press, but also state-owned radio and television stations—are especially influential in the public sphere because of their role in selecting and diffusing social and cultural criticism. Intellectuals in particular receive a great deal of attention from France's mass media. Voluntary associations and to a lesser extent religious groups in many cases appear to provide significant opportunities for accessibility and active participation. A revised portrait of the contemporary public sphere, at least for France, cannot neglect differentiation along these lines. Further, this study of the French case suggests that institutions contribute to the public sphere at two levels: they provide organizational settings that shape public discourse, but are themselves also participants in societywide communication. Hence, political parties, the mass media, religious organizations, and voluntary associations all have the capacity to speak in societal debates, where they typically claim to represent the opinions of entire groups of people.

[15] The public's perception of association financing also affects the availability of resources for communication. Among the respondents in one recent survey, 65 percent agreed that associations should be able to use modern means of communication, and 70 percent agreed that associations generally have difficulty being heard by the media and the public, yet over 53 percent found it unacceptable that associations finance their campaigns through donations (*Lettre du crédit coopératif* 1990:11, *La Croix* 1989:16).

STATE, MARKET, AND THIRD SECTOR

In the foregoing examination of how different institutional domains have shaped France's public sphere, the influences of the state and market sectors were encountered frequently. We would now like to shift attention to the state and market, and focus on developments that have influenced the growth of one area involved in the public sphere, the third or voluntary sector, which in France is composed of voluntary associations, cooperatives, and mutual-aid societies (Archambault 1990).

The Jacobin conception of the relationship between state and citizen, together with a corresponding system of centralized political institutions, has significantly determined the context within which the voluntary sector has developed in France: the preeminence of the centralized state in French society has direct institutional roots in the ancien régime, and it was during the reign of Louis XIV that the state was first construed as the exclusive representative of the common interest.

At the time of the Revolution, the universality of French citizens' rights and freedoms was seen to rest on the unity of the nation, with the state as the incarnation of disinterested reason. A speech to the Constituent Assembly in 1791 summarized the Jacobin perspective:

> It should not be permissible for citizens of certain occupations to meet together in defence of their pretended common interests. There must be no more guilds in the state but only the individual interest of each citizen and the general interest. No one shall be allowed to arouse in any citizen any kind of intermediate interest and to separate him from the public weal through the medium of corporate interests. (Bendix 1978:372)

During the Revolution the state pursued a persistent struggle against bodies such as guilds, the nobility, and political clubs, which stood between the citizen and the republic. Since then both the Left and the Right have at various times viewed with suspicion the church, voluntary associations, decentralization, and ethnic pluralism.

In the nineteenth century the unique position of the church vis-à-vis the state distinguished it from voluntary associations. Shortly before Napoleon banned associations in 1810, he recognized the church, and agreed that the state would remunerate bishops, canons, and priests. In return, he acquired a privilege once held by French monarchs, the right to nominate bishops. With the Restoration, the state also provided funds for seminaries and the maintenance of religious properties (Langlois and Tackett 1980:305–9). However, throughout the nineteenth century the state continued to distrust associations, fearing they would help the proletariat organize on the left, and the church to insinuate itself from the right.

In spite of restrictive laws during the second half of the nineteenth century, members of the bourgeoisie were joining illegal clubs and associations devoted to discussion, games, and the advancement of their class interests. When Napoleon's prohibition against unauthorized associations of more than twenty persons was rescinded in the late nineteenth century, only the middle and upper classes could afford the time and expense membership demanded. Although trade unions and mutual-aid societies became legal in 1884 and 1898 respectively, 1901 is the pivotal date in the history of French voluntary associations, for in that year the state formally recognized the right to freedom of association, aside from certain restrictions on religious associations. During this century, more relaxed relations between the state and the voluntary sector created an environment in which citizens have organized to meet social needs that government could not (Agulhon 1988; Archambault 1990).

Today, apart from the fact that it regulates associations through legislation, the state exercises a major influence by funding associations through its various agencies and ministries. Changes in government policy can therefore have a direct influence on how individual associations see their roles or structure their organizations, and indeed can determine whether or not they survive at all. This has remained true under a Socialist government. In the 1970s, the Socialist party promoted active associations as a key to the renewal of civil society, and the extensive connections the party nurtured with these groups were used to mobilize electoral support in the victory of 1981. Once in power, the Socialists initially boosted indirect state support to associations, but as unemployment worsened the latter were increasingly expected to create jobs in return for government aid. Thereafter, the "disengagement of the state" translated into shrinking grants, tax incentives to stimulate private support, and, for nonprofit organizations, official encouragement to help push back the state by doing good, through the market if necessary. Associations could go along with such initiatives by turning to banks, which had developed special financing programs for them (Bruneau 1986:16–19; Palard 1988:94–95).

While the Jacobin model of relations between the state and the organized voluntary sector no longer holds as much in the areas of funding and regulation, the same is not true with regard to the public sphere. Indeed, in France no group or institution outside the state can claim the prerogative of recognizing the general will through the exercise of disinterested reason. A deeply held concern with formal legitimacy leads many to perceive only universally applied measures and criteria as legitimate, so that the state's interlocutors are viewed as capable of representing only partial interests. It is thus not surprising that, compared with other Western nations, France's government maintains a remarkably aloof stance toward interest groups (Wilson 1987).

The decentralization of government under the Socialists holds potentially important consequences for national conceptions of the roles of state and citizen, as well as for the allocation of resources to the voluntary sector. This series of political, administrative, and fiscal reforms has already upset the old balance of power between authorities at the intermediate and local levels.[16] Though its long-term consequences are not yet clear, decentralization has so far disappointed those who hoped it would promote political participation. New forms of grass-roots democracy have been discouraged at the local level, and the reforms have reinforced local patron-client relations and the dependence of mayors on regional political bosses. Some observers have speculated that local participation may nonetheless benefit from decentralization once individuals and associations learn to work within the new system (Schmidt 1987). On the other hand, it has been argued that "decentralisation has straightened, to the detriment of the welfare associations, a rather chaotic structure of public subsidies which had enabled the associations previously to milk several public authorities at the same time" (Seibel 1990:54).

How is the voluntary sector affected by the market? This is a difficult question to answer, beyond the obvious observation that market pressures constrain voluntary associations, which borrow from banks, employ salaried workers, receive private donations, or offer courses, shows, or cut-rate travel. The main reason it is difficult to isolate the market's influence on the voluntary sector is that the economy is largely molded by the state. Indeed, the French state is still among the most interventionist in the West, as is suggested by indicators such as the share of government spending in the national economy, its responsibility for social welfare, and its participation in economic development (Pierce 1973; Hall 1986).

Recent employment trends in the third sector illustrate the state's importance in mediating economic forces. Government action has helped turn the economic crisis since the mid-1970s, with its high rates of unemployment and inflation, into a stimulus for France's voluntary sector. Indeed, while public- and private-sector employment stagnated during the early 1980s, employment in voluntary associations increased by 4.5 percent (Seibel 1990:44).[17] From the supply side, more personnel have become available to the third sector due to a combination of conditions: early retirement programs; the underemployment of women; legislation that shortened the workweek; and government programs designed to alleviate unemployment and provide training for certain groups, particularly youths (Le Net and Werquin 1985:14–22).[18]

[16] Executive power in the ninety-six *départements* of metropolitan France has shifted from the centrally appointed prefects to elected representatives, rationalizing administration and giving the latter more room for initiative.

[17] During the 1980s, the third sector employed an estimated 1,070,000 employees (6.1 percent of France's work force), including 664,000 in associations, 235,500 in cooperatives, and 138,500 in mutual-aid societies (Chomel 1985:8).

[18] A development since the mid-1970s has been the state's active promotion of association membership (see Ion 1988). Wolfgang Seibel (1989:188) has argued that in complex societies, the nonprofit sector provides an institutional arrangement that discharges government from responsibilities for unsolvable social problems (the other alternative, of course, is to privatize the delivery of collective goods). One way of testing this argument is to consider levels of government

Closer examination of one sector involved in the public sphere, the voluntary sector, confirms the important role of the French state. Its funding and regulatory powers influence the resources and roles available to the voluntary sector, while the Jacobin tradition gives it the sole legitimacy to articulate the nation's collective values. The economy partly influences the voluntary sector, of course, but its influence seems mostly mediated by the state, whose policies, even under the restrictive economic conditions of the 1970s and 1980s, appear to have strengthened the voluntary sector. The state's ability to structure the environment in which the third sector functions is but one aspect of its pervasive influence, for it is also the subject of much public discourse, which as a consequence is strongly politicized in comparison with the United States.[19]

THE IMMIGRATION-NATIONALITY ISSUE

The French have engaged in a number of important public debates over the past decade, such as calls for worker self-management and government decentralization, and conflict over the independence of private (mainly Catholic) schools. Consideration of any of these cases would help make the preceding discussion more specific. However, in order to illustrate how the public sphere works in France, we have chosen to focus on the immigration-nationality issue.

Since the founding of the nation-state after the Revolution, centralized institutions like the army and the school system have tried to assimilate native ethnic groups (Bretons, Alsatians, Savoyards, Corsicans) and immigrants (such as the Poles and Italians of the interwar period) into a French identity

---

subsidies and control over the voluntary sector. In France three types of legal status distinguish among voluntary organizations: a few organizations, mainly in the areas of health and welfare, are primarily or totally state-funded and possess quasi-public authority; a second group of sports, youth, and arts organizations have less government funding and greater autonomy; a third category includes organizations providing broadly defined public services that are subject to the least control and receive little funding. This breakdown by categories of funding and control suggests the French state is ill-equipped or reluctant to fulfill certain functions in the areas of health and welfare. Indeed, in 1982 associations operated 51 percent of all welfare institutions, in particular providing 80 percent of all facilities and services for the handicapped, while mutual-aid societies ran a total of over six hundred pharmacies, optical centers, dental offices, nursing homes, day-care centers, and convalescent centers (Théry 1986:7; Archambault 1990). The state nonetheless maintains a heavy, direct presence in the health sector: 95 percent of the nation's medical practitioners participate in state health plans, 70 percent of the nation's hospital beds are located in public hospitals, and 70 percent of the population belongs to a public insurance plan financed largely by employers (*Europa Year Book* 1988:1039; INSEE 1987; Lagrange 1986).

[19] The cultural insignificance of the market for France's public sphere is captured in one French writer's interpretation of Habermas's *offentliche Kommunikation*, which is able to define public communication exclusively in terms of state administrators and civil society, without mentioning the market (Miège 1989:121).

that "gave a Jacobin primacy to the individual's link to the State and relegated particularistic traits (different religion, language, or mores) to the private sphere of family life" (Pinto 1988:17). Yet since the early 1980s a nationwide discussion about the social status of recent immigrants and their children has forced the French to reexamine their national identity and the meaning of citizenship.

Because of a sustained decrease in fertility rates, France's population levels remained virtually the same between 1896 and 1946 (Carré, Dubois, and Malinvaud 1972:60). Relatively slow economic modernization had been one consequence of this long-standing demographic trend. Postwar planners therefore decided that immigration should be an essential ingredient for a successful reconstruction of the country's productive capacities. Portuguese, Belgian, and Algerian workers came first, but from the early 1960s until large-scale immigration was halted in 1974, immigrants came mostly from North Africa (Morocco, Algeria, Tunisia), often under temporary permits directing them into the worst-paid, least-desirable jobs in manufacturing, mining, and public works (Trotignon 1984:10). Later, a number of Southeast Asians received asylum.

Starting in the 1970s it became clear that, contrary to historical experience, the ongoing presence of less easily assimilable aliens was changing the profile of France. Half of the new immigrants were visible minorities, mostly Muslims who (thanks to official immigration policy) could now establish their families on French soil (Noreau 1989:8–9). In 1970 immigrants made up 5.2 percent of the total population, and today they represent over 8 percent (Arnaud 1986:16–18). The new immigrants settled mainly on the outskirts of major cities, where they met with a variety of problems—crime, drug and alcohol abuse, alienation—associated with poverty and poor housing. Young people experienced difficulties in school and showed particularly high rates of unemployment and underemployment. All this strained relations with local authorities and the law. Some of the immigrants' French neighbors, for their part, came to blame social problems and unemployment on the foreigners so visibly in their midst. The sense of invasion and competition eventually translated into xenophobia and calls for the repatriation of non-Europeans (Noreau 1989:8–11; Viard 1989:318–20).

Race, immigration, and law and order were first framed as national issues by the Communist party during the 1981 presidential campaign, when it was claimed that "immigrants from North Africa were too numerous; that they posed problems in racial/ethnic conflict; and that their presence was related to problems of law and order" (Schain 1987:238–39). Such a stand was a departure for the Communist party, which since the 1920s had engaged in the socialization and politicization of aliens. Back then it invoked the pan-nationalism of the working class and the right to be different as ideological justifications for its solidarity with immigrant workers. A transition took place during the 1970s when, on the one hand, the Communist party called for greater social and political rights for aliens, and on the other, conflicts arose between immigrants and the often Communist administrations of the suburbs they inhabited (Noreau 1989:23–25). Similar problems were encountered by the other political parties, but they remained unarticulated until the Communist party's initiative brought them onto the national scene (Schain 1987:238).

In the wake of the Socialist victory of 1981, the Communist vote nonetheless declined to a level never before seen in the Fifth Republic. But the Socialists' soft rhetoric on the legitimate place of visible minorities in French society failed to reassure a sizable portion of the electorate. As the Communists backed off the immigrant issue, the initiative passed to the National Front, a party of the extreme right. According to the Front's leader, Jean-Marie Le Pen, the combination of France's current immigration practices and the purported higher fecundity of immigrants will one day lead to "the substitution of a Third World population for the French population, which is condemned to become a minority in its own country. . . . Make no mistake about it: *it is the existence of the French people itself which is being challenged*" (emphasis in original; Taguieff 1989:217). Over the past decade, Le Pen has become a subject of all the national media, and thus an agenda-setter and a public figure with or against whom to take a stand. His high profile illustrates the crucial role political parties play in defining the French polity's collective orientations.

In 1981, the National Front received only .4 percent of the vote. Its popularity rose over the next two years, with a major breakthrough coming in the 1984 European parliamentary election, when it received over two million votes (11.2 percent of the vote). The vote for Le Pen's party was strongest in urban areas with high concentrations of immigrants; in some districts the National Front received one out of five votes. That election, in which only 56.8 percent of the French electorate voted, certainly favored a throwaway protest vote, since at the time few in Europe—experts or laypeople—could properly claim to understand the future import of the European parliament. But subsequent French elections, in which the stakes have been clearer and the participation higher, have demonstrated the stability of support for the National Front. Since 1984 the party has always won at least 9 percent of the vote nationally, though the regional variation in support is immense. It is highest in the major cities and industrial centers and along the Mediterranean coast. On average, between 1984 and 1988 electoral support for the party was highest among the self-employed, followed by the unemployed, then by those in the for-profit sector, with support lowest among public-sector employees (Perrineau 1989).

Defeated by the Left in 1981, the once dominant right-of-center parties now saw themselves outflanked on the right. For a time some of its leaders, such as then-mayor of Paris Jacques Chirac, borrowed the rhetoric of Le Pen:

Without accepting all of the theses of the National Front, the UDF and the RPR [the dominant parties of the Right coalition] share with it some common ideas: the particular contribution of immigrants to insecurity; the certainty that there are too many immigrants in France; the absolute necessity therefore to increasingly send them home; the affirmation that "naturally if there were fewer immigrants, there would be less unemployment, fewer tensions in certain cities and certain neighborhoods, and a lower social cost." (Schain 1987:241–42; translation ours)

Further, in a local election during 1983 the Right welcomed the National Front into its party coalition, and then proceeded to defeat the left-wing incumbent. However, such outright opportunism was markedly tempered by 1985, as opposition to an alliance with the National Front was consolidated among both supporters and leaders of the Right. The church and antiracist groups may have influenced this new resistance (Schain 1987:239–42).

With the rise of the National Front, a grass-roots movement grew among minority youths that attracted the sympathies of students, Socialist activists, and people involved in new social movements. An impetus to the participation of aliens in this whole question came in 1981, when the Socialist government provided an important revision to the 1901 law on associations. Henceforth, foreigners on French soil had the legal right to create their own associations. Around that time, two types of voluntary associations attracted young immigrants from major suburban areas. The first type used a more conflictual language: it promoted North African ethnicity and collective self-defense against the police. The second type was more accommodating, seeking to organize services and advance civil rights through legitimate channels. Its best-known representative, SOS-Racisme, had enlisted the support of influential Parisian intellectuals who brought the organization to the public's attention, then helped secure ongoing media coverage of its political positions and activities. By 1983, because the Socialists in power seemed to promise real possibilities for progress, young North Africans were clearly tending toward antiracist associations of the moderate type (Noreau 1989:31–33).

But that year leaders of immigrant youth groups were jolted by the rising popularity of the National Front, and the wounding and killing of over twenty young people in various police incidents. In the fall of 1983, these groups organized a cross-France march that provided a high-profile and legitimate outlet for the resentment of minority youths. Through the media, the public was introduced to a new antiracist movement whose most vocal leadership came from SOS-Racisme. Upon its arrival in Paris, the march gathered one hundred thousand supporters, who were met by top Socialist officials, representatives from unions and opposition parties, and the nation's president (Noreau 1989:33–34). Among other things, this Parisian reception symbolized the public consecration of the movement by the highest form of legitimacy on French soil: the state.

Since then, marches and well-publicized rock concerts have been held every year under the sponsorship of antiracist youth groups. There is no doubt that during the 1980s these movements did much to orient public discourse toward the ideal of a fraternal and multiethnic France (Noreau 1989:35). On the eve of an important antiracist rally, Marxist intellectual Etienne Balibar took aim at Le Pen's dismay over a "mongrel France." Writing for a large daily newspaper, Balibar celebrated a new "society of mixed-bloods" (société métissée) (Benot 1985:511).

However, a number of contradictions exist in the antiracist movement. Differences between conflictual and moderate immigrant groups have not been resolved, and factional splits occur periodically. Tensions also threaten to divide pro-Israeli Jews from pro-Palestinian North Africans. Further, high-profile groups such as SOS-Racisme could soon outlive their usefulness. They have won the enthusiasm of minority youths and their supporters by fighting for what are essentially legal rights and guarantees: no repatriation of aliens; an end to violence against visible minorities; French citizenship and the right to vote for all residents of France. It is not certain whether the movement could continue to mobilize supporters once its present legalistic goals had been met, or if the antiracist movement were to turn violent.

We saw earlier that in the public sphere the influence of voluntary associations is often structured by the state. This may turn out to be the case with the antiracist movement too, because it is in danger of losing its fiscal and political autonomy. Without government funding SOS-Racisme might have become insolvent, and the well-connected group has relied on government grants when organizing concerts in Paris (Philippe 1988). The Socialists have not been shy to reap the political capital gained from such ties. President Mitterrand has been an assiduous well-wisher of all the major antiracist concerts and rallies, and during the 1988 legislative elections, some leaders of SOS-Racisme ran as candidates for the Socialist party, while others campaigned on Mitterrand's behalf (Noreau 1989:40–48). Herein lies a threat to the group's ability to represent minorities. In an open letter published in a major French weekly, sociologist Alain Touraine began by calling SOS-Racisme "the most important and the most positive of the movements that have penetrated French society in recent years." But Touraine added that he feared for the autonomy of the movement. It should not become so eager for power that it "transformed itself into a transmission belt for a party," as had happened to other social movements in France (Touraine 1988).

When the Socialists first came to power in 1981, they liberalized policies affecting aliens, not only making it possible for them to form their own associations, but also giving legal status to 130,000 illegals (Pinto 1988:18). As the economic crisis worsened and Le Pen's popularity surged, the Socialists grew more cautious and along with the Communists quietly advocated stricter measures to control illegal immigration (Schain 1987:242). Faced with an impasse, in 1987 prime minister Jacques Chirac formed a temporary commission to study immigration and nationality. Throughout France public meetings were held in which diverse parties expressed their views: academics, government experts, minority youths, and representatives of the country's major religious denominations. The government-appointed commission, which consisted mostly of intellectuals, but also included high-level civil servants, physicians, a lawyer, and a theater director, saw itself as "a group of citizens without political legitimacy seeking to inform other citizens." Because the commission held the education of public opinion to be part of its task, some meetings were televised.

One of the commission's members, sociologist Dominique Schnapper (1988), described the exercise as an innovation with potentially important symbolic value: as the product of an independent inquiry involving public participation, the commission's meetings and final report could claim a form of moral and intellectual legitimacy. In a nation where only the state has been seen as capable of rising above partisanship to discern the common interest, this is not an insignificant event. Still, it is important to bear in mind that it was intellectuals, members of a state-appointed committee, who produced the report, and not leaders of religious and civic groups, let alone ordinary citizens or aliens.

The most recent episode of the immigration-nationality debate took place during the fall of 1989, when North African girls wore Muslim scarves to their school in the industrial town of Creil. The school's principal quickly moved to bar the girls from classes, interpreting the wearing of the scarves as "indiscreet . . . extremely aggressive, a form of proselytism" (*Libération* 1989:5). Speaking from the perspective of French Republicanism, his words upheld the century-old ideal of a lay educational system opposed to church authority. However, now that traditional conceptions of French nationality are under attack, the view of the French school as a neutral instrument of enlightenment and shaper of citizens has grown much less tenable. The events at the school in Creil made headlines, and "the scarf affair" rapidly assumed great symbolic importance as a test of the government's willingness to support a new pluralist vision of France: would the ministry of education overrule the principal at Creil?

As it turned out, the Socialist party was split on the issue, and the government eventually decided that although religious dress and insignia were not contrary to the principle of lay education, individual school administrations could prohibit such displays when they appeared exaggerated, politically motivated, or provocative (*Libération* 1989:2). Apart from the government's lack of decisiveness, what was striking were the amount of space the issue received in the press and the unusual alignments the debate produced. On one side stood feminists, intellectuals, and religious and ethnic groups who for various reasons upheld the right to be different. Opposing them were feminists who supported the principal of lay education, and saw the scarf as an antiquated symbol of Muslim domination over women; and the National Front, which called the government's decision a surrender to Muslims. Even SOS-Racisme was divided over the issue, and at least one prominent figure in the organization resigned over a disagreement with the group's leader, Harlem Désir.

Examination of the immigration-nationality debate shows how various institutions have actually contributed to France's public sphere, both as loci of critical discourse and as voices in larger contexts. The political parties have all taken widely publicized positions on the issues and, as we have seen, even within the parties discussions have revealed sharp differences in opinion. Through this case, we have also seen the reduced salience of the left-right split that normally characterizes French political life. It was the Communist party that first placed race on the public agenda, not the anti-immigrant National Front, and the "scarf affair" generated further alignments that undercut the usual ideological oppositions. At the societal level, voluntary associations, in this case notably SOS-Racisme, have in this national debate played a role equal to that of the political parties. At the same time, we suspect the group's leadership will be forced to restrict internal discussions to a core of unifying issues in order to avoid factionalism. Also, as in many social movements, the autonomy of SOS-Racisme has become compromised by its connections to the Socialist party.

It is more difficult to assess the role of religious groups in this debate. Certainly they testified before the government's commission on nationality, and religious figures have made public statements in the mass media. However, at this point it is hard to say how discussion within religious organizations has been affected by the debate. More research remains to be done in this area.

Finally, along with voluntary associations and political figures like Le Pen, Mitterrand, and Chirac, intellectuals must be considered among the principal actors in the immigration-nationality debate. A handful of them in Paris have been responsible for the vast amount of media attention directed at SOS-Racisme. Intellectuals also predominated on the commission of inquiry appointed by prime minister Chirac, and thanks to the press, readers across the country are familiar with the views of thinkers like Alain Touraine and Etienne Balibar. In France, intellectuals continue to be influential in nationwide debates, and as in the case of SOS-Racisme leader Harlem Désir, their reputation grows when they come to symbolize a particular point of view on public issues.

Conclusion

The present study has given a preliminary answer to an admittedly difficult question by examining the conditions for a critical and democratic public sphere in France. This analysis suggests that several institutions contribute to the public sphere in two ways: by providing environments that sustain critical-rational public discourse, and by functioning as voices in societywide discussions. At the intrainstitutional level, French political parties, voluntary associations, and religious organizations generally appear to offer individuals the best opportunities for active participation in public discussion. While the mass media reach the broadest public and provide important channels for the diffusion of the critical views of intellectuals and other high-profile public figures, they provide a forum for the opinions of only a tiny minority of the population.

At the societal level, the major political parties and intellectuals with access to the mass media provide the most prominent voices in French public discourse. It comes as no surprise that political actors receive much attention, since the state continues to influence so many aspects of French life. The nation's deeply embedded literary culture meanwhile accords intellectuals great influence as interpreters of social affairs. Religious organizations and voluntary associations (the major unions excepted) on the whole lack the resources, expertise, and prestige necessary to maintain a consistent presence in societal communication. Groups like SOS-Racisme that benefit from the backing of politicians or state administrations must balance the advantages of such support against the dangers of dependence.

Although our study of the factors shaping the voluntary sector, as well as a historical overview of the immigration-nationality debate, have demonstrated the effect of the French state on the public sphere, current developments in the European Economic Community may recast the state's influence. While the Socialists were soft-selling the immigrant issue in 1989, the European parliament decided with near-unanimity that in future EEC elections foreigners ought to have the right to vote (Feron 1989). To be sure, the possibility that France's present laws may one day conflict with those at the European level has sharpened the immigrant issue in France, at least for the time being. But the parliament's decision also contains more far-reaching implications for the public sphere in France. It signals the emerging influence of a supranational institution that apparently enjoys greater freedom from partisan pressures than the nation-state, yet makes law. The European parliament may soon be in a better position to advance the formal legal rationality from which liberal states like France derive their political legitimacy. Although the European parliament lacks the administrative and coercive powers of the nation-states, as a lawmaking supranational body it may win a special legitimacy that makes it a competitor for the Jacobin right to articulate France's collective good.

The public sphere is multidimensional, and institutions are both milieus that shape public discourse and actors in societywide communication. Long-standing relationships between the state and civil society structure civil institutions' access to the legitimacy, resources, and spheres of action necessary for the production of collective discourse. Consideration of the French case indicates that the portrait of the public sphere found at the end of Habermas's *Structural Transformation of the Public Sphere* lacks sufficient nuance and is overly pessimistic: much critical discourse is carried on in France, and a number of institutions allow some degree of access to open discussion.

References

Agulhon, Maurice. 1988. "L'histoire sociale et les associations." *La revue de l'économie sociale* (April): 35–44.

Albert, Pierre. 1983. *La presse française*. Paris: Documentation française.

Ambler, John S. 1988. "Educational Pluralism in the French Fifth Republic." Paper delivered at the conference "In Search of the New France," Brandeis University, Boston, May.

Archambault, Edith. 1984. *Les associations en chiffres*. Nanterre: Association pour le développement de la documentation sur l'économie sociale.

———. 1990. "Public Authorities and the Nonprofit Sector in France." In *The Third Sector: Nonprofit Organizations in Comparative and International Perspectives*, edited by Helmut K. Anheier and Wolfgang Seibel, pp. 51–79. Berlin: De Gruyter.

Arnaud, Rémy. 1986. *Panorama de l'économie française*. Paris: Bordas.

Baecque, Francis de, and J. L. Quermonne. 1981. *Administration et politique sous la Cinquième République*. Paris: Presses de la Fondation nationale des sciences politiques.

Beer, W. R. 1980. *The Unexpected Rebellion: Ethnic Activism in Contemporary France*. New York: New York University Press.

Bendix, Reinhard. 1978. *Kings or People: Power and the Mandate to Rule*. Berkeley and Los Angeles: University of California Press.

Benot, Yves. 1985. "Le racisme." In *L'état de la France et de ses habitants*, edited by Jean-Yves Potel, pp. 511–31. Paris: Découverte.

Bertrand, Michèle. 1989. Review of *Pouvoir religieux et espace social: Le diocèse de Bordeaux comme organisation*, by Jacques Palard. *L'année sociologique*, 351–53.

Birnbaum, Pierre, C. Baruck, M. Bellaiche, and A. Marie. 1978. *La classe dirigeante française*. Paris: Presses universitaires de France.

Borne, Dominique. 1988. *Histoire de la société française depuis 1945*. Paris: Armand Colin.

Bruneau, Chantal. 1986. "Associations et pouvoirs publics: Vingt années d'évolution." *Les cahiers de l'animation* 1 (55): 5–19.

Carré, Jean-Jacques, Paul Dubois, and Edmond Malinvaud. 1972. *La croissance française: Un essai d'analyse économique causale de l'après-guerre*. Paris: Seuil.

Cholvy, G., and Y.-M. Hilaire. 1988. *Histoire religieuse de la France contemporaine (1930–1988)*. Paris: Privat.

Chomel, André. 1985. "Les acteurs de l'économie sociale." In *Les cahiers français: L'économie sociale: Entre étatisation et capitalisme* 221:7–8. Paris: Documentation française.

Clark, Priscilla. 1987. *Literary France: The Making of a Culture*. Berkeley and Los Angeles: University of California Press.

CNVA (Conseil national de la vie associative). 1989. *Associations et communication*. Paris: Documentation française.

Cobban, Alfred. 1961. *A History of Modern France*. Vol. 2, *1799–1945*. Baltimore: Penguin.

Conan, Eric. 1978. "Démocratie locale." *Esprit* (June): 35–41.

Coutrot, Aline, and François G. Dreyfus. 1965. *Les forces religieuses dans la société française*. Paris: Armand Colin.

Crozier, Michel. 1964. *The Bureaucratic Phenomenon*. Chicago: University of Chicago Press.

Debray, Régis. 1979. *Le pouvoir intellectuel en France*. Paris: Editions Ramsay.

Donegani, Jean-Marie. 1984. "L'appartenance au catholicisme français." *Revue française de science politique* 34 (2): 197–228.

Ehrmann, Henry W. 1983. *Politics in France*. 4th ed. Boston: Little, Brown and Co.

Europa Year Book. 1988. "France." London: Europa Publications.

Feron, François. 1989. "La gauche, la droite, et les Tiers-votants." *Libération*, 15 March, 3.

Ferry, Luc, and Alain Renaut. 1985. *La pensée 68: Essai sur l'anti-humanisme contemporain*. Paris: Gallimard.

Flower, J. E. 1987. "The Church." In *France Today*, edited by J. E. Flower, pp. 170–89. London: Methuen.

Forsé, Michel. 1984. "Les créations d'associations: Un indicateur de changement social." *Les cahiers de l'animation* 4 (47): 3–23.

Garraud, Philippe. 1985. "Enjeux associatifs locaux et stratégies municipales." *Les cahiers de l'animation* 4 (52): 27–43.

Goguel, François. 1952. *France under the Fourth Republic*. Ithaca: Cornell University Press.

Grémion, Pierre. 1978. "Les associations et le pouvoir local." *Esprit* (June): 19–31.

Guéhenno, Jean-Marie. 1987. "France and the Electronic Media: The Economics of Freedom." In *The Mitterrand Experiment*, edited by G. Ross, S. Hoffmann, and S. Malzacher, pp. 151–77. Cambridge: Polity Press.

Habermas, Jürgen. 1989. *The Structural Transformation of the Public Sphere: An Inquiry into a Category of Bourgeois Society*. Translated by Thomas Burger. Cambridge, Mass.: MIT Press.

Hall, Peter. 1986. *Governing the Economy: The Politics of State Intervention in Britain and France*. New York: Oxford University Press.

Handbook of Nations. 1987. 7th ed. Detroit: Gale Records.

Hanley, David. 1986. *Keeping Left? Ceres and the French Socialist Party*. Manchester: Manchester University Press.

Hoffmann, Stanley, 1963. "The Paradoxes of the French Political Community." In *In Search of France*, edited by Stanley Hoffmann, pp. 262–83. Cambridge, Mass.: Harvard University Press.

Hohendahl, Peter Uwe. 1979. "Critical Theory, Public Sphere, and Culture." *New German Critique* 16:89–118.

Hughes, H. Stuart. 1968. *The Obstructed Path: French Social Thought in the Years of Desperation, 1930–1960*. New York: Harper and Row.

IMF (International Monetary Fund). 1988. *International Financial Statistics Yearbook*. Washington, D.C.: IMF.

———. 1989. *World Economic Outlook* (April). Washington, D.C.: IMF.

INSEE (Institut national d'études statisques et économiques). 1987. *Annuaire statistique de la France*. Vol. 92, no. 34. Paris: Documentation française.

Ion, Jacques. 1988. "Le modèle associatif entre l'idéal démocratique et la nostalgie de corps intermédiaires." *La revue de l'économie sociale* (April): 115–19.

Jenson, Jane. 1982. "The Modern Women's Movement in Italy, France, and Great Britain." In *Comparative Social Research*, edited by R. F. Tommasen, pp. 35–53. Greenwich, Conn.: JAI Press.

Kepel, Gilles. 1987. *Les banlieues de l'Islam: Naissance d'une religion en France*. Paris: Seuil.

La Croix. 1989. "Sondage: Les Français aiment leurs associations," 26 October, 16–17.

Ladrech, Robert. 1989. "Social Movements and Party Systems: The French Socialist Party and New Social Movements." *West European Politics* 12 (3): 262–79.

Lagrange, François. 1986. "Social Security in France from 1946 to 1982." In *Nationalizing Social Security in Europe and America*, edited by D. E. Ashford and E. W. Kelley. Greenwich, Conn.: JAI Press.

Lamont, Michèle. 1987. "How to Become a Dominant French Philosopher: The case of Jacques Derrida." *American Journal of Sociology* 93 (3): 584–622.

Langlois, Claude, and Timothy Tackett. 1980. "A l'épreuve de la Révolution (1770–1830)." In *Histoire des catholiques en France du XVe siècle à nos jours*, edited by François Lebrun, pp. 299–322. Paris: Privat.

Le Monde. 1989. "Une enquête du CREDOC: Les associations 'militantes' perdent leurs adhérents," 11 January.

Le Net, Michel. 1988. *La communication sociale*. Paris: Documentation française.

Le Net, Michel, and Jean Werquin. 1985. *Le volontariat*. Paris: Documentation française.

Lettre d'information de la Fonda. 1989. "Des chiffres marquants," no. 66.

Lettre du crédit coopératif. 1990. "Le poids économique du bénévolat," 37:11–12.

Libération. 1989. "Les sages intègrent le foulard dans la laïcité," 28 November, 2.

———. 1989. "Réactions," 28 November, 5.

Lipovetsky, Gilles. 1983. *L'ère du vide: Essais sur l'individualisme contemporain*. Paris: Gallimard.

McQuail, Denis. 1987. *Mass Communication Theory*. 2d ed. London: Sage.

Maire, Edmond. 1988. "La résistance syndicale." *Le Nouvel Observateur*, 3–9 June.

Mantrant, S. 1984. "La France à l'écart." In "Le mouvement pour le désarmement et la paix," edited by J. G. Vaillancourt and Ronald Babin, pp. 94–111. Special issue of *Revue internationale d'action communautaire* 12 (52).

Martin, Jean-Paul. 1988. "A la recherche d'un 'modèle associatif laïc.' " *La revue de l'économie sociale* (April): 133–43.

Mendras, Henri. 1988. *La Seconde Révolution française, 1965–1984*. Paris: Gallimard.

Michel, Patrick. 1985. "Christianisme: La désaffection des fidèles." In *L'état de la France et de ses habitants*, edited by Jean-Yves Potel, pp. 541–86. Paris: Découverte.

Miège, Bernard. 1989. *La société conquise par la communication*. Grenoble: Presses universitaires de Grenoble.

Mouriaux, R. 1988. "Stratégies syndicales face au chômage et à l'intervention industrielle de l'Etat dans la période 1962–87." Paper delivered at the conference "In Search of the New France," Brandeis University, Boston, May.

Mueller-Rommel, F. 1982. "Ecology Parties in Western Europe." *West European Politics* 5:68–74.

Noreau, Pierre. 1989. "L'action collective des jeunes issus de l'immigration en France (1981–1988)." Doct. diss., Institut d'études politiques de Paris.

Palard, Jacques. 1988. "Les associations nationales à l'épreuve de la décentralisation." *La revue de l'économie sociale* (April): 93–104.

Perrineau, Pascal. 1989. "Les étapes d'une implantation électorale." In *Le Front national à découvert*, edited by Nonna Mayer and Pascal Perrineau, pp. 269–95. Paris: Presses de la Fondation nationale des sciences politiques.

Petit, Pascal. 1988. "The Economy and Modernisation: An Overview." In *France and Modernisation*, edited by John Gaffney, pp. 1–35. Aldershot, England: Avebury.

Philippe, Patricia. 1988. "Les concerts de SOS-Racisme." *Le Nouvel Observateur*, 2–8 September, 51.

Pierce, Roy. 1973. *French Politics and Political Institutions*. 2d ed. New York: Harper and Row.

Pinard, M., and R. Hamilton. Forthcoming. "Intellectuals and the Leadership of Social Movements: Some Comparative Perspectives." In *Research on Social Movements, Conflicts, and Change*. Greenwich, Conn.: JAI Press.

Pinto, Diana. 1988. "Toward a Mellowing of the French Identity?" *Yearbook of French Studies* 18:1–19.

Porter, Vincent. 1989. "The Re-regulation of Television: Pluralism, Constitutionality, and the Free Market in the U.S.A., West Germany, France, and the U.K." *Media, Culture, and Society* 11 (1): 5–27.

Poujol, Geneviève. 1988. "Les créations d'associations dans une nouvelle problématique privé/public." *La revue de l'économie sociale* (April): 109–14.

Rand Smith, W. 1987. *Crisis in the French Labor Movement: A Grass-roots Perspective*. New York: St. Martin's Press.

Reader, Keith A. 1987. *Intellectuals and the Left in France since 1968*. London: Macmillan.

Rose, Arnold. 1954. *Theory and Method in the Social Sciences*. St. Paul: University of Minnesota Press.

Roudet, Bernard. 1984. "Réseaux d'associations, réseaux de militants: Une étude de cas." *Les cahiers de l'animation* 4 (47): 35–54.

———. 1988. "Bilan des recherches sur la vie associative." *La revue de l'économie sociale* (April): 11–28.

Schain, Martin. 1987. "The National Front in France and the Construction of Political Legitimacy." *West European Politics* 10 (2): 229–52.

Schmidt, Vivien A. 1987. "Decentralization: A Revolutionary Reform." In *The French Socialists in Power, 1981–1986*, edited by Patrick McCarthy, pp. 111–37. New York: Greenwood Press.

Schnapper, Dominique. 1988. "Sur la commission de la nationalité." *Esprit* (June): 54–63.

Seibel, Wolfgang. 1989. "The Function of Mellow Weakness: Nonprofit Organizations as Problem Nonsolvers in Germany." In *The Nonprofit Sector in International Perspective: Studies in Comparative Culture and Policy*, edited by Estelle James, pp. 40–73. New York: Oxford University Press.

———. 1990. "Government Third-Sector Relationship in a Comparative Perspective: The Cases of France and West Germany." *Voluntas* 1 (1): 42–60.

Service aux associations. 1987. *Guide pratique des associations*. Paris: Service aux associations.

Taguieff, Pierre-André. 1989. "Un programme 'révolutionnaire'?" In *Le Front national à découvert*, edited by Nonna Mayer and Pascal Perrineau, pp. 211–23. Paris: Presses de la Fondation nationale des sciences politiques.

Théry, Henri. 1986. "La place et le rôle du secteur associatif dans le développement de la politique d'action éducative, sanitaire, et sociale." *Journal officiel de la Republique française*, 29 July, 9–21.

Touraine, Alain. 1988. "Supplique à Harlem." *Le Nouvel Observateur*, 18–24 March, 40.

Trotignon, Yves. 1984. *La France au XXe siècle*. Vol. 2. Paris: Bordas.

Tuppen, John. 1988. *France under Recession, 1981–86*. London: Macmillan.

UNESCO. 1987. *Statistical Yearbook*. The Hague: UNESCO.

United Nations. 1987. *Statistical Yearbook*. The Hague: United Nations.

Viard, Jean. 1989. "Le dérangement marseillais." In *Le Front national à découvert*, edited by Nonna Mayer and Pascal Perrineau, pp. 301–20. Paris: Presses de la Fondation nationale des sciences politiques.

Wilson, Frank L. 1987. *Interest-Group Politics in France*. Cambridge: Cambridge University Press.

———. 1988. The French Party System in the 1980s." In *Parties and Party Systems in Liberal Democracies*, edited by Steven B. Wolinetz, pp. 15–30. London: Routledge.

Wright, Vincent. 1983. *The Government and Politics of France*. 2d ed. New York: Holmes and Meier.

Wylie, Laurence. 1973. *Village in the Vaucluse*. Cambridge, Mass.: Harvard University Press.

CHAPTER SIX

Italy: Why No Voluntary Sector?

Ted Perlmutter

THE SECTOR of private, nonprofit activity, the "third sector," does not play a determinant role in the Italian public sphere.[1] As Banterle and Cella (1984) have argued, a third sector requires a history of autonomous, pluralistic groups and the absence of deep societal cleavage. Italy lacks a rich tradition of grassroots, associational life. If a contemporary Tocqueville searched for autonomous groups on which to write on "democracy in Italy," he would produce a thin volume indeed.[2] In Italy, political parties have a firm purchase on all aspects of public life. Parties usurp space that in other advanced industrialized countries is held by bureaucracies and by local grass-roots organizations. It is hardly an exaggeration to say that they pervade all aspects of political, economic, and social life in Italy. Political parties also shape the oppositional forms that emerge. Social movements, which develop in reaction to the pervasiveness of the party system, play a far greater role than the third sector in changing the dimensions of the public sphere.

In Italy, political parties embody the divisions between left and right, and between secular and Catholic culture. Although these cultural divisions are in decline, they are still strong enough to make it difficult for any group to advance its claims in a universalistic language. These divisions are historically rooted in the process of state-formation, when power was concentrated in the hands of the central authority to the detriment of local initiative and when the divisions between church and secular authority became hardened.

This chapter will start by providing a historical overview of Italian political and societal development before 1945, showing how the weakness of that development in turn hindered the growth of the public sphere. The chapter will turn first to the actors—political parties, social movements, and the Catholic church—that have shaped the development of the public sphere, and then to the changes in the economy and the welfare state that structure the possibilities for the emergence of a third sector as an alternative. The final sections will

---

[1] This chapter has benefited from the critical readings of Alex Reichl, Mabel Berezin, and Robert Wuthnow. I also owe a debt of gratitude to Piero Gastaldo of the Fondazione Giovanni Agnelli for assistance in gathering materials for the project.

[2] Joseph LaPalombara's (1987) reflections on Italian democracy produced a detailed analysis (and defense) of the political elites and very little on grass-roots movements.

analyze the condition of the third sector and discuss the possibilities for changes in the Italian public sphere.

The Historical Legacy

The limits on the public sphere in Italy can be seen starting with its earliest phases of state building. Italy's experience as a republic is short-lived, dating only from 1948. It was unified as a country with its present boundaries in 1870. In its first fifty years, Italy was governed by a constitutional monarchy with a weak party system and, until 1913, a restricted franchise. From Mussolini's march on Rome in 1922 until the fall of fascism in 1943, there existed only the most manipulated form of a public sphere.

Italy's national unification and its subsequent political and economic development were characterized by an incomplete nation-building effort, described by Antonio Gramsci as a "passive revolution."[3] The unification of Italy grew out of the military domination of the North over the South. A large part of the population was not involved in or affected directly by the unification of the country. The physical unification of the Italian state was only the beginning of the difficult process of creating an Italian nation. The republics and monarchies that united to form Italy had diverse political heritages. In addition, the North and the South were at very different stages of cultural and economic development. Milan and Turin had far more in common with Paris and London than they did with Naples and Palermo. The lack of a common language further complicated the creation of an Italian national identity. More than 99 percent of Italy's largely peasant population was unable to read or write Italian. The creation of a public sphere required more than the unification of the country.

The economic policies of the liberal regime maintained this distance between the North and the South. In exchange for not disrupting political and economic arrangements within the South, northern elites were given a free hand to pursue policies that encouraged northern economic development at the expense of the South, where traditional feudal social relations and equally oppressive political relations were maintained. This policy exacerbated the economic differences between the two regions.[4]

The Catholic church refused to recognize or support the state of Italy. It forbade its members either to vote in Italian elections or to stand for political office. It was not until 1929, when the church signed a concordat and a treaty

---

[3] The latter phrase is Gramsci's description of a political revolution that did not include the peasantry (1975:1767, 1772–74). A concise, Gramscian interpretation of nineteenth-century Italian political developments is to be found in Ginsborg (1979).

[4] As Bagnasco argues, this economic union was not altogether in favor of the North, which had to embed its plans for economic growth within a society whose fundamental stasis could not be overcome (1987:30–31).

with Mussolini, that it finally regularized its relations with the Italian state. The pacts recognized the diplomatic autonomy of the Vatican, gave the church a significant role in religious education in public schools, and compensated it for the lands taken from the church during Italian unification (Smith 1969:441–43).

The constitutional monarchy that ruled Italy from 1860 to 1922 was ill-equipped to carry out the task of building an Italian nation. The republican aspirations that had animated Italy's unification remained frustrated. The constitution had granted considerable powers to the monarchy, most notably control over the military and hence foreign affairs, and the right for the king to choose which minister would form a government.

It was the narrowness of the franchise that most limited the growth of the public sphere. Until 1913, the parliament had been elected by a small minority who could meet certain property requirements. These restrictions meant that few groups were active or represented in public life. Political parties were coteries of nobles, with little in the way of firm policies or organizational strength. The fluidity of party boundaries was illustrated by the prevalence of transformismo—the willingness of opposition parliamentarians to abandon their parties and to become part of the dominant coalition. Similar concerns shaped the administrative structure of the state. Political authority was highly centralized, with prefects having strong control over provincial and local officials. Mayors, for example, were appointed rather than elected. The bureaucracy that emerged was directly subordinated to the political interests of the parties' elites.[5] Although there were movements sympathetic to more federalist systems, the ruling elites feared that decentralization would give the many opponents of the regime too much power.

The weakness of the public sphere was both a cause and a consequence of the unresolved tensions between church and state and between the North and the South. Because the state's legitimacy was slight, particularly among southern peasants, over whom the church exercised considerable influence, the state was reluctant to broaden the arena of conflict. These limits hindered the state's capacity to strengthen civil society. Fascism followed shortly on the heels of a mass franchise, which had undermined the previous electoral domination of the Liberal party. In the aftermath of World War I, labor militancy in northern industrial cities and agrarian unrest in the Po River valley disrupted the social order. In reaction to these movements and to the government's incapacity to respond, a Fascist party emerged to destroy these movements and to restore order.[6] Fascism shrunk the domain of the public sphere. It dimin-

[5] Unlike in England and Germany, this administrative apparatus failed to establish its own autonomy. For an intriguing argument tying this weak development to the strength of the state and to the timing of the growth of mass franchise in these three countries, see Shefter (1977).

[6] For an account that emphasizes all the missed opportunities and weakness of will on the part of the Socialists, and particularly the Liberals, see Smith (1969).

ished the role of parliament, abolished the free press, and manipulated the cinema and, to a lesser extent, the theater (Berezin, forthcoming). While the state requested symbolic allegiance to its rituals, it did not require that Italians act as citizens. In the words of Franco Catalano, fascism "had relieved them of the civic duty of looking after their own communities, and had accustomed them to taking no part in political life" (Catalano 1972:79).

The eventual defeat of fascism grew out of Italy's military debacles during World War II. The collapse of Mussolini's government in 1943 was followed by a military movement, dominated by the Communists, but including other groups of partisans as well, that helped defeat the German occupying army. The resistance was more a symbol than a military force. It provided a hegemonic myth of a country that fought to free itself of fascism. This myth would sustain the postwar governments and help erase the memory of Italians' acquiescence to fascism. It gave the Communist party a greater role in determining the postwar solution and also broadened the party's base and conception of a mass party. It taught the art of compromise across ideological divides between the various groups that were part of the committees that fought to liberate Italy.

Between 1943 and 1948, the fundamental shape of the postwar distribution of power was established. The governments that emerged after the war were dominated by parties that represented groups that had previously played a minor role on the stage of Italian politics—the Communists and the Christian Democrats. In 1946, the monarchy was abolished by popular vote, and subsequently a republican form of government with a strong parliament and a weak executive was established. The constitution reflected a compromise between left and right. The language of rights and obligations of the state, which would provide a justification for the rights of labor to organize and for the welfare state, reflected the interests of the Left. The provisions accepting the 1929 Vatican treaties into article 7 of the constitution were a significant and highly controversial concession to the Catholic church and the Christian Democratic party.

POLITICAL PARTIES

In the post–World War II era, political parties have become dominant in the Italian public sphere and they pervade all aspects of social and political life. They have politicized the bureaucracy, and, through it, have come to exercise a substantial influence over the Italian economy. An analysis of the public sphere and the possibilities for its transformation requires an understanding both of the structure of the party system and of the coalitions that have emerged over the past forty years. Party dominance is reflected in the term *partitocrazia,* or rule by party, used to describe the anomalies of the Italian party system.[7]

This domination by parties comes at the expense of the state's bureaucracy, which has been colonized by its clientelistic practices, and at the expense of other organizations of civil society, which find that all activity must be negotiated through parties. The Italian bureaucracy is similar in size to that of other European countries. It has 4,500,000 employees, or roughly 5.3 public employees per 100,000 people. This compares with rates of 5.9 in Germany, 6.2 in France, and 8.2 in Britain (Spotts and Weiser 1986:129). Its growth was more substantial in the 1970s than in the 1980s. If one considers only those who work directly for the state and the related quasi-public institutions, one sees a growth from 1,697,020 in 1970, to 2,145,960 in 1980, to 2,362,360 in 1986. This represents an annual growth rate of 2.6 percent in the decades of the 1970s, but only of 1.7 percent in the first six years of the 1980s.[8]

The state that the parties control is one that has more power over the market than do most European states. The most unusual economic instruments are the state-run industrial corporations. These corporations are holding companies, with government-appointed directors, that also raise capital on the private market. The largest of these is the Instituto per la Ricostruzione Industriale (IRI), with six hundred subsidiaries, including substantial holdings in metalworking industries, shipbuilding, transportation, and state radio and television. The second largest, the Ente Nationale Idrocarburi (ENI), is a major firm with three hundred subsidiaries in energy (nuclear and non-nuclear), chemicals, and petroleum, with textile and engineering holdings as well (Spotts and Weiser 1986:138). These holding companies were the third and seventh largest companies in Europe in 1976 (Sassoon 1986:140). Through its various banking institutions, the state also controls 80 percent of the credit (Spotts and Weiser 1986:139).

Italy has a multiparty system, with between nine and twelve parties in parliament at any one time. One party, the Christian Democratic party (Democrazia Christiana, or DC), has always been a part of the governing coalition, an event unparalleled in Western democracies. Another party, the Communist party (Partito Comunista Italiana, or PCI), has always been excluded from government. As the PCI's strength has oscillated between one-fourth and one-third of the electorate, this prejudicial strategy has introduced severe imbalances and immobility into the system.[9]

---

[7] In Sartori's more clinical language, "the Italian situation represents an extreme case of partisan hypertrophy" (1976:88).

[8] Although it is dated, the best account in English of the Italian bureaucracy remains Allum (1973:139–72). For an argument about how bureaucratic immobility leads to corruption, see Chubb and Vannicelli (1988).

[9] As Mershon (forthcoming) argues, it is the assurance that one political coalition will vary incrementally from the previous one that reduces the risks of rapid turnover of governments.

By demonstrating unparalleled strength and political durability, both parties are anomalies within the party systems of Western Europe. Both have continued to represent substantial parts of the electorate despite changes in society that have undermined their social bases. The Communist party has withstood a decline in the importance of industrial workers in the Italian economy. The Christian Democratic party has maintained its dominant role despite increasing secularization within the world of Italian catholicism. Other parties, primarily the Socialist, have tried to take advantage of the increasing political space available for alternatives, but have not fundamentally changed the rules of the game or founded a new governing coalition.

Understanding the barriers to change requires analyzing the formal rules of the game and the strategies different political parties have pursued. Despite the image of Italy as a country with constantly changing governments, the rules of the game and the underlying political structure have led to great continuities. The two factors that lead most directly to this continuity are the electoral system and the patterns of political subcultures.

The Italian system is a relatively pure form of proportional representation, with a low threshold for parties to gain entrance to parliament, and with candidates running on lists within various districts. This system of proportional representation means that, unlike in single-member district systems such as that of England, changes in votes are directly reflected in electoral outcomes.[10] The small number of votes required to elect a representative to parliament, roughly three hundred thousand votes with sufficient concentration to elect a single candidate in one district, facilitates social movements adopting an electoral strategy.[11]

The electoral balance between different parts of the political spectrum has remained relatively constant since 1948. The share of the vote for left-wing parties, the Communists and the Socialists, has varied between 35 percent and 40 percent; the share of the vote for secular parties of the center, the Liberal, Social Democratic, and Republican parties, has been 8 percent to 10 percent, and the vote for the Christian Democrats has varied between 35 percent and 40 percent. Parties of the extreme left and right, which have been beyond any political coalition, account for another 8 percent and 10 percent of the vote (Spotts and Weiser 1986:9). There has also been little variation between elections, particularly during the period between 1958 and 1972, with an average variation of no more than 3 percent per year (Parisi and Pasquino 1980:7).

The second aspect that lends continuity to Italian electoral patterns is the stability of subcultural voting. These votes tend more to be testimonies to who people are, and to the social networks in which they are embedded, than to

[10] For a comparison of electoral effects on voting changes, see Allum (1973:77–78).
[11] For a discussion of the effects of the Italian political system on ecological politics, see Diani (1988:177–78).

rational calculations as to which candidate will advance their individual interests.[12] This vote of "belonging" (*appartanenza*) tends to occur in specific regions where the subcultures are strong: in the Catholic or "white" regions in the northeast, including Trento-Alto Adige, Friuli Venezia Giulia, and Eastern Lombardia, and in the Communist or "red" regions in the center, including Emiglia-Romagna, Tuscany, the Marches, Umbria, and some of southern Lombardia.[13]

The evolution of postwar political coalitions shows a general, if limited, move to the left. The Communist party that emerged from World War II was a far different party from the one that went underground in 1922. The model of a *partito nuovo*, a new party, supplanted the Leninist model. Instead of a small, homogeneous party, in which members were committed to the ideology of the party doctrines, there would be an open party, in which membership required only an agreement on the party's political platform.[14] Particular efforts were made to be open to Catholic votes and participation within the party. The Christian Democratic party emerged out of fascism with a great deal of strength, which came from its relation to the Catholic church, whose lay association Catholic Action was one of the few organizations to have any autonomy during the twenty years of fascist rule. It was the grass-roots structure of the church that provided the Christian Democratic party with the organizational infrastructure for its electoral campaigns.

Fanned by the ideological competition of the cold war, the first national electoral campaigns were highly inflammatory and polarized. The church saw these elections as contests between the champions and the destroyers of civilization (Wertman 1982:87).[15] The United States intervened by encouraging and financing divisions within the unitary governmental coalitions and the union movement in the late 1940s.

The Catholic church sought to use the dependence of the Christian Democratic party to influence the party. This interference provoked increasing reaction on the part of Christian Democratic officials. In the mid-1950s, when Arnaldo Fanfani was prime minister, he used the state-run industries as a source of political patronage to develop an alternative base of support in lieu of the church. This development of patronage fragmented the party into factions but cemented the power of the Christian Democrats as a party of govern-

[12] On the development of this argument, see Parisi and Pasquino (1980). For an interesting elaboration, see LaPalombara (1987).

[13] The role of the clergy in the nineteenth century shaped these voting patterns. In the northeastern regions, the church was seen as representing the interests of the peasantry and defending Italian nationalism against Austrian rulers. In the central regions, the church was seen as an oppressive force linked to papal states (J. Hellman 1987:138–40).

[14] For an extraordinary synthetic essay contrasting the French and Italian Communist parties' development, see Tarrow (1977). For a discussion of the ambiguities and complexities within this doctrine of the *partito nuovo*, see S. Hellman (1988:20–40) and Lange (1980).

[15] To vote Communist was to risk excommunication (Kertzer 1980:106).

ment.[16] The strength of the Christian Democrats was the multiplicity of its bases of legitimacy and support. It was not just a Catholic party, a patronage party, or an anti-Communist party; it had all these components within it.

While the division of votes between the Left and the Right has been relatively stable, the coalitions increasingly took on partners of the Left in the 1960s and 1970s. Between 1963 and 1972, there was a center-left coalition between the Christian Democrats and the Socialists. Between 1976 and 1979, there was a government of the Christian Democrats supported by the Communist party. The center-left coalition sought to enact policy reforms, but found itself held hostage to the more conservative elements in its coalition, and floundered without making substantial progress.

In the early 1970s, the Communist party moved toward being a party of government. In the historic compromise, Enrico Berlinguer, the general secretary of the Communist party, theorized that for a country such as Italy, it was not possible for the Communist party to come to power with a minimal electoral majority. A coalition with the Christian Democrats was necessary. With its electoral support waning, the Christian Democratic party partially accepted this proposal after the 1976 elections. A government of the "constitutional arc" was founded, whereby the Communist party would support the government from the outside, in exchange for policy and patronage concessions and the expectation that it would become a full member of the government at a later time. As it became apparent that the DC would not let the Communist party into the government, and as the costs grew of being a part of a coalition that it could not induce to carry out serious reforms, but whose policies it was responsible for nonetheless, the Communist party withdrew its support in 1979.

Although its policy legacy was more substantial, as will be seen in the discussion of the welfare state, the outcome of the historic compromise, in terms of party coalitions, was similar to the fate of the center-left coalitions of the 1960s. Constructing an alliance between the DC and a party that had been previously considered too left-wing to govern presented the possibility of including a broader constituency in the government. In both cases, however, the incapacity of the DC fully to support reform meant that the coalitions dissolved without accomplishing their goals, much to the electoral and political damage of the partners.

In the 1980s, the party that seemed most capable of taking advantage of this breakdown of traditional loyalties was the Socialist party. Before Bettino Craxi took over and remade the Socialist party in the mid-1970s, its history had been one of internal fragmentation, rapid changes in political line, subor-

[16] The dominance in the party of those who came from Catholic positions of power was maintained until the early 1970s (Pasquino 1980:89). On the comparative weights and the modes of mobilizing business and religious elites within the DC, see LaPalombara (1964:252–348) and Martinelli (1980).

dination to the PCI, and gradual decline in political strength. Craxi rapidly centralized the power under his control and reversed the party's previous alliance with the PCI. He entered into a five-party alliance, or *pentapartito*, with the Christian Democrats and the other small centerist parties. The governing strategy was based on neoliberal policies that would decrease the power of the trade unions and cut back on the welfare state. The coalition sought institutional reform to make the government more efficient. The Socialist party had theretofore not substantially altered the system of alliances that shape the public sphere. It had not increased its vote enough to claim equal footing with the DC within the five-party coalition, nor had it diminished the strength of the Communists enough to claim hegemony over an alliance of the left. While its vote had increased to 15 percent, the Socialist party never achieved the electoral breakthrough that it always anticipated and often promised. Thus, the decade of the 1980s produced little transformation in Italian politics. Despite the pervasiveness of the party system, its frequent immobility provides the space in which social movements can flourish.[17]

SOCIAL MOVEMENTS

Social movements have provided the sharpest challenge to the traditional structure of the public sphere. Urban movements challenged the planning process, called for greater representation at the neighborhood level, and occupied public housing (Marcelloni 1981; Perlmutter 1988a, 1988b). Feminist movements called for a revision in the legislation on abortion, defended women's right to divorce, and demanded legislation on sexual violence (J. Hellman 1987; Beckwith 1987; Ergas 1986). Ecological parties challenged the development of nuclear power (Diani 1988; Biorcio and Lodi 1988). The cycle of protest movements that started in 1967 with student protests and lasted until the mid-1970s formed a generation of activists whose involvement would continue long after the protest wave stopped (Tarrow 1989b:330–33).

These movements challenged not only the values and policies of the Italian political establishment but also the modalities of political activity. They sought a new way of doing politics (*un nuovo modo di fare politica*), one that involved more direct and disruptive forms. This search for a different mode of opposition accounts both for the attractiveness of politics to a new generation of activists and for the difficulty these movements had in either sustaining an autonomous opposition or engaging in more traditional politics.

Italian social movements follow a pattern distinct from those in other European countries. The reasons for this can partially be found in the patterns of belated economic development and in the openness of the party system. From

[17] For a picture of the context in which the 1968 movements emerged, see Tarrow (1989b:35–38).

a European perspective, the urban movements are advanced and articulate, while the ecological movements are late, derivative, and weak. The urban movements were strong because they were direct responses to the costs placed on the northern industrial working class as a result of the massive migration of workers from the South and to the problems of lumpen groups in southern cities. This industrialization and regional equilibration had already occurred in most other European countries. Correspondingly, there is a smaller middle-class pool from which to recruit an ecology movement. Indeed, if one compares the size of professional classes, one sees that in Italy only 7.3 percent were so employed in the mid-1970s, as opposed to the European average of 11.2 percent, and 14.2 percent in the United States.

Italy has also been slow to move to a "postmaterialist" set of values. The centrality of working-class beliefs in Italy can be seen in the analysis Ronald Inglehardt has done on value change in Western Europe. Inglehardt claims that the fundamental value cleavage in Western Europe is between materialist values, concerning "material well-being and physical security," and postmaterialist values, concerning quality of life. Working with a data set of six countries (Britain, Germany, France, Belgium, the Netherlands, and Italy), he discerns a dramatic change between surveys done in 1971–1972 and 1986–1987 that occurs for most of the countries, but that does not hold for Italy. In the early period, for the set of countries an average of 29 percent more people described themselves as materialist than postmaterialist; by the latter period this difference had declined to only 10 percent. In Italy the difference changed only 1 percent throughout this time period, remaining at 24 percent.[18]

By the nature of its rules and its members, the Italian party system is open to new challengers, both in the way that parties support or compete with social movements and in the low electoral threshold for groups to elect members to parliament.[19] Particularly in Italy, social movements encounter the established parties not only as models of parliamentary behavior, but also as models of opposition. For example, in the mid-1970s, the Italian Communist party called itself a party of "movement" as well as a party of "government." Although the Radical party at times sought to elect its candidates to parliament, it criticized both the limiting of politics to parliament and parliamentary rules and norms.

The Communist party's dual role made for an ambivalent political posture toward social movements. As a party that challenged the system it presented a framework within which groups could develop. It provided resources, endorsed demands, and shaped legislation that supported the goals of various

[18] Data are taken from table 2.6 in Inglehardt (1990:95).

[19] It has also been argued that the strong left-wing parties provided a political training ground for those who would become leaders of the movements (Tarrowd 1989b:159–63) and who espoused a revolutionary ideology that movements could see themselves carrying out (Schnapp and Vidal-Naquet 1971).

social movements. As a party that aspired to government, the PCI defended the institutions of the state and sought to undermine the state's more radical opponents. The party's Marxist heritage led it to view conflicts as resulting from antagonisms between the working class and the capitalist class.[20] The party saw urban, ecological, and feminist issues as either secondary or as not within its direct purview, and it was therefore resistant to addressing them.[21] Throughout the 1970s, the party's strategies led it to dampen the more radical enthusiasms and tactics of social movements, and to seek alliances, or at least to avoid open conflict, with the Christian Democratic party. These ambiguities made the party a tempting but uncertain ally for social movements.

The Radical party illustrates the kind of party that can flourish in a proportional-representation system that has a low voting threshold. In national elections, its share of the vote ranges from 1.1 percent to 3.5 percent. Founded in 1955 as a left-wing offshoot of the Liberal party, the Radical party attained prominence in the early 1970s under its charismatic leader, Marco Pannella. The party has taken a progressive and anticlerical stance in its defense of liberalized laws on abortion and divorce (Clark, Hine, and Irving 1974). Its constituency is made up of young, liberal to left-wing voters. In the mid-1970s, it attacked the draconian laws aimed at terrorists that restricted the rights of the accused. It has generally supported the rights of embattled groups such as feminists, gays, and conscientious objectors. To accomplish these ends, the Radical party has been willing to adopt the tactics of social movements: demonstrations, sit-ins, and hunger strikes. Most critically for the political system, it has shown the value of the referendum as a political tactic, which, with a majority vote, can be used to abrogate the provisions of most laws. The party proved to be a natural, if at times overbearing, ally of certain wings of the ecological and feminist movements.

The openness of the party system and the potential for alliances heightened the strategic dilemmas of social movements. In all countries, groups could seek either to maintain an independent path or try to work within a partylike organization. The attendant risk of the latter strategy is that the benefits of increased resources and support would be offset by the difficulty of maintaining the protest groups's agenda. These groups could seek to become political parties, with the risk that a part of their constituency would favor dissolving the organization before they would participate in electoral politics. In Italy, the option to become involved in the political system was particularly attractive.

[20] On the problems the PCI had in carrying out these ambiguous politics in the 1970s and the debates regarding the "workerist" tendencies within the Italian left, see Golden (1988) and Tarrow (1989a).

[21] In comparison with other European countries, this resistance should not be exaggerated. Southern European countries, with their tradition of stronger left-wing parties, have been more powerful proponents of women's rights than northern Social Democratic parties (Klein 1987:41–42).

In the cases of urban, feminist, and ecology groups, an initial phase of distrust for activities within established political channels was followed by intense debates over how to respond to the political parties. In some circumstances, groups compromised; in others, they dissolved rather than become like the parties they had so strongly opposed. But in all cases, the possibilities of parliamentary politics were so enticing that they shaped the movements' responses.

It was the intense politicization of the Italian public sphere that made social movements such a powerful challenge. They were born in response to the problems of the party system, and their subsequent development was shaped by their interactions with that system. They brought new activists into political life, raised new issues, and broadened the range of political tactics (Tarrow 1989b:325–36). Concerns that in other countries would be addressed through more autonomous voluntary associations in Italy are taken up by social movements.

CHURCH AND SOCIETY

If social movements represent an episodic but potentially transformative possibility for the public sphere, then the church's presence is the opposite: constant, but steadily declining in importance. The church's declining political influence results from its diminishing role in civil society. These changes can be seen as following from the secularization of Italians' religious beliefs, the renegotiating of the juridical relations between the church and state, and changes within the organizational structure of the church. Although there are disagreements as to its exact dimensions, there has been a general decrease in religiosity in Italy.[22] Weekly church attendance, which was 69 percent in 1956, declined to 48 percent in 1968 and 35 percent in 1980 (Wertman 1982:100). While this decline in church support and membership has been on the same level as that in Spain and Portugal, and thus substantially smaller than in France, West Germany, and the Netherlands (Berger 1987:108), it has nonetheless undermined the church's capacity to influence society.

The numbers of those who consider themselves practicing Catholics have declined from 90.8 percent in 1970 to 83.6 percent in 1980, but the quantitative aspect is only part of the picture (*World Christian Encyclopedia* 1982:531). As Franco Garelli defines the problem, religion has ceased to

[22] For a disaggregation of the different trends in secularization in Italy, see Ricolfi (1988). Italy is, of course, overwhelmingly Catholic. Of the people who declare a religion, 97 percent describe themselves as Catholics. Starting in the mid-1960s, there was a minor growth in the number of evangelicals. The most recent estimates count eighty thousand traditional evangelicals, thirty-five thousand neopentecostal evangelicals, and one hundred fifty thousand members of the apocalyptic church. Other groups include forty thousand Jews and between thirty thousand and fifty thousand members of the Eastern Orthodox church (Dal Ferro 1988:296).

shape the identities of believers: "The decline of religion is not to be found in the falling away or in the weakening of faith, as much as in the fact that the coherence or internal congruence appears excessively flexible in confrontation with the conditions of life, persisting without generating in its subject a deep and significant re-definition of personal and social identity" (1988:117–18).

The public is ambivalent regarding the legitimacy of the church's involvement in politics.[23] Data from the mid-1970s suggest that on the church's right to be involved in "politics in general," there is very strong aversion (75 percent) and only weak approval (18 percent)—yet on specific issues such as abortion, the public seemed to accept the church's involvement in public issues. The church's participation does not mean that voters will follow the church's lead. Despite enormous church involvement, referendums intending to restrict Italians' rights to divorce and abortion were defeated in 1974 and 1981.

Another index of changing relations among state, church, and society in Italy was the change in the treaties with the Vatican, treaties which had been made in 1929 and incorporated into the constitution in 1947. These treaties, the renegotiation of which had begun in the early 1970s, were finally ratified in 1983. They substantially reduced the privileges of the church. They required that church law on marriage follow civil law. The treaties changed the status of religious education in public schools from required to voluntary. They eliminated certain financial privileges of the church, and required that the Vatican pay $244 million and admit moral responsibility for bank scandals in which its own bank had been involved.

The transformation in relations between church and society can fruitfully be examined by a brief survey of the changing patterns of political organization within the Catholic church. From the 1940s until the Second Vatican Council in 1962, the organizational structure of the church was tightly regulated and hierarchical. The Catholic church had a strong territorial organization structured by diocese and parish, and a series of lay organizations that encompassed the secular aspects of society. Active membership in the church required participation in these lay associations as well. The most important of these, Catholic Action, had over three million members in the 1950s.[24] These groups were organized toward maximum support of the church's political mission in Italy, at the cost, it has been argued, of its spiritual mission (Poggi 1967).

The 1960s and 1970s were characterized by innovation within the church hierarchy and the rise of new groups outside it. The church reduced the im-

[23] The effectivenesss of religious sentiment as a predictor of political activity also varies regionally. In the South, religious sentiment seems more difficult to translate into votes than in the northeastern areas of the country, where the Catholic subcultures are stronger and better organized (Cartocci 1989).

[24] On Catholic Action's early history, see Poggi (1967). For its later transformations, see Penco (1986:227–37).

portance it ascribed to such groups as Catholic Action. These changes were outrun by Catholic groups that formed dissenting groups outside the hierarchy of the church.[25] These groups in turn were eclipsed by the movements that emerged in the aftermath of the occurrences of 1968. Base communities, Christian groups searching for a reconciliation of Catholicism with Marxism, and New Left political experiences all overtook these earlier forms of religious dissidence.[26]

The insurgencies within the church diminished the church's political impact and organizational strength. Until the late 1960s, the Catholic unions (CISL) and the Association of Catholic Workers (ACLI) had funneled support of the Christian Democratic party. Increasing radicalism within these workers' organizations undermined their willingness to cooperate with the church. Catholic Action, the main lay organization, which had close to three million members in the early 1950s, had shrunk to six hundred thousand members in the early 1970s (Pasquino 1980:92).

After the decline of these movements in the mid-1970s, three new emphases in associative life emerged. First, new groups were formed that were more concerned with private religiosity than with public competition (Pace 1983). The second was a general tendency toward looser forms of association, with less direct connection to the church hierarchy. The third tendency was the growth of more "integralist" groups, which called for a return to religious influence over social issues that were increasingly being defined as secular. Communione e Liberazione, the most important integralist group, with seventy thousand members, would be extremely prominent in campaigning for the repeal of the abortion legislation. Through its explicitly political wing, the Movimento Populare, it ran candidates for office. Communione e Liberazione sought to replace Catholic Action as the central group of Christian laity.

These diverse tendencies—toward privatization of interest, diffusion in organizational structure, and political intergralism—have pulled the church in various directions. In its effort to regain control over this increasingly variegated associational life, the church in 1981 set out new criteria for regulating these groups, but it is unclear whether there will ever again be a center to Catholic associational life or whether the centrifugal tendencies, opposed to formal organization, will come to dominate.[27] In general, the picture of the church that emerges is one of an organization with decreasing impact over secular life. Its state-sanctioned powers have diminished; its hold over the

[25] On the emergence of Catholic dissent, see Malavolti (1969), Ristuccia (1975), and Cuminetti (1983). On the efforts to build a more united and coherent church after these years of strife, see the debates on the "recomposition" of the Catholic church in Sorge (1979, 1981).

[26] For a detailed portrait of the various trajectories of these groups in Turin, see Berzano et al. (1984).

[27] For a study that points to the latter tendency, and that sees an increasing tendency to "polycentrism," see Colozzi and Martelli (1988:39).

faithful has declined; and its organizational direction and capacities seem to be without (or with too many) points of reference.

THE CHANGING BOUNDARY BETWEEN STATE AND SOCIETY

In the last forty years, the boundary between state and civil society has shifted substantially. The state has taken an increasingly active role both in regulating industrial relations and in developing a welfare state. These transformations have a critically important impact on the possibilities of development of the voluntary sector. Economic regulation has led to the revitalization of certain regions, which are also those where the third sector might find its most promising territory. The increasing commitment to the welfare state has led to promises being made that the Italian state has not been able to keep, providing a space in which the voluntary sector could expand.

The Regionalization of the Italian Economy

The post–World War II economic order has been tightly circumscribed by the historic weakness of Italian economic development. This economic weakness has meant that until the 1960s economic development had occurred primarily in the industrial triangle found by Genoa, Milan, and Turin, and that the infrastructure necessary for further expansion was lacking. The Italy that emerged after the war was predominantly agricultural, with 44 percent of its total employment in that sector, 29 percent in the industrial sector, and 27 percent in the third sector (Boccella 1987:9).

Following World War II, Italy chose to open its economy to the international order and to base its development on exporting midlevel technology to Western Europe. Its advantage was its lower labor costs. In a sense, Italy had little choice regarding free trade. Its lack of primary commodities required low tariffs so that it could import necessary raw materials. This decision was also influenced by the government's desire to make a clean break with fascism, where trade policy had been highly protectionist, dictated by Mussolini's desire to build an Italian empire. The United States' interest in free trade also played a role in opening up the Italian economy.

The export strategy that Italy chose depended on and exacerbated the internal divisions in the country. The low-wage strategy counted on the reservoir of southern labor to migrate north to work in the factories.[28] It strengthened northern industries, while the acceptance of agricultural imports undermined the agrarian southern economy. The export strategy pushed the modernization of these industries. Wages increased, but not as much as did productivity. On the other hand, the smaller firms, predominantly in the South, that were ori-

---

[28] For an assessment of alternative development strategies, see Sassoon (1986:18–20).

ented to the internal market tended to stagnate. From 1945 to 1963, during the time of reconstruction and then the economic miracle, this low-wage strategy produced high growth rates and transformed the class structure of Italy.

The tightening of the labor market diminished business's control over labor, which became increasingly militant. Through an exceptional wave of militancy, labor dramatically improved its position.[29] Wages caught up with previous productivity gains. Between 1969 and 1973, workers' share of national income increased 8 percent (Salvati 1975:106). This increase in wages and labor's rigidity undermined Italy's primary advantages in the world economic market. From the early 1970s to the early 1980s, the Italian economy was in great difficulty. OPEC's price increases showed how Italy's lack of energy resources made it vulnerable to fluctuating prices. Inflation was running at about 15 percent from the mid-1970s until the early 1980s, approximately twice as high as elsewhere in Europe. Together with budget deficits that drove up domestic interest rates, these economic problems combined to make Italy's economy the sick man in Western Europe. In the past five years, the Italian economy has rebounded, but unemployment is still high (particularly in the South), inflation is still above the European average, and the budget deficits have not been reduced.

What little success Italy had in weathering the crisis of the 1970s and reviving in the 1980s was due largely to new forms of factory organization that developed in regions outside the traditionally strong Northwest. The state and the unions imposed limits on the autonomy and profitability of larger firms in the Northeast in their capacities to hire and fire and control work routines and this coincided with changes in the international economic order to benefit small, flexible firms. There, wages were lower, unions weaker, and hiring and firing (for firms with fewer than fifteen employees) could be carried out without state involvement. These firms are predominantly found in the "Third Italy."[30] These areas had never been incorporated into the model of large economic development that had predominated in the North. For the past twenty years, they have played a critical role in the resilience of the Italian economy.

The Third Italy is characterized by small and medium-sized enterprises linked in a pattern of close cooperation. In contrast with the model of large factories that predominate in the Northwest, there is little class differentiation within these areas. The areas have strong local cultures. They represent the antithesis of the assembly-line industries in the Northwest that had been the base for the economic miracle in the 1950s and 1960s. Missing in all these portraits is the South, which has not responded to the national government's economic development projects. Forty years of projects have not altered the

[29] Italy had 302 million person-hours of strikes in 1969 and 146 million in 1970 (Sassoon 1986:62).

[30] The concept of the Third Italy has been most fully developed by Arnaldo Bagnasco (1977–1987).

South's share of the gross domestic product, which has remained at about 24 percent. Incomes in the South still remain 40 percent below the national average (Spotts and Weiser 1986:239).

The vast regional economic variations mean that any unitary, national form of governmental regulation such as neocorporatism is likely to fail. It also means that there will be vastly different possibilities for the voluntary sector in the highly industrialized Northwest, an underdeveloped South, and in the Third Italy, where there are strong intermediate institutions.

The Particularity of the Italian Welfare State

The evolution of the Italian welfare state is critical to the possibility of Italy's development of a third sector. Its patterns of development show how political parties have manipulated the welfare system for partisan purposes and thereby weakened autonomous groups. The present difficulties of the welfare state in fulfilling its responsibilities provide a reason for expanding the reach of the third sector and the categories in which the debate is framed.

Italy's welfare state presents us with an anomaly. In the resources allocated to it, the Italian welfare state resembles the rest of Western Europe. In its mode of allocating these resources, it is most unusual. This anomaly can most clearly be seen by placing Italy within the theoretical frameworks developed by Richard Titmuss.[31] Titmuss distinguishes between the "institutional-redistributive" model, where benefits are universal and seen as an extension of citizenship rights, and the "industrial achievement-performance" model, where benefits depend on labor market position. The first pattern, also referred to as the Scandinavian model, is more prominent in Northern Europe, including England and Scandinavia, whereas the second is the Continental pattern, including Austria, France, Belgium, and West Germany—and Italy, albeit in a qualified way.

The Italian welfare state is characterized by its clientelistic practices, centralization, and subordination of civil society to the interests of political parties. Italy has traditionally provided benefits to particular groups and has rarely adopted universalistic policies. Although its origins date to the late nineteenth century, the Italian welfare state did not fully mature until the late 1970s, and even then its development was contradictory, marked by generosity in some areas and penury in others.

The clientelistic character of the Italian welfare state was prefigured in the first laws passed during the period of liberal governance, following the unification of Italy in 1870. Initially, the liberal state seemed willing to delegate many social-service functions to the Christian charitable organizations and to workers' aid societies (Ascoli 1984:25; Piperno 1984; Ferrara 1984:27). In the

---

[31] This mode of analysis is applied to Italy by Ascoli (1987a, 1987b) and Paci (1984).

1880s and 1890s, Italy adopted workers' compensation and subsidized, voluntary social insurance. The policies were aimed at integrating northern workers, primarily those in the steel and metalworking industries, into the political system (Ascoli 1984:26). The proposals tended to be paternalistic, reminiscent of Bismarck's, although there were precedents for more progressive proposals that would have granted more autonomy and control to unions and related local institutions. The leverage of the less economically advanced and less liberal South proved dominant, and the legislation was state-centered, patronage-oriented, and paternalistic (Paci 1984:310).

During the period between 1900 and 1920, and particularly in the aftermath of World War I, popular mobilization combined with organizing efforts by political leaders to push social-policy demands onto the political agenda. Popular pressure increased as a result of the introduction of universal male suffrage in 1913, the intensifying industrialization of the country, and the growth of the Socialist unions and party. In 1919 and 1920, mandatory social security and unemployment insurance were discussed by politicians of all parties, and legislation passed that addressed both issues (Ferrera 1984:30–31). The Fascist period did not produce any ruptures in this system. The initial policy was to resist this postwar thrust of progressive legislation. Not until 1926 did the Fascist state develop social policies of its own. The Fascist policies tended to benefit middle-class groups, and to construct tight relations among these groups, the public bureaucracy, and the Fascist party (Paci 1984:315). The Fascist legacy strengthened two tendencies: first, to provide benefits primarily to workers and employers, and second, to distribute these resources (following principles of political expediency) to groups that would then support the regime (Paci 1989:85).

A broad commitment to the welfare state emerged only after World War II (Bassinini et al. 1977:10). The Republican constitution of 1948 stated that "every citizen unable to work and without the necessary means for living has the right to maintenance and to social assistance" (article 38, clause 1). Other clauses specified the need to defend the rights of the family, the young, and the handicapped in ways that suggested a commitment to a full-fledged welfare state (Paci 1989:87). This constitutional authority was not accompanied by any systematic legislation. Plans were discussed and developed by the Commissione d'Aragona that showed the resonance of the universalistic claims of Beveridge plans in England, but they were never enacted. After the split in the government between Communists and the Christian Democrats in 1948, such policy innovation was impossible. What occurred was an incremental expansion for the next twenty years.[32]

[32] This was the first of two "missed opportunities" for reform. The second came in the 1960s when a center-left government would come to power with a mandate for social reform (Ferrera 1984:220). In both cases, one sees that political divisions within the country (and the Left) vitiated this mandate.

In the early 1950s, Italy had the least-complete social insurance coverage of any Western European country. Its policies were limited primarily to uneven coverage of pensions and unemployment programs (Ascoli 1984:20). Despite some reforms in pensions and the housing sector, the period was characterized by only slight attention to these problems. Economic growth and recovery from the devastation of the war were the government's priorities during this period. The changes that did occur involved expanding the coverage of the system, not reforming its distributive principles. The incremental pattern of changes and the attention to targeting particular groups can be seen in the growth of the welfare state in the late 1950s and early 1960s. Health insurance was extended to farmers (1956), artisans (1957), and merchants (1966). Pensions were expanded to include farmers (1957), artisans (1959), housewives (1963), and merchants (1966). Family support (assegni familari) was granted to farmers (1967) and to the unemployed (1968) (Paci 1989:89). It was the national government that led this process: "The initiative always came from the government, interested in guaranteeing the electoral support of these social groups; the unions generally did not oppose them . . . and even though they always showed little sympathy for this fragmentary, unplanned expansion . . . , they were not strong enough to oppose them" (Ascoli 1984:32).[33]

These jerry-built systems were greatly unequal in the contributions required, the way they were managed, and the benefits they paid (Ascoli 1984:89). The major expansion and change in the structure of the welfare state occurred after 1968. The period of the late 1960s and early 1970s was one of intense social mobilization. It resulted in the development of a union movement that demanded wide-ranging political and social reforms.[34] Government spending increased rapidly during this period (Ascoli 1984:29). Existing programs were rationalized, most notably the financing and administration of hospitals (1968) and pension plans (1969). The results were a greater correspondence between contributions and benefits, and a minimum pension provided for all citizens. There was also an expansion of unemployment insurance (Ferrera 1984:42) and a centralization of control over public housing.

The 1970s were, in general, a period of modernization in Italian society. Legislation was passed legalizing divorce (1971 and 1974), giving new rights to women in the family (1975), lowering the age of majority (1975), providing new rights in the workplace (1977), and legalizing abortion (1978). The public began to see the welfare state in an increasingly favorable light. The national government worked to redeem the claims written in the Republican constitution regarding increased decentralization of political authority to neighbor-

[33] See Ferrera for a discussion of how particular policies were rewards given to constituencies in the elections of 1957, 1963, and 1968 (1986:194–96).

[34] On the problems posed by union involvement in the politics of reform, see Pizzorno (1978). For a comparative analysis of the Italian strategy, see Lange, Ross, and Vannicelli (1982).

hood, local, and regional authorities, and regarding institutional democratization.[35] In 1978, important health-care legislation revised and substantially extended coverage. This innovation happened much later than in other welfare states, and it was the high-water mark of the Italian welfare state.

The Italian system ranked in the middle of the European social-welfare systems in expenditure levels. It covered a similar percentage of the population, and offered similar services. Between 1954 and 1980, the share of GNP allocated to social services in Italy grew slightly faster than in France, Britain, Germany, and the United States. Particularly striking was the increase during the period between 1973 and 1980, an increase of 4.2 percent at a time when increases in these other states were substantially smaller (Ascoli 1984:29). The Italian welfare state was more heavily weighted to pensions than most, with 48.2 percent of all social expenses coming under this category, as opposed to the European average of 36.5 percent (Ascoli 1984:22). In the South in 1971, more money was paid out in pensions than in salary (Bassinini et al. 1977:11). The welfare state tended to neglect social expenditures, allocating roughly half as much for unemployment (2.2 percent versus 4.8 percent) and for social assistance (5.2 percent versus 9.2 percent) as the European average (Ascoli 1984:22 citing Albers 1983:97). For all the efforts at rationalization, the welfare system was not substantially moved from its particularist tradition.[36]

The oil shock of 1979 and the economic crisis that followed it increased pressures for austerity on all the welfare states in Western Europe. This need was particularly compelling in Italy as the GNP declined in real terms from 1981 to 1983, and as social expenses continued to rise, increasing the importance of the budget deficit as a political issue. In the early period, from 1978 to 1983, there were cuts in health, education, and family subsidies. These cuts were somewhat offset by improvements in pensions. The result was a mild austerity plan (Ferreara 1984:235–40). In the mid-1980s, greater efforts were made to enact neoliberal austerity policies.[37] These measures included raising the costs of services to all users, encouraging the more affluent to seek out private-sector services, and restricting certain benefits to the neediest recipients. These moves away from "universalistic" policies tended to exacerbate tensions between workers, who were paying for these services, and the most

[35] As one analyst put it, "Above all, on the terrain of social service policy, the level of government must be as close as possible to the clients" (Bassinini et al. 1977:19). In fact, the pressure for decentralization meant that national authorities often lost control over the patronage-oriented use of local funds, producing a system that was even less easy to control than the one it replaced (Paci 1984:320).

[36] In the distribution of services, clientelistic relations are not surprising; it is the manipulation of the categories of transfer payments that makes the Italian case unique (Paci 1989:275).

[37] These efforts did not increase the percentage of GDP that went to the national government. This percentage rose from 28.7 in 1975, to 36 in 1980, to 41.4 in 1984. This percentage, which had been in line with the OECD average in 1975, was substantially above it by 1985.

disadvantaged, who were increasingly the only beneficiaries. Although there was never a concerted policy, the net effect seems to have been to weaken the protections of the welfare state and to augment its more "particularist" leanings (Paci 1989:115–17).

THE THIRD SECTOR

In this context the third sector became an issue in national politics—an alternative that could ease the state's financial burdens of service provision and also contribute to building a more autonomous civil society. The third sector, or *volontariato*, is a small but growing part of the public sphere. As the discussion of the welfare state suggests, the state has historically tended to undermine rather than to promote local initiatives. The policies that have linked civil society to the state have been based on clientelistic relations. The *volontariato* and the debate surrounding it grew substantially in the early 1980s, much of this growth coincident with, if not caused by, the deficiencies in the Italian welfare state.

Though the voluntary sector does have certain roots in the secular, liberal culture, it has had the greatest resonance within the Catholic culture.[38] Given the historic role Catholic charities have played in the administration of social services, this should come as no surprise. The third sector's growth has not been looked on favorably by the Left, which initially saw it as a covert attack on the welfare state. Also, the Communist subculture already had a broad array of flanking institutions that served its purpose of trying to enrich civil society. However, the Left has increasingly recognized the need for new associational forms that give greater opportunity to movements in civil society (Ascoli 1984:9).[39]

Another factor that has impaired the third sector's growth (and made it difficult to study) is the lack of a national center. There is no national legislation defining a voluntary sector, although there were proposals in 1984 and 1985 for such legislation. In fact, there is no law on social associations in general.[40] The laws regarding social associations are established by sector and by fiscal relation to the state. The laws regarding contributions by the state to private associations have been defined as "an overgrown forest." A recent govern-

[38] The analysis from a Catholic standpoint has been prominently developed by Ardigò (1980, 1984) and Donati (1981, 1983) and the circles around them. While the liberal viewpoint does not have a policy network of similar depth, see the publications by the Fondazione Giovanni Agnelli (1979) and the writings of its president, M. Pacini (1980). A good local study of Catholic organization is found in Colozzi and Martelli's research on Bologna (1988).

[39] See Balbo (1984) and comments by the Communist senator Taramelli, cited in IREF 1988:420).

[40] The terms "associations," "base associations," "free associations," "associations without monetary ends," "associations with social means," "associations of volunteers," and "volunteers" are used interchangeably in various laws and proposals for new ones (IREF 1988:419).

mental study, which noted that 8.3 percent, or 421 billion lire, of the budget goes to private associations, suggests, in its own opaque and bureaucratic prose, the possibilities for abuse of this system: "In not a few cases, the total lack of directive and limiting criteria regarding the beneficiaries . . . in the face of this quite diffuse associational phenomenon could obscure the image of impartiality that, also according to constitutional mandate, is a necessary connotation for public administration."[41]

At the national level, legislation regulates voluntary activity in various sectors, including health care (1978), drug-addiction treatment (1982), civil defense (1982), and cultural and environmental protection (1982) (Colozzi 1984). The regional legislation is more ample and far-reaching, but no more coherent. The question of what constitutes a voluntary group remains poorly defined. For example, some of the legislation seems oriented to individuals, and some to the groups themselves.

A little less than one-fifth (18.9 percent) of the Italian population between the ages of eighteen and seventy four engage in some form of organizational activity. Those who are members of social organizations (*associazionismo sociale*) come to 7,345,000 (IREF 1988:21). Not all of these activities are purely voluntary. A substantial percentage also involve work for unions and political parties. In purely voluntary activity, 11.7 percent of the population, or 4,547,000 people, are active. Other studies indicate that this is a growing phenomenon, with an increase between 1983 and 1985 from 10.7 percent to 11.7 percent of the population: this is an annual increase in participation of 4.7 percent (IREF 1988:22).

The regional variation is quite striking. As is to be expected, given the lower levels of economic development and social infrastructure, the South lags far behind the other regions.[42] The areas with the strongest and most rapidly growing sectors of voluntary activity are in the Third Italy—the center and the Northeast, where the Communist and Catholic subcultures have traditionally been most rooted in local associational life, and where there has been an upsurge in economic development. In the Northwest, the area associated with the large industrial cities, there has been a slight decline, which can perhaps be attributed to a more difficult economic situation.

There has never been a complete census of voluntary groups. In 1983, a government-sponsored survey analyzed the activity of 7,024 local voluntary associations. The survey showed that the largest numbers of groups were involved in social assistance (56.2 percent), followed by cultural and educa-

[41] "In non pochi casi la totale mancanza di criteri direttivi e limitativi reiguardanti i soggetti beneficiari (ma anche l'entita dell somme erogate), a fronte del femonomeno assai diffuso dell'associzionismpuo offuscare l'immagine di imparzialita che, anche secondo il dettato costituzionale, e doverosa connotazione per la pubblica amministrazione."

[42] The most detailed analysis of the voluntary sector in the South is to be found in FORMEZ (1986).

TABLE 6.1
Adults (18–74) Involved in Voluntary Activity, by Region

| | Northwest | Northeast | Geographic Distribution | | Total Italy |
			Center	South	
1983	14.3%	13.5%	7.1%	8.3%	10.7%
1985	12.5%	16.1%	13.2%	8.1%	11.7%
Change	− 1.8%	+ 2.6%	+ 6.1%	− 0.2%	+ 1.0%

Source: IREF (1988:23).

tional activities (52.7 percent), health care (33 percent), civil defense (21.9 percent), and environmentalism and cultural preservation (17.1 percent).[43]

These groups represent a range of political and religious orientations. Those of religious inspiration include 44.6 percent of the total, those of a lay-humanitarian and nonreligious nature account for slightly more (49.9 percent), while those coming from a "socialist solidarity" viewpoint only account for 5.5 percent of the groups (Colozzi 1988:118). In more than half of the groups, religious activists (religosi) are involved. This analysis confirms the standard assumptions that liberal and Catholic groups make up the backbone of these movements, and that left-wing groups are marginal. In those activities that concern social welfare exclusively, we can see a religious preponderance, with 69 percent of these groups of Catholic inspiration. One sees a similar preponderance of liberal activity in health care (80.2 percent).[44] Again, this suggests that the roots of Catholic charity continue to have a profound effect on the handling of welfare functions, and that medical activities are the province of liberal, professional groups.

Although the role of the third sector is gradually increasing, it is unlikely that the third sector will come to play a very significant part in Italian society. A key aspect of the future of the voluntary sector depends on how the government chooses to establish its legal parameters. There have been recent efforts to write more coherent national legislation, concerning both the voluntary sector and social concerns in general, but no significant legislation has yet been

---

[43] The sum of these participation rates being substantially greater than 100 percent indicates the tendency of almost half of these groups to intervene in more than one sector (Colozzi 1984:132).

[44] There has been a general trend toward privatization in the health-care system in recent years. Spending on private health care increased from 16.7 percent to 21.7 percent of all health expenditures from 1980 to 1987. Spending for public services contracted to private institutions went from 34.6 percent to 40.6 percent (CENSIS 1989:100). For a more detailed treatment of the relation between the voluntary sector and the health-care system, see Colozzi (1988). For a greater elaboration of the data on the health-care system, see Colozzi (1988:137–39) and Boccacin (1988:49–63).

passed.[45] An equally important element is how these diverse bodies react to governmental proposals. There are grounds for these groups to be skeptical. The first is that governmental institutionalization might undermine the autonomy of the groups. The second is the fear that the government might use these groups as a way of passing on the costs of the welfare state.[46]

CONCLUSION

Given its position in the aftermath of World War II as a defeated power, with a legacy of twenty years of fascism, Italy has made significant strides in the past forty years. Its economy has advanced to the point where it is the fifth or sixth largest industrial power, moving from a primarily agricultural base to a modern, high-technology industrial profile. Despite challenges from terrorism and the Mafia, its political institutions have held remarkably firm. It has increasingly accommodated parties of the Left, although the party system still suffers from the exclusion of the Communist party, which prevents full alternation between coalitions.

This progress has not fully overcome the historical weakness in civil society grounded in the nineteenth-century patterns of state formation. The weak bourgeois forces that failed to produce a strong market economy or to undermine the southern feudal relations left Italy with a legacy of uneven development that has yet to be overcome. The failure to develop an autonomous bureaucratic state that can withstand politicization by the parties also weighs heavily on the possibilities of future developments within the third sector. As the evolution of the Italian welfare state illustrates, the links between state and civil society have consistently favored patronage ties between political elites and preferred constituencies.

This weakness in economic and political formation can be seen most strikingly in the patterns of regionalism in Italy. The South has clearly borne the burden of this path of development; its economy is underdeveloped and its civil society is demobilized. The northwestern regions, witness to the purest bourgeois-modernizing influence, still play a critical role in the financial and industrial development of the country, although the crisis in industy has both weakened these regions' productive capacities and caused greater strains in their associational lives. In the northeastern and central regions of the country, those tied to a more flexible and decentralized model of industrial develop-

---

[45] For a summary of the legislation affecting the voluntary sector and other legislative proposals that have not been enacted, see IREF (1988:456–66). For a detailed analysis of health-care legislation, see Manganozzi (1988:65–97). For an authoritative list of all regional legislation through 1984, see Manganozzi (1988).

[46] On the issue of costs, see IREF (1988:302, 444). On the question of autonomy, see Colozzi (1988:113).

ment, with strong political subcultural networks, one sees an increasing development of voluntary activities.

In looking to the broadening of a public sphere in Italy, it is easier to say which groups are unlikely to effect a dramatic change than to say which would. It seems unlikely that either the Catholic church or the voluntary sector will play an important role in these activities. Although it is still a formidable actor in Italian political and social life, the church has less purchase than before on political parties and on private consciences. An overwhelming number of Italians see themselves as Catholic, but fewer and fewer of them think the church has the right to pronounce on secular matters (Spotts and Weiser 1986:262). The referendums on divorce and abortion in the past twenty years attest to that decline.

It is also difficult to foresee the voluntary sector playing a great role. As Banterle and Cella (1984) have argued, a tradition of autonomous groups and a lack of political cleavage provide the space in which a third sector can flourish. At present, the tendencies toward either an increase in autonomous, pluralistic groups or a decrease in political cleavage are too weak to generate the space for the development of universalistic claims. Even though the Left and the Right increasingly recognize the need to strengthen grass-roots associational life, they disagree as to which groups should perform these functions; they tend to view the voluntary sector quite differently. For Catholics, that sector is similar to traditional forms of charitable activity, and can be seen as a response to the crisis of the welfare state. For Communists, a voluntary sector is a threat to the welfare state, and one that would not help the flanking organizations to which the Communists are already committed. Social movements, which on the whole have favored increased (and rationalized) state intervention, would also be skeptical of the voluntary sector.[47]

From the perspective of voluntary groups themselves, the state's lack of organizational or legislative coherence undermines the possibility of the growth of a regulated *volontariato*. In all contexts, formal affiliation with the state could cost voluntary organizations their autonomy. In Italy, the state's weakness and tendency to be overly politicized present additional difficulties. The failure to develop a national policy regulating the voluntary sector, and the maze of regional laws this failure has left in its wake, bespeak the state's legislative incapacities. The jumble of laws that shape the relations between the government and private organizations, and the patronage-oriented growth of the welfare state itself, evidence an unfortunate politicization.

The most dominant actors in the public sphere are the political parties. Changing the public sphere could be accomplished by a different political co-

---

[47] In this sense, they are profoundly dissimilar to the "anti-political" (Berger 1978) and "anti-welfare state" (Offe 1985) social movements that are seen in other European contexts during this period.

alition, either by the accession of the Socialists to a dominant position within the existing five-party coalition, by a government of the Left headed by the Socialists and Communists, or by a substantially greater role for the fledgling ecological parties. Given the electoral stability of Italian politics, such changes seem improbable.

A second source of changes in the public sphere would be a resurgence of social movements. We have seen how they have enriched public discourse and provided new forms of militancy. In a country such as Italy where political parties are powerful and diverse, the parties' university and cultural associations offer an opportunity for the political socialization of future leaders in social movements, and models to which social movements will inevitably be compared. Initiatives that in other countries would emerge directly out of civil society and remain autonomous from the political system for a longer period, come from and return to the realm of political parties more rapidly in Italy. The recurrence of student movements, which detonated the post-1968 cycle of protest and also occurred in 1977, 1986, and 1990, increases the likelihood of social-movement activity. Though social movements have difficulty sustaining themselves, their potential influence should not be discounted.

It is this oscillation between party stability and social-movement activity that provides the dynamism of the Italian public sphere. The voluntary sector is still too strongly identified with the church and the weak liberal tradition to make the universalistic claims that would free it from its present marginal status.

References

Albers, Jens. 1983. "Some Causes and Consequences of Social Security Expenditure Development in Western Europe, 1949–77."*Stato e Mercato*, no. 7.

Allum, P. A. 1973. *Italy—Republic without Government?* New York: W. W. Norton and Company.

Ardigò, A. 1980. "Volontariato, welfare state, e terza dimensione." *La ricerca sociale* 25

———. 1984. "Nuovi valori e nuovi attori per la rifondazione del welfare state." *La ricerca sociale* 32.

Ascoli, Ugo. 1984: "Il sistema Italiano di welfare." In *Welfare state all'Italiana*, edited by Ugo Ascoli, pp. 5–46. Bari: Laterza.

———. 1987a. "Il sistema Italiano de welfare tra ridimensionamento e riforma." In *La società Italiana degli anni ottanta*, edited by Ugo Ascoli and Raimondo Catanzaro, pp. 283–312. Rome: Laterza.

———. 1987b. "Le iniziative di solidarietà e di volontariato nei moderni sistemi di welfare." Ugo Ascoli, pp. 9–33. In *Azione volontaria e welfare state*, edited by Ugo Ascoli, pp. 9–33. Bologna: Il Mulino.

Bagnasco, Arnaldo. 1977. *Tre Italie: La problematica territoriale dello sviluppo Italiano*. Bologna: Il Mulino.

———. 1987. "Borghesia e classe operaia." In *La società Italiana degli anni ottanta*, edited by Ugo Ascoli and Raimondo Catanzaro, pp. 30–49. Rome: Laterza.

Balbo, Laura. 1984. "Tra pubblico e mercato, il ruolo del volontariato." *Inchiesta* 7–8:85–89.

Banterle, Clara Busana, and Gian Primo Cella. 1984. "Il welfare e l'allocazione politica: Alcune alternative." In *Welfare state all'Italiana*, edited by Ugo Ascoli, pp. 265–97. Bari: Laterza.

Barnes, Samuel Henry. 1979. *Political Action: Mass Participation in Five Western Democracies*. Beverly Hills: Sage Publications.

Bassinini, Maria Chiara, et. al. 1977. *I servizi sociali: realtà e riforma*. Bologna: Il Mulino.

Beckwith, Karen. 1987. "Response to Feminism in the Italian Parliament: Divorce, Abortion, and Sexual Violence Legislation." In *The Women's Movements of the United States and Western Europe: Consciousness, Political Opportunity, and Public Policy*, edited by Mary Fainsod Katzenstein and Carol McClurg Mueller, pp. 153–71. Philadelphia: Temple University Press.

Bellah, Robert N. 1980. "The Five Religions of Modern Italy." In *Varieties of Civic Religion*, edited by Robert N. Bellah and Phillip E. Hammond, pp. 86–118. San Francisco: Harper and Row.

Benedetti, Pierpaolo. 1971. "Dove Sono finiti i gruppi spon tanei." *Quaderni di azione sociale* 22 (1): 79–92.

Berezin, Mabel. Forthcoming. "Created Constituencies: Fascism and the Middle

Classes in Inter-War Italy." In *Splintered Classes: The Politics of the Lower Middle Class in Interwar Europe,* edited by Rudy Koshar. London: Holmes and Maier.

Berger, Suzanne. 1978. "Politics and Antipolitics in Western Europe in the Seventies." *Daedalus* 107:27–50.

———. 1987. "Religious Transformations and the Future of Politics." In *Changing Boundaries of the Political,* edited by Charles S. Maier, pp. 107–49. Cambridge: Cambridge University Press.

Berzano, Luigi, et al. 1984. *Uomini di frontiera: "Scelta di classe" e transformazioni della coscienza cristiana a Torino dal concilio ad oggi.* Turin: Lorenzo Milani.

Biorcio, R., and G. Lodi. 1988. *La sfida verde: Il movimento ecologista in Italia.* Padua: Liviana.

Boccacin, Lucia. 1988. "Il volontariato sanitario fra tradizione e innovazione: Alcuni aspetti del caso Italiano." In *Volontariato e salute,* edited by Ivo Colozzi and Luciano Tavazza, pp. 49–63. Bologna: EDB.

Boccella, Nicola. 1987. "Uno sviluppo eterogeneo." In *La società Italiana degli anni ottanta,* edited by Ugo Ascoli and Raimondo Catanzaro, pp. 5–29. Rome: Laterza.

Cartocci, Roberto. 1989. "Secolarizzazione, voto cattolico, e voto democristiano." *Rassegna Italiana di sciologia* 30 (1): 69–102.

Catalano, Franco. 1972. "The Rebirth of the Party System, 1944–1948. In *The Rebirth of Italy,* edited by S. J. Woolf, pp. 57–94. London: Longmans.

CENSIS. 1989. *Italy Today: Social Picture and Trends, 1988.* Rome: Franco Angeli.

Cervellin, Pietro Sergio. 1988. "Evoluzione dell'associazionismo cattolico nel Veneto." In *Religione e religiosità nel Veneto ieri e oggi,* edited by Giuseppe Dal Ferro, pp. 193–273. Vicenza: Rezzara.

Chubb, Judith, and Maurizio Vannicelli. 1988. "Italy: A Web of Scandals in a Flawed Democracy." In *The Politics of Scandal: Power and Process in Liberal Democracies,* edited by Andrei S. Markovits and Mark Silverstein, pp. 122–50. New York: Holmes and Meier.

Clark, Martin, David Hine, and R. E. Irving. 1974. "Divorce—Italian Style." *Parliamentary Affairs* 33 (Autumn): 333–58.

Colozzi, Ivo. 1984. *Nuove prospettive di politica sociale: Una analisi sociologica sul presente e sul futuro del welfare state.* Bologna: Editrice CLUEB.

———. 1988. "Introduzione: Il volontariato nel sistema sanitario complesso." In *Volontariato e salute,* edited by Ivo Colozzi and Luciano Tavazza, pp. 11–45. Bologna: EDB.

Colozzi, Ivo, and Stefan Martelli. 1988. *L'arcipelago cattolico: Analisi sociologica dell'associazionismo ecclesiale a Bologna.* Bologna: Tecnoprint.

Cuminetti, Mario. 1983. *Il dissenso cattolico in Italia.* Milan: Rizzoli.

Dal Ferro, Giuseppe. 1988. "Minoranze religiose nel Veneto." In *Religione e religiosità nel Veneto ieri e oggi,* edited by Giuseppe Dal Ferro, pp. 275–347. Vicenza: Rezzara.

Diani, Mario. 1988. *Isole nell'arcipelago: Il movimento ecologista in Italia.* Bologna: Il Mulino.

Donati, Pierpaolo. 1981. *Per una rifondazione del welfare state.* Milan: Franco Angeli.

———. 1983. "Volontariato e nuove risposte alla crisi del welfare state: Per una 'so-
luzione staturaria.' " *La rivista di servizio sociale,* no. 2.

Ergas, Yasmine. 1986. *Nelle maglie della politica: Femminismo, istituzione, e poli-
tiche sociali nell'Italia degli anni '70.* Milan: Franco Angeli.

Ferrera, Mauricio. 1984. *Il welfare state in Italia.* Bologna: Il Mulino.

———. 1986. "Italy." In *Growth to Limits: The Western European Welfare States
since World War II,* edited by Peter Flora, 2: 385–482. New York: Walter de Gruyter.

Fondazione Giovanni Agnelli, 1979. *Volontariato e società.* Turin: Fondazione Giovanni Agnelli.

FORMEZ. 1986. *Volontariato e mezzogiorno.* Bologna: Edizioni Dehoniane.

Garelli, Franco. 1984. *La generazione della vita quotidiana: I giovani in una società
differenziata.* Bologna: Il Mulino.

———. 1988. "Forme di secolarizzazione nella società contemporanea: Il caso Italiano." *Rassegna Italiana di sociologia* 29 (1): 89–121.

Ginsborg, Paul. 1979. "Gramsci and the Era of the Bourgeois Revolution in Italy." In
Gramsci and Italy's Passive Revolution, edited by John A. Davis, pp. 31–66. New
York: Harper and Row.

Girotti, Fiorenzo. 1973. "Partecipazione politica e crisi di legittimità." In *Il sistema
politico Italiano,* edited by Paolo Farnetti, pp. 395–414. Bologna: Il Mulino.

Golden, Miriam A. 1988. "Historical Memory and Ideological Orientations in the
Italian Workers' Movement." *Politics and Society* 16 (1): 1–34.

Gramsci, Antonio. 1975. *Quaderni del carcere.* 4 vols. Critical Edition of the Gramsci
Institute, edited by Valentino Gerratana. Turin: Einaudi.

Graziano, Luigi. 1984. *Clientelismo e sistema politico: Il caso dell'Italia.* Milan:
Franco Angeli.

Hellman, Judith Adler. 1987. *Journeys among Women: Feminism in Five Italian Cities.* New York: Oxford University Press.

Hellman, Stephen. 1987. "Italy." In *European Politics in Transition,* edited by Mark
Kesselman and Joel Krieger, pp. 319–450. Lexington, Mass.: D. C. Heath and Co.

———. 1988. *Italian Communism in Transition: The Rise and Fall of the Historic
Compromise in Turin, 1975–1980.* Oxford: Oxford University Press.

Inglehardt, Ronald. 1990. *Culture Shift.* Princeton: Princeton University Press.

IREF. 1988. *Rapporto sull'associazionismo sociale 1986.* Milan: Franco Angeli.

Kertzer, David I. 1980. *Comrades and Christians: Religion and Political Struggle in
Communist Italy.* Cambridge: Cambridge University Press.

Klein, Ethel. 1987. "The Diffusion of Consciousness in the United States and Western
Europe." In *The Women's Movements of the United States and Western Europe:
Consciousness, Political Opportunity, and Public Policy,* edited by Mary Fainsod
Katzenstein and Carol McClurg Mueller, pp. 23–43. Philadelphia: Temple Univer-
sity Press.

Lange, Peter. 1980. "Crisis and Consent, Change and Compromise: Dilemmas of Italian Communism in the 1970s." In *Italy in Transition: Conflict and Consensus,* edited by Peter Lange and Sidney Tarrow, pp. 110–32. London: Frank Cass and Company.

Lange, Peter, and Marino Regini. 1987. *Stato e regolazione sociale: Nuove prospettive sul caso Italiano.* Bologna: Il Mulino.

Lange, Peter, George Ross, and Maurizio Vannicelli. 1982. *Unions, Change, and Crisis: French and Italian Union Strategy and the Political Economy, 1945–1980.* London: George Allen and Unwin.

LaPalombara, Joseph. 1964. *Interest Groups in Italian Politics.* Princeton: Princeton University Press.

————. 1987. *Democracy, Italian Style.* New Haven: Yale University Press.

Magister, Sandro. 1979. *La politica vaticana e l'Italia, 1943–1978.* Rome: Riuniti.

Malavolti, Alberto. 1969. "Gruppi spontanei e dissenso politico." *Quaderni di azione sociale* 20 (2): 201–9.

Manganozzi, Gian Paolo. 1988. "Volontariato e SSN nel piano sanitario nazionale e in quelli regionali." In *Volontaiato e salute,* edited by Ivo Colozzi and Luciano Tavazza, pp. 65–97. Bologna: EDB.

Marcelloni, Maurizio. 1981. "Qualche riflessione su dieci anni di lotte sociali in Italia." In *Lotte urbane e crisi della società industriale: L'esperienza Italiana,* edited by Maurizio Marcelloni et al., 1:17–50. Rome: Savelli.

Martinelli, Alberto. 1980. "Organized Business and Italian Politics: Confindustria and the Christian Democrats in the Postwar Period." In *Italy in Transition: Conflict and Consensus,* edited by Peter Lange and Sidney Tarrow, pp. 67–87. London: Frank Cass and Company.

Melucci, Alberto. 1979. *Sistema politico, partiti, e movimenti sociali.* Milan: Feltrinelli.

Mershon, Carol A. Forthcoming. "Government Coalitions in Postwar Italy: The Logic of Sudden Death and Sure Resurrection." In *Coalition Theory and Coalition Governments,* edited by Norman Schofield. New York: Oxford University Press.

Miccoli, Giovanni. 1976. "Chiesa, partito cattolico, e società civile." In *L'Italia contemporanea, 1945–1975,* edited by Valerio Castronovo, pp. 191–252. Turin: Einaudi.

Offe, Claus. 1985. "New Social Movements: Challenging the Boundaries of Institutional Politics." *Social Research* 52 (4): 817–68.

Pace, Enzo. 1983. *Asceti e mistici in una società secolarizzata.* Venice: Marsilio.

Paci, Massimo. 1984. "Il sistema di welfare italiano tra tradizion clientelare e prospettive di riforma." In *Welfare state all'Italiana,* edited by Ugo Ascoli, pp. 297–324. Bari: Laterza.

————. 1989. *Pubblico e privato nei moderni sistemi di welfare.* Naples: Liguori.

Pacini, M. 1980. Introduction to *Volontariato, società, e pubblici poteri,* edited by Luciano Tavazza et al., pp. 11–26. Bologna: EDB.

Parisi, Arturo, and Gianfranco Pasquino. 1980. "Changes in Italian Electoral Behavior: The Relationships between Parties and Voters." In *Italy in Transition: Conflict and Consensus,* edited by Peter Lange and Sidney Tarrow, pp. 6–30. London: Frank Cass and Company.

Pasquino, Gianfranco. 1980. "Italian Christian Democracy: A Party for All Seasons." In *Italy in Transition: Conflict and Consensus,* edited by Peter Lange and Sidney Tarrow, pp. 88–110. London: Frank Cass and Company.

Pasquino, Gianfranco. 1987. "Partiti, società civile, e istituzioni." In *La società Ital-*

iana degli anni ottanta, edited by Ugo Ascoli and Raimondo Catanzaro, pp. 69–95. Rome: Laterza.

Penco, Gregorio. 1986. *Storia della chiesa in Italia nell'età contemporanea*. Vol. 2. Milan: Jaca Book.

Perlmutter, Ted. 1988a. "Intellectuals and Urban Protest: Extraparliamentary Politics in Turin, Italy, 1968–1976." Ph.D. Diss., Harvard University, Cambridge, Mass.

———. 1988b. "Using Urban Protest as a Guide to Political Structures: The Neighborhood Councils in Turin." Center for Research on Politics and Social Organization Working Paper Series, Department of Sociology, Harvard University (June).

Piperno, A. 1984. "La politicà sanitaria." In *Welfare state all'Italiana*, edited by Ugo Ascoli. Bari: Laterza.

Pizzorno, Alessandro. 1978. "Le due logiche dell'azione di classe." In *Lotte operaie e sindacato: Il ciclo 1968–1972 in Italia*, edited by Alessandro Pizzorno et al., pp. 7–43. Bologna: Il Mulino.

Poggi, Gianfranco. 1967. *Catholic Action in Italy: The Sociology of a Sponsored Organization*. Stanford: Stanford University Press.

Ricolfi, Luca. 1988. "Il processo di secolarizzazione nell'Italia del dopoguerra: Un profilo empirico." *Rassegna Italiana di sociologia* 29 (1): 37–87.

Ristuccia, Sergio. 1975. *Intellettuali cattolici tra riformismo e dissenso*. Milan: Edizioni di Comunità.

Salvati, Michele. 1975. *Il sistema economico Italiano: Analisi di una crisi*. Bologna: Il Mulino.

———. 1980. "Muddling Through: Economics and Politics in Italy, 1969–1979." In *Italy in Transition: Conflict and Consensus*, edited by Peter Lange and Sidney Tarrow, pp. 31–48. London: Frank Cass and Company.

Sartori, Giovanni. 1976. *Parties and Party Systems: A Framework for Analysis*. Cambridge: Cambridge University Press.

Sassoon, Donald. 1986. *Contemporary Italy: Politics, Economy, and Society since 1945*. London: Longman Group Limited.

Schnapp, Alain, and Vidal-Naquet, Pierre. 1971. *The French Student Uprising: November 1967–June 1968: An Analytic Record*. Boston: Beacon Press.

Shefter, Martin. 1977. "Party and Patronage: Germany, England, and Italy." *Politics and Society* 7 (4): 403–51.

Smith, Denis Mack. 1969. *Italy: A Modern History*. Ann Arbor: University of Michigan Press.

Sorge, Bartolomeo. 1979. *La "ricomposizione" dell'area cattolica in Italia*. Rome: Città Nuova Editrice.

———. Ed. 1981. *Il dibattito sulla "ricomposizione" dell'area cattolica in Italia*. Rome: Città Nuova Editrice.

Spotts, Frederic, and Theodor Weiser. 1986. *Italy: A Difficult Democracy*. Cambridge: Cambridge University Press.

Tamburrano, Giuseppe. 1979. *L'iceberg democristiano: Il potere in Italia oggi domani*. Milan: SugarCo Edizioni.

Tarrow, Sidney. 1977. "Communism in Italy and France: Adaptation and Change."

In *Communism in Italy and France,* edited by Donald L. M. Blackmer and Sidney Tarrow, pp. 575–640. Princeton: Princeton University Press.

————. 1989a. "Mutamenti nella cultura di opposizione in Italia, 1965–1975. *Polis* 3 (1): 41–64.

————. 1989b. *Democracy and Disorder: Protest and Politics in Italy, 1965–1975.* Oxford: Oxford University Press.

Verucci, Guido. 1988. *La chiesa nella società contemporanea: Dal primo dopoguerra al concilio vaticano II.* Rome: Editori Laterza.

Wertman, Douglas A. 1982. "The Catholic Church and Italian Politics: The Impact of Secularization." In *Religion in West European Politics,* edited by Suzanne Berger, pp. 87–107. London: Frank Cass and Company.

World Christian Encyclopedia. 1982. Nairobi: Oxford University Press.

CHAPTER SEVEN

Israel: State, Religion, and the Third Sector

Eliezer D. Jaffe

ISRAEL DOES NOT SHARE many basic normative characteristics with the other countries described in this book. For example, the final borders of the country have yet to be determined; the eastern and northern borders consist of cease-fire lines from the Six-Day War in 1967. Most of the neighboring countries for thousands of miles around call for the destruction of the state and the exile of those Jews who did not live there before the First World War. Despite goodwill from the Western countries, only the Israeli Army has prevented the elimination of this Western-Jewish enclave in the Arabian-Muslim Middle East.

There are not only no adjacent economic markets, but an Arab economic boycott, fostered worldwide, hinders maximum development. The West Bank (Judaea and Samaria) and the Gaza Strip areas, referred to as "occupied" or "liberal" territories, depending on one's political views, contain nearly one and a half Arabs, kin to six hundred thousand Israeli Arabs living within Israel's pre-1967 borders. External and internal defense needs, an arms race with its neighbors, and the cost of sophisticated weaponry have resulted in 30 percent of the state budget being targeted for defense, and another 30 percent for repayment of debts.

Israel was created in 1948 as a homeland for the Jews. Some call it the Third Jewish Commonwealth, coming after mass exile and loss of national independence twice before, during the destruction of the First Temple by the Babylonians and the destruction of the Second Temple by the Romans. Its creation was perhaps a direct result of the Holocaust in Europe in which six million Jews were murdered by Nazis. These three events—the Diaspora experience, the Holocaust, and the war of independence—shape the fears and hopes of most Israelis today.

Since the late 1800s, pioneering Jews left Europe for Turkish-controlled Palestine, severing themselves from the bourgeois and religious life-styles of their parents. They purchased land with funds from worldwide Jewish philanthropies and set out to establish a Jewish, Socialist, agrarian-based culture and communal economy. They founded rural settlements, kibbutzim, and moshavim (cooperative farms); they established monolithic trade unions, social services, self-help programs, health services, and industries. These young Zionists revived a worldwide movement for the return to Zion and the eventual establishment of a Jewish state. They are referred to as the Yishuv Hehadash, the origins of the modern Zionist community in Palestine.

Alongside this community and more venerable by far was the Yishuv Hayashan. This community was composed of Orthodox Jews who were part of a chain that had remained for centuries in the Holy Land, clustered with their sages in the cities of Jerusalem, Tiberias, and Safed. They dedicated themselves almost totally to Jewish learning and religious life, living in poverty and as a small minority among the Muslims. Much of their income came from emissaries (*shlichim*) sent to prosperous Jewish communities abroad who raised funds for their respective organizations, which were then doled out on their return (Kellner 1977).

While the settlers were busy building their new Socialist-secular state, the religious Talmudists were counting on the Messiah for salvation and change. Between them was a relatively small group of religious Zionists who bridged the chasm between the secular and the ultra-Orthodox, eventually establishing a chief rabbinate, several religious Zionist political parties, and a network of settlements and educational and economic institutions.

During the 1920s and early 1930s, the previous trickle of new immigrants from Europe gave way to a minor flood of shopkeepers and businesspeople from Poland and then from pre-Nazi Germany, seeking escape from anti-semitism in both countries. Many more Jews immigrated to North and South America, England, South Africa, and Australia. These fateful decisions and the separation of families became the bases for strong kinship relationships, and for international Jewish philanthropic support for Israel to this day.

The immigration of traders and shopkeepers quickly resulted in an urban-based society and economy, rather than an agrarian-based one. Kibbutz members initially exerted disproportionate influence on the government and social institutions, but by the 1980s, the kibbutzim, with less than 3 percent of the total population, retained only a shadow of their former influence. Nevertheless, social institutions established by the Labor Movement of David Ben-Gurion, Yitzchak Ben Zvi, Golda Meir, Berl Katznelson, and Levi Eshkol left strong Socialist imprints on contemporary Israeli social institutions.

The history of modern Israel can be understood in terms of the interrelated themes of immigration and physical and cultural survival. Because of the constant state of tension with all of Israel's neighbors except Egypt, any increase in immigration also increases the sense of security, as well as fulfilling the desired return-to-Zion values and the job of "nation building." Immigration, in turn, has provided the labor, ideas, competition, talent, and often the capital needed for the development of the state.

But absorption of immigrants, especially in large numbers over short periods of time, has not been easily accomplished. Every citizen of Israel can trace his or her modern origins to a specific wave of immigration, each with its distinct label. These include the pre-Nazi wave, the Teheran children, the Holocaust survivors, the Sephardi Jews (1948–1956), the Rumanians, the Anglo-Saxons (after the 1967 war), the "early Russians" (1976), the Ethiopians (1982), and now, the *glasnost* Russians. The Sephardi Jews, coming from Arab lands, refugees from the destruction of the First Temple, numbered 750,000, and they were "absorbed" by 600,000 Jews living in the state at the time. To make things more difficult, the country fought two major wars during the ten years of the Sephardi immigration. It can be compared with the United States doubling its population today while at war with Russia, Canada, and Mexico.

Within forty years (1948–1988), the population of the state multiplied 5.5 times, and the Jewish population increased by 5.6 times during that period. Over 1.8 million Jewish immigrants arrived between 1948 and 1988, half of them during the first decade after independence, from over a hundred different countries. The average annual population growth rate from 1950 to 1985 was 6.6 percent, followed by Brazil, with a 4.57 percent average growth rate (United Nations 1957, 1961, 1975, 1985).

The socioeconomic, political, and cultural accommodations and changes that inevitably took place as a result of immigration are still in progress and are very important to an understanding of present and future developments.

THE POLITICAL SECTOR

The formative years for Israel's political institutions were those of the British Mandate in Palestine. This period lasted from 1917, when the Allied armies under the British general Allenby's command drove out the Turks, to 1948, when the United Nations decided to partition Palestine into separate Arab and Jewish sectors. When the Jews declared their sector the state of Israel, seven Arab nations went to war to destroy it.

The British Mandate, in Palestine as in India, was generally benevolent to the local population. The government invited self-rule in selected areas of life for Jews and non-Jews alike, and it encouraged each of the communities to establish its own services and commerce within an overall British departmental structure.

Because of the contribution of Jewish scientists, soldiers, and others to the British war effort, Lord Balfour in 1917 committed the British to supporting the Zionist program for "a homeland in Palestine." In preparation for implementation of this principle, the Jews were asked to establish a "Jewish Agency" to represent the Jewish community, with a national council as its governing body. The Jewish Agency then established a quasi-governmental structure, with education, finance, health, and other departments to rule the affairs of the Jewish community. One of its last departments was the social work department, created in 1932 and headed by a new immigrant, Henrietta Szold, the founder of Hadassah Women in America. The only departments not established in the agency by British demand were those related to immigration and internal security (police and armed forces).

When the British left in 1948, most of the Jewish Agency departments became the ministries of the state of Israel. The Knesset was established, based on the electoral strength of the same political parties formerly represented in the Jewish Agency. The first prime minister, David Ben Gurion, had initially wanted to terminate the Jewish Agency, but then decided to maintain it as a vehicle for bringing immigrants to Israel and helping in their initial absorption, and primarily, to serve as a nonprofit, fund-raising body and receptacle of Jewish Diaspora philanthropy and a forum for Zionist world Jewish leadership acting on behalf of Israel.

The roof organization of the trade unions, the Histadrut General Federation of Labor, created in 1920, had already established a well-organized, service-providing structure for the Jewish working class, based on the same political party structure used for the Knesset elections. From the beginning, control of both the Knesset and the Histadrut went to the Mapai Labor party. This tight coalition with its overlapping directorates concentrated enormous power in the hands of the Labor party. Faced with impossible problems of defense, massive immigration, low food supply, and low income, the centralization of power complemented the need for centralized planning in all public spheres, and is a basic component of Israeli bureaucratic government today.

The various ministries developed a vertical hierarchical structure for implementing their various mandates. Each has great responsibility for supervising municipal standards, services, and budgets. Most of the power of the ministries stems from the fact that they distribute government (tax) funds to the municipalities, none of which can survive on local taxes alone. Only the largest municipalities (Tel Aviv, Jerusalem, and Haifa) have more leeway in service allocation due to their larger local tax bases and electoral clout. In similar fashion, most nonprofit associations attempt to contract for services with the ministries, or seek block grants.

A major change in the Israeli political scene took place in 1977 when the largest opposition party, the Likud, headed by Menachem Begin, succeeded in forming a coalition cabinet and ousting the Labor party for the first time. This was due in part to public anger and demoralization over the surprise attack of the Yom Kippur War in 1973 and heavy Israeli losses, but also to rising inflation, and the appearance of a new Center-Democrat party headed by Prof. Yigael Yadin, which split Labor voters. Most crucial in this mix was massive voting by Sephardi Jews for Begin and his party. Since 1977 there has never been a Labor-led coalition. At most there has been a rotation of the prime minister's position between Likud and Labor.

The majority of Sephardi voters, Jews formerly from Islamic countries, identified more with the Likud party, which projects a right-of-center political stance, a more capitalistic, liberal, free-enterprise economic ideology, and a

Jewish-traditional orientation in general. This development has also led to much greater involvement of Sephardi Jews in senior and other government and civil-service positions, and somewhat more reallocation of resources in projects and programs of development towns and less to the economic strongholds of Labor, such as the kibbutzim and Histadrut industries.

In the 1989–1990 "unity" coalition, the Likud held the prime minister's office and Labor held the finance ministry portfolio. This unwieldy coalition was brought about by two factors: a peace process with the Arabs was sought by both major parties, and Israel's economy continued to weaken. In August 1989, inflation was at an annual rate of 17 percent, unemployment reached 8.3 percent, and tax burdens and government spending were nearly double their relative shares of GNP twenty to thirty years before. Barely half of Israel's potential working-age population (fifteen and older) participates in the civilian labor force, as opposed to 66 percent of the United States population (Rabushka and Hanke 1989).

The efficiency and productivity of Israel's labor force have steadily declined. Total productivity grew at an average annual rate of 4.2 percent during 1961–1973, but was only 6 percent during 1973–1981. Capital per employee grew at about the same rate during both periods, but annual output increase per worker fell from 6.1 percent to 1.9 percent. During 1980–1987, real unit costs for manufacturing increased more rapidly than productivity, while real wages increased 21 percent during 1987–1988, far exceeding gains in productivity and necessitating a series of currency devaluations to keep Israeli goods competitive in world markets (Rabushka and Hanke 1989).

Lower labor-force participation applies to Israeli men and women as well. The respective rates for American and Israeli men in 1989 were 76.2 percent and 62.4 percent; for women the respective rates were 56 percent and 38.9 percent. Between 1973 and 1986, real economic growth in Israel averaged only 3.4 percent a year, compared with 9.2 percent during 1960–1962. In per capita terms, growth during 1973–1976 was almost stagnant at 1.1 percent. While the per capita GNP jumped to 3.6 percent in 1987, it slowed again in 1988 and 1989 (Rabushka and Hanke 1989).

Despite the general economic recession, the standard of living in Israel continued to increase dramatically. For example, the average annual growth rate for TV sets (per thousand people) was 496.6 percent from 1960 to 1985; during the past thirty years the number of phones installed jumped by an average of 40 percent each year; university enrollments increased each year by an average of 17 percent over thirty-five years. More significant was the increase in apartment owners, car owners, persons traveling abroad, and private companies.

Undoubtedly, part of the reason for the unaffordable rise in the standard of living was the injection of funds from foreign governments and private sources, the black market, tax evasion in certain sectors, and deficit spending by both the government and many private citizens.

These objective factors and a public consensus have resulted in a series of Likud-Labor coalition governments trying to provide some unified economic policy, if not foreign policy, and cooperative leadership and planning efforts.

Another closely related development is the increasing public demand for electoral reform, effectively spearheaded by several nonprofit, broad-based social movements. Since any party receiving 1 percent of the total election votes receives a seat in parliament, the number of minor parties has proliferated, enabling no majority party to emerge. Instead, since 1948 Israel has always had coalition governments of various degrees of fragility, all of which are very expensive, as each of the minor partners demands its contractual plums. In 1989 and 1990 bills for electoral reform reached near-final stages in the Knesset, and many Israelis are hoping that the frustrated Likud and Labor parties can reach an agreement to enable electoral reform to become law. This would greatly change the electoral scene and pave the way for only a handful of parties to compete. This may mean somewhat less-participatory politics, but it might lead to more-stable government, fewer ministries, and the merging of the smaller parties.

ISRAEL'S ECONOMIC SECTOR: THE POST-SOCIALIST ERA

Major favored sectors in Israel's economy over the years have been the Labor- and Histadrut-associated industries and services, including for a long period the kibbutz movement enterprises. Their success was undifferentiated from and tied to the success of the Labor party and the country as a whole.

The Likud electoral success brought an end to this protectionism, and in 1987 the Likud initiated a tax reform that gave billions of shekels to the top 1 percent of income earners, with no tax relief to the middle-income groups. The Likud fought inflation with a price and wage freeze, which led to economic stagnation, and it refused to bail out four hundred million dollars of kibbutz debts. During the five-year period from 1984 to 1989, the price of education rose by 250 percent in real terms, and the price of health care rose by over 120 percent. Subsidies for basic food products and public transportation disappeared. Many Israelis blame part of this situation on the Likud's spending billions of shekels to finance projects and settlements in the West Bank and Gaza (Maoz and Temkin 1989).

In November 1989 the former government coalition gave the finance ministry back to the Labor party, with Shimon Peres as finance minister. Within eight months the kibbutzim received a massive subsidy to wipe out part of their debts, and several of the Histadrut enterprises were also aided. All these debts were transferred to the taxpayers.

But once again, all this experience and the new political and economic realities have caused a major ideological change among the Labor leaders. These leaders like those of most of the Western and Eastern-bloc countries (and apparently China), have concluded that the socialist bureaucracy prevents the country from moving forward. In 1989 the government began selling off national companies, those in which the government held the majority of the shares. It has actively sought to privatize government services, and has declared its intention to "liberate the economy," relying more on internal and external private enterprise. In June 1989, the Labor leader and finance minister Shimon Peres announced that the Labor Federation economic enterprises and nationalization of the means of production have damaged initiative, "diminishing creative motivation, giving rise to arbitrary, blind, distorted and paralyzing bureaucracy, It did not lead to class equality, but created a preferred class of managers and an oppressed and mute class of workers. Nationalization dispensed poverty more than it did equality" (Doron 1989).

Actually, socialism slowed to a crawl in Israel in the 1980s as the extensive social insurance and workers' benefits resulted in 25 percent of the GNP being devoted to transfer payments. Since most of the social benefits, including some maintenance, pensions, and wages, are tied to the cost of living, it became impossible to fund these programs. Although most of the social-insurance networks created by the Labor party during the heyday of the welfare state are still intact, they have been greatly trimmed and will be further clipped in the future. A move has already been made in this direction by lowering current unemployment compensation benefits, and by drastically reducing the number of hours of compulsory public-school education.

These trends toward a market economy and less state intervention have alarmed many Israelis who fear a survival-of-the-wealthiest situation such as exists in many capitalistic countries. Already, a large network of "grey" (private) educational institutions has sprung up in every city, with parents creating nonprofit associations to hire teachers to provide extra classes (usually in English, math, arts, and computers) to their children—on the public-school premises, after hours. Private medicine is also beginning to flourish as never before, using existing government or Labor Federation health facilities, after hours. Private health-insurance policies have become standard, guaranteeing faster service and private physicians.

Social workers fear that clients will lose access to personal services. Foster-care placements have been greatly reduced, as have dormitory placements, day care, and social service staff in general. Many young graduates have abandoned the social work for white-collar jobs or other professions. Many more have gone into private practice, along with other health and education professionals.

As Israel gears up to market goods in the new European Economic Community in 1992, more resources are being invested in export industries and producers of foreign currency. Israel has entered a long period of economic restructuring, where previously subsidized companies have gone bankrupt or retrenched, and where retraining of workers for science-based, high-tech industries is taking place. This has created temporary unemployment in some of the larger cities and enormous unemployment in one-industry development towns located away from the major population centers. As the government seeks new industrial investments, these towns are in great distress, often losing their young people to jobs in the large cities on the coastal plain. These are the new core of the disadvantaged who, along with the urban poor and lower-income workers, make up the underclass. Generally, they also belong to the Sephardi population; this may create serious ethnic tension as the stratification continues.

In this climate thousands of nonprofit groups from the third sector have moved in to try to fill the service vacuum, each in its own particular way, and each reflecting the values of Judaism and Israeli society.

SELF-HELP AND NONPROFIT ORGANIZATIONS: THE THIRD SECTOR

The British Mandate saw the development of the Jewish Agency, the Kupat Holim Health Services, Youth Aliya, and services to the aged (Malben and the Joint Distribution Committee), day care (WIZO, Na'amat, the Federation of Hebrew Women, Mizrachi, and Emuna Women's Organization), children's villages, and loan funds for the poor. Most of these prestate organizations and programs still thrive today as major enterprises within the nonprofit sector (Jaffe, 1982b).

With statehood in 1948, volunteer activity waned somewhat as taxpayers felt government should or would take over many of the nonprofit services. But as the country moved rapidly from a semirural agrarian economy to an urban-industrial economy, fighting simultaneously for physical and economic survival, there was a great upsurge in voluntarism and a growth in the nonprofit sector that has not yet peaked. Also, as more casualties of modern life and fateful experiences accumulated (victims of cancer, birth defects, and other illnesses, widows, the handicapped), many of these populations banded together into nonprofit associations seeking rights, services, and status. In addition to these groups, other self-help, social-action, and nonprofit groups were created, twelve thousand of them, including immigrant groups (the most recent is the Association of Ethiopian Immigrants), battered women's groups, civil and women's rights groups, theatrical and cultural associations, ethnic associations, Arab-Jewish friendship associations, and associations of foster parents, the elderly, and large families.

The network of self-help, nonprofit, and volunteer organizations in Israel constitutes a major area of social activity and economic influence. The nonprofit sector employs 11 percent of Israel's labor force. Out of a total of 233,000 workers in health and education, 98,000 (41 percent) were nonprofit-

sector employees (Roter et al. 1985). The value of services supplied by organizations and institutions in this sector is about 8 percent of Israel's GNP and
14 percent of total civilian consumption (Central Bureau of Statistics 1985).
Nonprofit organizations in Israel are the main providers of services in the fields
of health, immigrant absorption, education, welfare, culture, research, and
religion. They are partners with government; 75 percent of the income of non-
profit-sector organizations is transferred from other sectors, primarily (66 percent) from the government sector (Offer 1987).

Volunteer activity in Israel has tripled from five thousand person-years in
1962 to fifteen thousand person-years in 1985 (Roter et al. 1985). The civil-
defense guard alone has over one hundred thousand volunteers, and compulsory volunteering as part of the public-school curriculum accounts for tens of
thousands of additional volunteers. Self-help groups abound in Israel, and social-action groups have become increasingly sophisticated in lobbying for legislation and resources (Danino 1978; Jaffe 1980).

State Relationships with the Third Sector

Israel is a postwelfare state, marked by a relatively large number of universal
social insurance programs such as income maintenance, children's allowances, old-age and survivors' insurance, unemployment insurance, free compulsory education, and insurance for the chronically ill (Cohen and Antler
1985). The overwhelming feature of the formal service-delivery network is
the pervasive role of government, with its tax-funded services, civil-service
employees, and state control. This major core is supplemented by thousands
of nonprofit organizations and agencies, which sometimes serve as vanguard,
catalytic demonstration programs, but more often sell their services to the government (Kramer 1981). This is particularly true in the areas of medical and
child-care services.

In many cases, nonprofit organizations serve their own members rather than
the general population. This is the case for most religious organizations, which
also solicit funds from specific support groups and Jewish and gentile donors
abroad who identify with their religious views and goals. This is also the case
for other organizations, such as the Histadrut Federation of Labor Unions,
which operates the largest health and hospital (nonprofit) service in Israel for
its members.

The government is generally very outwardly supportive of the nonprofit sector, but it is also ambivalent as to how much service territory to allocate to the
nonprofit sector and how much to control it by tax restrictions and accountability measures. The government tends to do its social planning on a relatively ad hoc basis, leans heavily toward centralization of services, and requires constant public recognition and acknowledgment of its work. The
nonprofit sector is seen by some government and political personalities as

threatening to their own needs and goals. This has delayed serious, well-planned, long-range, efficient cooperation and divisions of labor between government and nonprofit agencies in Israel, and is an important area for research and policy change.

During the Turkish administration, public associations were viewed as a potential threat to the government. Consequently, they were forced to register with the authorities, giving full details of their purposes, members, and rules of organization. The "Ottoman Associations" became the nonprofit sector, and the British inherited the registration system, also using it as a way of keeping tabs on public gatherings, activities, and financial transactions.

The Israeli government kept the registration process and the fiscal reporting requirements, but changed the name of these associations to Amutot, or nonprofit public associations. The Ministry of Interior is responsible for the simple registration procedure and keeps a computer record on each organization, which is open to the public for perusal at the ministry offices.

Far more stringent, however, is the procedure for obtaining tax-deductible status. This is handled by the Ministry of Finance and requires the Amuta permit, an annual report from a certified public accountant, an expanded governing body, and direct accountability to a special office for public associations in the ministry. Unfortunately, these records are not open to the public, preventing important research and public scrutiny of the sector. Only the signature of the minister of finance can neutralize the Private Information Law that restricts the availability of these records to the public.

In 1989, over five thousand organizations were registered as tax-deductible nonprofits. In recent years, the ministry has become more stringent, seeking to weed out profit-making organizations disguised as nonprofits attempting to benefit from exemptions from corporate income tax, property tax, capital gains tax, reductions of value added tax, and tax credits for individual and corporate donations. Recently, the commissioner of internal revenue in the Ministry of Finance appointed a professional commission to examine this issue (Center for Social Policy Studies in Israel 1989).

A major finding, however, indicates that current tax incentives for nonprofit organizations and donations to them are not effective as an encouragement for philanthropic work and giving (Center for Social Policy Studies in Israel 1989).

Nonprofit associations in Israel and elsewhere often perform two compatible but diverse functions: they act as pressure groups, prodding government to meet citizens' demands for services, and as functional groups, cooperating with government to formulate and implement public policies. According to current theory, the first type of relationship occurs within a pluralistic configuration in which groups retain their autonomy vis-à-vis the state. In the second case, a corporatist pattern evolves, based on concerted action and partnership between the state and groups. However, research in Israel with a sample of eight welfare (health and disability) associations determined that the associations are generally autonomous and not controlled by the state; they rarely were granted the right of integrated participation (but groups of disabled people take part in formulating policies); the state held fast to its power, unwilling to share it with "outsiders"; and the state did not seek legitimacy by devolving power. It could always command support by virtue of its central role in providing services (Yishai 1989). In brief, the "exchange" or "cost-benefit" theory does not apply to the Israeli situation.

In some cases, the government initiates nonprofit services to fill a service vacuum. This was the case with 150 Community Service Agencies (CSAs), neighborhood community centers founded in the early 1970s. Gradually, the government decreased its financial support and the CSAs introduced a fee-for-service policy and adjusted their programs to new markets. The strategy resulted in a vital network for thousands of families with only catalytic government funding. This model has been repeated many times in different areas of nonprofit work (Yanai 1989; Joint Distribution Committee—Israel 1989). Increasingly, the search for funds has led many Israeli nonprofit organizations into profit-making ventures, selling vital services that government cannot provide in sufficient quality or quantity. The problems posed by the changing clientele of these organizations, especially those in need of government subsidies for purchase of services, is fast becoming an ethical and practical issue in the postwelfare state (Perlmutter and Adams 1989).

Kramer (1981:85) noted in his pioneering comparative study of voluntary agencies in welfare states that "negative public attitudes towards the Ministry of Social Welfare have also been used to justify the development of parallel services by voluntary agencies on the grounds that it is easier for their clientele to utilize a non-governmental service." This observation remains true today, with new nonprofit agencies starting up in the areas of adoption, foster care, and services to the frail elderly, brain-damaged infants, and other groups. In most instances, however, these voluntary agencies will receive government subsidies or reimbursements. Kramer correctly characterized Israel as a close partnership between government and voluntary sectors. However, his description of civic culture as "little citizenship participation outside of political parties and unions" (1981:95) does not reflect the current situation. Today, volunteer associations are the offspring of interest groups, protest and quasi-political ideological groups, and self-help organizations of all kinds, the former reflecting Kramer's description of the "improver role" and advocacy functions as the special domain of the voluntary sector, and the latter focusing on service-dispensing programs.

Some organizations combine advocacy and service, maintaining a fine balance between cooperating with government and eternally pressuring it for policy changes and resources. The Zahavi Association for Rights of Large Families is one such organization, founded in 1971 by seven parents of large families (four or more children). Members of this group were angry over the negative image of large families in Israel, the lack of resources spent on children from these families, and the absence of any government demographic policy.

The association promptly introduced the phrase "families blessed with children" to describe its membership and launched branches and organized self-help activities around the country. Today, there are forty-nine branches throughout Israel, with a total membership of thirty thousand families. It has greatly increased the buying power of families, and has pressed for housing benefits and nonprofit deductions, water-rate reductions, municipal services, organizational facilities, and many other benefits. It is a volunteer, parent-run organization, cutting across all the barriers of ethnic backgrounds (Ashkenazi and Sephardi), religious backgrounds (Orthodox and secular), and income groups. It operates an interest-free loan fund of nearly one hundred thousand dollars, and it provides highly subsidized home reference libraries, tutorial help for children, college entrance exam preparation, counseling, legal advice, educational seminars, and discounts on clothing, food, supplies, appliances, hotel and tourist services, and more. In the early days, it was hardly possible for Zahavi members to appear before the Knesset welfare or finance committees. Today, the national chairman of Zahavi has a pass to park in the Knesset members' lot and can appear on request before committees interested in the view from the grass-roots level.

Until these lobbies are duplicated to the point where they dull the sensitivity and no longer meet the public-relations needs of Knesset members, they will continue to be the prototypes for other grass-roots citizens' organizations.

RELIGION, STATE, AND THE NONPROFIT SECTOR

Israel is the only country in the world in which Jews are the majority of the population (82 percent) and the Jewish religion is the dominant religion. In this small state the size of New Jersey, with 4.4 million citizens, 82.2 percent of the population is Jewish, 13.8 percent Muslim, 2.3 percent Christian, and 1.7 percent Druze or members of other religious groups such as Bahai, Karaites, and Samaritans (Central Bureau of Statistics 1987).

Each of the three major groups can be subdivided into different religious communities with diverse rites and religious leaders. The one hundred thousand members of the Christian community in Israel, for example, are represented by thirty-five different churches, sects, and streams, with over five hundred education, health, welfare, pilgrim, and hospice organizations to serve their needs and to supervise their holy sites. The six hundred thousand members of the Muslim community live primarily in ninety-four towns and villages, and the 250 *kaddim* (clerics) serving in 138 mosques are salaried employees of the Israel Ministry of Religious Affairs. The Druze community numbers sixty-five thousand, and, like the Islamic community, has its own religious court and performs its own wedding rites and many other basic communal services (Ministry of Religious Affairs 1987). This pluralistic but separate religious coexistence is a normative phenomenon, but it has been threatened somewhat in recent times by nationalistic fundamentalist influences within both the Muslim and the Jewish religious groups.

The history of the state of Israel, the Jewish people, and their relationship with other cultures and countries can best be understood within the framework of Jewish religious history, literature, and values. The course of Jewish history and of the state of Israel has been shaped immeasurably by religious values and actions, and by the varied reactions of non-Jews to Jews and Judaism. The roots of modern Israeli institutions, social policy, and services, the national language (Hebrew), the creation and location of the state itself, its foreign policy, and its social, political, and ethnic fabric, population, and divisions, all lead inevitably to Jewish religious foundations, interpretations, and developments. While Israel is not a theocracy, and only 25 percent of the people are observant Jews, the role and control of religion is pervasive in many areas of national and personal life, especially those involving marriage, divorce, family law, and immigration law. "Who is a Jew?" and "who is a (state-recognized) rabbi?" are determined by state as well as by religious law and by the state-sanctioned rabbinical *Beit-Din*, or court of Jewish law. The same clerical authority exists regarding marriage and divorce in the *Shaaria* (Islamic) courts and the Christian and Druze courts.

Unlike in the United States, religion in Israel has state-delegated and tax-funded responsibilities; there is no rigid separation of religion and state, although the secular supreme court has final say when it chooses to exercise its ultimate judicial authority.

Thus religion in Israel does not fall exclusively into the third sector. Rather, it falls into all three spheres of social activity: the public, the nonprofit, and the private. Religious services are provided by all the sectors, with a clear division of labor. All matters of family law are the domain of the religious tax-supported courts, and the Ministry of Religious Affairs subsidizes religious facilities, infrastructure, holy sites, places of religious instruction, and many Jewish and non-Jewish nonprofit religious organizations. The third-sector religious organizations provide direct services to synagogue congregants, operate private religious schools at all grade levels, and fund holiday celebrations and observances in every community and neighborhood in Israel. In the private, for-profit sector, some agencies and entrepreneurs provide religious services for groups and individuals—Bar Mitzvahs at the Western Wall in Jerusalem, tutorial help to obtain religious knowledge and skills.

For Jewish Israelis with even minimal Jewish socialization, education, or involvement with Jewish religion and culture, the imperative to help themselves and be philanthropic is a basic tenet of the tribe and the nation. The Old

Testament, the Jewish Bible, speaks constantly of "charity, prayer, and repentance" (*tzedaka, tefilla,* and *teshuva*) as the formula for redemption, for finding favor with God, and for long life and connection with the Holy Land (Rabinowicz 1982). People are urged to copy the attributes of God: practicing loving-kindness, and mercy; clothing and raising up the poor, the widow, and the stranger. Jews are urged to "hold up your brother when he becomes impoverished" and "let your brother live with you"—in other words, help him while you are still around to do it (Peli 1988b).

Through the ages after the patriarchs, the prophets, and the Jewish kings, the sages and the religious literature of each generation reinforced these injunctions to voluntarism, charity, and justice. Even during the darkest periods of Jewish history, mass religious movements such as Hasidism in the eighteenth century came forth with a hopeful message and a prescription of altruism rather than individualism (Rotenberg 1983). Some even viewed the kibbutz movement as a new semireligious movement, and the religious kibbutz as the fullest realization of religion, nationalism, and socialism (Fishman 1983).

Beyond the biblical literature, the single most important factor that led to institutionalized philanthropy, a self-help mentality, and, self-help services among the Jews was the destruction of the First and Second Temples (and Jewish Commonwealths) in 587 B.C. and A.D. 70. The forced wandering of the Jews, in exile from their homeland for almost two thousand years, and life in predominantly hostile host countries, coupled with a collective religious decision to remain Jewish, reinforced religious values concerning self-help, redemption, and religious identity. These values led to specific indigenous services and charitable and educational institutions and a sophisticated network of mechanisms for coping with religious survival in exile.

It is surprising that the two groups of exiles (the Sephardi, or Middle Eastern, exiles created by the destruction of the First [Solomon's] Temple by the Babylonians, and the Ashkenazi, or Western, exiles created by the destruction of the Second Temple by the Romans) developed very similar coping mechanisms and institutions to ensure survival as Jews. The major task of the Jews during those long centuries of exile was to survive as Jews. The following is a brief description by this author of what this actually meant:

> Remaining Jewish meant maintaining a separate religious life and set of values and priorities dictated by that way of life. It also meant development of family, education, income maintenance, and self-help institutions that could support and reinforce Jewish religious life and prevent assimilation and loss of Jewish identity. In every Jewish community there emerged Jewish leadership and a network of autonomous self-help services, separate from the non-Jewish community and geared to the problems of fellow Jews. These services were anchored deeply in the Biblical commandments, Biblical commentary, religious scholarship, and the personal example of

charismatic religious leaders throughout the centuries. Religious themes that underpinned the social services included the personal accumulation of *mitzvot* (''good deeds''), reward in the Garden of Eden or in the ''World to Come'' after death, following the example of the Biblical patriarchs and matriarchs, hastening the coming of the Messianic era by good deeds, and giving of charity to avoid misfortune and as a concrete sign of repentance for misdeeds. Above all, the central theme behind charitable behavior is the belief that it is commanded by God, that one must ''do'' and not just ''be,'' that there is good and evil in the world and in people (the *yetzer tov* and the *yetzer ra*), and that man has the free choice to decide his actions. Norman Linzer . . . has written expertly about these themes in Judaism and their relationship to social work. The Jewish scholar-philosopher Maimonides spelled out these values and their practical behavioral implication in his famous works *Mishneh Torah* and *Guide to the Perplexed*.

The religious momentum for creating concrete social services to Jewish communities in exile (the Diaspora) was greatly magnified by the constant persecution of Jews because of their clinging to Judaism and religious separatism. Names like Nebuchadnezzar, Titus, Haman, Petlura, Chemelnitzki, Hitler, and thousands of others in cities and villages across the world and throughout time are chronicled in Jewish history as arch anti-Semites who have wreaked havoc and death on Jewish families. These events conditioned Jewish communities to pull together to maintain their way of life and well-being.

The heart of the Jewish community is the family and its children, and the preservation of the family as an institution was primary to the survival of the Jewish People. Child welfare was not a creation of benevolence or paternalism in Jewish life. Thus, every Jewish community boasted day schools (*talmud torah*), religious elementary and high schools and teachers' seminaries (*yeshivot*), a free or low-cost kitchen (*tamchui*) for the poor, free lodging and board in private homes for visitors (*hachnasat orchim*), stipends for support of adult Torah scholars and their families (*killel*), financial support for poor families and individuals (*kapat tzedaka*), and interest-free loan funds (*gemilut chasadim*).

In the traditional Jewish family, children are seen as a blessing, and large families were the norm. The sexual act that resulted in childbirth was ''a reflection of divine creativity; man becomes a creator like God. The human family is a reflection of the divine family. The home is a miniature sanctuary'' (Linzer 1974). The extended family was the norm among early Jewish communities and remained so among the Middle Eastern (also known as Sephardi or Oriental) Jews who lived for centuries among the Muslim population. On the other hand, Jews who lived in the West gradually adopted the prevailing nuclear family pattern of the Western technological and mobility-oriented societies.

One need not look too far to find a modern replica of Jewish social services during the long period of Jewish life without political autonomy, outside the homeland. Every Jewish community in the United States, for example, has a well-established Jewish Community Federation. Jews pay dues to the Federation and fund the Hebrew

204 · Eliezer D. Jaffe

schools, day-care programs, and Jewish community centers. Each community has
its Jewish children's and family service agency, which provides foster care, adoption, family counseling, and other classic social work functions provided by government and other private agencies, In each of these communities there are variations
of all of the services that existed in the Jewish communities of Europe and the Middle
East, including the interest-free loans, the charity and educational funds, and especially the religious educational institutions, with the synagogue at the center of religious life. The network of services may be modernized, but it is all in place, including the basic Jewish values and the pressures of life in exile that created them
centuries ago. (Jaffe 1982: 4–5)

The return to Zion in large numbers from 1880 to 1968, from both Diaspo-
ras, brought with it the social and religious institutions developed and influenced over the years in the various host countries in which the Jewish people
had lived. Some of these institutions were incorporated into the Israeli ministries, such as those of labor, welfare, and religion. The intense necessity for
and experience with successful self-help activity provided the prominent motivations and basic features of the Israeli nonprofit sector.

Along with political Zionism, which sought statehood for the Jews based
on an ingathering of the exiles, came politicization of religion in Israel. Although there was general agreement on the need for a Jewish state, there was
much less consensus on exactly what "Jewish" meant. The religious Zionists
were convinced that dialogue and personal example would not be enough to
secure laws regarding the sanctity of the Sabbath (business closed and no public transportation on Saturday), religious education (separate religious and secular public-school tracks, government support for yeshivas, academies, and
religious institutions), marriage and divorce according to Halacha (Jewish
law), kosher food in all government offices (including army bases and at all
official gatherings), and observance of religious holidays as national holidays.

They felt that in Israel, as in the Diaspora, they would have to establish a
complex infrastructure of self-help services for "their" community to preserve their Orthodox Jewish culture from assimilation into the predominant
(75 percent) non-Orthodox Israeli Jewish society. However, unlike their prior
experience in the Diaspora, Orthodox Jews wanted to create state policy for
themselves and for the nonreligious, more conducive to Jewish values. In Israel this could only be done politically. Consequently, the religious Zionists
established a number of religious political parties and ran for parliament. The
foundations of these parties began with the development of the Zionist movement in Europe in the early 1900s. For example, the Mizrachi Movement was
founded in 1902 in Vilna, and became a political party in Israel in 1948,
changing its name to the National Religious Party in 1956. Similar parties
were established by the ultra-Orthodox Agudat Yisrael, the Poalei Agudat
Yisrael, and more recently, the Sha'as party (Talmi and Talmi 1973). These

parties were successful in securing religious legislation primarily because under Israeli electoral procedure no single party in Israel has ever been able to obtain a majority of the votes in any of the past elections to the Knesset. Thus, any large party that seeks to establish a firm coalition government and to rule has to cater to the religious-party bloc (Jaffe 1990).

This situation explains how most of the religious laws mentioned above were devised. It also explains why government transfer payments are provided rather generously to a relatively large number of religious nonprofit educational, medical, child-care, settlement, and other institutions operated by the religious movements throughout Israel. Many Orthodox Jews in Israel still view politicization of religion as antithetical to religion (Spero 1988), but others see it as self-defense against the non-religious Socialist parties that were tapping government funds for their own nonprofit social, educational, and medical projects and for settlements. There is no doubt that the religious parties, originally interested in the preservation and growth of their institutions and in their definition of Judaism for the Jewish state, have now become major funders and suppliers of nonprofit services. They have also become very involved in efforts to determine the final borders of the country and the fate of the West Bank, or Judaea and Samaria.

The relative success thus far of the religious parties in obtaining religious legislation nationally and locally cannot be explained only by their success at coalition bargaining tables. There is much cultural sympathy and benevolence in the general population for the religious side of statehood. David Hartman, a rabbi, teacher, and philosopher in Jerusalem, expresses the modern Israeli view that while Israel is not a theocracy, it is also not a purely secular state in the sense that most Western democracies are:

> Which democracy would show so much tolerance toward any religious group as our secular authorities are tolerating so many anti-Zionist, ultra-Orthodox Jews who are making life unbearable here? Why do the secularists show as much tolerance as they do of legislation that enforces *halacha* (Jewish religious law)? Are we a people or a faith? We are neither, and we are both. If you are a Jew, you cannot remember Jewish history and ignore the prophets. You cannot touch the land without being awake to the teachings of Amos or Rabbi Akiva. . . . Where was it ever seen that a people staked it all on a promise? (Hartman 1988)

Electoral reform could have radical implications for the religious parties. They might have to merge into larger religious blocs, and they might lose their ability to force government decisions on religious questions, leaving these to rabbinical authorities and their respective followers. Spero (1988), a prominent immigrant rabbi from the United States and professor of Jewish philosophy, calls for a rejection of religious political parties as effective instruments of religious change in Israel. He is joined in this view by the late Israeli rabbi Pinchas Peli (1988), who wrote that "the voice of the politician and the dealmaker is almost the only voice of religion that is heard in the land." These views are quickly countered by Kirschenblum (1988), a member of the Mizrachi movement and chairman of the Jewish Great Synagogue, who "cannot imagine a proud religious life in Israel without the central rabbinic authority of the Chief Rabbinate which is the bridge between Torah-true Jews the world over and the State of Israel. Using politics for religion, as we do, to strengthen its institutions and assure its dignified continuity by democratic means is not only permissible, but even laudable."

Thus the ideological and philosophical divisions are clear within the Orthodox community. On another front is a growing young, politically active, and vocal bloc of liberal and secular Israelis bent on obtaining eventually the total separation between religion and state.

The Diaspora Connection and Religious Kinship

Because of the growth of the nonprofit sector and the need for resources to support it, fund-raising has again become a profession in Israel, with instruction and technology available for those organizations that can afford it. This development includes increasing use of knowledge about the resources of the international foundation community as it affects Israel (Jaffe 1988b). In this regard, Israel's connection with Diaspora Jewry in other countries is a major factor in the politics, mechanics, and values of the unique international support system that has been developed for Israel's nonprofit social-service network.

Less than one-third of the Jews alive today returned to live in the state of Israel, and most of those who did came from "countries of distress"—pre- and post-Holocaust Europe, refugees from Islamic countries (seven hundred thousand), Russian refuseniks, and Ethiopian Jewish refugees (fifteen thousand so far, with another fifteen thousand trapped in Ethiopia). Only a relatively small number of Jews came to Israel from the free, democratic countries of the West—forty-five thousand born in North America and Oceania; forty-one thousand born in Latin America (Central Bureau of Statistics 1987: 77). Thus, ever since the days of Ezra and Nehemiah, when a relative handful of Jews returned from Babylonia, the prosperous Diaspora communities have sent primarily financial support to those brethren refugee Jews who settled under difficult economic, political, and physical conditions in the Holy Land. This ancient philanthropic relationship, forged primarily in religious duty, remembrance, and love of the Holy Land and its refugee Jews, also became part of the ethos of modern Judaism. Charity for Jews in Palestine became institutionalized and organized between 1810 and 1860 in the form of the Haluka, or distribution of Diaspora charity to poor Jews in Palestine (Rothschild 1986). In 1852, the "North American Aid Association for Indigent Jews of Jerusalem" was established by the chief rabbi of England, Rabbi Nathan Adler

(Jaffe 1987). In the 1970s Israel was described as the heart and spiritual center of the Jewish people by foremost Conservative and Reconstructionist educators and religious leaders such as Abraham Joshua Heschel and Mordechai Kaplan in the United States. They fully supported efforts among their congregants to provide financial and political support for Israel, but were less enthusiastic about the need for massive Jewish immigration from the West. In 1921, Jewish communities pioneered in developing methods and leadership for modern, sophisticated mass fund-raising by Jewish federations and organizations around the world. The UJA (United Jewish Appeal) in North America and the Keren Hayesod Appeal in Europe, South America, and elsewhere are two of the largest charitable funds, sending $420 million to Israel *each year*. These funds arrive via the Jewish Agency, which is a nonprofit Israeli welfare organization (United Israel Appeal 1987; Sheffer and Manor 1980). For perspective, this amount exceeds the total annual revenue of each of eleven of the fifteen largest charities in America, just behind Goodwill Industries and UNICEF (Kinkhead 1987). The $350 million in UJA funds sent from North American Jews in 1987 represented 1.5 percent of Israel's $23.5 billion budget, and 9.8 percent of the government's total social-services budget—health, education, welfare, housing, and absorption of immigrants (Ministry of Finance 1987). In the early years of the state, income from foreign philanthropy exceeded the total economic assistance from the United States (Stock 1987).

These sums do not include direct philanthropic grants from private donors, foundations, associations, corporations, synagogues, community federations, or other sources, which in total at least equal the UJA annual income for Israel (Jaffe 1985, 1988b). The Diaspora financial connection, its religiohumanitarian anchorings, and the donor-recipient relationships that nurture it are all important topics for concern, research, and discourse. Obviously, many nonprofit Israeli organizations would wither without these funds, yet many Israelis are deeply concerned about the almost exclusively money-oriented donor-recipient relationship (and related negative stereotypes) between Israel and Diaspora Jews. Many Jews have substituted donating to Israel for religious practice, Jewish scholarship, and Jewish education.

The Politicization of Mainstream Philanthropy

One of the fruits of the politicization of religious activity was access to mainstream funds (UJA, Keren Hayesod, legacies) coming to Israel from the Diaspora. As noted above, the funds gathered for Israel by organized Jewish communities abroad are sent to the Jewish Agency in Israel. During the British Mandate, the Jewish Agency was the Jewish "government in waiting." Once the state was created, the agency became a large service organization in the areas of slum renewal, immigrant absorption, settlement, and child placement (Hoffman 1986a). The agency's governing bodies are made up half of donors from the Diaspora and half of representatives of the World Zionist Organization (WZO). Since the WZO consists primarily of Israeli Zionist political parties, this means that these parties control 50 percent of the Diaspora charitable funds given to and distributed by the Jewish Agency.

This arrangement and the politicization of collective Diaspora philanthropy has allowed Israeli parties, including the religious parties, to benefit, directly and indirectly, from their own nonprofit enterprises in Israel. Recent sensitivity to and increased awareness of this situation has caused some Diaspora donors to seek reforms (although they are only cosmetic thus far) in Jewish Agency governance, and many have begun to give to Israeli nonprofit groups or to private foundations serving Israel. The PEF Israel Endowment Funds, located in New York, sent eleven million dollars directly to Israeli nonprofit organizations in 1987. The New Israel Fund (1987) allocated two million dollars; the Doron Foundation donated eight million dollars in six years. The Tel Aviv Foundation, the Jerusalem Foundation, the Rothschild Foundation, and the American-Israel Cultural Foundation are only a few of the rapidly growing number of private foundations operating in Israel, allocating Diaspora funds to a large variety of nonprofit organizations. In partial response to this important development, the Jewish Agency has now established its own Innovative and Creative Programs Fund to finance projects of nonprofit organizations, external to the Jewish Agency departments. It is hoped that this will be a nonpolitical effort.

Nonprofit Activity among Non-Jewish Religious Groups in Israel

Some of the dynamics presented above are also relevant for minority religious groups in Israel. For example, Christian and Islamic nonprofit groups benefit greatly from financial assistance from coreligionists abroad. Scores of nonprofit associations assist the blind, the invalid, the ill, and children in need of aid. These are in addition to the network of government services existing in Arab Israeli towns and communities, as in the Jewish community (Jaffe 1982b).

The rapid integration of Israeli Arabs (Christian and Muslims) is resulting in an increase in indigenous self-help organizations, fund-raising, and volunteer services. Several Jewish Knesset members have suggested mandatory volunteer service (in Arab or other social, educational, and medical settings) for all Arab young people, since they are not inducted into the Israeli Army for three years of duty, as is the case for Jewish youths. If such a law is passed, the implications for voluntarism and a whole series of other social issues could be far-reaching.

It is important to study in depth, from historical, religious, national, and economic perspectives, the nature and direction of voluntarism, philanthropy, and the nonprofit sector among Israeli minority groups. This has never been done in a systematic way, neither for Arabs in the territories nor for Arabs and other minorities in Israel proper.

Finally, there has developed an ambivalent interdependence between minority religious groups in Israel and the dominant Jewish secular and religious establishments. It is important to examine these relationships in order to facilitate maximum participation and religious expression in Israeli society by all religious groups.

THE PUBLIC SPHERE IN ISRAEL

The past few decades in Israel have been outstanding in the persistent polarization of social groups and the breakdown of consensus on many issues central to the public and the state. For example, until late 1989 the ingathering of the exiles, a sacred task in prestate days and a central principle of Zionism, received only sporadic attention from the government and the public. There was no public sense of mission regarding immigration ever since the Holocaust survivors arrived. This was characterized by ad hoc planning and follow-up for the Ethiopian Jews and the expected immigration of tens of thousands of Russian Jews. The government machinery and programs for handling immigration were not in place, and there still is a constant battle for territory between state and nonprofit organizations dealing with immigrants and immigration.

All of this has now drastically changed because of current Russian emigration policy and American immigration policy. Jews can now freely leave the Soviet Union and are doing so in huge numbers due to their (not unfounded) fear of anti-Semitism resulting from increased Russian religiosity, scapegoating regarding the ills of communism, and ultranationalism now blossoming in the Soviet Union.

Most Jews leaving Russia would undoubtedly prefer to settle in America, seeking the best that capitalism has to offer. However, American immigration quotas do not allow this any longer, and from January 1990 to July 1990 over 50,000 Russian Jews arrived in Israel. A government interministrial coordinating committee anticipates 150,000 Soviet immigrants arriving each year at a cost of $2.3 billion annually through 1992. Senior Jewish Agency and government officials now predict that 2,000,000 Soviet Jews will eventually come here. More than 1,000,000 already possess entrance visas for Israel.

The establishment of a new, narrow Likud government (62 out of 120 seats) in the spring of 1990 focused primarily on gathering in the mass exodus from Russia. Emergency regulations were passed to begin a massive housing program, job training, and airlifts from Eastern Europe, and to enlarge the socioeducational infrastructure for the new immigrants. Diaspora Jews were asked to raise six hundred million dollars in three years for the Russians, and all signs point to this being accomplished in half the time, with more funds to be collected in addition to the original quota. Private philanthropy also contributed large sums, one American donor alone giving twenty million dollars directly to the Russian Immigrant Association, headed by Natan Sharansky, for housing mortgages.

This development will have a huge impact on the Israeli society, economy, and political power structure. Approximately 41 percent of the Russian immigrants are scientists and academicians, and 25 percent are technicians, teachers, and professionals. For Israel, now moving into high-tech enterprises for local and export purposes, this highly educated Western population could revolutionize the economic and social scene. The political leanings of the immigrants are not clear, but some observers suggest a tendency to the right, with important policy implications, in any case. The Russian immigration must not come at the expense of disadvantaged, mostly Sephardi, families and of young Israeli couples, a development that could create serious social havoc. Fortunately the government understands this issue, and is attempting to share new housing and jobs with these veteran Israelis. Almost every other major issue, including the "peace process," has been placed on the back burner in favor of absorbing the Russian immigrants into Israel. Most Israelis welcome the immigrants and have shown an outpouring of hospitality and sympathy. Many are also convinced that such a large immigration may provide the strength and security needed to achieve peace with Israel's neighbors.

Regarding the most crucial of all issues for Israelis, the attainment of peace with the Arabs, the public is sharply divided between hawks and doves over what solutions to pursue. One camp has done everything possible to help promote a Palestinian state in the West Bank and Gaza, convinced that total separation and sovereignty for the Palestinians will save the Jewish state demographically from an eventual Arab majority in general and in the Knesset and from continued violence in the territories, and will lead to peace with the other Arab states. They cite the squandering of $125 million in resources each year in the West Bank, and the loss of two-thirds of Israel's current annual economic growth due to the *intifada* or uprising in the territories.

Other Israelis are doing everything possible to build more Jewish settlements in Judaea and Samaria. They are extremely fearful of another aggressive, terrorist-run Arab state a few miles from Israel's major population centers and see a Palestinian state as part of a salami-slicing of Israel and a springboard for an eventual destructive, combined military attack on the Jewish state. Still others will countenance no other border than the Jordan River as Israel's final eastern boundary, as part of what they see as God's promise to the children of Israel.

Where consensus on the defense of the country and national survival was once clear to all, the 1967 Six-Day War created a bitter controversy deeply felt in the military, economic, religious, social, and political spheres of Israeli society. Not one citizen is unaffected by this controversy. Most have a clear opinion about it, and tens of thousands are active in publicly pursuing their views in one form or another, including through nonprofit citizens' associations.

Another sector where consensus has fallen apart is the struggle between secular and religious Jews. As Western materialistic culture pervades society, young people have often become alienated from Judaism and from the roots of their parents and grandparents. The secular educational system, administered for decades by secular Labor party officials and educators, feared any form of religious educational content, thus depriving generations of youth from receiving basic information about Jewish ritual, philosophy, and religious thought, even as history and cultural anthropology. As a result, generations of Jews came out of the public education system ignorant of the basics concerning their own religion, if not antireligious. Some lost touch with their attachment to the country, and the raison d'être of a unique Jewish state. Beyond ignorance of Jewish values and sources, the secular kibbutz movement had only revulsion for and misconceptions about the Jews of the Old Yishuv, especially the politically involved Orthodox.

Many ultra-Orthodox Jews today simply dismiss the secular Jews as "non-Jews," beyond help. A few of the ultra-Orthodox consider the state itself to be sacrilegious, a blasphemy against God who alone can bring Jewish redemption in the Holy Land by ushering in the Messianic Era. All other human attempts to establish a state are doomed and illegitimate in their eyes. The non-religious have no part in their world. This is a far cry from the Mandate days and the 1948 war of independence, when everyone, secular and religious, fought together to bring in illegal Jewish immigrants, harass the British, and fight off the invading Arab armies. Although there is some attempt at dialogue, primarily by nonprofit associations of modern Orthodox Zionist Jews acting as a bridge, these are meager and do not touch the masses on either side.

Lack of consensus also exists concerning the Sephardi and Ashkenazi Jews, although much objective progress has been made. Fighting for equal educational opportunity and for political power, the Sephardi Jews have improved their status economically, socially, and politically, but stereotypes on both sides persist and there is a very high positive correlation between being disadvantaged and being Sephardi (Jaffe 1988b). Ben Gurion's dream of having a Sephardi commander of the army may yet be exceeded by the election of a Sephardi prime minister.

Jews and Arabs in Israel (inside the pre-1967 "Green Line" borders) have very different political views about what peaceful borders mean. Israeli Arabs clearly identify with West Bank Arabs as to the need for a Palestinian state, and some hope eventually to link the predominantly Arab Galilee to such an adjacent state. This causes tremendous friction between Arabs and Jews, with occasional violence on both sides by extremists.

Beyond these indigenous conflicts, the Israeli public sphere is split on issues common to the Western world. These include abortion, women's rights, constitutional reform, nuclear arms, religious and political pluralism, civil rights, and social services such as utilities and higher-education policies.

Many of these pressures in Israeli society have resulted in *mediating services*, both in the public sector and in the third sector. For example, civil-rights activists have blossomed and flourished, insisting on equal treatment and the clarification of the rights of contending parties. The prime minister has appointed official government representatives to deal with high-pressure social issues, encouraging debate and defusing conflict. Nevertheless, without basic policy decisions many of these issues cannot be resolved.

CONCLUSION

The public sphere in Israel is characterized by dynamic interactions among the sectors of society. Events take place rapidly, with many and varied actors involved, many of them from outside Israel. Israel's public sphere encompasses not only citizens of Israel, but Jews around the world in countries in distress, as well as those from prosperous and free countries.

Bureaucratic norms are part of the legacy of the British Mandate, massive immigration, scarce resources, and defense needs. While these are pervasive, there is also a very strong partnership with the third sector, a rapidly growing symbiotic relationship. Religion, like most other institutions, has been highly politicized and expertly exploited by small political coalition partners. Israel's third sector plays a major role in the provision of services, and in the future will probably contract for many services now provided by the government. Private enterprise will also provide far more services than before, but to a more economically privileged clientele. The Israeli government cannot afford to continue extensive funding and centralization of services, nor does it ideologically now want to do so. Over ten billion dollars have been spent on the Lebanese war, the *intifada*, and the settlements in Judaea and Samaria. Funding must now be found for jobs for new immigrants and the unemployed, and housing and services must be provided for immigrants as well as the four hundred thousand additional adults (native-born and immigrants) who will reach the age of twenty-one during the next five years. The economic miracles of the first two decades of the state may be hard to repeat in the next decades, with a largely middle-class population eager to further improve its standard of living.

These are major conceptual and economic changes that will drastically change the scope and future content of the public, private, and nonprofit sectors.

Third-sector organizations will continue to mobilize resources to satisfy new demands that cannot be satisfied by the state or the market. But they will have to be much more creative and aggressive in raising funds, labor, and skills for the job. If they fail, it will not mean a return to bureaucratic government services, but a dramatic reduction of services and an increase in unmet human needs. In effect, the postwelfare state has lowered its sights, encouraging the nongovernment organizations, especially in the third sector, to take more initiative.

The nonprofit sector in Israel increasingly finds itself providing goods and services that are unavailable in the other sectors. In the process, it has clearly created an important social by-product that has frequently resulted in the improved integration of a very polarized, divided society. In every area of Israeli social conflict and ideological contention, there are nonprofit, third-sector organizations that have been created to mediate, inform, and create a dialogue between the parties involved. In numerous cases, the third sector has defused serious conflicts in the public sphere, and has helped the government formulate policy and resource-allocation decisions when the government could not clearly perceive the public will or was in a political stalemate. This mediation function, whereby third-sector organizations emerge as influential forces in the bureaucratic public sector, is a major feature of Israeli society.

This little-recognized but extremely important mediation by-product may be the first important contribution to Israel of those unsung organizations standing between the state and the market.

References

Center for Social Policy Studies in Israel. 1989. *Interim Report, April, 1989*. Jerusalem: Center for Social Policy Studies in Israel.

Central Bureau of Statistics. 1985. *Survey of Income and Expenditures of Nonprofit Institutions, 1980–1981*. Jerusalem: State of Israel.

———. 1987. *Statistical Abstract of Israel, 1987*. Jerusalem: State of Israel.

Cohen, Shlomo, and Yaakov Antler. 1985. *The Pension System in Israel*. Jerusalem: Brookdale Institute.

Danino, Avraham. 1978. *The Child-Favored Family: Large Families in Israel*. Haifa: Zahavi Association.

Doron, Daniel. 1989. "The Economy May Have Its Messiah: Shimon Peres." *The Jerusalem Post*, 28 June.

Fishman, Aryei. 1983. "The Religious Kibbutz: Religion, Nationalism, and Socialism in a Communal Framework." In *The Sociology of the Kibbutz*, edited by Ernest Kranz, pp. 115–25. New Brunswick, N.J.: Transaction Books.

Goldscheider, Calvin. 1986. *The American Jewish Community*. Atlanta: Scholars Press.

Hartman, David. 1988. "Faithful to Our Memory." *Israel Scene* (April): 6–7.

Hoffman, Charles. 1986. *Project Renewal: Community and Change in Israel*. Jerusalem: Halberstat Publications.

———. 1986b. "Where Do All Our Dollars Go?" *Baltimore Jewish Times*, May–June.

Jaffe, Eliezer. 1979. "Non-Conventional Philanthropy," *Moment* 4.

———. 1980. *Pleaders and Protesters: Citizens' Organizations in Israel*. New York: American Jewish Committee.

———. 1982a. *Child Welfare in Israel*. New York: Praeger.

———. 1982b. *Giving Wisely: The Israel Guide to Nonprofit and Volunteer Social Services*. Jerusalem: Koren.

———. 1985. *Givers and Spenders: The Politics of Charity in Israel*. Jerusalem: Ariel Press.

———. 1987. "The Crisis in Jewish Philanthropy." *Tikkun* 2.

———. 1988a. *A Private Foundation in Israel: The Doron Foundation for Education and Welfare*. Jerusalem. Manuscript.

———. 1988b. *Unequal by Chance*. Jerusalem: Gefen.

———. 1990. "The Role of Nonprofit Organizations among the Haredi (Ultra-Orthodox) Jewish Community in Israel." In *The Nonprofit Sector in the United States and Abroad*, edited by Russy Sumariwalla and Kathleen McCarthy. San Francisco: Jossey-Bass.

Jewish Agency for Israel. 1990. *Operation Exodus: An Israel Report, June 1990* (in Hebrew). Jerusalem: Information Department.

Joint Distribution Committee—Israel. 1989. *The Israel Association of Community Centers—Facts and Figures*. Jerusalem: Joint Distribution Committee.

Kellner, Yaakov. 1977. "Beginnings of Social Policy in the Yishuv of the Land of Israel." *Megamot* 14–15:175–91.

Kinkhead, Gaven. 1987. "American's Best-Run Charities." *Fortune*, 9 November, 145–50.

Kirschenblum, Mordechai. 1988. "Religion and Politics." *The Jerusalem Post*, June 19.

Kramer, Ralph M. 1981. *Voluntary Agencies in the Welfare State*. Berkeley and Los Angeles: University of California Press.

Liebman, Charles. 1977. *Pressure without Sanctions: The Influence of World Jewry on Israeli Policy*. Rutherford, N.J.: Fairleigh Dickinson University Press.

Linzer, Norman. 1974. "On the Role of Volunteerism in the Jewish Tradition." In *New Directions in the Jewish Family and Community*, edited by Gilbert Rosenthal. New York: Federation of Jewish Philanthropies.

Maoz, Shlomo, and Avi Temkin. 1989. "The Devaluation of (Shimon) Press," *The Jerusalem Post*, June.

Ministry of Finance. 1987. *Budget of the State of Israel*. Jerusalem: State of Israel.

Ministry of Religious Affairs. 1987. *Budget of the Ministry of Religious Affairs*. 1987. Jerusalem: State of Israel.

Musher, Sidney. 1987. *PEF Israel Endowment Funds, Annual Report*. New York: PEF.

New Israel Fund. 1987. *New Israel Fund Annual Report*. New York: New Israel Fund.

Offer, Gur. 1987. "National Expenditure for Social Services." In *Allocation of Resources for Social Services. 1986–1987*, edited by Yaakov Kop. Jerusalem: Center for Social Policy Studies in Israel.

Peli, Pinchas H. 1988a. "A Religious Renaissance: Can It Happen in Israel?" *Moment* (December).

———. 1988b "Welfare State in the Torah." *The Jerusalem Post*, 6 May.

Perlmutter, Felice, and Carolyn Adams. 1989. *The Voluntary Sector and For-Profit Ventures: The Transformation of American Social Welfare?* Manuscript, Hebrew University, Jerusalem.

Rabinowicz, Harry. 1982. *Hasidim and the State of Israel*. London: Associated University Press.

Rabushka, Alvin, and Steve Hanke. 1989. "Where Has Israel's Labour Force Gone?" *The Jerusalem Post*, 2 August.

Rotenberg, Mordechai. 1983. *Dialogue with Deviance: The Hasidic Ethic and the Theory of Social Contraction*. Philadelphia: Ishi Press.

Roter, Raphael, et al. 1985. "The Nonprofit Sector and Volunteering." In *Israel's Outlays for Human Services, 1984*, edited by Yaakov Kop, pp. 181–229. Jerusalem: Center for Social Policy Studies in Israel.

Rothschild, Meir M. 1986. *The Haluka: A Facet of the Relationship of Diaspora Jews to the Jews of Eretz Israel from 1810 to 1860*. Jerusalem: Reuben Mass.

Shapiro, Daniel. 1987. "A Perspective on North American–Israeli Relationships." In *Summary of Board Leadership Institute*. New York: Council of Jewish Federations.

Sheffer, Gabriel, and Yohanan Manor. 1980. "Fund-Raising: Money Is Not Enough." In *Can Planning Replace Politics? The Israeli Experience*, edited by M. Bilski, et al., pp. 282–319. Hague: Martiners Nighoff.

Spero, Shubert. 1988. "Who Needs Religious Parties?" *The Jerusalem Post*, 26 May.

Stock, Ernest. 1987. *Partners and Pursestrings: A History of the United Israel Appeal.* New York: University Press of America.

Talmi, Efraim, and Menachem Talmi. 1973. *The Zionist Lexicon.* Jerusalem: World Zionist Organization.

United Israel Appeal. 1987. *Annual Report, 1987.* New York: United Israel Appeal.

United Nations. 1957, 1961, 1975, 1985. Population Statistics. *United Nations Demographic Yearbook.* New York.

Yishai, Yael. 1989. *State and Welfare Groups: Competition or Cooperation?* Manuscript, Hebrew University, Jerusalem.

Yanai, Uri. 1989. *Organization in Transmission: From Government to Non-Government Service Centers.* Manuscript, Hebrew University, Jerusalem.

CHAPTER EIGHT

Japan: The Public Sphere in a Non-Western Setting

Helen Hardacre

THE PUBLIC SPHERE in Japan is characterized by a broad consensus favoring continued economic growth as the nation's major priority. Implied in this is the idea that Japan should be essentially a mercantilist nation, leaving most questions of political ideology out of its foreign policy and out of its dealings with other nations. This consensus was developed in the postwar decades in the face of the overwhelming and obvious need to reestablish economic stability after Japan's disastrous defeat in World War II, and under considerable pressure from the Allied Occupation to accept peace and democracy as the nation's guiding ideals. The success of this pressure from the central government and from foreign countries for a consensus about the national identity has been evidenced by the steady improvement in the nation's standard of living during the postwar decades. The basic commitment to sustained economic growth has been supported by the media, and by voluntary associations across the board, including religious ones. The consensus is further supported by the formation of individual values conducive to it, building on value patterns deeply rooted in Japanese history.

The goal of sustained economic growth and prosperity provides the broad umbrella under which other issues of values are debated. Of these, two in particular stand out: the issues of brain death and organ transplants. The concept of brain death is not widely accepted in Japan, and it has no legal status; thus transplant operations resulting in the death of the donor are not performed. There is, however, a growing pressure to establish brain death as the official medical standard of death so that such operations might be performed. To this, however, there is strong opposition, including from most religious associations, based on traditional concepts of life and death and a distrust of modern medicine. Contributions to this debate from religious leaders have only just begun, however, and are not presently very influential.

In contemporary discourse on public values, Japan is distinguished by an ongoing dynamic of comparison and confrontation with the West. Such questions as the following underlie this discourse: How can the nation retain its distinctive cultural heritage and ethos while still incorporating so much from the West? How can the people retain a distinctive identity as Japanese when their society is so pervasively influenced by the West, and when the country in contemporary times is constantly called on by foreign governments to lift a variety of barriers to further cultural, economic, and political interchanges? These and similar questions have dominated Japanese discourse on public values throughout the nation's modern history.

One of the distinctive issues in the Japanese case is the assumption in discussions about public values that Japan is under pressure from the outside to incorporate Western values, styles of life, and ways of thinking. In this sense, the discourse on public values in Japan is not entirely an internal affair; it presupposes the existence of external "conversation partners" who want, for reasons of their own, the Japanese to continue to assimilate Western values, which are further understood to privilege the individual and the quest for self-fulfillment. This assumption of an ever-present foreign pressure on the national identity is welcomed by some as a much-needed catalyst for change, and decried by others who call on the nation to return to "tradition"—which is cast in increasingly narrow, sometimes nationalistic, terms.[1]

THE PUBLIC SPHERE IN JAPAN

The idea of the public sphere refers originally to the domain of social life where public opinion is formed, an arena of discourse on values that stands between the state, on the one hand, and the market, on the other. Built on a liberal idealization of the autonomy of citizens gathering together to discuss the public good apart from the coercive power of the state and the marketplace, the concept is embedded in Western ideals of freedom and liberation of the self from various constraining forces as a primary goal of individual and social life.

Habermas's critique of the classical formulation of the idea of the public sphere holds that the liberal view of a public sphere masked significant ideological aspects. Whereas statements of the common good may appear to have arisen from the free and disinterested application of the light of reason to questions of social significance, in reality they "scarcely [can] be understood in terms of a consensus achieved by private persons; in public discussion, they correspond, in more or less undisguised form, to compromises between conflicting private interests."[2] Habermas thus calls attention to the heavy influence of private interests on public discourse on the public good in modern democracies. This point is particularly salient in considering the nature of the

---

[1] The issue of tradition is closely linked to that of national identity. There is a popular genre of writing seeking to clarify the national identity, which is known variously as *nihonjinron*, "theory of the Japanese," *nihonbunkaron*, "theory of Japanese culture," *nihonshakairon*, "theory of Japanese society," or *nihonron*, "theory of Japan." These writings seek to identify an essential "Japaneseness" in terms of language, blood, culture uniqueness, and strong contrasts with the West. See Harumi and Hiroshi 1983.

[2] Habermas (1989:235).

public sphere in Japan, and should be addressed in combination with an understanding of the role of the state.

The nation's modern history has been characterized by extensive and perduring expansion of the state, dating from the Meiji Restoration of 1868, when under pressure from the West Japan opened its doors to international relations of all kinds and embarked on the course of modernization. The state and the most powerful market forces joined hands and cooperated in seeking the nation's advancement in a variety of ways, and have been joined inextricably. Both have shaped and molded public discourse on the public good in such a way that it is extremely difficult to discern the existence of a public sphere standing between the two. The scope for a public sphere in the classic, liberal sense, therefore, has throughout modern Japanese history been extremely limited, in addition to being dominated by marketplace issues. Discourse about the public good has, in fact, been dominated (through state direction in consultation with the leaders of the nation's economic powers) by essentially economic issues. Other issues that have come before the nation have been cast within a framework that assumes the desirability of the economic goals affirmed by the state in concert with economic interests. There is simply little room for issues cast in other terms to come before the public for its consideration or debate. The evolution of this situation can best be understood through a brief examination of some relevant historical issues.

HISTORICAL CONSIDERATIONS

Premodern theories of statecraft promoted core values that have harmonized well with modern goals of economic development. Japan's early modern period (1600–1868) saw the official adoption of Confucian and Buddhist thought as the rationale for government, and values emanating from these traditions, such as loyalty, filial piety, harmony, diligence, sincerity, and modesty, found virtually universal acceptance at all levels of society. These traditional virtues were the basic elements of all discourse on public values. While philosophers of the era differed in their interpretation of them, these values were made a part of educational curriculums in most domains[3] without reference to minute philosophical distinctions. Public discourse about values was dominated by these concepts and remained rather static until the opening of the country to the West with the Meiji Restoration.[4]

During the Meiji period (1868–1912), Japan created the institutional infrastructure of a modern nation-state, including compulsory education, military conscription, and parliamentary government. Industrialization proceeded rapidly, first through the establishment of textile factories and later through the

[3] During this era Japan was divided into a number of domains (*han*), whose rulers (*daimyō*) governed their subjects with considerable autonomy.
[4] Bellah (1957) and Ooms (1985).

creation of heavy industries of all kinds. Large families of corporations, united by a holding company at the top called a *zaibatsu*, controlled much of the economy through complex relations with the government. Urbanization was pronounced because many sought work in the cities, partly due to the inducements of urban life, and in many cases to escape rural poverty. The Japanese empire was established with the annexation of Taiwan, the Korean peninsula, and Manchuria, and many Japanese went as settlers to these areas. In addition, many Japanese, especially from western Japan, immigrated to Hawaii, the West Coast of the United States, and South America.

The first decades of the Meiji period were a time of intense enthusiasm for Westernisms of all kinds. Many people went abroad to study the science, technology, philosophy, and legal systems of the West. Western dress was adopted as the norm for all state functions. Western-style houses and public buildings were constructed in great number. Christianity, especially American Protestant denominations, made numerous converts, and Christian-sponsored campaigns for the education of women and the eradication of prostitution and concubinage, as well as general drives for social welfare, were extremely influential. Study of the English and German languages became popular. Western philosophies of education and law were made the basis of the modern Japanese educational and legal systems.[5]

The distinctive bond between the state and business that has been so influential in shaping the nature of the public sphere in Japan was forged at the beginning of the Meiji Era. The demand in 1854 by the United States, in the person of Admiral Matthew Perry, for Japan to open its doors made Japan suddenly realize its vulnerability. A small group of domains from western Japan overthrew the Tokugawa shogunate and established a government with the emperor as its titular head (hence the term "restoration"—"that is, restoration of imperial rule). The struggle to industrialize and to create the institutions of a modern nation proceeded with foreign trade, which began almost immediately, under pressure from the West.[6]

Foreign trade was initially controlled by foreign traders, and a series of humiliating encounters stimulated the new nation to gain an independent footing. It was clear that the conduct of foreign trade would require specialized knowledge and skills, and substantial financial reserves. Foreign trade became a matter of high priority not only because of the drive for autonomy, however, but also because of trade's potential for securing foreign capital to finance the purchase of foreign advice, machinery, and weapons. A number of firms emerged that specialized in foreign trade; of these, Mitsui Bussan, or Mitsui Trading Company, is typical. The House of Mitsui had strong ties to the winning side in the struggles surrounding the Restoration and had provided the

[5] Sansom (1949).
[6] Yoshino and Lifson (1989:9–10).

winners with important financial backing. Thus the new government granted it the first chance to enter banking, mining, and trading. These privileges were to some extent a recognition of past favors, but, more importantly, they registered an expectation of future service to the state.[7]

The House of Mitsui soon acquired a semiofficial status under this government patronage, and it expanded its businesses rapidly. It acquired exclusive rights to export coal from the government's richest mine. It became a major promoter of the cotton textile industry. It procured spinning and weaving machines abroad and imported raw cotton from China and India. It organized Japanese spinners and weavers into export guilds and became their sole representative. It expanded into ocean shipping, warehousing, and insurance. It became the head of a *zaibatsu*, evolving "diversified groups of giant companies under the control of family-owned holding companies."[8]

The decades immediately preceding World War II saw the blossoming of urban culture modeled on that of the West, with the growth of consumerism; democratic, socialist, and anarchist political movements; and an emerging feminist movement. This was also an era of rapid expansion by the state into virtually all areas of life, and many of these political movements were severely suppressed, as were numerous religious associations. Militarism and imperialism were supported, for the most part, by religious groups, but even small inconsistencies between their doctrines and state orthodoxy left them open to heavy punishment. *Zaibatsu* like Mitsui, including Mitsubishi, Sumitomo, Yasuda, and other, smaller groups, proliferated, and their power increased markedly after World War I.

Expansion of state supervision over religious affairs was quite marked, and the state patronized Shinto in a variety of ways while, in the twentieth century, suppressing the growth and free expression of many voluntary religious associations. Before 1945 it was understood that all voluntary associations should contribute to the nation materially and with unqualified allegiance. With the exception of a very few groups, some of them Christian, nearly all did so.

One example of state suppression of religious groups is the case of Omotokyo, a new religion founded in 1892 by a peasant woman, Deguchi Nao (1837–1918), and her son-in-law Deguchi Onisaburô (1871–1948). Especially under Onisaburô's leadership after Nao's death, the religion's followers increased dramatically, becoming the fastest-growing new religion in prewar Japan. Onisaburô traveled to the Asian mainland and there became affiliated with several religious associations, including Taoists and the Red Swastika Society. He took to riding a white horse, a privilege ordinarily reserved for the emperor. These flamboyant gestures were minor annoyances to the state, however, compared with the threat it perceived in the religion's utopianism,

---

[7] Ibid., 10–11.
[8] Ibid., 11–13.

which prophesied an apocalypse when the present rulers of the world would be put down and those presently without power exalted. The group was first suppressed in 1921, and in 1935 a much harsher suppression was carried out, including the bombing of Omoto headquarters and the reduction of all materials to pieces no larger than one foot long, lest diehards sought to rebuild.[9]

These and other instances of suppression of religious groups within the Japanese main islands and also in the colonies arose when religious groups were seen to be infringing on the state's prerogative to establish a national mythology with the imperial house at its center. Most persecutions came not from any lack of loyalty to the prewar regime, but because of the association in question assuming too high a profile and seeming to usurp the state's authority by proclaiming any kind of independent doctrine.[10]

The centrality of the emperor, in whose person national sovereignty was officially vested by the Meiji constitution, became a matter of intense concern with regard to the state's ideological self-presentation. The emperor's authority was in theory absolute, so that any assertion from a platform independent of the imperial house could be interpreted as lèse-majesté.

All official links between Shinto and the state came to an end in 1945, and Japan began the difficult task of rebuilding after its defeat. The system of government was radically altered, and there were important changes in previous patterns of relations between the state and business, as well as between religion and the state.

Government by political parties was established. Since 1945 the country has been ruled almost exclusively by the Liberal Democratic party (LDP, or Jiyû minshûtô).[11] The LDP has enjoyed a broad base of support from farmers, business people, professionals, and civil servants. Although it is by no means monolithic, it is conservative within the spectrum of political parties in Japan. The LDP's support from business is substantial, and in the 1960s and 1970s business provided over 90 percent of the LDP's publicly reported income.[12]

Business makes its interests felt in government through the agency of such business federations as Keidanren (Federation of Economic Organizations), having as members about 110 groups representing such industries as mining, manufacturing, trade, finance, and transportation. Formed in the wake of the Allied Occupation's dissolution of the *zaibatsu* in 1946, Keidanren is a prominent voice of big business. It exists to forge a consensus within the business community on matters of economic policy and to forward proposals on economic policy to the government. Its influence is impressive; the LDP was

[9] Shigeyoshi (1980:70–75, 96–98).

[10] Garon (1986).

[11] The only interruption of LDP rule was the period from 1947 to 1948, when Japan was ruled by a coalition government headed by a Socialist prime minister.

[12] Haruhiro (1983).

actually created in response to the Keidanren demand that two smaller parties merge, and it helped bring down the Kishi cabinet in 1960.[13]

The relation between business and government does not, of course, take place in a vacuum, but within the framework of law. The postwar constitution represents a significant departure from the prewar past and has charted the nation's political course throughout the postwar decades.

The postwar constitution was largely written by the Allied Occupation (1945–1952), and became effective on 3 May 1947. The constitution is distinctive in its assertion of popular sovereignty and fundamental human rights, and in its renunciation of war. Sovereignty resides in the people; this is a departure from the prewar Meiji constitution, under which sovereignty resided in the emperor. Now the emperor is described as a symbol of the state, and all his acts in matters of state require the advice and approval of the cabinet. The postwar constitution guarantees freedom of religion, forbids compulsory participation in any religious activities, and prohibits the state from patronizing any religion. No restrictions are placed on the freedom to write, speak, assemble, or form associations. Discrimination based on race, creed, social status, family origin, or sex is officially banned; there is universal suffrage. The most famous passage in the constitution is that renouncing war:

Article 9. Aspiring sincerely to an international peace based on justice and order, the Japanese people forever renounce war as a sovereign right of the nation and the threat or use of force as means of settling international disputes. . . .

(2) In order to accomplish the aim of the preceding paragraph, land, sea, and air forces, as well as other war potential, will never be maintained. The right of belligerency of the state will not be recognized.

Public-opinion polls throughout the postwar decades have regularly shown strong popular support for article 9, while the nation also favors the continued existence of the Self-Defense Force, the nation's alternative to regular military forces.

World War II destroyed the economic infrastructure of Japan. The nation embarked on its reconstruction following the defeat, and that period of rebuilding is referred to as the postwar era (1945–1955). Beginning in the mid-1950s the economy began to expand and soon entered a period of great economic growth. The period of great economic growth began to slow with the oil embargoes of 1973. Although economic growth has never regained the pre-1972 level, the average annual rate of growth from 1981 to 1986 was 3.6 percent, and the GNP in 1987 was $1,979 billion (at 167.1 yen = US $1).

The Japanese recovery after the war and the beginnings of the era of great economic growth were supported by a centrally supported direction in the for-

[13] Masami (1983).

224 · Helen Hardacre

mation of national goals and values. In this, no one was more important than the nation's first postwar prime minister, Yoshida Shigeru (1878–1967).

When Yoshida became prime minister in 1946, Japan was a defeated nation occupied by foreign power; it was impoverished, and its economic infrastructure lay in ruins. When he left office in 1954, the country was on the brink of an era of great economic growth that was sustained at unprecedented levels until the oil shock of 1973. Yoshida's strategy, called the Yoshida Doctrine, had the aim of rebuilding the nation, establishing its long-term security, and enabling it to concentrate single-mindedly on economic growth.

Kenneth Pyle has described the Yoshida Doctrine as having three major tenets:

1. Japan's economic growth should be the prime national goal. Political-economic cooperation with the United States was necessary for this purpose.
2. Japan should remain lightly armed and avoid involvement in international political-strategic issues. Not only would this low posture free the resources and energy of its people for productive economic development, it would avoid divisive internal struggles—what Yoshida called a "thirty-eighth parallel in the hearts of the Japanese people."
3. To gain a long-term guarantee for its own security, Japan would provide bases for the U.S. Army, Navy, and Air Force.[14]

In order for Japan to achieve economic growth, cooperation with the United States was a necessity. Yoshida resisted U.S. pressure to rearm and to contribute troops to the Korean War effort, but agreed to the building of U.S. military bases on Japanese soil. This made Japan, in effect, a protectorate of the United States, a humiliating position in the opinion of many. Nevertheless, swallowing this bitter pill was understood to be key to containing defense expenditures and thereby facilitating economic growth.[15]

This dependence on the United States in the area of defense continued to receive widespread, if not unanimous, support in Japan in the 1980s. Miyazawa Kiichi, a powerful politician in the LDP and a protégé of Yoshida Shigeru, has described Japan as a "special state" that must pursue a somewhat passive style of foreign policy, "a diplomacy that precludes all value judgments," leaving Japan without much scope for initiative on the international scene: "All we can do when we are hit on the head is pull back. We watch the world situation and follow the trends."[16]

That economic growth itself represents a value was not debated; by the 1980s the idea was so entrenched as to appear natural and inevitable, and not the result of the conscious choices of Yoshida Shigeru and his advisors. This

[14] Pyle (1987:246–47).
[15] Ibid.
[16] Ibid., 249.

assimilation and assumption of the desirability of continued economic growth has thus become a precondition for any discussion of public values. Other than this, the nation can function in its relations with other nations, Miyazawa implies, without reference to questions of value. The master value of economic growth thus exerts a controlling influence over the public sphere in Japan today.

The central initiative in the formation of a national discourse on values has been echoed by the formation of individual values that harmonize well with the consensus supporting economic growth. Since Japan's large corporations, some established in the postwar dissolution of the former *zaibatsu*, have provided the principal engines of postwar economic growth, membership in them carries considerable prestige. Gaining employment in them has become a goal appealing to a broad range of the population.

The large corporations hire new university graduates on the basis of complex criteria, of which the greatest is educational achievement. Educational achievement is measured most importantly by the university from which a prospective employee has been graduated, and there is a widespread perception of a single ranking system that creates a hierarchy among universities. At the top of the list are the former imperial universities such as the universities of Tokyo and Kyoto, followed by such prestigious private universities as Waseda and Keio. A graduate of one of these universities has a much greater chance of employment by one of the large corporations than a student from a low-ranking prefectural university.[17]

Because the employment prospects of a student are directly influenced by the university's rank, there is intense competition to enter the best ones. This competition has given rise to an intense focus within families on children's educational attainments. Since the purpose of this concentration on educational achievement is itself ultimately driven by the marketplace, it is not a great exaggeration to say that much of family life is indirectly shaped and colored by the public sphere's preoccupation with economic growth.[18]

RELIGION AND THE NONPROFIT SECTOR SINCE 1945

The Allied Occupation (1945–1952) made important changes in the relation between religion and the state. It wanted to sever the link between Shinto and the state, which it perceived to be a powerful mechanism for inculcating the Japanese people with a militaristic and chauvinistic ideology. The Shinto Directive of 1946 ordered the state to cease all patronage of Shinto and to remove Shinto influences from the schools, while the postwar constitution granted freedom of religion and the separation of religion and state (article 24) and

[17] Rohlen (1983).
[18] Shields (1989).

prohibited the state from patronizing religion (article 89). Education has been profoundly affected by the removal of Shinto ideology. Educational curriculums at all levels are thoroughly secular and increasingly oriented toward science and technology. Shinto and religion in general have virtually dropped out of public discourse on values.[19]

Buddhism and Shinto were both closely associated with the prewar regime, which they supported without qualification. Thus they were seen to be discredited by the defeat, and they have not regained the moral authority they once had in public discourse. Buddhism is presently associated most prominently with funeral and mortuary ritual and with ancestor worship, which is highly institutionalized and generally, though not exclusively, performed in Buddhist mode. Shinto shrines are visited by millions of people every year, especially at the new year, but few could identify any distinctive Shinto doctrine because the Shinto priesthood is not a proselytizing order. Instead, shrine management tends to be passed from father to son (this is true of the Buddhist priesthood also), and thus few in the priesthood are there because they feel a calling. Both Buddhism and Shinto lost important economic resources in the Occupation-directed land reforms, and their economic base was further eroded by urbanization. Hereditary parishioners' groups in rural areas have suffered severe depopulation, and while urban members may visit their temples once or twice a year to attend to family graves, urbanization has drastically attenuated the links between parishioners and their temples or shrines. Most clergy of either Buddhism or Shinto find it necessary to take on secondary employment of some kind. Numbers are declining, especially in Shinto, and the priesthood is in nearly all cases a hereditary profession rather than a "calling."[20]

Most Japanese observe the rites of both Buddhism and Shinto, religions that are understood to be complementary, not mutually exclusive. Christians make up less than 1 percent of the total population. Between one-fourth and one-third of the population are affiliated with one of the associations collectively known as the "new religions." This term refers to voluntary religious associations established since 1800, which are largely or entirely independent of Buddhist and Shinto clergy, and in which laypersons can perform virtually all important religious functions.[21]

The new religions have attracted many converts since 1945, and without a doubt they represent the most vigorous area of post-1945 religious life. They have succeeded well in urban areas and have developed interlocking organizational forms that speak to the cultural, social, and intellectual interests of members as well as their religious concerns. Their members are more active

[19] Hardacre (1989), chapter 7.
[20] Ibid.
[21] Hardacre (1986), chapter 1.

than observers of Buddhism or Shinto in welfare and social-service activities. In many cases, though by no means all, the new religions are wealthy organizations that continue to expand at a modest but steady rate, following a period of phenomenal growth in the immediate postwar years. Their economic base is generally at least stable, and in some cases affluent.

Voluntary associations, especially religious associations, have been very important in the perpetuation of the traditional values enumerated above. They have been less important, however, as participants in discourse about public values, and on the whole, with a few exceptions, have been very reticent to identify themselves publicly with distinctive moral theories or ethical positions not already widely accepted in society. This state of affairs represents a significant change from the prewar era, when religious groups of all kinds (though not without exception) spoke out strongly in favor of the state's goal of expansion of empire and competed with each other in promoting state values at the local level.[22]

Compared with that in other developed nations, the nonprofit sector in Japan is small. The most significant area of the sector is occupied by religious organizations, but in addition such organizations as the Red Cross and Rotary International are represented. A small number of foundations sponsor academic research in science and medicine, but few support research in the humanities and social sciences. Philanthropic foundations sponsoring the promotion of public values are not unknown, but are small in scale and few in number.

Two reasons for the relative lack of development of a nonprofit sector outside religious organizations may be cited. The first is the minor emphasis on altruism and philanthropy in Japanese religious traditions compared to the major importance of these themes in Western religions. The second lies in the recency of the appearance of large amounts of disposable wealth. Only since the period of great economic growth have there emerged numerous individuals with the resources to support philanthropic projects.

Welfare and social service are minor themes in Buddhist and Shinto history, constituting recognized but distinctly secondary functions. While some branches of Buddhism are concerned with such issues as eliminating the discrimination faced by the outcasts (*burakumin*, descendants of members of such stigmatized occupations as slaughtering and tanning), welfare efforts in Buddhism are by no means widespread, and in Shinto they are virtually nonexistent. Voluntarism and philanthropy as a whole are little-developed in Japan, and only a minority of the population is involved in such activities, which are regarded as exceptional.[23]

[22] Ibid.

[23] Information on the political social-welfare activities of the new Japanese religions is based on interviews conducted at the headquarters and branch churches of Reiyūkai Kyōdan, Risshō Kōseikai, and Sōka Gakkai in 1988 and 1989. Interviews were also held with MPs of Kōmeitō

Some of the new religions sponsor hospitals in Japan, contribute to such international organizations as UNICEF and UNESCO, and send medical teams to Southeast Asia. In addition, on the model of the Peace Corps, they sponsor teams of young members to go to Southeast Asia to engage in reforestation efforts or projects to provide pure drinking water.

New religious organizations coordinate some of their efforts with such secular, nonprofit organizations as the Red Cross, but such cooperation is occasional and not institutionally regularized. An exception to this generalization lies in the designation of one new religion, Sôka Gakkai, as a Non-Governmental Organization recognized by the United Nations.

The new religions vigilantly guard their tax-exempt status and believe that it is endangered. Politicians interact with religious organizations mainly during election campaigns, when they seek the support of these groups in the hope of securing bloc voting. The new religions are generally targeted by conservative candidates of the Liberal Democratic party or by independent candidates with strong ties to that party. It is virtually unknown for religious organizations to support candidates of the Communist party, because the organizations perceive in communism a threat to religion as a whole; the expression "opiate of the people" is widely known and offered as a reason why it is impossible for a religious organization to lend support to the Communist party. The Socialist party and the Democratic Socialists are distrusted for the same reason, but it sometimes happens that a religion will support candidates from those parties.

The religions concerned typically support candidates who are either pro forma members of the group or who are generally conservative and take no particular positions that are offensive to the group. In national elections, a religion may sponsor numerous candidates from several factions of the Liberal Democratic party more on the basis of personal ties than in support of the candidates' particular platforms.

Political candidates are well aware of the tightly knit organizations of new religions, and they know that religions can deliver bloc votes. In fact, in the larger Buddhist organizations other than Sôka Gakkai, which invariably supports Kômeitô[24] candidates, branch churches during campaigns will display bulletin boards listing the candidates they support, and members are made well aware of the persons for whom they are encouraged to vote.

Political candidates also seek financial support from religious organizations,

and the Kokumin Kaigi. These interviews were generously supported by the Lilly Endowment, and that support is gratefully acknowledged.

[24] A party established in 1964 by Sôka Gakkai, Kômeitô has been the third or fourth largest political party throughout much of its history and thus is important as a "swing vote." It generally works in cooperation with the LDP, with which it has much in common in general conservative orientation. It consistently favors an expansion of social-welfare measures and resists LDP initiatives to boost the defense budget.

and at least in the case of the new religions, they typically receive strong financial backing. Though exact figures are lacking, it is widely believed that these organizations support conservative candidates handsomely.

The reasons why the new religions support conservative politicians so well (and, one might add, so indiscriminately) are not entirely clear. The new religions were regarded by the press with considerable suspicion during the immediate postwar period, and even now an informal taboo operates within all the media on coverage of the new religions, except when some titillating scandal occurs. The new religions are all quite wary of scandal, and they may wish nothing other than friends in high places should they ever need to exert political influence over the press. Further, they may wish to create channels whereby they *could* make their opinions known in the political world, even if, in fact, they rarely do so. They do not speak out on moral or ethical questions with any insistence or with any distinctive position. Finally, they may simply find it impossible to say no when approached by a politician with his hand out, for fear that a refusal might create in that person a will to challenge these organizations' tax-free status or otherwise jeopardize their existence.

The Buddhist organization Risshô Kôsei Kai is something of an exception in this regard. Founded in 1938, this organization has now roughly five million members, making it the second largest of the new religions after Sôka Gakkai, which has around twelve million members. Because it is the principal financial backer of the League of New Religious Organizations, which includes some three hundred member organizations, its influence in the religious world is considerable. Until around 1985 Risshô Kôsei Kai took the essentially passive political position described above as characteristic of the new religions. Thereafter, however, it developed a four-point litmus test for the politicians it would support, requiring them to promote world peace, to support freedom of religious belief, to promote ethics in government, and to work for administrative reform. More concretely, politicians are asked to resist attempts to increase the defense budget, to oppose state support for the Yasukuni Shrine (an emblem of religious persecution under the prewar regime), to support article 9 of the constitution (which renounces war), and to act ethically in all political dealings.

These positions were advanced as the core of Risshô Kôsei Kai's political stance. That the group felt it necessary to articulate a political position at all was in part the product of its rivalry with the much larger Sôka Gakkai, which had founded its own political party in 1964. Risshô Kôsei Kai is not in a position to found a political party, but it may be seen as having developed its four-point platform as an alternative way to exert political influence, and to attempt to be a voice for religion in the public sphere.

The four points established Risshô Kôsei Kai's opposition to the Liberal Democratic party's sporadic postwar efforts to resurrect elements of the prewar regime's symbolism of chauvinistic patriotism. The Yasukuni Shrine, which memorializes the war dead, was used to promote nationalistic and patriotic sentiments in such a way as to sanction persecution of dissent and diversity of all kinds before 1945. Risshô Kôsei Kai and many other religious groups were persecuted and suppressed by the prewar regime on the pretext of minor points in their doctrines that, with reference to the Shinto mythology promoted by the state and glorified at the Yasukuni Shrine, could be interpreted as lèse-majesté. When the Liberal Democratic party several times sought to reestablish state support for the shrine, Risshô Kôsei Kai perceived that suppression of religions might be the next step.[25]

Risshô Kôsei Kai promotes support for the postwar constitution for much the same reason it opposes state support for the Yasukuni Shrine. The articles of the constitution with which the group is most concerned are those dealing with the separation of religion and state and granting Japanese citizens freedom of religious belief. In particular, article 89 prohibits state expenditures for religious activities, and support of the Yasukuni Shrine would be disallowed.

With the exception of Risshô Kôsei Kai, religious associations seldom become involved in discourse on public values. In the cases of Buddhism and Shinto, this silence can be traced to their loss of moral authority by virtue of their association with the prewar regime. The new religions do not, themselves, directly address public values. The reason for their silence are complex.

The phenomenal growth of new religions after 1945 inevitably included some organizations that later were shown to be fraudulent. The media exposed them through extended, sensational journalism, and the press is ever-watchful for scandal in the religious world. This being the case, it seems that religious associations find silence the better part of valor and rarely speak out. There are, however, significant exceptions to this generalization.

The most significant of the exceptions is Sôka Gakkai, a Buddhist organization founded in 1925, which in 1964 established a political party, Kômeitô. Kômeitô supports the expansion of state welfare as well as measures aimed at ensuring ethics in government. In its early years it also supported a specifically religious agenda, but now it is a party of the center. As the third largest political party in the nation, it occupies an important, swing-vote position and commands considerable support beyond the membership of Sôka Gakkai, who are believed to vote as a bloc for Kômeitô. In general the party has opposed rapid expansion of the military and favors greater appropriations for education and welfare.

All members of the Diet from Kômeitô are also members of Sôka Gakkai, and it is expected that they will keep the interests of the religion in mind. In addition, however, Sôka Gakkai and Kômeitô support a limited number of

---

[25] Hardacre (1989), chapter 7.

independent MPs known as the People's Congress (Kokumin Kaigi), which is made up of experts in such fields as labor legislation, energy, and defense whom Sôka Gakkai and Kômeitô have identified as opinion leaders in their fields and whom they wish to keep in the Diet to offer expertise.

The Honorable Nakanishi Tamako of the House of Councillors is one such member of the People's Congress. After many years in the Tokyo office of the International Labor Organization, Nakanishi served as head of the alumni association of Tsuda Women's College, one of the most prominent Japanese women's colleges, in which position she founded a school to prepare Japanese to serve in the United Nations. She was first elected as a member of the People's Congress in 1985 and since that time has introduced important legislation to improve working conditions for part-time workers, the majority of whom are women, as well as continuing liaison work with the United Nations in the areas of housing and habitat. Her work has been highly significant as a force to eliminate discrimination and to create equitable labor conditions. She is a Christian.

Religion supports the broad consensus affirming the present conservative government. Only a minority of the people questions the goals of economic stability through increased productivity, efficiency, and the progressive adoption of high technology.

THE DEBATE ON BRAIN DEATH AND ORGAN TRANSPLANTS

Some religious leaders have announced positions opposed to such issues of medical ethics as the transplantation of organs and the adoption of brain death as a standard for determining the death of the human person. Some are opposed to abortion, but abortion is not so important an issue for current ethical thinking in Japan as brain death and organ transplants. Religious leaders do not exert much moral suasion beyond their own adherents, however, because the government agencies charged with the legal and policy decisions in these areas do not consult them, and they apparently are not so committed to their positions that they will risk exposing their ideas in a more public way.

The questions of brain death and organ transplants are two of Japan's most hotly contested issues in contemporary ethical thinking. The problem does not precisely oppose values to norms of effectiveness, nor does it impinge directly on the master value of sustained economic growth; rather, it seems to indicate a more basic questioning of technology in relation to standards of life and death. Indirectly, the primacy of economic growth as a controlling value of the society is called into question.[26]

Brain death and organ transplants are the major issues preoccupying Japanese medical ethics today, and they are treated as inseparable. At present Ja-

[26] On the evolution of the debate, see Lock and Honde (1990) and Tamayo (1990).

pan has no code of law recognizing the phenomenon of brain death as the basic standard for determining that an individual has died. Instead, national law specifies that a person shall be declared dead when three conditions have been met: cessation of heartbeat, cessation of respiration, and opening of the pupils.

Brain death is the cessation of brain waves, which is understood to indicate an irreversible termination of brain functions. With the aid of a respirator, heart and lung functions can continue even after brain death has occurred, but if the respirator is removed, heartbeat and respiration will also cease. As Japanese commentators present the issue, the question of substituting brain death for the three traditional criteria of death would not have arisen in the absence of the possibility of organ transplants.[27] The two are linked because organ transplants (except in the case of a single kidney from a living donor) are premised on the inevitable death of the donor, and the success of a transplant from a donor whose heart is still beating is much greater than from one whose heartbeat has terminated.

Thus if it could be established that the death of the human person is equivalent to brain death, then that person, as a donor of organs, would be officially "dead" at the time of transplant surgery. There would be no room to argue that removal of the organs in question resulted in the death of the donor and hence was tantamount to homicide. If the donor was brain-dead at the time of surgery, then death of the individual had already occurred, and the operation would be performed on a corpse whose respiration and heartbeat were artificially prolonged for the purpose of completing the transplant surgery.

As of 1988 there were some seven thousand persons in Japan judged to be brain-dead, but whose lives are sustained by respirators and other technologies. As popular discourse has developed on this issue, the question is not, as it was in the celebrated case in the United States of Karen Quinlan, whether to discontinue the use of life-support systems, but whether to permit organ transplants from the brain-dead to sustain lives of those with failing hearts, livers, lungs, kidneys, and other organs. The history of the twin issues of brain death and organ transplants reveals much about the construction of health and illness and cultural concepts of life, death, and the body, as well as unsuspected aspects of the symbiotic relations existing between Japan and other developed nations.

The world's first heart transplant operation was performed in Capetown in 1967. Japan's first and only heart transplant operation was performed in 1968 by Dr. Wada of Sapporo Medical University. At first Wada was heralded for his achievement, even though his patient died eighty-three days after the operation.[28] Later, however, the tide of public opinion turned against Wada, and he was accused of murder. In the end, the public prosecutor's office declined

[27] Miura (1987:144) and Nakayama (1989:235).
[28] The Capetown patient died twenty days after his operation.

to prosecute the case. Since then, no heart transplants have been performed in Japan, and the public prosecutor's office's manner of handling the case—failing to bring it to legal adjudication—left hanging in the air the suspicion that transplant operations can be linked to murder.

Until the late 1980s religious organizations have contributed virtually nothing to this debate, and even their most recent pronouncements on the subject are rather insular and seem ad hoc and out of touch with the aspects of the question that have been most significant in the debate carried on by other parties.[29] For example, Shinto priests who have spoken on the subject simply say that it goes against the sentiments of the Japanese people, while Buddhist priests of the True Pure Land school assert that a soul has difficulty reaching the Pure Land unless the body is intact. An argument from sentiment fails to engage the question of the potential benefits of life to be derived by the recipient of an organ transplant. The Buddhist argument is difficult to comprehend, given that virtually all Japanese are cremated at death, the vast majority attended by Buddhist ritual, including those from the True Pure Land School.

Religious commentary on this issue only began to appear in Japan in 1989. It is likely that the associations in question have not yet had time to grapple with the complex medical and ethical issues involved. Thus they are not yet prepared to respond in a systematic way, and their opposition is not yet clearly thought out. According to one commentator on the issue, religion's opposition is based on the same distrust of modern medicine one finds in the general population; it does not spring primarily from doctrine.[30]

Instead of significant religious influence in the current Japanese debate on brain death and organ transplants, as would be expected in a country like the United States, we find that a variety of cultural constructions of life, death, health, and illness play a much more important role. In particular, the following ideas are central: (1) a premium on funeral rites for the whole body; (2) the sense that organs must not be treated as "spare parts"; and (3) the desire for a "beautiful death." Let us take these up in turn.

First, the premium on funeral rites for the whole body. Linked to a folk-religious notion that death signals the beginning of a new life in another world, Japanese have a strong desire to send the *whole* body, via funeral rites, to the other world so that this new life can be begun intact and undamaged. Nowhere does this desire manifest itself more strongly than in war and disaster. A recent example is the great preoccupation with recovering the bodies from the Korean Airlines jet shot down in 1985, including many fruitless trips by sea by the survivors to the spot where the plane was thought to have entered the ocean, there to throw bundles of flowers into the sea. Grief over this tragic incident

[29] See the section of essays by religious leaders in Nakayama (1989).
[30] Prof. Yamaori Tetsuo (Nihon Bunka Kenkyûsho, Kyoto), private communication, June 1990.

by the survivors from other countries did not take the form of a preoccupation with recovering the bodies. A very contemporary example is provided by the behavior of the parents of one of three preschool girls murdered and dismembered in 1989 near Tokyo. The parents of one of the girls delayed her funeral for more than two months, hoping that the confessed murderer would reveal the location of missing parts so that the entire body could, as they put it, "be able to play with the other children in the other world."

Second, the idea that organs must not be treated like spare parts.[31] A more positive statement of the same sentiment would say that the body is something entrusted to the individual, but that it is not a private possession. According to more specific religious convictions, a person might say that the body was entrusted by parents, or by the *kami*, or that it comes to one as the result of accumulated karma. Whoever is believed to be the entrustor, however, the implication is that the individual does not have the right to dispose of the body.

A corollary is the idea that the individual's family has a right to contradict the individual's preference with respect to the disposition of the body or parts thereof, an idea embodied in the Autopsy Preservation Law and the Law concerning the Transplantation of Kidneys and Corneas. These laws stipulate that even when an individual has directed that the kidneys and corneas be made available for transplant, that directive cannot be implemented unless all the survivors give their consent.[32] Thus, in effect, the individual's wishes are a prerequisite for transplant surgery, but they are only sufficient to bring it about in concert with the wishes of surviving family members.

Third is the desire for a "beautiful death," one in which the individual is, so to speak, "prepared" to die, resigned to death, and mentally composed. The opposite situation is one in which the individual is perceived to cling unreasonably to life for its own sake, irrespective of the inevitability of death, and without considering that death might be "fated" to occur at any time. An extreme example, and one that many Japanese would find anachronistic, is the suicide of the author Mishima Yukio at the age of forty-five, motivated in part by the powerful image of the cherry blossom that falls at the zenith of its beauty rather than withering on the tree. Such a death is regarded as beautiful, and, conversely, to cling to life to the point of taking organs form someone else is regarded by some as grasping, covetous, and ugly.[33]

The above are three major sentiments that incline the Japanese people not to accept transplant surgery. The dislike of transplant surgery is a major reason why the nation is disinclined to accept the idea of brain death. As I mentioned above, the idea of brain death would only become relevant as a prerequisite for transplant surgery; no one argues that brain death should be recognized as

[31] Miura (1987:153).
[32] Fujii and Tanaka (1986:187).
[33] Ibid., 188.

a prerequisite for the removal of life-support systems, nor are arguments made, as they might be in less-wealthy nations, that brain death ought to be recognized because it is simply too expensive to keep brain-dead persons alive. Let us survey the opinions of influential social groups in Japan on the brain-death issue.

In January 1988 the directors of the Japan Medical Association voted unanimously to accept the idea of brain death as a standard for determination of death.[34] This is not, of course, to say that all physicians in Japan accept either the idea of brain death or the implied green light for organ transplant. For example, Dr. Takagi Kentaro, former president of Nagoya City University with a Ph.D. in medicine, has gone on record as saying that transplant surgery is not properly a part of medicine at all,[35] while Dr. Ide Kazuzo, professor at the Self-Defense Medical University, pointing to a news report claiming that a United States heart transplant patient spent his last days on gambling and other forms of dissipation, said that organ transplant surgery should not be undertaken until recipients can legally be forced to repay their debt to society by living a responsible life.[36] A more serious consideration forms the basis of the rejection of the idea of brain death by the Japanese Neurologists' Association: the fear that the disadvantaged, the handicapped, and the mentally impaired will be disproportionately diagnosed as brain-dead, motivated by the desire to use their organs for transplant surgery. Similarly, the Japan Patients' Rights Association rejects the idea of brain death because of a fear that basic human rights will not be protected.[37]

While there are thus many doctors and members of the medical community who would not accept the verdict of their major professional association, many would agree with Dr. Shibata Takashi, director of the Shibata Hospital, who advocates transplant surgery as a means to elevate the level of medical technology as a whole.[38] But the idea that organ transplants should be promoted as a means to promote the overall technological progress of medicine has a particularly crass ring for those inclined to question the value of technology for its own sake.

Notable among the reasons for rejecting the brain-death standard is a basic distrust of the medical profession, its competence, and its economic profit motives. In the absence of these considerations, recognition might be granted more broadly to the idea of brain death and the implications of more widespread transplant surgery. In fact, the Patients' Rights Association in 1988 charged a Niigata hospital and its head with murder for taking the kidneys of a brain-dead patient for transplant surgery. And in 1984, a group of doctors

[34] Nakayama (1989:15–16).
[35] Ibid., 5.
[36] Miura (1987:139).
[37] Nakayama (1989:248–50).
[38] Ibid., 168.

opposed to brain death and transplant surgery charged that doctors at the University of Tsukuba Hospital who removed the heart, liver, kidneys, and pancreas of a brain-dead person and subsequently transplanted the kidneys and pancreas were guilty of murder. As in the 1968 case of Japan's only heart transplant operation, the public prosecutor's office refused to reach a decision whether to prosecute the case, citing a lack of public consensus on the issue of brain death.[39]

These cases suggest that there is a significant discrepancy between the social reasoning of the medical profession and that of the judiciary in Japan. The result is that the implied association of a brain-death diagnosis with organ transplants can be construed as murderous. Of the developed nations, only Japan, Israel, and Denmark do not recognize brain death.[40]

If the medical and judicial situation in Japan regarding brain death is virtually at a stalemate at this time, that is not to say that many Japanese do not in fact receive organ transplants. Let us first examine the question of kidney transplants versus dialysis. The first Japanese kidney transplant operation was performed in 1964, and while these operations were not markedly successful until the 1972 development in Switzerland of the drug cyclosporine-A, which suppresses the body's rejection of the foreign organ, the success rate of transplants from living donors is about 75 percent, while about 40 percent from deceased donors succeed. Nevertheless, it must be noted that the medical profession does not publicize its failures widely, and patients' groups estimate that in some hospitals the rate of failure is as high as 50 percent, forcing many patients to return to dialysis.[41]

Dialysis is centrally involved in the current distrust with which the Japanese medical profession is regarded by the public. Patients on dialysis are typically outpatients who travel two to four times a week to a hospital for three- to four-hour sessions for the purification of their blood. During that time, they are prone on a hospital bed, attached to a machine that is essentially a pump and a filter. The pump conveys the patient's blood to the filter element, which purifies it, after which the pump conveys the blood back into the patient's body. As of 1986 there were 73,537 patients on dialysis in Japan, and their number is estimated to be increasing at the rate of about 5,000 per year. The yearly cost of dialysis on an outpatient basis is about five million yen, while on an inpatient basis it is eight million yen.[42]

As against the astronomical costs of dialysis, the following costs are associated with kidney transplants when carried out in Japan. In the first year the cost would be 4,232,000 yen, and in the second year 2,308,000.[43] In other

[39] Ibid., 250–51.
[40] Ibid., 276.
[41] Asahi shinbun (1983:6–7).
[42] Nakayama (1989:276).
[43] Ibid., 96.

words, the monetary costs associated with kidney transplants are far lower over time than those associated with dialysis.

In 1982 it was discovered that of the thirty richest persons in Japan, four were operators of hospitals specializing in dialysis. Investigative reporting uncovered major abuse of the national health insurance system and a cynical disregard for the rights and welfare of dialysis patients. Physicians were discovered to be charging inpatient rates for persons who were actually outpatients and claiming as much as three times the fluids actually used. Furthermore, while the filter element on a dialysis machine should be disposed of after each use, physicians were in fact using them many times over while claiming that a new one was used each time.[44] Not only were they guilty of massive fraud in their insurance claims, but because patients pay a proportion of these costs, patients were also being charged far more than their treatments actually cost.

The exposures regarding physician abuse of dialysis patients and related false claims on the insurance system have forged a connection between the preexisting distrust of the medical profession and the questions of organ transplants and brain death. This distrust includes several aspects: the suspicion that physicians create unnecessarily intense dialysis regimens in order to inflate their own profits; the prospect that many patients could be relieved of the necessity of dialysis if kidney transplant operations were more widely carried out; and the contradictory fear that those doctors who advocate transplant operations might be doing so to increase their own profits, while lacking the necessary experience and skill.

While kidney transplants have become increasingly common in the industrialized countries, the total of such operations ever performed in Japan is less than six hundred. Physicians explain that lack of donor organs is the principal reason why more kidney transplants are not carried out. We have seen that significant cultural barriers exist to strengthen Japanese reluctance to become either donors or recipients of organs for transplant.

At the same time, however, physician reliance on the argument that there are insufficient donor organs is advanced as if cultural reluctance were a fait accompli, rigid and unmalleable,[45] and as if physicians had no responsibility to promote organ transplants or the awareness of the need for such operations. Failure by the medical establishment actively to promote such awareness strengthens the suspicion that the reason it does not is that dialysis has become a golden egg. One commentator on this situation, Nakayama Taro, foreign minister in the Kaifu cabinet, has said:

Japan is the nation which has donated the smallest number of kidneys. Over one hundred sixty kidneys have been imported to Japan from the United States, but Japan

[44] Asahi shinbun (1983:6–11).
[45] Miura (1987:135–42).

has never sent even a single kidney to the United States. The European nations have a system of mutual organ donation, but Japan is entirely one-way. This situation is not limited to kidneys. Given this, we have no reply when charged that our so-called international exchange and mutual aid are just lip service. . . . The question is exactly like that of Japan's whole history in the application of scientific technology. Japan contributes almost nothing to its development but merely uses the technology and research results of Europe and the United States. Moreover, because Japan has almost no deceased donors of organs, in terms of organ transplant, it is just like an underdeveloped country. Because of that, many who might have been saved die after a short life.[46]

Because heart and liver transplant surgery are unavailable in Japan, a growing number of people go abroad for these services, but in fact, only the wealthy or those financed by a public fund-raising drive are able to exercise this option. The Royal Brisbane Hospital is a frequent site for these operations in pediatric cases. The prospective patient receives a diagnosis specifying that transplant surgery is the only option. The patient's history is sent to the hospital, which then decides whether to admit. Upon procuring a six-month visa, the patient and family move to Brisbane, where they find housing. When their fee is paid, they commence waiting for a donor organ to become available. The fee is $110,000 Australian; this represents the actual cost for the operation and the cost of transporting the organ. Neither the hospital nor the operating surgeon receives any special fees.[47]

As of April 1989, twenty Japanese children had received liver transplant surgery abroad; of these, thirteen operations were performed in Australia and the remainder in Canada and the United States.[48] Ten of the operations were financed by private means and ten by public fund-raising drives.

The fact that the possibility of sustaining life by liver transplant surgery is effectively restricted, first to children and second to the wealthy among them, illustrates the inequities that develop now that transplant surgery in Japan itself has become deadlocked in judicial indecision and public confusion about it and the associated issue of brain death.

Transplant surgery, as we have seen, is in fundamental conflict with deeply held sentiments regarding the body. Transplant surgery represents a graphic example of a mechanistic image of the body, in which its parts are interchangeable, and in which parts can be disposed of in accord with such factors as social need and the availability of physicians competent to perform the relevant surgical techniques. After transplant surgery, what is left of the donor is incomplete, unfit, according to widespread religious sentiments, for beginning

---

[46] Nakayama (1989:6).
[47] Ibid., 15.
[48] Ibid., 254–55.

a new life in another world. Brain death is far indeed from the "beautiful death" Japanese so highly esteem.

Distrust of transplant surgery, of its basis in the notion of brain death, and of those physicians who advocate it implies a distrust of the reliance on technology as the ultimate standards for a human life. Implied is a questioning of the value of life achieved at the expense of another's death, and as an alternative to facing one's own death with dignity and calm, and as something rightly conceived of as sustainable in the first instance by technological means. These questions are indistinct, vague, and sometimes obscurantist. They sometimes rest on an uniformed distrust of medicine. They have yet to develop into systematic ethical thought, and this may be attributed to the undeveloped character of ethical thought in Japanese religious history or in the study of philosophy in Japan. Nevertheless, in the twin issues of brain death and transplant surgery we can see the beginnings of reappraisal of the role of technology in health care.

CONCLUSION

This essay has described Japan as having a very limited public sphere, in which the state and the marketplace cannot be excluded from consideration. Japan is thus a case that tends to confirm Habermas's thesis that the public sphere becomes increasingly eroded in advanced capitalist democracies. The reasons for the dominance of the state and the marketplace may be located historically in Japan's coming comparatively late to modernization. Latecomer status was accompanied by a sense of considerable urgency, occasioned by the not unreasonable fear that if Japan did not modernize quickly it would be consumed or conquered by the West, as China had been during the opium wars. The drive to modernize meant most importantly military and economic security, and the effort to achieve these guided Japan until 1945.

After World War II, Japan's reliance for its defense on the United States allowed it to pursue economic growth as a primary goal, and the partnership between state and market that began in the Meiji period facilitated the achievement of this goal. Religion and voluntary associations have generally supported the state and business in the quest for sustained economic growth. In the immediate postwar decades, the obvious dependence of the nation's survival on achieving economic rebuilding, stability, and growth was clear to all. Religious institutions were substantially eroded by various postwar reforms and social changes, with the exception of some new religions, and thus religious people of virtually all persuasions shared the society's preoccupation with recovery and growth.

Religion did not emerge as a critic of the goal of sustained growth in future decades. With the exception of some of the new religions, it had been discredited after 1945 and lacked confidence. Furthermore, there are only a few examples in Japanese religious history of religion assuming a role critical of the state, so there was little precedent for such a position. Finally, the growing secular cast of the society as a whole disinclined the nation seriously to consider religious claims of any kind. Thus when religion has spoken out on such issues of the public good as brain death and organ transplants, it has not done so from a position of strength nor from a tradition inspiring it with confidence. It seems likely that the public sphere in Japan will continue to be little influenced by religion.

References

Asahi shinbun kagakubu iryō shūzai han. 1983. *Iryō saizensen* (Medical Treatment—The Front Line). Tokyo: Asahi shinbunsha.

Bellah, Robert. 1957. *Tokugawa Religion: The Values of Pre-Industrial Japan*. Glencoe, Ill.: Free Press.

Coleman, Samuel. 1983. *Family Planning in Japanese Society*. Princeton: Princeton University Press.

Fujii Teruhisa and Tanaka Minoru. 1986. *Iryō no hōritsu funsō* (Legal Disputes Regarding Medical Treatment). Tokyo: Yuhikaku.

Garon, Sheldon. 1986. "State and Religion in Imperial Japan, 1912–1945." *Journal of Japanese Studies* 12 (Summer): 273–302.

Habermas, Jürgen. 1989. "The Public Sphere." In *Jürgen Habermas on Society and Politics: A Reader*, edited by Steven Seidman, pp. 235–58. Boston: Beacon Press.

Hardacre, Helen. 1986. *Kurozumikyō and the New Religions of Japan*. Princeton: Princeton University Press.

———. 1989. *Shintō and the State, 1868–1988*. Princeton: Princeton University Press.

Haruhiro, Fukui. 1983. "Liberal Democratic Party." In *The Encyclopedia of Japan* 4:385. Tokyo: Kôdansha.

Harumi Befu and Hiroshi Mannari, eds. 1983. *The Challenge of Japan's Internationalization: Organization and Culture*. Tokyo: Kwansei Gakuin University and Kôdansha International.

Lock, Margaret. 1987. "Introduction: Health and Medical Care as Cultural and Social Phenomena." In *Health, Illness, and Medical Care in Japan*, edited by Margaret Lock. Honolulu: University of Hawaii Press.

Lock, Margaret, and Christina Honde. 1990. "Reaching Consensus about Death: Heart Transplant and Cultural Identity in Japan." In *Social Science Perspectives on Medical Ethics*, edited by G. Weisz, pp. 99–119. The Hague: Kluwer Academic Publishers.

Long, Susan Orpett. 1987. "Health Care Providers: Technology, Policy, and Professional Dominance." In *Health, Illness, and Medical Care in Japan*, edited by Margaret Lock. Honolulu: University of Hawaii Press.

Masami Hirata. 1983. "Keidanran." In *The Encyclopedia of Japan* 4:188. Tokyo: Kôdansha.

Miura Kazuo. 1987. *Nōshi* (Brain Death). Tokyo: Tokyo shoseki.

Nakayama Tarō. 1989. *Nōshi to zōki ishoku* (Brain Death and Organ Transplant). Tokyo: Simul Press.

Ooms, Herman. 1985. *Tokugawa Ideology: Early Constructs, 1570–1686*. Princeton: Princeton University Press.

Pyle, Kenneth B. 1987. "In Pursuit of a Grand Design: Nakasone Betwixt the Past and the Future." *Journal of Japanese Studies* 13 (Summer): 243–70.

Rohlen, Thomas P. 1983. *Japan's High Schools*. Berkeley and Los Angeles: University of California Press.

Sansom, Goerge B. 1949. *The Western World and Japan*. New York: Vintage Books.

Shields, James J., Jr. 1989. *Japanese Schooling: Patterns of Socialization, Equality, and Political Control*. University Park and London: Pennsylvania State University Press.

Shigeyoshi Murakami. 1980. *Japanese Religion in the Modern Century*, translated by H. Byron Earhart. Tokyo: University of Tokyo Press.

Sonoda Kyoichi. 1988. *Health and Illness in Changing Japanese Society*. Tokyo: University of Tokyo Press.

Streslicke, William. 1987. "The Japanese State of Health: A Political-Economic Perspective." In *Health, Illness, and Medical Care in Japan*, edited by Margaret Lock. Honolulu: University of Hawaii Press.

Tamayo Okamoto. 1990. "The Brain-Death Controversy in Japanese Medicine." Paper presented at the Forty-Second Annual Meeting of the Association for Asian Studies, Chicago, April.

Yoshino, M. Y., and Thomas B. Lifson. 1989. *The Invisible Link: Japan's Sogo Shosha and the Organization of Trade*. Cambridge, Mass.: MIT Press.

CHAPTER NINE

United States: Cultural Challenges to the Voluntary Sector

David Harrington Watt,
  with the assistance of Michael Simon

THE WORK OF SCHOLARS such as Alan Brinkley, Richard Wightman Fox, and T. J. Jackson Lears suggests that the historiography of twentieth-century America involves three major themes. The first theme centers on the development of an economic system of exceeding complexity, whose inner workings were, to most Americans, incomprehensible, and which produced both remarkable economic inequity and impressive prosperity. The second theme speaks of the creation and development of governmental structures that were far more expansive than those that had existed in previous eras of American history. The final theme traces the emergence of a culture whose central tenets seem to include the following motifs. One's life is shaped by shadowy institutions beyond one's control. There is little one can do to produce fundamental positive changes in the nation's economic or political structures. It seems wise to concentrate one's energy on achieving satisfactions in one's private life—either through the acquisition of consumer goods or through the attainment of psychic health (Brinkley 1984; Fox and Lears 1983).

This chapter starts from the assumption that such a reading of the central themes of the recent history of the United States is essentially correct, and then goes on to consider the ways in which a public sphere may and may not be said to be functioning in the contemporary United States. The chapter is divided into five sections. The first section, which is relatively brief, is concerned with the meaning of the term "public sphere." The second section surveys the political sector of American society; the third is concerned with the economic sector. The fourth section explores the relationship between religious organizations (which in America take the form of voluntary associations) and the public sphere in contemporary America; the fifth looks at secular voluntary associations, paying particular attention to their relationship to the public sphere. A number of points emerge with some clarity:

1. The understanding of the public sphere that grows out of the work of scholars such as Jürgen Habermas turns out, despite its apparent exoticism within the

American context, to raise a number of issues that, in a somewhat different form, are near the heart of American political culture.

2. In the United States, religious organizations play an important role in shaping society in general and politics in particular. Their relationship to American public life is a matter that attracts much attention.

3. The scholarly literature on religion in the United States suggests, however, that religious organizations in the United States make, generally speaking, only very modest contributions to public discourse (as that term is used in this volume).

4. American voluntary associations are not much different. They too play a fairly large role in American society. But the third sector, taken as a whole, is a better argument for the evisceration than for the utility of the American public sphere.

5. The groups to which the terms "religious organizations" and "voluntary associations" refer are, in the United States, extraordinarily diverse, so conclusions should not be taken to apply to all religious organizations or all voluntary associations.

6. Indeed, there is some evidence to suggest that some voluntary associations and religious organizations actually do embody some of the characteristics that would have to be present in a vital public sphere.

THE PUBLIC SPHERE

The phrase "public sphere" will be used in this chapter to refer to that place where people, having chosen not to focus their attention purely on the private realm, may rationally discuss questions of the common good in a manner that is not distorted by either the power of the state or that of the marketplace. This definition of the public sphere is, of course, hardly original: it draws on (though it is not identical to) the understanding of the public that informs Jürgen Habermas's *Structural Transformation of the Public Sphere* (1989b).

It is not, of course, simply a recapitulation of an American consensus. The assertion that "public" is somehow the opposite of "private" is not one with which many Americans would take issue. But each of the other clauses in the definition would strike many Americans as odd. Many Americans would insist that public discourse is almost always something less than or more than rational. Public discourse is, for instance, often taken to include symbolic speech. Thus many Americans are quite willing to say that either waving or burning an American flag is the sort of public discourse that is protected by the Bill of Rights. Similarly, many Americans would take issue with the claim that public discourse, in the fullest sense of that term, is about matters of the common good—and therefore not simply the outcome of the competing voices of special-interest groups. Indeed, one standard interpretation of what American public life should be—the one that draws on theories of "pluralism"—might reject the "common good" claim out of hand. Pluralists would argue that American public life is, and should be, a free-for-all of competing interest groups. According to their view, moreover, asserting that public discourse has to revolve around matters of the common good is naive, utopian, romantic, and perhaps even—though this is, admittedly, an unusually harsh way of putting the matter—fascistic.

The juxtaposition of state and public—a juxtaposition that implies that in some contexts "public" and "state" are antonyms—would also strike many as strange, for in America "public" is often used as a synonym for "government." Nor do many Americans have much affinity for a definition that implicitly stresses the way that marketplace forces can eviscerate public discourse. The assumption, often found in many of the works influenced by Habermas's ideas, that when discourse becomes thoroughly commodified it ceases to be truly public, would strike most thoughtful Americans as unwarranted. The point is obvious but still worth making: American political culture provides many ways to talk about how the state can limit free speech; it provides far fewer ways to analyze how the marketplace limits what is sayable.

It should not be supposed, however, that this working definition of the public sphere has no connection whatsoever to American political discourse. The appearance of the English translation, in 1989, of Habermas's book on the public sphere was widely heralded. Habermas's ideas on the public sphere had begun to influence English scholars (such as Terry Eagleton and John Keane) with large American audiences, and American scholars such as Joan Landes, Peter Uwe Hohendahl, David Tracy, and John Forester, well before 1989. Moreover, Habermas's ideas on the public sphere were not developed in complete isolation from American thought. When Habermas tried, in the final pages of *The Structural Transformation*, to move toward "a sociological attempt at clarification" of what the "public" was, he found it helpful to quote at length from C. Wright Mills's *Power Elite*. When he was trying elsewhere in the manuscript to show some of the ways that the public sphere was eroding, he found it helpful to quote from William Whyte's *Organization Man*. But of course the parallels between Habermas's concerns and American thought go much deeper than that. For what Habermas was up to, in part, in *The Structural Transformation* was taking liberal notions concerning the public sphere and then trying to see how well they fit the realities of modern democracies. Accordingly, some of the issues treated in *The Structural Transformation* are closely related to those addressed by two great thinkers who can hardly be said to rest at the margins of American political thought—John Dewey and Alexis de Tocqueville. It is a rare text in this field that does not address itself to the insights of Alexis de Tocqueville. The relationship that Tocqueville discerned between voluntary associations, especially religious organizations, and the public realm of American society seems the requisite starting point for most discussions of the public sphere.

Tocqueville observed that Americans' proclivity for forming associations might enjoin the totalitarian tendencies of their large, democratic government.

He argued that by forming associations and by advocating the values and interests of the members of those associations, two forces would be brought to bear within the democratic populace. First, associations represented the mobilization of private interests and thus could provide spaces for claims against local or state governments on behalf of those interests. And second, the fact of associations as *public entities* might pull against those "individualistic" tendencies he observed in American democracy, in favor of forging more communal bonds. In short, the realm of voluntary associations might function as a mediator between the authority of the state and the "will of the people," in the process forging communitarian links and politicizing the citizenry.[1] Tocqueville recognized, however, that these processes were contingent on the maintenance of some degree of autonomy between the realm of voluntary associations and that of the state. If the state was increasingly to put its own efforts "in the place of associations," then the attraction for individuals to associate would eventually wane. "Feelings and opinions are recruited, the heart is enlarged, and the human mind is developed only by the reciprocal influence of men upon one another. I have shown that these influences are almost null in democratic countries; they must be artificially created, and this can only be accomplished by associations" (Tocqueville [1835] 1963, 2:108).

Tocqueville's observations and arguments foreshadowed what most see as our current situation: the expansion of state power fostering privatization and depoliticization of the masses. (See, for example, Schroyer 1985; Wuthnow 1989.)

Whereas Tocqueville was concerned with the threats raised by the state to what Habermas today calls the "life-world,"[2] Habermas extends these concerns and points us in the direction of the threats posed to "democratic will formation" by the rapid rise of industrial capitalism.[3] "In the political systems of advanced capitalist societies, we find compromise structures that, historically considered, can be conceived of as reactions on the part of the life-world to the independent systemic logic and growth in complexity proper to the capitalist economic process and state apparatus with a monopoly on force. These origins have left their traces on the options that remain open to us in a social-welfare state in crisis" (Habermas 1989a:355–56).

[1] This is not to ignore, however, that Tocqueville also warned against the "tyranny of the majority" and the relationship between public opinion as majority and as a critical force against unlimited power (Tocqueville [1835] 1963, 1:258).

[2] See, for example, Habermas's own discussion of the components of the life-world, taken as a resource for contestatory action in Habermas (1989a:340–50).

[3] In *Philosophical Discourse*, Habermas draws on Niklas Luhmann's systems theory to argue for both the necessity and the (near) impossibility of maintaining "free spaces," in order to recognize what Luhmann calls a "consensus functional for society as a whole about what is and what is valid" (Habermas 1989a:358). One is thus reminded of Tocqueville's interest in the emancipatory possibilities of voluntary associations in Habermas's insistence on democratic will formation apart from the twin "steering" influences of money and state power.

This additional focus on the erosion of potential public spheres by advanced capitalist practices has much to recommend it. Because it both echoes and modifies the concerns of Tocqueville, Habermas's work gives us analytical leverage into the *mutually enhancing* processes of a burgeoning capitalist economy and an expanding state.

THE GOVERNMENTAL SECTOR

Since the United States is (in the language of old-fashioned political science) a federal republic, its governmental structure is far less centralized than those of many of the other countries discussed in this volume. In 1987, the last year for which reliable statistics are available, there were 83,237 distinct governmental entities in the nation (U.S. Bureau of the Census 1989b). Many of these organizations were subject to the direct control of the electorate, and in theory all of them derive their authority from the American people, for in the American political tradition it is there that sovereignty resides. Nevertheless, a number of the most important constituent structures of the United States government—the Supreme Court, the National Security Council, the Central Intelligence Agency, and the Federal Reserve Board, for example—have been deliberately insulated from popular control.

A suspicion of the state has always been an important part of American political culture. It was, as historical inquiries have made plain, a central feature of both the republican ideology that fueled the American Revolution and decisively shaped the framing of the American Constitution and of those forms of liberalism that dominated the American political imagination throughout the nineteenth and twentieth centuries (W. P. Adams 1984; Ross 1984). Suspicion of the state is still an important part of American political culture. When polling organizations ask Americans whether big business, big labor, or big government poses the gravest threat to the nation, nearly twice as many people answer "government" as say either "labor" or "business" (Gallup 1986). A great deal of the recent political history of the United States involves various attempts to gain access to the levers of governmental power by appealing to voters' antipathies to government.

In part because Americans have feared the state so deeply and for so long, the expansion of the American state, when compared to the expansion of most of the other states examined in this book, looks quite modest. In 1983, for example, governmental revenue in the United States accounted for only 37.3 percent of the GDP. That contrasts with the comparable figures for West Germany (45.7 percent), the United Kingdom (45.9 percent), France (47.4 percent), and Sweden (62.7 percent) (Organisation for Economic Cooperation and Development 1989). Such figures (and one could cite many others to the same effect) remind us that the conventional wisdom that America is a "strong" nation with a "weak" state contains a measure of truth.

But to return to one of the points mentioned at the outset of this chapter, the various governmental structures in the contemporary United States are, when compared to the governmental structures in all the other eras of the nation's history, extraordinarily expansive. Total governmental expenditure—federal, state, and local—stood at $20 billion in 1940; $70 billion in 1950; $151 billion in 1960; $333 billion in 1970; and $959 billion in 1980. The pattern was not, by any means, reversed by the Reagan revolution: in 1986 total governmental expenditures reached $1,696 billion (U.S. Bureau of the Census 1975, 1989b).

The expansion of the federal government has been particularly striking. In 1901, the federal government employed under 240,000 civilians. By 1940, it employed just over 1,000,000; by 1988, over 3,100,000. In 1900, the chief executive of the federal government had 140,000 active-duty military personnel at his command; in 1940, just under 460,000; in 1988, about 2,200,000 (U.S. Bureau of the Census 1975, 1989b). In 1900, the total outlays of the federal government were $520 million; in 1940, they were $1 billion; in 1980, $617 billion (U.S. Bureau of the Census 1975, 1989b). Allowing for inflation does not make the trend disappear: when expressed in constant dollars (fiscal year 1982), total federal budget outlays increased from $83 billion in 1940 to $699 billion in 1980 and to an estimated $870 billion in 1988. Thus between 1940 and 1988 federal outlays increased tenfold.[4]

We know far less about the effects of this state expansion than we should, for the literature on the American state, especially in comparison to the rich body of literature on the history of the state in Western Europe, is distressingly thin. Morton Keller's slightly lame pun summarizes the point nicely. "To say 'there is still much to be learned about the state in America is a major understatement. There is close to everything to be learned about the state" (Leuchtenberg 1986:594). Given these circumstances, and the need for brevity, perhaps it is not too much of an oversimplification to suggest that what state expansion did not do is probably as important as what it did.

Because the United States spent a larger proportion of its GNP on the military than did nations such as Japan, France, West Germany, or the United Kingdom (Arms Control and Disarmament Agency 1989), and because its GNP was far larger than that of any other nation in the world, the United States developed a military arsenal that far outstripped those of its allies and rivals and that was without precedent in world history. But although its military strength gave the United States remarkable power to shape international events, it did not give the nation sufficient power to enable it to accomplish its most important foreign-policy goals—think of Cuba, Iran, Nicaragua, and, of

[4] The increases in governmental expenditures were concentrated in two areas: military spending, which at times in the postwar era accounted for as much as 62 percent of total federal expenditures, and expenditures on social welfare, which had by 1984 risen to $671 billion—a figure equal to 52 percent of total government outlays and 18 percent of the GNP.

course, Vietnam. Nor did U.S. military strength provide its inhabitants with a foolproof defense against potentially devastating attacks from other nations.

The way the American state expanded its social-welfare provisions did, as writers such as John Schwarz have documented, ameliorate the living conditions of the poorest portion of the American populace (Schwarz 1988).[5] And it created a system of providing social-welfare services and payments that directly linked a large percentage of the American population to the American state. Between 1983 and 1986, for example, it is estimated that over forty-four million people received help from at least one of the so-called major assistance programs sponsored by the federal government (U.S. Bureau of the Census 1989a).

The Social Security system is a case in point. In 1991, almost two hundred billion dollars will be spent annually on the program. In 1940, 222,488 Americans received Old-Age, Survivors, and Disability Insurance (OASDI) payments. By 1986 this figure had reached almost thirty-eight million. And from the time the Social Security Act was signed in 1935, more than twenty-two trillion dollars in cash benefits have been paid (Social Security Administration 1987). The program has achieved some notable results. In 1986, for example, the program helped raise well over fifteen million people above the "poverty line," reducing the "official poor" to less than thirty-six million.

OASDI is but the largest—38.6 million people covered for an outlay of $217 billion in 1988—in the network of federal and state "social insurance" programs (U.S. Department of Health and Human Services 1988).[6] The widening of the state's "safety net" covers a vast array of what have come to be called "income-support" programs. On average, during 1986, over twenty-two million Americans per month were linked with the American state through Medicaid payments representing a yearly outlay of close to forty-one billion dollars. Close to twenty-one million people were food-stamp recipients; eleven million received Aid to Families with Dependent Children (AFDC) monies (well over sixteen million in 1987 dollars); nearly four and one-half million received Supplemental Security Income (SSI) at an average (individual) benefit payment of almost two hundred fifty dollars per month. And between low-income housing programs and general-assistance aid programs such as the National School Lunch Program, the food program for Women, Infants, and Children (WIC), and the Child Care Food Program, another four and one-half million Americans received federal assistance from 1983 to 1986. In sum, 20.5 percent of the American male population received federal or state assistance for one or more months during the early 1980s, as did 15.2 percent of the female population.

[5] Between 1959 and 1987 the percentage of Americans living below the poverty line declined from 22.4 to 13.5 (U.S. Bureau of the Census 1989b).

[6] All social-service statistics are from U.S. Department of Health and Human Services (1988).

State expansion did not, however, drastically alter the distribution of income in the United States. In 1987, the lowest one-fifth of America's households received 5.1 percent of the nation's aggregate income; the second fifth received 11.6 percent; the third received 17.5 percent; the fourth, 24.3 percent; the highest, 41.6 percent (U.S. Bureau of the Census 1989b). Those figures do not differ dramatically from the comparable statistics for 1940, 1950, 1960, or 1970 (U.S. Bureau of the Census 1975). Nor did state expansion lead to the creation of a fully functioning welfare state in which, through the creation, maintenance, and predominance of social-service activity, a transfer (or legal redistribution) of resources was effected from "rich" to "poor" (Titmuss 1969:38).[7]

State expansion ensured that the state, acting through its courts, schools, regulatory bodies, and social-welfare agencies, would influence the lives of ordinary people more profoundly than ever before. It ensured—to put the matter in the sort of language that is especially appropriate for a volume inspired by Habermas's works—that the colonization of life-world by system could progress with ever-increasing celerity. But state expansion did not, on the whole, lead to Americans taking a deeper interest in the affairs of state. Rather, it was accompanied by a depoliticization of American society. The society that the expanding state helped fashion is one in which a relatively small proportion of the populace know even the most basic facts about the political system under which they live (Wald 1987), in which barely half of the voting-age population actually votes in presidential elections (U.S. Bureau of the Census 1989b), and in which political parties attract less and less of the energy of the citizenry (Burnham 1982; Ginsberg and Shefter 1990:9–16). Burnham notes that into the 1980s, the

> party was increasingly replaced by interest-group ascendancy in the formulation of public policy, and, with the passage of time, the results came to be condemned explicitly by conservatives and, more or less tacitly, by liberals as well. The stage was set for the filling of this vacuum by Ronald Reagan and the policies of the economic and cultural Right. The politics of excluded alternatives, based on the

[7] Titmuss delineates three types of "welfare," though he indicates that inasmuch as the social division of welfare is bound to changing conceptions of "need," the content of service delivery will constantly change. "Considered as a whole," writes Titmuss, "all collective interventions to meet certain needs of the individual and/or to serve the wider interests of society may now be broadly grouped into three major categories of welfare: social welfare, fiscal welfare, and occupational welfare" (1969:42). The "welfare state" is created insofar as the state's activities represent the means by which collective provision is made for what Titmuss calls "culturally determined dependencies" (1969:42–44). Ralph M. Kramer's *Voluntary Agencies in the Welfare State* provides a more formal definition of the welfare state as one that provides "government-protected, minimum standards of income, health, nutrition, housing, and education for all citizens as a legal right, not as a charity" (Kramer 1981:3). Alternative definitions (cited in Kramer) include "employment" and "personal social services" in the above list of minimum standards provided by the welfare state.

uncontested hegemony of the "liberal tradition in America," had come full circle. (Burnham 1982:19)

While it seems to be the case that presidential electoral politics saw a re-alignment toward the Republican party in the 1980s, it is also evident that overall citizen participation in political parties continues its post–Progressive Era downward slide. Gone are "direct organizational ties to rank-and-file vot-ers," in favor of a new constitution of party activities as "coalitions of public officials, office seekers, and political activists" (Ginsberg and Shefter 1990:10). Increasingly, battles are fought by third-sector groups willing to wage protracted fights in the courts, illustrating the growing importance of nonelectoral conflict—activity perhaps better suited to voluntary associations other than political parties.

The expansion of the state did certainly affect and (arguably, at least) sys-tematically distort the sorts of communication that took place in the American public sphere. Indeed, it helped produce a society in which political parties, labor unions, and educational institutions are all to a great extent the creatures of the state. The effects of state expansion on American public discourse have not been examined very thoroughly. But it does seem clear that because those in the media look to government officials for descriptions of what is really going on, and because government officials can, at least in certain situations, manipulate the media into accepting and disseminating their version of reality, the version of reality that Americans ingest daily is rooted, at least partly, in the state. Thus one cannot reject out of hand the possibility that the public sphere in America is being eroded by the power of the state as well as by the power of the marketplace.

But the American state did not expand in a way that curtailed public-sphere activity nearly so dramatically as did state expansion in societies such as the Netherlands (Kramer 1981). Thus it seems likely that one of the questions raised by the American example is this: in what ways, if any, is the public sphere being eroded in societies where the state is, by most standard defini-tions, relatively weak?

THE ECONOMIC SECTOR

Although the origins and effects of a number of the fundamental transforma-tions that the American economy is currently undergoing are not fully under-stood, a few observations can be made with confidence. It is clear, for in-stance, that the labor force of the American economy now includes a much larger percentage of women than it did only a few decades ago. In 1960, women constituted 33 percent of the American labor force. By 1987 44 per-cent of the nation's labor force was female. That figure is slightly lower than the comparable figure for Sweden (48 percent), but higher than those for West

Germany (39 percent), France (42 percent), the United Kingdom (41 percent) and Japan (40 percent) (Organisation for Economic Cooperation and Development 1989).

It is clear, too, that the economy of the United States is increasingly centered on services rather than on manufacturing. In 1960, services accounted for 58 percent of the nation's GDP. By 1980 they accounted for 64 percent. In 1987, the last year for which there are reliable figures, the percentage was 69. (This last figure is higher than the comparable statistics for Sweden, Japan, Italy, France, and West Germany.) The percentage of the American labor force in services also increased in the postwar era. In 1960, 56 percent of American laborers were in the service sector; by 1987, 70 percent of American workers were in that sector (ibid.).

The move away from manufacturing has been accompanied by a decline in the relative strength of organized labor. In 1954, 25 percent of the nation's total labor force was unionized. In 1987 that figure stood at 17 percent. And the willingness of American laborers to engage in work stoppages—traditionally one of the most important weapons in labor's arsenal—has declined dramatically in recent years. In 1970 there were 381 work stoppages; in 1980, 187; in 1987, 46. The work stoppages that took place in 1970 involved 2,468,000 workers; those that took place in 1987 involved only 174,000 (U.S. Department of Labor, Bureau of Labor Statistics 1988). Most observers would surely agree that there are few reasons for optimism among the supporters of organized labor in the contemporary United States.

Some would say there is little warrant for optimistic assessments of the future of the entire economic sector of American society. Textbooks on American economic history used to end with glowing descriptions of American capitalism's latest accomplishments and roseate predictions concerning its future. The tone of the textbooks' final chapters is considerably less ebullient these days, reflecting as often as not the widespread suspicion that the American economy may well have already seen its best days.

The change in tone is not, by any means, groundless. The growth rate of the American economy, for example, has been somewhat disappointing for decades. Between 1960 and 1987, the average annual growth rate for the GDP of the United States was 3.2 percent. This growth rate was more impressive than that of either the United Kingdom or the USSR. But the annual growth rate of America's GDP in the years between 1960 and 1987 compares poorly with many Western European countries and Japan (Organisation for Economic Cooperation and Development 1989).

Then, too, there are definite signs of weakness in the American banking system. In no year between 1980 and 1988 were there fewer than forty-two failures at federally insured banks; in 1988 there were two hundred. In 1988 there were more than 350 insolvent savings-and-loan organizations in the United States. And though (at the time of this writing) the American stock market is near its all-time high, it has been extremely volatile. On a single, much-discussed day in 1987, the Dow-Jones Industrial Average fell 508 points: it was, by some measures, the worst single day in the market's history. The vastness of the federal debt is another disturbing sign (totaling over $2,350 billion in 1987). So, too, is the fact that the American economy is now dependent on foreign capital in a way it has not been at any other time in this century.

Accompanying the shift to a service economy and the decline in organized labor since the 1950s—trends in full throttle by the 1980s—the United States has been witnessing a rather dramatic redistribution of the national wealth, one unparalleled since the period between 1890 and 1910. In the 1970s and especially in the 1980s, the percentage of U.S. assets owned by the wealthiest 1 percent of the population rose sharply from 28 to nearly 35, up from a century-low 23 percent (in 1950) (Harvey 1989:193; U.S. Bureau of the Census 1975). Increasingly evident in the 1980s were severe inequalities in income distribution, symptoms of "the emergence of an ill-remunerated and broadly disempowered underclass" (Harvey 1989:192). And, finally, although some point to the current all-time high of the stock market as proof of the solubility of American financial markets, one thoughtful critic views the "explosion in new financial instruments and markets" as a symptom of fundamental structural problems—as a "search for financial solutions to the crisis-tendencies of capitalism" evidenced by the bank failures and massive Third World debt, rather than as a sign of the continuing success story of American capitalism (ibid., 194).

But by many standards of judgment, American capitalism's performance has been stunningly strong. Its strengths were particularly evident in the years between 1945 and 1970. During those years, as politicians and journalists loved to point out, the American people enjoyed a level of prosperity that was without precedent in world history. In part because of American economic performance in that era, the economies of all the countries discussed in this volume are part of what might be usefully thought of—as a recent work by John Hall and G. John Ikenberry suggests—as "the American system" (Hall and Ikenberry 1989). Moreover, the weaknesses the American economy displayed in the 1970s and 1980s, as Hall and Ikenberry argue, can easily be exaggerated. Its performance in those decades does not look very good when compared with what happened in Japan; when compared with what was going on in Canada, West Germany, France, the United Kingdom, or Italy, it looks fairly strong (Organisation for Economic Cooperation and Development 1989). Observers such as John Schwarz warn us to be cautious in our glum assessments of American economic performance in the 1970s and 1980s and to remember the tremendous increase in the labor force that took place after 1965:

To appreciate the context of the times enables one to recognize the success of the nation in managing the economic situation it faced. By all counts, unemployment in the United States should have grown by leaps and bounds as the crowded generation surged into the labor market. Despite this, the nation's rate of unemployment for 1980 (7.1 percent) stood less than two points higher than it did in 1960 (5.5 percent) . . . miraculously, no massive rise had taken place in the nation's unemployment rate. Potentially, more than 10 million Americans had been spared joblessness . . . [and the] nation achieved a record that neither Japan, nor West Germany, nor France, nor Britain surpassed, or in most cases even equaled. . . . The American performance was truly remarkable and might well have been the cause of celebration. But few of us thought more than casually about the challenge set by the crowded generation for the nation, and so few of us celebrated the achievement. (Schwarz 1988:137–38)

Those who wanted to argue that the downturns seen in the 1980s in particular were exceptions to the rule of American capitalism's triumph had several arguments at their disposal. Schwarz draws on the tremendous challenges to the economy in the post-Eisenhower years and argues that America's economic "failures" were, in part, the result of misperceptions of relative successes, given these challenges. He cites the increase in real gross national product (after inflation) as being as substantial during the 1970s (3.7 percent yearly) as during the 1950s (3.5 percent yearly). The nation saw sharp growth in the Industrial Production Index (at rates higher than those for any major West European nation), rapid increase in personal income and real disposable income (at a rate double that of the 1950s), a rise in housing starts and home ownership (up 15 percent between 1973 and 1980), a very moderate increase in income taxes, and other "great advances in material well-being to ever-larger percentages of Americans, just as had earlier characterized the 1950s" (ibid., 112–13).

Following sociologist Peter Berger's formulations in *The Capitalist Revolution*, many argue that the perils of modernization that may leave tradition vulnerable in either a socialist or a capitalist economy are more tempered by the linkage between capitalism and democracy. At base, capitalist economics—even with any attendant "risks" such as unequal distribution of wealth, the continual growth of "individualism," or "massive state interventions in economic life" (Berger 1986:157)—simply provides a more successful system for the preservation of those values most Americans deem paramount. Thus, while observers like Berger are not insensitive to the "tragedies" of capitalism, they caution us to remember the "superior productive power of industrial capitalism," and not to ascribe to capitalism the "faults" of modernization (ibid., 173). One might argue thus that the American system during the 1970s and 1980s was not working well enough to satisfy utopian expectations, but especially when compared to the performance of most Eastern and some Western European economies, it was, in some sense, working (if not for everybody). Besides, if part of the problem of modernization lay in the awesome development of the modern state, then, as Berger argues, America still needs an economy that, "even when subjected to all sorts of governmental interventions, creates its own dynamic that confronts the state as a relatively autonomous reality. Whatever else the government then controls, it does not fully control this zone, which ipso facto limits state power. The 'fit' between capitalism and democracy is the consequence of this" (ibid., 79).

But even Peter Berger, whose work often emphasizes the virtues of the American economic system, asserted that

> the world created by capitalism is indeed a "cold" one. Liberating though it may be, it also involves the individual in countless relations with other people that are based on calculating rationality . . . superficial . . . and inevitably transient. Human relations too become subject to the "creative destruction" of capitalism. There is, therefore, an overriding need for a world of "warmth" to balance all this "coldness." Family, church, private friendships, and freely formed associations have provided this balance throughout the development of bourgeois culture; they continue to do so today, despite the tensions and "contradictions" of this culture. (Ibid., 113)

Berger's observations suggest two important points. First, there is, in one of the most capitalist nations on earth, palpable ambivalence about the sort of society that capitalism produces. Second, that ambivalence influences the way Americans view both their religious organizations and their voluntary associations. Ambivalence is not (and this point can hardly be overemphasized) the same as opposition: comparatively few Americans have ever been willing to go to the polls, much less to the barricades, to overthrow capitalism. Anticapitalist parties have achieved notoriously few successes in the United States. In the early twentieth century, Socialists won control of some municipalities and even served in the United States Congress. But even at the height of its power and prestige the Socialist movement could not garner more than 6 percent of the votes in a presidential election.

But neither is nonopposition the same as untroubled celebration. The ambivalence to which I referred earlier is evident, for instance, in Americans' conversations about what is usually called the "plight of the homeless," in their comments on how they see "suffering in the midst of plenty," and in their observations about the unequal distribution of wealth and economic power in the United States.[8] It is evident, too, in the concerns expressed by many Americans that business is exercising too much influence on the govern-

[8] Public-opinion polls suggest that there are twice as many Americans who believe that the nation's wealth should be more evenly distributed as there are who believe that the present distribution of wealth is fair (Gallup 1986).

ment (Lindblom 1977; Stern 1988). And though the prediction is expressed most frequently and forcefully by intellectuals and social activists, it is evident, too, in the pages of mass-circulation magazines and daily newspapers: capitalism will, many Americans say, be unable to outlast the environmental disorder it produces. Other less-obvious and more-widespread concerns about capitalism are also worth noting. Complaints about materialism, overly rapid change, disintegrating families, excessive hedonism, and the like are the worn-smooth coinage of much informal discourse in America. What they signify about Americans' attitudes toward capitalism needs further investigation.

Of particular interest, in the present context, are some observers' comments about the way the so-called commodification of culture affects public discourse. For instance, Ben Bagdikian has argued that the American media's overwhelmingly commercial orientation has produced a situation in which the media is "sensitive to failures in [governmental] bodies, but insensitive to equally important failures in the private sector, particularly in what affects the corporate world. This institutional bias does more than merely protect the corporate system. It robs the public of a chance to understand the real world" (Bagdikian 1987:xvi). Neil Postman's somewhat popular study of "public discourse in the age of show business" concludes that a good deal of such discourse is based, as it were, on "a theory of anticommunication, featuring a type of discourse that abandons logic, reason, sequence and rules of contradiction (Postman 1985:105). Sut Jhally's more sophisticated essay on the political economy of culture concludes that "more and more areas are being drawn into the sphere of domination by exchange-value so that the cultural realm (where healthy societies think about their past, present, and future) become more and more intertwined with narrow economic concerns. Capitalist interests are moving forcefully into the one area of society where there may still exist alternative social visions—a process of increasing colonization and control" (Angus and Jhally 1989:81).

There is, I think, a great deal of truth in such an analysis. But it would be a mistake to conclude that the commodification of public discourse in America—or for that matter (if you will pardon the neologism) the "statification" of public discourse in America—means that there are no contemporary American conversations that are truly public in the sense suggested at the outset of this essay. A recent work by Herbert Schiller, one of the more prominent students of communications in America, includes a few lines that helpfully undercut the tendency (to which Schiller himself is not immune) to write as if Jeremiah had said all there was to say about American public life: "The corporate enclosure of cultural space, however extensive in the last fifty years, has not been total. There remain a number of centers of democratic and public expression, though they may be small-scale and geographically dispersed" (Schiller 1989:163).

RELIGIOUS ORGANIZATIONS

It is generally acknowledged that traditional religion has fared better in the United States than it has in most other advanced capitalist societies, and there is no shortage of recent works on the stubborn perseverance of traditional religion in America. Kenneth Wald, for example, writes that modernization and class-conflict theory notwithstanding, "by all the normal indicators of religious commitment—the strength of religious institutions, practices and belief—the United States has resisted the pressures toward secularity" (Wald 1987:7). In terms of practice and affiliation, a 1982 Gallup poll indicated that almost 70 percent of all adults belonged to a church and 72 percent had attended church within the past six months, accounting for much of the almost $25 billion given to religious institutions that year. Over half of those surveyed prayed frequently, participated in church social life, and encouraged others to seek religious guidance (ibid., 9). When compared with another activity given vital importance—at least rhetorically—voter turnout for all postwar presidential elections among voting-age Americans has consistently been lower than the recorded level of church membership, and not ironically, more American adults claim to speak in tongues than worked for a party or candidate in 1980 (ibid.).

The more elusive measure of American religious vitality—the persistence of religious "feeling"—was celebrated in Caplow's 1983 reexamination of traditional religion, a revisitation of the Lynds' famous 1929 study of Muncie, Indiana. "Against all expectations, the most recent study of Muncie uncovered a community with reverence for the sacred and faith in religion as a source of strength and guidance. . . . There can be little doubt about the durability of religion in the United States" (ibid., 11).

As to why traditional religion seems to have weathered the storm in the United States, arguments are not difficult to find. First, scientific and political activities and ideologies have been unable to meet "basic human needs," those needs most often called "spiritual." Second, religious groups in the United States have been able to respond to rapid social change through the formation of denominations that, unlike in many European countries, are not solely supported by the financial resources of the state. Third, the heterogeneity of American religion has ensured that "no single denomination today comprises more than about 40 percent of the church membership" (ibid., 15). This last argument, one version of Tocqueville's commentary on the importance of factions within a democracy, implies that the health of traditional religion is linked to the fact that no single denomination is in the majority. What is variously called "pluralism," "denominationalism," or simply the expression of democratic tendencies within our religious lives is also a concomitant of our economic lives. Traditional religion, too, is in the marketplace, and successful or unsuccessful attempts to "reach the consumer," it is argued, have created an atmosphere of healthy competition where churches must continually project messages of relevance, and at a pace that keeps up with the rapidity of commercial images. Thus, the argument runs, what some say is the increasing secularization of the churches is also the necessary process of adaptation that has kept church involvement steady, and in some cases, booming. Images of God, like the stream of television images, fluctuate according to perceived need, now as "the almighty power of the universe and source of redemption," and now again as "psychologist, economic advisor, athletic trainer, and friend" (ibid., 12).

Then, too—and this does not exhaust the arguments for the vitality of American religion—the churches in the United States, in avoiding (the appearance of) exclusive association with any one political party or ideology, have been able to thrive despite the specter of deep suspicion leveled at the state, for example, in the aftermath of Watergate. Wald is correct to point out that, as the churches take increasingly visible political stances, the link between religious affiliation and political ideology is increasingly harder to conceal; as the American tradition of distrust of the state increases, so with it may go a decline in religious attachment at the institutional level.

To be sure, there are already signs of decline among some religious bodies in the United States, particularly among those denominations that make up what used to be called the Protestant mainstream (Roof and McKinney 1987). To say that traditional religion has "fared better" is, perhaps, to invite a conflict of interpretations. It can be construed in a way that makes it possible to argue, with considerable plausibility, that traditional religion in America is in very poor condition. Thus one could say that the apparent "vitality" displayed by many of the religious groups in America is the result of their willingness to accommodate themselves to values and practices whose origins are thoroughly secular.

But the more general point still holds: by most conventional standards, religious organizations in America are doing quite well—doing better, perhaps, than religious organizations are doing in any of the other countries discussed in this volume. Many of the founders of modern social inquiry thought that the vitality of religious practice and affiliation would erode in the presence of advanced industrialization. But when the United States (perhaps the overindustrialized "model" of secularized society) is compared with countries such as Canada, Great Britain, France, West Germany, and Japan, the results are intriguing. In a study comparing fifteen countries with the United States, all fifteen countries, including those mentioned above, showed a "decline in religious sentiment" in proportion to an increase in economic development. The notable exception is the United States, which shows the highest ranking on the index of economic development right alongside its ranking as the "most religious" of countries (Wald 1987).

Measures of belief and practice bear out these same conclusions. Gallup surveys show that close to 60 percent of the American public considers prayer and "growing into a deeper relationship with God" to be "very important" (Wuthnow 1988:303). Contemporary measures of religious sentiment often echo a kind of psychotherapeutic stance that, as some observe, may "serve a positive role in sustaining the plausibility of communication with an invisible God in the modern era" (ibid.). And, as noted earlier, contemporary images of *relationship* to God do not appear wholly arbitrary in light of the apparently deep impact of psychological theory. Sixty-four percent of the public linked their relationships with God to their "own sense of self worth," and most (90 percent) surveyed expressed "satisfaction" with their relationships with God, reporting that God loved them (80 percent), and that they rarely felt afraid of God (16 percent). Among those gratifications often cited by regular church-goers, 77 percent reported feeling close to God, 60 percent mentioned the experience of worshiping God, and over 50 percent spoke of a "sense of companionship or fellowship" (ibid., 304).

One conclusion, then, is that the degree to which religious practices, beliefs, and affiliations are linked to modern cultural forms—such as psychotherapeutic images of a "good relationship with God"—is a fairly good predictor of the "vitality" of those practices and beliefs. It is difficult to argue with those who say that, overall, "religion" is in decline. By 1986 estimates, inclusive membership in religious bodies totaled almost 143 million (Jacquet 1988),[9] and the 1987 edition of *The Encyclopedia of American Religions* now lists almost 1,350 denominations of churches and synagogues, up from the 1,200 listed in the 1979 edition of that volume (Melton 1979).

Whether in membership in one of the (over) 338,000 churches in the United States (Hodgkinson and Weitzman 1986:19), or through membership, voluntarism, or employment in close to 370,000 religious organizations, Americans continue to express a well-documented proclivity for forming associations with specifically "religious" aims (ibid., 128). It would be no surprise, then, that the greatest percentage of those who volunteered in 1985 volunteered for religious organizations and causes (48 percent of all who volunteered). In 1984, religious organizations accounted for over 60 percent of all third-sector organizations and (though this is difficult to estimate) spent well over seventeen billion dollars that year. And it is significant that when we want to find

[9] In 1986, 71 percent of the American people were affiliated with Christian organizations (Wald 1987). In 1987, estimates of the number of Jews holding membership in synagogues or temples of the four main branches of Judaism totaled about 3.75 million. The total number of Jews in the United States was estimated at about 5.8 million (U.S. Bureau of the Census 1989b). As of 1988 there were estimated to be about six million adherents of Islam in the United States (Jacquet 1988). In spite of these significant Jewish and Muslim minorities in the United States, there can be no question that the Christian religion occupies, in certain respects, a privileged position in American society. (The election of either a Jew or a Muslim as president is, for instance, still unimaginable.) But in just which respects Christianity is or should be privileged are matters on which there is no consensus.

out who gives to charity, the single best predictor of individual giving is whether or not the person attends weekly religious services; the 86 percent of Americans who attended religious services in 1984 made 94 percent of all contributions to charity that year (ibid., 46). Perhaps most suggestive is the fact that whether we consider the United States, England, France, Latin America, India, Kenya, or most other countries, religious groups are the major founders of all nonprofit service institutions (James 1987:404).

One of the points that should by now, be quite clear is the extraordinary heterogeneity of American religion. One can get some sense of how heterogeneous it is by simply noting that there are, if one uses a rather broad definition of "denomination," over thirteen hundred denominations in the United States (Melton 1987), and that there are, in addition, thousands of religious "special-purpose groups"—organizations that perform functions ranging from encouraging Christian magicians to have a "fellowship" with other Christian magicians to trying to affect the foreign policy of the United States government (Wuthnow 1988). But the heterogeneity actually goes deeper than such numbers suggest, for many of the denominations in the United States are themselves deeply divided, often along lines that can be called, somewhat loosely, liberal and conservative (ibid.). The divisions go so deep that some observers have interpreted them as symptomatic of a Kulturkampf.

In *The Restructuring of American Religion*, Robert Wuthnow points out that although the 1980s saw a much greater interaction across denominational lines, there were growing barriers within denominations, and those appeared to be political ones. Whether one considers Americans' education levels, their stands on religious and social issues, or a majority of Americans' beliefs that there are great tensions between religious liberals and conservatives,[10] all factors point to a "more important basis of cleavage in American religion than . . . denominationalism" (ibid., 218). Both the 1980 and 1984 elections evidenced increasing segmentation within denominations. The special-interest groups to which I have referred tended to show the same pattern: much of the activity within them took place in settings—such as healing ministries and Bible study groups or antinuclear coalitions and group therapies—that seemed to peg the participants right away as either religious liberals or religious conservatives.

Though it is offensive, it is not surprising that in the 1980s conservative Baptist leader Bailey Smith could warn Jews about the superfluousness of their prayers while supporting a strong pro-Israel policy or aligning himself with Jewish neoconservatives on abortion or national-defense issues (ibid., 222). Wuthnow writes of the division within denominations along political lines:

[10] Wuthnow reports that about 66 percent of Americans believe there is a great divide that exists between denominations on the basis of political stances on key issues such as abortion and social-service spending (Wuthnow 1988).

"Overall, the issues that discriminated best between the two (in order of strength) were: government spending on social programs, abortion on demand, homosexual teachers in schools, view of Moral Majority, and pornography laws. These issues, in fact, divided liberals and conservatives more strongly than did most of the theological and religious orientation examined in the study" (ibid., 223).

Passion-filled discussions about the relationship between the various religious groups in America and American public life are nothing new: they stretch back to and beyond the founding of the republic. But to many observers, the topic does seem especially, though not uniquely, pressing just now. The precise reasons for this new sense of urgency are not altogether clear. It seems almost certain, however, that a number of the controversies surrounding the "church-state" issues that have received a great deal of attention in recent years have directed Americans' attentions to the topic (Morgan 1980; Watt 1986–1987). And the sense of urgency is connected, too, to a number of disputes that have taken place in recent years over the political activities of various religious groups (Chidester 1988; Wald 1987).

A great number of scholarly and quasi-scholarly works on religion and the public have been published in recent years (see, for example, Lovin [1986], Reichley [1985], and Wilson [1986–1987]). But although the literature on this important topic is vast, it is not, for the most part, very impressive. With a few important exceptions (most notable among which are Robin Lovin's *Religion and American Public Life* and John F. Wilson's "The Public as Problem") it consists, to a very large degree, of the sort of banal bromides and pious simplicities to be found on the Op-Ed pages of the *New York Times*. It rarely evinces either a sense of history or a willingness to question old assumptions (see, for instance, Reichley [1985]). And it is—except for a very few works such as Trent Schroyer's "Corruption of Freedom in America"— isolated from the broader intellectual debate about the nature of the public that Habermas's work exemplifies. Thus we are not in a position to answer the question of religion's relationship to an American "public sphere" (as that term is used in this essay), once and for all. But we are certainly in a position to sketch a series of hypotheses. More specifically, four separate topics—religion and privatization, religion and rationality, religion and the common good, and religion's relations with the nation-state and capitalism—merit particular attention. Each question will be answered in a somewhat general fashion that will nevertheless reflect, I hope, some of the central themes in scholars' current thinking about religion in contemporary America.

Privatized Christianity

Religion in America is often said to be linked to privatization and to a focus on otherworldly matters. Its adherents are not concerned, the argument runs, with the public sphere because they are concerned instead with otherworldly salvation. Thus one could say—and have both religious and nonreligious Americans concur—that the relationship between religious commitment and commitment to the public sphere is an inverse one. There is some truth to this position. There *is* a strong link, as the work of scholars in several different disciplines and writing on a number of different topics demonstrates, between religion and privatization in the United States (see, for instance, Frank [1986]; Cherry [1972]; also, cf. Garrett [1976]). The link is a very old one, and it is rooted partly in the sorts of religious traditions that were transplanted to the United States (they were, to greater degree than is the case for most of the other countries studied in this volume, "pietistic" in outlook) and in the "failure" (that is how most contemporaries surely experienced it) to transplant the European state-church model to the United States. Thus in America it has generally been assumed that there are, as Reinhold Niebuhr once remarked, "constitutional limitations in the genius of religion which will always make it more fruitful in purifying individual life, and adding wholesomeness to the more intimate social relations, such as the family, than in the problems of the more complex and political relations of modern society" (Niebuhr 1932:63).

But a good deal of the recent literature on religion and politics indicates that the relationship between privatization and politicization is not simply inverse. The new religious right is probably the best single instance of that point. Rhetoric about an endangered private sphere figured prominently in many of the public pronouncements of the adherents to that movement: they said they were joining the political fray as a way of defending their families from the attacks of secular humanists. Although such pronouncements can hardly be taken at face value, they do contain a kernel of truth. If you are religious, have staked a great deal of hope on your family, and perceive that family to be endangered by systems that are fundamentally secular and also fundamentally beyond your control, it does make some sense to enter politics in an attempt to affect those systems. The paradox is only apparent: private religious hopes can very naturally push you into political action (Watt 1990). Thus one of many significances of the emergence of the new religious right is that in an era in which life-worlds are increasingly colonized by systems, it is quite possible that previously privatized groups will be increasingly drawn into public action. Yet more often than not, the paradoxes that pushed the new religious right into political action were, to say the least, deepened by the medium to which they turned to broadcast their private hopes. One of the most illustrative cases in point is the stunning impact of technological advances on the rise of religious television.

Robert Wuthnow has observed just this paradoxical relationship between the apparent vitality of evangelical religion and the medium "linked to some of the most thoroughly secularized forces currently operating" (Wuthnow 1989:115). Wuthnow's study of the media and privatization does not question the validity of the televangelists' mission but rather interrogates the ways in which the rise of religious television influences and signals a retreat from and an advance into public life.

The relationship is not easy to discern. On the one hand, religious television brought private hopes and concerns into the public realm in ways previously unimagined. The relationship between religious programming and the individual viewer went far beyond anything Nielsen ratings could measure. Religious television helped sell Robert Schuller's books and Pat Robertson's presidential candidacy. It also brought us Jimmy Swaggart's public confession of sin and Jerry Falwell's intense mix of religion and politics via the Moral Majority. Television audiences gave freely of their money in support of the evangelists' messages. Those likely to feel dispossessed and marginalized by their strong convictions that the Bible is the actual word of God or that America is in perilous moral decline were now connected (at least symbolically) with millions of others who shared their viewpoints. They, too, had vocal, charismatic leaders willing to translate their religious views into political demands. "For example, arguments about abortion, homosexuality, and personal morality have taken issues out of the bedroom and placed them on the national agenda. The televangelists have argued that such matters really cannot be left purely to individual discretion; instead, morality bears on the collective strength of a nation and thus must become an item of political policy and legislation" (ibid., 134).

On the other hand, the ways in which these private issues became public may have shadowed a deeper privatization that was consonant with "listening to a single authoritative voice, as opposed to engaging in open dialogue with fellow believers who may represent a wide variety of views and experiences" (ibid., 136). Wuthnow notes that the rise of religious television did not, for the most part, inhibit local church growth but it did, perhaps inevitably, drive a deeper wedge between the "religiously dispossessed" and the "liberal churches . . . universities, and high-tech institutions of the secular society" (ibid., 141). Those who already watched a lot of television now watched both more religious and more conventional television—an activity more likely than not to privatize experience, religious or otherwise. Among those who watched the televangelists, their dissatisfaction with the moral climate of American public life deepened. Although this dissatisfaction could have been channeled, for instance, into the political campaign of one prominent televangelist or into public discussion within one's local church about a recent "700 Club" presentation on abortion, or even into the act of turning off the television to pray, more often than not "the religious television programmers do not encourage most of these spontaneous actions. . . . Their work succeeds best when they can program millions of viewers to watch at the same time every week, to sit passively and listen (even, one sometimes wonders, to listen at more of a subliminal level than to listen critically), and to send in one's check dutifully for the amount prescribed. On this criterion, then, the role of religious television is not so much to privatize faith as to render it passive" (ibid., 127–28).

The conclusions are thus mixed. The example of televised religion illustrates both the reinforcement of the role religion plays in the public sphere and, perhaps, its decline. In characteristic, if not confusing, fashion, we became more "connected" with the "public" world beyond our front doors, and we did not have to step through those doors to do it.

Religion and Rationality

But simply being interested in the world beyond one's front door is not the same as engaging in public activity in Habermas's sense of the word: there are several other requirements that have to be met. Rationality is, as I have already suggested, traditionally seen as one of the hallmarks of public discourse. Theologian David Tracy writes that "a public realm is that shared rational space where all participants, whatever their other particular differences, can meet to discuss any claim that is rationally redeemable." Indeed, Tracy asserts that "a public realm, by definition, is dependent on a shared concept of reason" (Tracy 1988).

That religious discourse is, allegedly, not rational is one of the traditional rationales for concluding that religion cannot play much of a role in the public sphere. A. James Reichley, for instance, has argued that one of the reasons religious groups should think twice about entering into public debate is that they so often lack the sort of competence—a competence that seems to me to be almost precisely the same as a mastery of technical rationality—that is a prerequisite for speaking authoritatively on matters of the public good (Reichley 1985:354–55). An encounter between a political scientist named Kenneth Wald and a delegate to the 1980 Republican National Convention illustrates another facet of the widespread belief that religion's entry into public discourse tends to be perniciously irrational. Wald was wearing a pro-ERA button on his lapel and it caught the delegate's eye. She stopped, pointed to it, and asked him to justify his support for a measure that would "undoubtedly lead to incest." Wald, taken aback, asked how the ERA could possibly lead to such a result. The delegate did not answer. Instead she looked Wald in the eye, scowled, and asked if he was a Christian. When Wald said that he was not, the delegate proclaimed that that meant there was no point in carrying the discussion any further. She then "pointedly turned her back on [Wald] and strode away angrily—as if escaping a leper" (Wald 1987:269).

Such stories certainly give one pause. But the proposition that all public discourse must be rational is not nearly so evident now as it was three decades ago: indeed, no other aspect of Habermas's seminal work on the public sphere now seems so suspect as his treatment of rationality. Joan Landes's *Women and the Public Sphere in the Age of the French Revolution*, published in 1988, makes it clear that the "prediction of the category of the public sphere on a disinterested, universalizing principle of rational discussion can hardly be regarded as unproblematic" (Landes 1988:44). John Keane spends a good deal of time in *Public Life and Late Capitalism* trying to show how Habermas's understanding of the norms of public discourse is too restricted; the definition of public life that Keane uses carefully avoids ruling out nonrational conversation (Keane 1984:2–3).

Keane and Landes are, of course, part of a much broader movement that directly bears on the present topic, but whose causes and consequences are still only dimly understood (Bruns 1988; Schweder 1984). It does, however, seem clear to me that Habermas's understanding of rationality is far more supple than his critics sometimes imply. His work is, to a much greater extent than most scholars realize, a criticism of certain forms of rationality as well as a celebration of others. It seems clear, too, that the critics of reason have not by any means succeeded in showing that there have been no times and no places where an appeal to reason was not genuinely liberating. Furthermore, Habermas's response to such critics of reason as Foucault and Derrida—as elaborated, for instance, in *The Philosophical Discourse of Modernity*—possesses considerable force.

Yet it does seem apparent now, in a way that it was not when *The Structural Transformation of the Public Sphere* was written, that rationality, as a governing principle of public discourse, is somewhat parochial. It now seems obvious that rationality is by no means unrelated to social power. It is all too clear that telling the dispossessed that they have to speak rationally can be a way of keeping them quiet. Moreover, there are—and this is a point that writers such as Tracy sometimes seem to forget—aspects of our common life that cannot be fully explored rationally. Telling people that they have to be rational to enter into public debate marginalizes all those people for whom life is finally about something—such as art, or serving God and enjoying him forever—other than rational discourse.

Given all this, one of the traditional arguments against religion playing any role whatsoever in the public sphere—that it is insufficiently rational—now seems to have lost much of its force. The manner in which religious language and religious symbols can enrich our public debate is now open for exploration in a way that it had not been before. An encounter between Daniel Berrigan and the judge before whom he was tried for burning the local draft-board files in Catonsville, Maryland, illustrates the sort of language that is not, when judged by conventional standards, fully rational, but that is nevertheless a potential contribution to public discourse. Berrigan's attorney asked him to tell the court what his intent was in burning the files. Berrigan said, "I did not want the children or the grandchildren of the jury or of the judge to be burned with napalm." The judge asked for clarification: "You say your intention was to save these children, of the jury, of myself, when you burned the records? That is what I heard you say. I ask, if you meant that." Berrigan did not back off. "I meant that. Of course I mean that or I would not say it. The great sinfulness of [the] modern way is that it renders concrete things abstract. I do not want to talk about Americans in general.'' The judge did not find the clarification helpful. ''You cannot,'' he said, ''think up arguments now that you would have liked to have had in your mind then.'' At another point in the trial, after Berrigan had complained that the moral passion of the defendants was being banished from the courtroom, the judge commented on Berrigan's demeanor. ''Father Berrigan, you have made your points on the stand, very persuasively. I admire you as a poet. But I think you simply do not understand the function of a court.'' ''I am sure,'' Berrigan said, at once agreeing and disagreeing, ''that is true'' (Fenn 1982:187).

Religion and the Common Good

Yet there are, as will become increasingly clear, a number of considerations that undercut the relatively optimistic assessment of religion's potential contributions to American public life that I have advanced thus far. For instance: religious groups in the United States have, for at least three reasons, a great deal of difficulty presenting themselves as speaking on behalf of the common good.

The first reason is that religious groups in America seem forced to choose (or at the very least, believe themselves to be forced to choose) between adopting the techniques of secular special-interest groups or else having no influence whatsoever on American public life. When the leaders of the new religious right came into public prominence they did so as the representatives of a movement that had been mobilized in a manner obviously similar to that in which secular groups were organized, financed, and publicized. The Moral Majority was widely, and no doubt correctly, perceived as just another player—albeit a fairly important player—in the game of special-interest politics. And the Moral Majority was by no means the only religious group to join in the game. A great number of the religious special-interest groups to which I have referred are directly involved in it (Wuthnow 1988). As they play that game they tend to behave in ways that make it natural to compare them, as one writer has, with the Pipefitters Union and with the National Association of Realtors (Reichley 1985:356).

The second reason grows out of a matter I have touched on previously: the strong links between religion and the private sphere. It seems clear that privatized religious groups are, because of the ongoing penetration of life-world by system, increasingly jettisoning their reluctance to enter the public fray; it is also true that whenever religious groups in the contemporary United States do try to speak authoritatively about public matters, they cause controversy. That is because such claims strike large segments of the American population as a violation of a long-standing, informal religious settlement. According to that settlement, religion's primary contribution to public life is the fostering of private virtue. Whenever it tries to do more than that it will be perceived by many thoughtful Americans as overstepping its proper bounds. In order to speak about the common good, religious organizations have to find ways of proving they have a right to do so. Such attempts are almost always divisive.

The third difficulty has to do with the heterogeneity of religion in America. Whenever religious language surfaces in the public sphere, few Americans can completely ignore the obvious question: from which religious tradition or traditions should such language be drawn? Given the degree to which religion is a centrifugal force in American life, it is nearly—or perhaps completely— impossible to find a religious tradition whose language can be unproblemati- cally appropriated. The appropriations tend to produce language that is either ineffectually vague and abstract or else offensively specific. Consider for in- stance the assertion of Robin Lovin:

> If those who are concerned about this relationship between religion and American public life speak primarily in Christian and, indeed, Puritan, Protestant symbols, that is largely due to historical accident. What is important is that there be some set of meanings that are shared, that provide a language of commitment which can be widely understood to values which are larger than personal purposes. For all the important differences between them, the Moral Majority and the sociologists of civil religion have in common the conviction that a culture survives and functions only on the basis of a specific set of meanings that everyone can share. Religion, which has a widely acknowledged capacity to invest those meanings with reality and inter- subjective power, has the public role of contributing to social order by supporting the framework of shared meanings. (Lovin 1986:12)

Lovin's formulation is a thoughtful one, but it is still bound to strike many of his fellow citizens as unacceptable. Interestingly enough, it is unacceptable because it is both so deracinated that it is not likely to have much power *and* because it seems to point, in spite of the author's intentions, toward a privileg- ing of Christianity. I do not mean to say that this language problem—which is, of course, a great deal more than a language problem—is absolutely un- solvable: surely many sophisticated attempts have been made to get around it. There is a vast literature on the religious conflicts that give rise to this language problem. But neither would I be willing to say that any of those attempts is finally successful.[11]

Religion, the Nation-State, and Capitalism

In recent years a number of religious organizations in the United States have tried to perform a role that Habermas ascribes to the public sphere of the eigh- teenth and nineteenth centuries: checking the claims of an increasingly pow- erful state. In part because of the strong tradition of church-state separation in

[11] See, for instance, Bellah (1988, 1989); Bellah and Greenspahn (1987); Hadden (1969); Handy (1971); Hoge (1976); Menendez (1985); Morgan (1980); and Wuthnow (1988).

the United States and in part because the expansion of the state posed (as noted in Wuthnow 1988) some genuine threats to their traditional prerogatives, when religious organizations in America mobilized for political purposes in the 1960s, 1970s, and 1980s, they tended to do so in ways that were oppositional to the American state. In those decades a fair proportion of the American religious organizations sometimes spoke as if they believed that, if they did not define their social roles as systematically challenging the American state's claims, then they would, in the future, have no social roles whatsoever (cf. Eagleton 1984:124).

The sort of apocalyptic rhetoric one associates with such a belief was very often present, for instance, in the pronouncements of religious groups, on the left of the American political spectrum, that protested the United States' involvement in the Vietnam War or its policies concerning nuclear weapons. It was present, too, in many of the public statements of the new religious right. Those statements typically began with an assertion that the American state had fallen into the hands of secular humanists who were using its power and prestige to undermine the religious beliefs and moral standards of the American people; therefore, if the secular humanists were not overthrown with great dispatch, America would soon witness the demise of all religious liberty and all sound morality (Watt 1990). Apocalyptic language was also adopted by religious groups on both the left and the right in discussing questions—such as in what ways, if any, affirmative-action guidelines should apply to religious organizations or the policies of the Internal Revenue Service—that were, from the point of view of the state, simple matters of administration (Kelly 1982).

From time to time in recent years, religious organizations have also taken up explicitly adversarial stances toward American capitalism. The United States' Catholic bishops, some of the intellectual and ecclesiastical leaders of mainline Protestantism, and even a few evangelical Christians have said, with varying degrees of stridency, that there are tensions between capitalism as it is expressed in the contemporary United States and the social implications of the Christian faith (Fowler 1982; Gannon 1987; Grelle and Krieger 1986). Those sorts of explicit criticism of capitalism, and a number of signs that even those religious bodies that do not advance them nevertheless embody some values and practices with few affinities for modern capitalism, have attracted a great deal of attention in recent years. Neoconservatives such as Michael Novak have complained about the tendency of religious groups to "denigrate capitalism" (Novak 1979). And leftists, even those as doctrinaire as the ones associated with the *Monthly Review*, have started to explore the possibility that Christian groups in America can provide resources in their battles to radically restructure the American economic system (Tabb 1986).

But most of the attention to the tensions between capitalism and religion in contemporary America takes another, less dramatic form—a form outlined in the passage from Berger that I quoted earlier and nicely exemplified in

A. James Reichley's *Religion in American Public Life*. Reichley does not see these tensions creating any real possibilities for religious organizations to undermine the American economic system. Rather, he believes that religious organizations are going to continue to embody values and practices that cannot be fully expressed in the marketplace, and thus help "humanize" capitalism. This is, Reichley says, one of the two most important contributions religion can make to the public good (Reichley 1985:359). Ben Primer has shown, for instance, that a number of the religious organizations in America modeled themselves after business enterprises.

The ability of religious groups in America to make even that relatively modest contribution to public life is easy to overestimate. When one looks through the recent literature on religion in America what seems most striking is not the degree to which religious organizations in contemporary America counterbalance capitalism, but rather the degree to which they have been molded by capitalist values and practices. Neil Postman and many others have noted the degree to which the means religious organizations use to spread their views are commercial in nature. Tomaskovic-Devey and many others have discussed how often the political pronouncements and political actions of American religious organizations support the free-enterprise system. As recent works by Wayne Elzey and Charles Lippy suggest, at the popular level, religion in America consists (to a much greater degree than standard treatments of American religion suggest) of a celebration of the joys and comforts to be found in capitalism. So although it is quite true that the various religious groups in America are all based, to a greater or lesser extent, on traditions that predate the rise of modern capitalism and that are therefore potentially in tension with the sort of society capitalism produces (cf. Williams 1980), it is also true that religious groups in America have been accommodating their traditions to capitalism for quite some time (Lundén 1988). Indeed, it could be said that the willingness of various religious groups to enter into a sort of Erastian settlement with American capitalism is one of the keys to its apparent vitality.

The limits on the ability of American religious organizations to foster debate that is not distorted by the power of the state are no less real. This is in part because (as the vast literature on American civil religion makes clear) religious organizations in America are as deeply influenced by values and practices that are rooted in the nation-state as they are by values and practices rooted in modern capitalism (Bellah 1985; Gehrig 1981). Then, too, no one in America seriously questions that in the final analysis it is the state and not the religious organization that decides the rules under which conflicts between religious organizations and the state interact. If religious groups differ with the state, the differences are going to be settled in a courtroom abundant with symbols of the state's authority, and with the claims of religious people explicitly undercut (Fenn 1982).

Moreover, when religious groups take oppositional stances toward the United States government they often engage the state in ways that presuppose the values and practices of the nation-state and that result in those organizations taking up those assumptions themselves. One plausible way of interpreting the significance of the politicization of conservative religious groups in the 1970s and 1980s was as an instance of this pheneomenon. The emergence of the new religious right was, one can argue, an example of the increasing "statification" of certain religious traditions in the United States. The difficulties that leftists within American religious organizations have had in maintaining an essentially religious outlook have been commented on so frequently that they have become clichés. But the difficulties are nevertheless quite real. If one is convinced that a clearheaded reading of the truths contained in the Scriptures show that the present policies of the United States government concerning nuclear war are absolutely repugnant, and then devotes one's life to trying to change those policies, will it not become increasingly difficult to find much time to read the Bible? (Cf. Norman 1979.) Or, to return to the case of the new religious right, if the state makes it illegal in certain selected times and places to pray, and one puts a great deal of effort into political activity aimed at overturning that policy, will not one tend to spend less time praying?

Any clearheaded response to the question of what religious organizations in the United States can do to foster communication that is not distorted by the power of either the state or the marketplace must be fairly pessimistic. One would no doubt want to avoid saying that religious organizations contribute nothing whatsoever to such communication. But one would also have to say that its potential contributions can easily be exaggerated and that they are likely overwhelmed by religious organizations' contributions to the forces that make such communication so difficult in the contemporary United States.

THE THIRD SECTOR

There are several definitions of the "third sector." One can, for example, say that the third sector is made up of all the voluntary associations in a given society—that it is, in other words, made up of all those organizations in which membership is neither mandatory nor acquired by birth, which are not part of the state, and which are not primarily concerned with making a financial profit (cf. Sills 1968). Alternatively, one can say that the third sector is that portion of the economy that includes all 501(c)(3) and 501(c)(4) tax-exempt organizations as defined by the Internal Revenue Service; all religious institutions, such as churches and synagogues; all social-responsibility programs of corporations; and all persons who give time or money to some charitable purpose. This second definition, which relies in large part on an arm of the state to define a sector that is often said to be independent of both the state and the marketplace, is, in several respects, inferior to the first one. It has, however,

the great advantage of corresponding precisely to the definition that governed
the best statistical survey of the size and scope of the third sector in the United
States: *Dimensions of the Independent Sector* by Virginia Ann Hodgkinson
and Murray S. Weitzman.

One of the points that emerges most clearly in that book is the extraordinary
heterogeneity of the American third sector. From the Bulgarian Eastern Orthodox Church to the United Methodists, the third sector represented, in 1984,
well over 338,000 churches in the United States (Hodgkinson and Weitzman
1986:19). However significant they are, religious organizations account for
only a portion of the extraordinary range of third-sector interests (Rudney
1987:55). The 501(c)(3) umbrella provided by the Internal Revenue Service
finds the Friends United Meeting and the Buddhist Churches of America
alongside such organizations as the National Rifle Association, the ASPCA,
and the Marin Community Foundation, which alone is responsible for the distribution of one private philanthropic trust worth in excess of $430 million.[12]
In 1984, females represented over 66 percent of third-sector employees (as
opposed to 45 percent in the total labor force); one out of every ten working
women was employed in the third sector. Blacks made up 14 percent of all
employees in this sector, compared with 9.5 percent for all employees (Hodgkinson and Weitzman 1986:5). According to 1985 figures, Americans volunteered for religious organizations (48 percent), education (27 percent), recreation (21 percent), health (19 percent), social-service and welfare
organizations (15 percent), political organizations (8 percent), and the arts and
culture industries (8 percent), and almost 40 percent said they contributed time
"informally, alone" to some organization or activity.[13] Whether it be in the

[12] Though all these organizations can be classed within what Powell calls the 501(c)(3) "char-
itables" circle, there is a further partitioning—some suggest that it is the creation of a "class"
system—between 501(c)(3) organizations subject to section 509 of the IRS code and those that
are not. The former group was supposed to represent those organizations, like the Marin Community Foundation and other large grant-making entities, where activities like fiscal abuse, political activism, and problems associated with "unaccountable wealth" were thought more likely.
The latter group, the "publicly supported" charitable organizations such as schools, churches,
and hospitals, was thought to represent activities in support of the broader "public good," and
was thus subject to different state regulations. One of the results of these complicated distinctions
is that those organizations deemed "public-service" organizations provide tax deductions for
individual and corporate contributions. Gifts to fraternal organizations, veterans' groups, and the
like fall, for the most part, under less-generous tax-deduction regulations. Regardless of the classification of the vast number of 501(c)(3) organizations as "voluntary" or "independent," federal, state, and local regulations regarding the tax treatment of the nonprofit sector establish a
strong, ongoing link between the "state" interests and the activity of the "independent" segment
of the economy (see Powell 1987:68–72).

[13] Ideologically speaking, as the choice of examples suggests, the voluntary associations that
constitute the third sector present a striking, if not often contradictory, range of political and social
interests. There often appears to be some link between the race, ethnicity, and socioeconomic
status of those who work for or volunteer for an organization and those who fund the organization.

over 52,000 human-service agencies, almost 14,000 hospitals and health-care facilities, 35,000 civic, social, and fraternal organizations, or close to 340,000 religious organizations, Americans continue to express a well-documented proclivity for forming associations (ibid., 128).

In 1984 Hodgkinson and Weitzman reported that third-sector organizations purchased about $209 billion worth of goods and services. In 1984, for example, the third sector accounted for only about 9 percent of the nation's total employment and for about 7 percent of the wages and salaries Americans received. Moreover, there are some indications that the third sector's share of the national economy, which had been expanding in the late 1970s and early 1980s, has now begun to shrink.

In 1975, the third sector accounted for 5.2 percent of the overall GNP, representing a 50 percent increase since 1960 (Rudney 1987:56).[14] Between 1977 and 1982, the sector's share of the national income grew faster than that of business (a 62 percent increase) or government (a 65 percent increase) but this trend reversed between 1982 and 1984, with the business sector posting the highest growth rates. From 1982 to 1984 the third sector's share of the national income dropped from 5.8 percent to 5.6 percent (Hodgkinson and Weitzman 1986:9). Indications of a slowdown in third-sector growth are evident in employment trends as well. From 1977 to 1982, the third sector saw close to a 20 percent increase in the overall number of employees, but this trend seemed to slow rapidly beginning in 1982. Employment increased only 1.5 percent from 1982 to 1983 and then seemed to come to a halt in 1984. When compared with the 6.1 percent increase in employment in the private, for-profit sector from 1983 to 1984, employment in the third sector looked to be on the decline. And though average wages and salaries are typically lower in the third sector than those in other segments of the economy, from 1977 to 1984 average wages and salaries in the third sector continued to drop in relation to all other sectors (ibid., 37). Moreover, the 86 percent growth in total funding for the third sector from 1977 to 1982 saw a sharp slowdown to 10 percent growth from 1982 to 1983 and 8 percent from 1983 to 1984. Per capita expenditures of private, nonprofit organizations have virtually stalled since 1981 (ibid., 21), and operating expenditures in the third sector have slowed significantly

---

This range of interests can be viewed by considering the differing sources of support for subsectors of the independent sector. For example, whereas religious organizations rely almost completely on "private contributions" for financial support, health services and education and research subsectors are dependent on private-sector and government payments for their survival (Hodgkinson and Weitzman 1986). And though arts and cultural organizations, like religious institutions, rely mainly on private contributions for the promotion of their activities, this "private support" also includes such activities as, say, Exxon's sponsorship of a traveling art exhibition. In some cases "private" means large, multinational corporations and in other cases it means "individuals" of varying economic status (ibid., 49).

[14] This 5.2 percent increase includes the assigned value for volunteer time and unpaid family workers (Hodgkinson and Weitzman 1986:9).

from 3.2 percent per year in 1976 to 1.6 percent per year in 1980—more evidence of the general slowdown in overall economic growth of the third sector.

Nevertheless, the question John Boli asks in his chapter on Sweden about whether or not that country even has a third sector could not really be asked about the United States: the United States does have a third sector, and it is still fairly large. Although precise comparisons are impossible, for reasons I will later suggest, United States third-sector spending is impressive when compared with Sweden, for example, where gross spending by nonprofit organizations totals barely 1.6 percent of GNP (James 1987:399). In 1974, Quebec nationalized and incorporated the greater portion of the voluntary sector, and in West Germany about half the social services are funded by the state but are administered by voluntary agencies. In contrast, gross spending by nonprofits in the Netherlands reached almost 15 percent of total GNP in 1982, with 61 percent of the nonprofit expenditures in Sweden going toward education (the comparable figure for the United States nonprofit sector's education expenditure is 21 percent). In the Netherlands over 90 percent of all health, education, and social-welfare services are provided by nongovernmental, nonprofit organizations, which Ralph Kramer, a careful student of the relationship between voluntary associations and the state, calls PIs (for *particulier initiatief*). Most of these PIs were organized under religious auspices (Kramer 1981:19). Though the Dutch system has been noted for its degree of independence from governmental control and influence, responsibility for funding the PIs rests primarily with the Dutch ministerial government. Thus it seems apparent that the size and scope of the United States third sector stands somewhere between that of Sweden and that of the Netherlands.

But, as Estelle James points out in her cross-national comparisons of the nonprofit sector, deciding just what is and what is not "third sector" is quite difficult. Although such diverse countries as Sweden, the Netherlands, Israel, Italy, France, England, Japan, and India appear to enjoy similar nonprofit activities such as education and the promotion of religious activities, there is great variation in the size of the nonprofit sector in these countries. To be sure, the major founders of nonprofit organizations in all countries are organized religious groups (James 1987:397), but this variation in size and function of the third sector is difficult to trace, in part because of complex factors of welfare-state expansion evident in these countries. The difficulty in precisely determining the boundaries of third-sector activity arises in relation to the sociopolitical context of voluntary associations and to the source and amount of funding contributed to nonprofit activities by the government in each of these countries. The Netherlands offers a prime example: the PIs, organized as independent entities along religious lines, provide almost all social services to the Dutch people, but this is done within a complex web of social and health insurance funded primarily by the government. The context of voluntary associations, then, is an interweaving of private initiative and state funding. In contrast to the Netherlands, citizen participation and voluntarism in the United States—in the form of "civic culture" or "social services"—is fueled by a kind of self-help ethos and a distrust of government. In Israel, unlike both the United States and the Netherlands, there appears to be little citizen participation outside the political parties and unions. Within Israel's highly centralized bureaucracies, voluntary agency activity can often be indistinguishable from government support and administration of social services (Kramer 1981:91). What makes all cross-national comparisons problematic, though, is that information on "public subsidy" versus "government expenditure," voluntary contributions, tax returns, and "household" versus "nonprofit" expenditures is not kept by many countries (James 1987:399). As noted above, definitions of the United States third sector, which is said to be independent of both the state and the marketplace, are constructed by an arm of the state. So, for example, in comparison to the United States, just what kind of conclusions can be drawn from trends in Italy such as the payment of volunteers or increased public funding of private agencies? Do these represent the growth or the erosion of a third sector (as "independent" or "purely voluntary") in Italy? One fact seems clear: the extraordinary growth of the third sector in the United States has not disabled the development of the welfare state (Kramer 1981:6).

The most important point for our purposes is that in the United States, the third sector performs some of the functions that, in other societies, are performed by the state. In the United States, funding is often provided to private, nonprofit welfare agencies for service delivery.[15] What some call the New Federalism of the 1970s is an astute response from a state that understands a crucial dilemma: how to respond to an ever-increasing need and desire for social services without raising taxes or increasing government spending in a population that seems basically to distrust the big government implied by the welfare state. One answer, characteristic of the 1970s and 1980s, was to enforce a separation between financing and administration of many voluntary agencies (Kramer 1981:73).

In *Democracy in America*, Tocqueville asserted that "nothing . . . is more deserving of our attention than the intellectual and moral associations of America" ([1835] 1963:110).

> Americans of all ages, all conditions, and all dispositions constantly form associations. They have not only commercial and manufacturing companies, in which all take part, but associations of a thousand other kinds, religious, moral, serious, futile, general or restricted, enormous or diminutive. The Americans make associations to

---

[15] One of the dominant trends in third-sector activity parallels that wider economic trend toward a service-producing economy. Between 1972 and 1982, private service-sector employment experienced the fastest overall growth in both for-profit and nonprofit segments of the economy (Rudney 1987:56). This is, perhaps, reflective of the increasing burden of social-service delivery being shifted from the state to the third sector.

give entertainments, to found seminaries, to build inns, to construct churches, to diffuse books, to send missionaries to the antipodes; in this manner they found hospitals, prisons, and schools. . . . Wherever at the head of some new undertaking you see the government in France, or a man of rank in England, in the United States you will be sure to find an association. (Ibid., 106)

In the years since the publication of Tocqueville's views, the importance of voluntary associations has become an American commonplace. Standard reference works on the social sciences traditionally note that studying voluntary associations carries one to the heart of some of the most important questions with which the social sciences are concerned (Sills 1968). Ethicists, most notably James Luther Adams, have argued for decades that voluntary associations play a crucial role in the creation of just societies. For over half a century, ever since Arthur M. Schlesinger, Sr., published his "Biography of a Nation of Joiners," students of American history have emphasized the place of voluntary associations in the sweep of American history.

Although John D. Rockefeller III's assertion, in the late 1970s, that throughout most of America's history "virtually every significant step forward in social progress sprang originally from the third sector" amusingly outran the evidence unearthed by professional historians, it does suggest an important point: in America interest in the third sector seems to have increased—and increased quite markedly—in the past two decades (O'Connell 1983:358; cf. Bremner 1988). In the 1970s and 1980s the third sector seems to have received more attention from scholars, from journalists, and from policy analysts than it ever had before. It also attracted what was perhaps an unprecedented amount of governmental interest: Congress held numerous hearings on the subject; the United States Treasury published a multivolume collection of papers on the third sector; President Bush's speeches referred to the third sector in remarkably glowing terms.

Much of the interest in the third sector comes, as my mention of Bush and Rockefeller suggests, from the right wing of the American political spectrum: the argument advanced by conservatives that voluntary associations should be assigned a larger and government a smaller share of the task of providing social services was at the center of much of the recent debate on voluntary associations (see, for instance, Cornuelle 1965). It would, however, be a serious mistake to think that only conservatives care about such associations. American liberals argue with some force that voluntary associations are an exemplary means of overcoming what they see as the excessive individualism of the American people (Bellah et al. 1985). Some American leftists, convinced that American society as a whole is in need of drastic change, but doubtful that such reforms are a present possibility, have began to focus their efforts of building strong voluntary associations that will, they hope, both embody their ideals and serve as launching pads for subsequent efforts at more general reform (Evans and Boyte 1986).

In *Beyond Preference* (1984), Franklin I. Gamwell, the dean of the divinity school at the University of Chicago, directed his readers' attention to voluntary associations' potential contributions to American society in a manner that bears directly on the themes explored in this book. Gamwell suggested that "independent associations"—a phrase he used to refer to a carefully delineated group of voluntary associations—in fact constitute the first and not the third sector of American society. That is so, he said, because in a specific but nevertheless significant sense, they constitute "the most important class of associations in our public life" (1984:12).

I cite Gamwell because I want to draw attention to the fact that Americans from nearly every band of the political spectrum often describe the functions voluntary associations perform in ways reminiscent of the way scholars such as Habermas describe the functions a public sphere is supposed to perform. To be sure, the question of what these groups do and do not contribute to making public discourse rational seldom surfaces in Americans' discussions of voluntary associations. But each of the other four clauses in the definition of the public sphere that I gave at the beginning of this essay is paralleled in Americans' discussions of voluntary associations.

Gamwell's work implies, for instance, that in order for an organization to be an "independent association" in the fullest sense of that word it must be "community regarding." Expressions of similar sentiments can be found in Dewey and embedded in the very names—Common Cause, United Way, Community Chest—that Americans have given some of their more prominent voluntary organizations. Voluntary associations are, moreover, sometimes seen as a crucial vehicle for Americans' expressions of concern and compassion for those beyond the circle of their private lives. They are seen, to put it somewhat crudely, as organizations that combat the excessive privatization of American culture. Thus it is only natural that the authors of the much-discussed *Habits of the Heart* cover voluntary associations in a chapter entitled "Reaching Out."

Americans' conversations about voluntary associations often emphasize the importance of these organizations embodying values and practices other than those that originate in either the state or the marketplace. This emphasis is present, for instance, in the American habit of referring to the third sector as "independent." The term "independent sector" appears quite frequently in both political polemics and scholarly works—more frequently perhaps than does the phrase "third sector." Revealingly enough, the organization that has probably done the most to encourage debate about the role nonprofits should play in American life calls itself Independent Sector. The term is clearly illustrative of a widespread sentiment that in the final analysis the third sector's value and importance rests on its independence from both business and government.

Although scholars such as Harry Boyte, Sara Evans, and Franklin Gamwell have made a strong case for seeing some voluntary associations in America as independent, the claim of independence for the sector *as a whole* is—as an important article by Peter Dobkin Hall convincingly argues—simply untenable. It is certainly hard to argue that the third sector is independent of the business sector. Historically, the development of nonprofit organizations and that of business corporations are intertwined. Capitalist enterprises still provide, either directly or indirectly, much of the third sector's income. Recent studies show that nonprofits often behave in ways that conform closely to models first worked out to explain how business corporations work. There is, moreover, a growing sentiment within the third sector that voluntary associations should wholeheartedly embrace entrepreneurial values and practices. Many of the leaders of nonprofit organizations in the United States are entirely convinced, as one publication put it, that "profit-making enterprise is a legitimate and necessary way of sustaining a nonprofit organization" (McNulty 1983).

Nor can one make a plausible case that the third sector as a whole is independent of the state. As I have already suggested, our understanding of which groups do and which do not belong to the third sector has been decisively influenced by the policies of the United States government: there is a sense, then, in which the third sector is defined for us by the state. Governmental policies, most obviously the provisions of the tax code and the way the state chooses to deliver its social services, account for a large part of the difference between the size of the third sector in the United States and in countries such as Sweden. That the American state has chosen to deliver many social services indirectly has produced, moreover, a situation in which a large proportion of the funds of many American voluntary organizations comes from the state.

"Nonprofit federalism," though not by any means a new development, has greatly expanded in the post-1960 years. Prior to 1960, most federal support was channeled to state and local governments and took the form of cash assistance programs for social services such as care for the disabled, the needy, the elderly, and orphans. But changes in the Social Security Act in 1962 and 1967 shifted the burden of actual social-service delivery from state agencies to nonprofit organizations (Abramson and Salamon 1986:58). Federal engagement of nonprofits to deliver health services, for example, was significant. In 1964, the Economic Opportunity Act provided for the establishment of community health clinics in poor neighborhoods. By 1980, almost nine hundred community health centers existed, funded by federal legislation and administered by nonprofit organizations. The continuing trend toward federal funding of the nonprofit sector is impressive. Though exact estimates are difficult to make, Abramson and Salamon's 1981 study concluded that, for example, 1980 fiscal-year federal support to the nonprofit sector reached over $40 billion, accounting for almost 35 percent of total nonprofit revenue. This was in comparison with $26.8 billion in contributions to nonprofit organizations from individuals, corporations, and foundations combined. "In other words," Abramson and Salamon tell us, "nonprofit organizations other than churches now derive a larger share of their revenues from the federal government than from all of private giving combined" (ibid., 62). 1986

Examples abound. A 1982 survey of twelve metropolitan human-services delivery sites indicated that, in every case, government funding accounts for the major source of nonprofit human-services delivery. (Along with "fees, dues, and charges" and "private giving," these three revenue sources account for 89 percent of total revenue for these cities' nonprofit human-services organizations [Hodgkinson and Weitzman 1986:140].) Indeed, in almost all areas of human services, from mental-health and social services to housing, employment training, legal services, and residential care, government funding provides the largest proportion of total nonprofit revenues (ibid., 141). In 1980 dollars, federal support accounted for 55 percent of social-service revenue, 48 percent of community and civic-development funds, 22 percent of education and research funds, 36 percent of health-care revenues, and 15 percent of all arts and culture-related nonprofit revenues (Abramson and Salamon 1986:65). It is clear that the nonprofit sector has, as Salamon puts it, "far more than a casual stake" in federal budget decisions. What is notable in these examples is that the third sector can be (however implausibly) identified as the "business" of private funding, private efforts, outside the frame of government but in support of public interests. What much of the literature suggests, however, is that the voluntary associations that constitute the third sector perform typical social-service institutions' functions, though they are not technically part of the state (Hall 1987; Salmon 1987). The existence and growth of the third sector vis-à-vis social-service delivery allows for the continuing conception of the sector as a place for voluntary, non-statish association while obscuring the reality of the modern American welfare state. "Independent" is, then, a remarkably inappropriate adjective to apply to what I am calling the third sector. That the phrase "independent sector" is used with some frequency in America tells us something about American political culture: namely, that Americans find the thought that corporate models might describe their nation's social structure with any accuracy whatsoever extremely distasteful. But the phrase tells us almost nothing about the realities of the third sector in contemporary America.

Voluntary associations' claims to speak on behalf of the common good rather than as special-interest groups must likewise be viewed with a great deal of skepticism. Such skepticism seems particularly appropriate when one reads the vast literature (which voluntary organizations have helped create) that argues that the good of the commonweal depends on a strong third sector and that government officials must, therefore, adopt tax policies that will ensure the sector's continuing vitality. But even when the claim to speak on behalf of the common good is not so obviously sophistic, it is still usually delusory. A sizable body of recent works—some scholarly, some journalistic—shows that America's most prominent voluntary associations behave in ways that are hard to interpret as growing out of a systematic and principled devotion to the common good, but are quite easily seen as rooted in the (often terribly idiosyncratic) personal concerns of the women and men who manage them and who sit on their boards (Nielsen 1985; Hall 1987).

Whether or not voluntary associations may be correctly seen as counteracting privatization depends, in part, on what one thinks privatization means. If one uses the phrase "privatization" to refer to a decision to focus most of one's energy on cultivating a strong family life or on finding psychic well-being, then one can plausibly argue that a good many of the voluntary associations in the United States do counteract privatization. But one would also have to note that it is not the case that all voluntary associations play this role. Self-help groups that promise their members psychic well-being account for an increasingly large proportion of American third-sector organizations; family-centered organizations such as the Boy Scouts and the PTA have traditionally been organizations that Americans have supported most loyally. If one is using the term "privatization" to refer to a way of looking at the world that assumes there is little one can do to produce fundamental positive changes in the nation's economic or political structures, then it seems clear that only a relatively small proportion of the voluntary associations in America actually offset privatization. More typically, they attempt to find nonpolitical ways of "helping people" or "doing good" without trying to make any significant changes whatsoever in the basic economic and governmental structures of the United States.

All in all, then, it seems clear that voluntary associations in America cannot, when considered collectively, be taken to constitute elements in a vital public sphere, in the sense that that term is used in this essay. They do less to show the benefits that accrue from such a sphere than they do to illustrate the pressures that eat away at the public sphere in advanced capitalist societies. But I do not mean to suggest that Jeremiah Schiller was altogether correct. As I read it, the literature on the third sector does not rule out the possibility that some of the hundreds of thousands of voluntary associations in the United States fulfill, at least partially, some of the important functions of the public sphere. Indeed, it seems likely that they do. As I read it, the literature suggests, moreover, that in contemporary America an association's ability to do that varies inversely with its size and with its integration into the rest of American society. The Pew Charitable Trusts are, for example, probably less likely to be a microcosm of the public sphere than are neighborhood associations in South Philadelphia. In contemporary America, I would like to suggest, voluntary associations that are closest to being a part of the public sphere are unlikely to have much power or prestige; influential associations are unlikely to embody the characteristics of a genuine public sphere. We are left then with an apparent oddity: in contemporary America, the literature on voluntary associations suggests, the public tends to be sectarian.

References

Abramson, Alan J., and Lester M. Salamon. 1986. *The Nonprofit Sector and the New Federal Budget*. Washington, D.C.: Urban Institute Press.

Adams, James Luther. 1986. *Voluntary Associations: Socio-cultural Analyses and Theological Interpretation*. Edited by J. Ronald Engel. Chicago: Exploration Press.

Adams, Willi Paul. 1984. "Republicanism." In *Encyclopedia of Political History*, edited by Jack P. Greene. 3 vols. New York: Scribner's.

Agger, Ben. 1985. "The Dialectic of Deindustrialization." In *Critical Theory and Public Life*, edited by John Forester. Cambridge, Mass.: MIT Press.

Angus, Ian, and Sut Jhally. 1989. *Cultural Politics in Contemporary America*. New York: Routledge.

Arms Control and Disarmament Agency. 1989. *World Military Expenditures and Arms Transfers, 1988*. Washington, D.C.: Government Printing Office.

Au, William A. 1985. *The Cross, the Flag, and the Bomb: American Catholics Debate War and Peace, 1960–1983*. Westport, Conn.: Greenwood Press.

Bagdikian, Ben H. 1987. *The Media Monopoly*. 2d ed. Boston: Beacon Press.

Bell, Daniel. 1976. *The Cultural Contradictions of Capitalism*. New York: Basic Books.

Bellah, Robert N. 1967. "Civil Religion in America." *Daedalus* 96 (Winter): 1–21.

———. 1988. "The Kingdom of God in America: Language of Faith, Language of Nation, Language of Empire." In *Religion and the Public Good*, edited by William L. Miller et al., pp. 41–80. Macon, Ga.: Mercer University Press.

———. 1989. "Christian Faithfulness in a Pluralist World." In *Postmodern Theology*, edited by Frederic B. Burnham, pp. 74–91. San Francisco: Harper and Row.

———, et al. 1985. *Habits of the Heart: Individualism and Commitment in American Life*. Berkeley and Los Angeles: University of California Press.

———, and Frederick E. Greenspahn, eds. 1978. *Uncivil Religion: Interreligious Hostility in America*. New York: Crossroads.

Berger, Peter. 1986. *The Capitalist Revolution*. New York: Basic Books.

Block, Fred. 1988. *Revising State Theory: Essays in Politics and Postindustrialism*. Philadelphia: Temple University Press.

Bluestone, Barry, and Bennett Harrison. 1982. *The Deindustrialization of America*. New York: Basic Books.

Bremner, Robert H. 1988. *American Philanthropy*. 2d ed. Chicago: Chicago University Press.

Brinkley, Alan. 1984. "Writing the History of Contemporary America: Dilemmas and Challenges." *Daedalus* 119:121–41.

Bruns, Gerald L. 1988. "The New Philosophy." In *Columbia Literary History of the United States*, edited by Emory Elliott et al. New York: Columbia University Press.

Burnham, Walter Dean. 1982. *The Current Crisis in American Politics*. New York: Oxford University Press.

Cherry, Conrad. 1972. "Nation, State, and Private Religion: The Emergence of an American Pattern." *Journal of Church and State* 14 (Spring): 222–33.

Chidester, David. 1988. *Patterns of Power: Religion and Politics in American Culture*. Englewood Cliffs, N.J.: Prentice-Hall.

Cochran, Thomas C. 1985. *Challenges to American Values: Society, Business, and Religion*. New York: Oxford University Press.

Cornuelle, Richard C. 1965. *Reclaiming the American Dream*. New York: Random House.

Delaat, Jacqueline. 1987. "Volunteering as Linkage in the Three Sectors." *Journal of Voluntary Action Research* 16:97–111.

Douglas, James A. 1983. *Why Charity?: The Case for a Third Sector*. Beverly Hills: Sage Publications.

Douglas, Mary, and Steven Tipton, eds. 1983. *Religion and America: Spiritual Life in a Secular Age*. Boston: Beacon Press.

Eagleton, Terry. 1984. *The Function of Criticism*. London: Verso.

Elzey, Wayne, 1988. "Popular Culture." In *Encyclopedia of the American Religious Experience*, edited by Charles H. Lippy and Peter W. Williams, 3 vols., pp. 796–821. New York: Scribner's.

Evans, Sara M., and Harry C. Boyte. 1986. *Free Spaces: The Sources of Democratic Change in America*. New York: Harper and Row.

Fenn, Richard K. 1982. *Liturgies and Trials: The Secularization of Religious Language*. New York: Pilgrim Press.

Forester, John, ed. 1985. *Critical Theory and Public Life*. Cambridge, Mass.: MIT Press.

Fowler, Robert Booth. 1982. *A New Engagement: Evangelical Political Thought, 1966–1976*. Grand Rapids: Eerdmans.

———. 1985. *Religion and Politics in America*. Metuchen, N.J.: Scarecrow.

Fox, Richard Wightman, and T. J. Jackson Lears, eds. 1983. *The Culture of Consumption*. New York: Pantheon.

Frank, Douglas W. 1986. *Less than Conquerors*. Grand Rapids: Eerdmans.

Gallup, George H. 1972. *The Gallup Poll: Public Opinion, 1935–1971*. New York: Random House.

———. 1986. *The Gallup Poll: Public Opinion, 1985*. Princeton: The Gallup Organization.

Gamwell, Franklin I. 1984. *Beyond Preference: Liberal Theories of Independent Associations*. Chicago: University of Chicago Press.

Gannon, Thomas M. 1987. *The Catholic Challenge to the American Economy*. New York: Macmillan.

Garrett, James Leo, Jr. 1976. "Does Church-State Separation Necessarily Mean the Privatization of Religion?" *Journal of Church and State* 18 (Spring): 209–16.

Gehrig, Gail. 1981. *American Civil Religion: An Assessment*. Storrs, Conn.: Society for the Scientific Study of Religion.

Ginsberg, Benjamin, and Martin Shefter. 1990. *Politics by Other Means*. New York: Basic Books.

Grelle, Bruce, and David A. Krieger, eds. 1986. *Christianity and Capitalism: Per-*

spectives on Religion, Liberalism, and the Economy. Chicago: Center for the Scientific Study of Religion.

Habermas, Jürgen. 1989a. *The Philosophical Discourse of Modernity*. Translated by Frederick Lawrence. Cambridge, Mass.: MIT Press.

———. 1989b. *The Structural Transformation of the Public Sphere*. Translated by Thomas Burger. Cambridge, Mass.: MIT Press.

Hadden, Jeffrey K. 1969. *The Gathering Storm in the Churches*. Garden City, N.Y.: Doubleday.

Hall, John A., and G. John Ikenberry. 1989. *The State*. Minneapolis: University of Minnesota Press.

Hall, Peter Dobkin. 1987. "Abandoning the Rhetoric of Independence: Reflections on the Nonprofit Sector in the Post-Liberal Era." *Journal of Voluntary Action Research* 16:11–28.

Hallin, Daniel C. 1985. "The American News Media: A Critical Theory Perspective." In *Critical Theory and Public Life*, edited by John Forester, pp. 117–36. Cambridge, Mass.: MIT Press.

Hammond, Phillip E., ed. 1985. *The Sacred in a Secular Age: Toward Revision in the Scientific Study of Religion*. Berkeley and Los Angeles: University of California Press.

Handy, Robert T. 1971. *A Christian America: Protestant Hopes and Historical Realities*. New York: Oxford University Press.

Harvey, David. 1989. *The Condition of Postmodernity*. New York: Blackwell.

Higham, John. 1974. "Hanging Together." *Journal of American History* 61:5–28.

Hodgkinson, Virginia Ann, and Murray S. Weitzman. 1986. *Dimensions of the Independent Sector: A Statistical Profile*. 2d ed. Washington, D.C.: Independent Sector.

Hoge, Dean R. 1976. *Division in the Protestant House*. Philadelphia: Westminster.

Hohendahl, Peter Uwe. 1982. *The Institution of Criticism*. Ithaca: Cornell University Press.

Hook, Sidney. 1967. *Religion in a Free Society*. Lincoln: University of Nebraska Press.

Jacquet, Constant H., ed. 1988. *Yearbook of American and Canadian Churches*. Nashville: Abingdon Press.

James, Estelle. 1987. "The Nonprofit Sector in Comparative Perspective." In *The Nonprofit Sector: A Research Handbook*, edited by Walter W. Powell, pp. 397–415. New Haven: Yale University Press.

Karl, Barry D., and Stanley N. Katz. 1982. "The American Private Philanthropic Foundation and the Public Sphere, 1890–1930." *Minerva* 19:236–70.

Keane, John. 1984. *Public Life and Late Capitalism*. Cambridge: Cambridge University Press.

Kelley, Dean M. 1979. *The Battle for the Catholic Church*. Garden City, N.Y.: Doubleday.

———, ed. 1982. *Government Intervention in Religious Affairs*. New York: Pilgrim Press.

Kerrine, Theodore M., and Richard John Neuhaus. 1979. "Mediating Structures: A Paradigm for Democratic Pluralism." *Annals of the American Academy of Political and Social Science* 446 (November): 10–18.

Kramer, Ralph M. 1981. *Voluntary Agencies in the Welfare State*. Berkeley and Los Angeles: University Of California Press.

————. 1985. "The Future of the Voluntary Agency in a Mixed Economy." *Journal of Applied Behavioral Sciences* 21:377–91.

Landes, Joan. 1988. *Women and the Public Sphere in the Age of the French Revolution*. Cambridge: Cambridge University Press.

Lasch, Christopher. 1977. *Haven in a Heartless World*. New York: Basic Books.

————. 1979. *The Culture of Narcissism*. New York: Norton.

Lasch, Scott, and John Urry. 1987. *The End of Organized Capitalism*. Madison: University of Wisconsin Press.

Leuchtenburg, William E. 1986. "The Pertinence of Political History: The Significance of the State in America." *Journal of American History* 73:585–600.

Levitt, Theodore. 1973. *The Third Sector: New Tactics for a Responsive Society*. New York: AMACOM.

Lindblom, Charles. 1977. *Politics and Markets: The World's Political-Economic Systems*. New York: Basic Books.

Lippy, Charles H., ed. 1989. *Twentieth-Century Shapers of American Popular Religion*. New York: Greenwood Press.

Lovin, Robin W. 1986. "Religion and American Public Life: Three Relationships." In *Religion and American Public Life: Interpretations and Explorations*, edited by Robin W. Lovin, pp. 12–28. New York: Paulist Press.

Lundén, Rolf. 1988. *Business and Religion in the American 1920s*. New York: Greenwood Press.

McNulty, John. 1983. Foreword to *Enterprise in the Nonprofit Sector*, by James C. Crimmins and Mary Keil. New York: Rockefeller Brothers Fund.

May, Henry F. 1949. *Protestant Churches and Industrial America*. New York: Harper and Brothers.

Melton, J. Gordon. 1979–1987. *Encyclopedia of American Religions*. 2 vols. Wilmington, N.C.: McGrath (vol. 1); Detroit: Gale Research Co. (vol. 2).

————. 1982. *Directory of Religious Bodies in the United States*. Wilmington, N.C.: McGrath.

Menendez, Albert, comp. 1985. *Religious Conflict in America: A Bibliography*. New York: Garland.

Molesworth, Charles. 1988. "Culture, Power, and Society." In *Columbia Literary History of the United States*, edited by Emory Elliott et al., pp. 415–36. New York: Columbia University Press.

Moore, R. Laurence. 1986. *Religious Outsiders and the Making of Americans*. New York: Oxford University Press.

Morgan, Richard E. 1980. *The Politics of Religious Conflict: Church and State in America*. 2d ed. Washington, D.C.: University Press of America.

Neuhaus, Richard John. 1984. *The Naked Public Square: Religion and Democracy in America*. Grand Rapids: Eerdmans.

Niebuhr, Reinhold. 1932. *Moral Man and Immoral Society*. New York: Scribner's.

Nielsen, Waldemar A. 1979. *The Endangered Sector*. New York: Columbia University Press.

————. 1985. *The Golden Donors*. New York: E. P. Dutton.

Noll, Mark A., Nathan O. Hutch, and George M. Marsden. 1983. *The Search for Christian America*. West Chester, Pa.: Crossway Books.

Norman, Edward V. 1979. *Christianity and the World Order*. Oxford: Oxford University Press.

Novak, Michael. 1979. *The Denigration of Capitalism: Six Points of View*. Washington, D.C.: American Enterprise Institute.

O'Connell, Brian. 1983. *America's Voluntary Spirit*. New York: Foundation Center.

Offe, Claus. 1985. *Disorganized Capitalism*. Cambridge, Mass.: MIT Press.

Organisation for Economic Cooperation and Development. 1989. *Economic Outlook: Historical Statistics, 1960–1987*. Paris: OECD.

Page, Ann L., and Donald A. Clelland. 1978. "The Kanawha County Textbook Controversy: A Study of the Politics of Lifestyle Concern." *Social Forces* 57:265–81.

Pemberton, Prentiss L., and Daniel Rush Finn. 1985. *Toward a Christian Economic Ethic*. New York: Winston Press.

Postman, Neil. 1985. *Amusing Ourselves to Death: Public Discourse in the Age of Show Business*. New York: Viking.

Powell, Walter W., ed. 1987. *The Nonprofit Sector: A Research Handbook*. New Haven: Yale University Press.

Primer, Ben. 1979. *Protestants and American Business Methods*. Ann Arbor, Mich.: UMI Research Press.

Pugliese, Donato. 1986. *Voluntary Associations: An Annotated Bibliography*. New York: Garland Publishing.

Reichley, A. James. 1985. *Religion in American Public Life*. Washington, D.C.: Brookings Institution.

Reynolds, Charles H., and Ralph V. Norman, eds. 1988. *Community in America*. Berkeley and Los Angeles: University of California Press.

Rogers, Daniel T. 1987. *Contested Truths*. New York: Basic Books.

Roof, Wade Clark, and William McKinney. 1987. *American Mainline Religion*. New Brunswick, N.J.: Rutgers University Press.

Ross, Dorothy. 1984. "Liberalism." In the *Encyclopedia of Political History*, edited by Jack P. Greene, 3 vols., pp. 596–601. New York: Scribner's.

Rudney, Gabriel. 1987. "The Scope and Dimensions of Nonprofit Activity." In *The Nonprofit Sector: A Research Handbook*, edited by Walter W. Powell. New Haven: Yale University Press.

Salamon, Lester M. 1987. "Partners in Public Service: The Scope and Theory of Government-Nonprofit Relations." In *The Nonprofit Sector: A Research Handbook*, edited by Walter W. Powell, pp. 99–117. New Haven: Yale University Press.

Schiller. Herbert I. 1989. *Culture, Inc.: The Corporate Takeover of Public Expression*. New York: Oxford University Press.

Schlesinger, Arthur M., Sr. 1944. "Biography of a Nation of Joiners." *American Historical Review* 50:1–25.

Schroyer, Trent. 1985. "Corruption of Freedom in America." In *Critical Theory and Public Life*, edited by John Forester, pp. 39–57. Cambridge, Mass.: MIT Press.

Schwarz, John E. 1988. *America's Hidden Success*. Rev. ed. New York: W. W. Norton.

Schweder, Richard A. 1984. "Anthropology's Romantic Rebellion against the Enlightenment, or There's More to Thinking than Reason and Evidence." In *Culture Theory*, edited by Richard A. Schweder and Robert A. Levine. Cambridge: Cambridge University Press.

Silk, Mark. 1984. "Notes on the Judeo-Christian Tradition in America." *American Quarterly* 36 (Spring): 65–85.

Sills, David L. 1968. "Voluntary Associations: Sociological Aspects." In *International Encyclopedia of the Social Sciences*, edited by David L. Sills. New York: Macmillan.

Sinha, Surajit. 1966. "Religion in an Affluent Society." *Current Anthropology* 7 (April): 189–95.

Skocpol, Theda. 1980. "Political Response to Capitalist Crisis: Neo-Marxist Theories of the State and the Case of the New Deal." *Politics and Society* 10:155–201.

Skowronek, Stephen. 1982. *Building a New American State: The Expansion of National Administrative Capacities, 1877–1920*. Cambridge: Cambridge University Press.

Smith, David Horton. 1983. "Churches Are Generally Ignored in Contemporary Voluntary Action Research: Causes and Consequences." *Review of Religious Research* 24:295–303.

Social Security Administration, 1987. *Publication 50:4*. Washington, D.C.: Government Printing Office.

Stern, Philip M. 1988. *The Best Congress Money Can Buy*. New York: Pantheon.

Stout, Jeffrey. 1988. *Ethics after Babel*. Boston: Beacon Press.

Tabb, William K. 1986. *Churches in Struggle: Liberation Theologies and Social Change in North America*. New York: Monthly Review Press.

Titmuss, Richard M. 1969. *Essays on the Welfare State*. Boston: Beacon Press.

Tocqueville, Alexis de. [1835] 1963. *Democracy in America*. 2 vols. Translated by Henry Reeve, revised by Francis Bowen, edited by Phillips Bradley. New York: Alfred A. Knopf.

Tomaskovic-Devey, Donald. 1986. "The Protestant Ethic, the Christian Right, and the Spirit of Recapitalization." In *The Political Role of Religion in the United States*. Boulder, Colo.: Westview Press.

Tracy, David. 1988. "Theology, Critical Social Theory, and the Public Realm." Manuscript, University of Chicago.

U.S. Bureau of the Census. 1975. *Historical Statistics*. Washington, D.C.: Government Printing Office.

———. 1989a. *Characteristics of Persons Receiving Benefits from Major Assistance Programs*. Washington, D.C.: Government Printing Office.

———. 1989b. *Statistical Abstract of the United States: 1989*. 109th ed. Washington, D.C.: Government Printing Office.

U.S. Department of Health and Human Services. 1988. *Fast Facts and Figures about Social Security*. Washington, D.C.: Government Printing Office.

U.S. Department of Labor. Bureau of Labor Statistics. 1988. *Current Wage Developments (June)*. Washington, D.C.: Government Printing Office.

———. Monthly. *Employment and Earnings*. Washington, D.C.: Government Printing Office.

Wald, Kenneth D. 1987. *Religion and Politics in the United States*. New York: St. Martin's Press.

Watt, David Harrington. 1986–1987. "Religion and the Nation: 1960 to the Present." In *Church and State in America: A Bibliographic Guide*, edited by John F. Wilson. 2 vols. Westport, Conn.: Greenwood Press.

———. 1991. *A Transforming Faith: Explorations in Twentieth-Century American Evangelicalism*. New Brunswick, N.J.: Rutgers University Press.

Weber, Max. 1972. "Proposal for the Sociological Study of Voluntary Associations." Translated by Everett C. Hughes. *Journal of Voluntary Action Research* 1:20–23.

Weber, Paul J., and Dennis A. Gilbert. 1981. *Private Churches and Public Money: Church-Government Fiscal Relations*. Westport, Conn.: Greenwood Press.

Weisbrod, Burton A. 1988. *The Nonprofit Economy*. Cambridge, Mass.: Harvard University Press.

Wiebe, Robert H. 1975. *The Segmented Society*. New York: Oxford University Press.

Williams, Raymond. 1980. *Problems in Materialism and Culture*. London: Verso.

Wilson, John F., ed. 1986–1987. *Church and State in America: A Bibliographic Guide*. 2 vols. Westport, Conn.: Greenwood Press.

Wuthnow, Robert. 1988. *The Restructuring of American Religion*. Princeton: Princeton University Press.

———. 1989. *The Struggle for America's Soul*. Grand Rapids: Eerdmans.

CHAPTER TEN

Tocqueville's Question Reconsidered: Voluntarism and Public Discourse in Advanced Industrial Societies

Robert Wuthnow

WERE IT ONLY a question of voluntary associations contributing to democracy, the evidence of voluntarism in advanced industrial societies would seem to provide indisputable confirmation of Tocqueville's ([1835]1945) central assertions. In all the societies we have examined, democratic government has prevailed without interruption since World War II and in most instances since at least the 1870s. During this period voluntary associations of all kinds have also flourished. Many factors have contributed to the strength of democracy in these societies, but voluntary associations have played an important part. They have served as nuclei for the formation of political parties and for reform movements within parties, brought direct and indirect pressure on political leaders and government bureaus, provided services that might otherwise have occasioned political alienation or resulted in centralized state programs, and cut across socioeconomic and cultural divisions that impeded the democratic process in other societies. How much the origin and evolution of democratic traditions in each society has depended on a healthy voluntary sector, as opposed to a variety of other conditions, is nevertheless impossible to determine in any exact sense. Certainly there is much variation both in patterns of democracy and in the strength of voluntary associations, and the precise strength of one does not seem to be connected to the precise strength of the other (Carnoy 1984). The connection between voluntarism and democracy is thus, as Tocqueville suggested, a feature of historic patterns that cannot easily be disentangled.

The larger question that has concerned social observers since Tocqueville, however, is the question of collective values (Habermas 1976, 1985). Democracy itself may be one of these values, but it is cherished chiefly as a means for the pursuit of individual and collective values. It can be, as in the American case, conceived of as a means for the protection of life, liberty, and the pursuit of happiness. It can also be conceived of as a system for the protection of class privilege, for the aggrandizement of certain political leaders, or for the pursuit of greed and narrow material ambitions. What these values are, where they come from, and how they are discussed and legitimated are questions that lead beyond democracy to considerations of the quality of collective life itself (Bellah et al. 1985).

Historically, the social institutions in which people in democratic societies, or in societies with nascent democratic institutions, came together to discuss collective values consisted chiefly of two major varieties: representative political assemblies and voluntary associations (Bendix 1977:39–65; Adams 1986:250–53). The former were well established throughout much of western Europe at the end of the Middle Ages, but became embroiled increasingly during the early modern period in struggles with the rising centralized monarchies (Poggi 1978). Not only questions of political power but also matters of class interests, regional claims, and religious doctrines dominated the deliberations of these assemblies. By the end of the seventeenth century there was thus a strong precedent for public discourse about collective values to be concentrated primarily in the various mixed patterns of government that had been worked out between the centralizing forces of the monarchs and the more decentralized tendencies embodied in legislative assemblies. Voluntary associations grew out of these governmental arrangements but also responded to their limitations.

Several trends that became increasingly apparent during the seventeenth century—economic growth, population increase, colonization, war, religious turmoil, and technological innovation—all contributed to the gradual expansion of the social situations in which public discourse about collective values could take place (Bendix 1978). As the leaders of the dominant nation-states competed with one another for economic and military advantage, administrative bureaus multiplied in size, required greater educational sophistication from their personnel, and concentrated these elites in central places, such as London, Paris, Edinburgh, and Berlin (Wuthnow 1989). During the eighteenth century these centers became the principal locations in which a vast number of voluntary associations came into being. Through a combination of official encouragement and private initiative, scientific societies were formed, salons and reading clubs emerged, and a host of more diverse associations developed, with interests as varied as agricultural improvement, poetry, freemasonry, and alchemy. While many of these groups depended on state subsidies and for this reason limited their memberships to a select minority of the educated elite, the larger share were truly voluntary, depending on free commitments of time and energy from their members to keep their collective activities alive. Some were clearly oriented toward charitable and benevolent causes as well. Drawing inspiration both from religious tradition and from the newer ideas of secular progress, they sought to help the poor, find solutions to urban problems, and challenge elites to consider issues of civic and humanitarian importance.

The nineteenth century witnessed the further broadening of these voluntary associations. Throughout Europe and North America, established religious organizations responded to the challenges of demographic and geographic expansion by forming missionary societies, associations for the distribution of Bibles and tracts, and movements aimed at educating the poor and encouraging them to practice temperance (Bremner 1983). As the franchise was gradually extended to larger segments of the population, political parties developed and made direct use of local methods of enlisting individuals in voluntary causes (Lipset 1968). Communal, utopian, socialist, and Marxist clusters emerged, also as voluntary associations (Billington 1980). And the various republican, liberal, and social-democratic movements that spread across the European continent in the final decades of the nineteenth century relied heavily on voluntary associations of all kinds—cycling clubs, reading rooms, choirs, brass bands—to cultivate loyalties among workers and members of the middle classes alike (Michels [1915] 1962).

In the twentieth century, therefore, no advanced industrial society has had to invent a voluntary sector from scratch. Traditions of free association have a long legacy on which to draw. At the same time, the challenges facing the voluntary sector in the twentieth century are largely unprecedented. Especially since World War II, the centralized activities of the nation-state have grown considerably (Boli 1980; Meyer 1980), and, although voluntary associations have from the beginning operated in close proximity to the state, recent growth has placed new demands on the voluntary sector and confronted it with different limitations (Wolch 1990). Even within a relatively short time, the economic conditions in which voluntary associations function have also changed dramatically. It is thus necessary to draw together what we have described in the foregoing chapters about these political and economic developments in order to summarize what we can now identify as the main contours of the voluntary sector in advanced industrial societies.

EXPANSION IN THE POLITICAL AND MARKET SECTORS

Standard indices for measuring the social role of government activity uniformly demonstrate the magnitude of this growth in nearly all advanced industrial societies since World War II (Alford and Friedland 1985). Despite the fact that GNP in all these societies has grown markedly, government revenues have at least kept pace with this growth as a proportion of GNP, and government expenditures have often outstripped government revenues. Government employment has made up an increasingly large share of the total labor force, with few reversals, and an increasing number of occupations in the nongovernmental sectors depend heavily on government for training, contracts, and indirect subsidies.

Although the term "welfare state" is often used to capture the essence of government activity in the contemporary period, it should be clear that the overall expansion in government budgets can be explained only in part by the growth in welfare services to the needy as such (Lindblom 1977). The more substantial areas of expansion, including ones that account for much of the welfare budget itself, are concerned with the promotion of economic affairs. These include the provision of collective services, such as highways and correctional facilities, the regulation of finance, the staffing of worldwide bureaus of diplomats and liaisons with other governments, expenditures on science and education, and various programs of insurance aimed at facilitating confidence in the business community and dampening the side effects of business practice (Bell 1973). Sizable sums are expended in most advanced industrial societies through these various programs in the form of transfer payments to the elderly and disabled and to educational institutions, and through loans and contracts from private individuals and firms to the government for the supply of goods and services. Even with recent efforts to "privatize" industries formerly operated by the state itself, and with tax limitations that have forced reductions in the size of government staffs, the overall size and scope of the government sector remains at a much higher level today than it did at midcentury.

The main point emphasized in the foregoing chapters, however, is that the critical feature of state expansion, so far as the voluntary sector is concerned, is not so much government expenditure (or ownership) but government control. As James Beckford points out in the British case, even during the recent period of privatization, centralized control by the state over activities and services previously left to the discretion of individuals or local communities has advanced considerably. Moreover, government control has not been limited to, and therefore should not be confused with, the growth of centralized state bureaucracies. The German case, for example, presents a contrast with societies such as France and England where governmental staff and functions are concentrated in central agencies, yet the German case also demonstrates the extent to which government control—exercised at regional and local levels of administration—can penetrate all aspects of civil society.

The other main effect of government expansion in the period since World War II has been a greater tendency toward the politicization of culture and society (Bell 1976). The main threat of this expansion to the voluntary sector has thus not been the absorption of previously voluntary services into monolithic agencies of the state, but a more subtle reorientation of the aims and aspirations of voluntary associations (Salamon 1987). Increasingly, the very status of these associations has been defined by legal statutes and by tax categories. The threat of lawsuits influences the kind of services likely to be provided; more importantly, voluntary associations that wish to influence public discourse assume their success depends on gaining the ear of political officials.

Although the variations in rates of economic growth among nations or from one year to the next capture the greatest interest among public officials and in the mass media, the most striking feature of economic development in advanced industrial societies since World War II is the sheer magnitude of this overall growth itself. This growth notwithstanding—and despite the efforts of the welfare state—the degree of economic inequality in advanced industrial societies has not been substantially reduced in recent decades. The need for services provided by the voluntary sector to the poor and disadvantaged has thus remained relatively unaffected by economic change and by the efforts of government officials. This is not to say, of course, that specific programs have been inconsequential or that such efforts should be abandoned. But in no advanced industrial society can it be said that the voluntary sector has been relegated to the dustbin of history simply because social needs have been eradicated (Gilbert 1983; Murray 1984).

If economic expansion has not eradicated social needs or socioeconomic disparities, it has nevertheless contributed in mixed ways to the voluntary sector's capacity to address social needs. On the one hand, average levels of personal income have risen sufficiently that small donations can be given to voluntary associations without much sense of personal sacrifice and, perhaps even more importantly, the vast concentrations of wealth that a few individuals have been able to amass make it more possible than ever before for charitable organizations to seek funding from private foundations and from individual philanthropists (Odendahl 1987a, 1987b). On the other hand, the increasing reliance of advanced industrial economies on the creation of markets for new consumer goods, combined with the rising costs of social services, leaves the typical breadwinner with little discretionary income that is likely to go either for savings or for charitable contributions (Hodgkinson 1988). Moreover, the increases in average numbers of hours worked per week and in the number of families in which both spouses work have limited the amount of time available for direct participation in voluntary activities.

THE VOLUNTARY SECTOR IN ADVANCED INDUSTRIAL SOCIETIES

What would perhaps have surprised Tocqueville most, had he been able to visit the United States a hundred and fifty years after his first visit and to compare it with other advanced industrial societies, is the extent to which voluntary associations continue to flourish in all these societies, despite the massive expansion of the state that he so much feared and warned against (Anheier and Seibel 1990; James 1987, 1989). While it is true that none of the societies we have examined can be described as having a totalitarian government of the kind Tocqueville most feared, it is certainly the case that governments in all these societies provide many more services than even Tocqueville could have imagined, and they penetrate the lives of their individual citizens in extraordinary ways. Much of the growth in government welfare, moreover, was advanced over the past century with the specific intention of replacing voluntary charities and mutual-aid societies that were deemed inadequate, patronizing, and archaic. Yet, if anything, the growth of government welfare services appears to have stimulated, rather than eroded, voluntary activity.

Several reasons can, at least in retrospect, be found to account for this continuing vitality in the voluntary sector. One is that governments in most societies have found it easier to enact legislation that guaranteed people basic rights and that acknowledged certain basic needs than to find ways of actually meeting those needs. As a result, the demand for services and the expectations about the importance of these services rose faster than governments could meet them, thus opening opportunities for voluntary associations to play an enlarged role. A related reason is that governments have often found it more efficient to channel public funds through voluntary associations than to start whole new bureaucracies for distributing welfare benefits. This infusion of public monies can be seen as a significant reason for the growth in voluntary associations, although the symbolic importance of government working together with the voluntary sector may be even more significant (Salamon 1987). Whether funds have been transferred by governments to the voluntary sector or not, public officials have often called on voluntary agencies to do more and have encouraged the citizenry to contribute time and money to the work of these agencies. Still another reason for the continuing prominence of voluntary associations is that many of these associations are not concerned with charitable or service activities at all but are oriented more toward the organization of middle- and upper-class interests and the representation of these interests in the political arena (Odendahl 1987a). Peak associations in the German case provide perhaps the clearest example of this powerful component of the voluntary sector, but professional, business, trade, and educational associations abound in all developed societies.

The most significant effects of economic development on the voluntary sector, at least among advanced industrial societies, are probably the consequences of cultural changes associated with economic growth, rather than direct effects of shifts in the composition of the labor force or in industry. For example, raw statistics on the industrial makeup of modern societies show an enormous rise in the role of services, as opposed to manufacturing and agriculture. This rise has sometimes been taken to suggest an increasing level of competition between for-profit firms and nonprofit firms offering the same kinds of services. Competition of this type has indeed been notable in some areas. But most of the growth in for-profit services has not occurred in areas formerly occupied by the nonprofit sector. The for-profit growth has instead occurred in areas such as fast-food restaurants, beauty parlors, and the servicing of automobiles and computer equipment. Similarly, the fear that women's inclusion in the labor force may create competition between job pressures and time available for volunteer activity may be exaggerated because women in a number of advanced societies still work more at part-time jobs than at full-time jobs. To the extent that part-time work draws women out of the home and into the community, it could even increase the likelihood of their participating in voluntary associations.

Even the effects of rising levels of education and professionalization on the voluntary sector seem less than straightforward. Although most studies of individual voluntarism suggest that involvement in the work of voluntary associations is more common among the better educated and among professionals than among members of the lower strata, these patterns do not necessarily imply that voluntarism will continue to increase as levels of higher education and professionalization rise. Indeed, these levels have already risen dramatically in advanced industrial societies over the past quarter century, whereas levels of voluntarism hardly seem to have grown at the same pace. The reasons for this lack of comparable growth have not been examined systematically, but several possibilities can be adduced. One is that countervailing tendencies are also at work; for example, the effects of longer working hours or a more general alienation from public life. Another is that professionals may simply exaggerate their reports of voluntary activity, either because of social desirability (wanting to appear involved) or because professional associations themselves are counted as voluntary activities. Still another is that changes within the ranks of professionals themselves—a smaller proportion in the classic helping professions and a larger proportion working as salaried members of bureaucracies—may be altering the relationship between professionalization and volunteer participation.

The cultural consequences of economic expansion are more difficult to assess, but on the whole have raised worrisome questions about the vitality of the voluntary sector. As international markets have become more fully integrated, forcing countries to compete more directly with one another, increasing emphasis has been placed on technical and instrumental values at the expense of more open consideration of a full range of human needs. Foundations and individual philanthropists are encouraged to support educational programs, for example, that will buttress the basic knowledge of the labor force or increase the mathematical skills of youngsters, rather than to give to the humanities or to support art museums and concerts. Businesses may contribute to community causes, but a bottom-line mentality pervades this philanthropy, causing it to be colored increasingly by media opportunities and by cynical calculations of return on investment.

One cultural consequence of economic development that may bode well for the voluntary sector is the degree of alienation from business and from work that appears to exist in most advanced industrial societies. Although this alienation has generally been thought to result simply in passive private leisure activities (such as watching television), studies of volunteers often indicate that wanting something more from life than meaningless work is one of the major sources of attraction to voluntary associations. The voluntary sector is often valued as well because it symbolizes a more personal or communal form of association than is often found in the competitive and hierarchical business environment.

ALTERNATIVE MODES OF CONTRIBUTING TO THE PUBLIC SPHERE

It is evident in a number of advanced industrial societies that the voluntary sector is no longer a protected zone that differs from the state and the economy, but has become a highly bureaucratized and increasingly centralized arena that cooperates fully in the activities initiated by the state and the marketplace. As pointed out most clearly by Helmut Anheier in his discussion of Germany, the result of increasing centralization in the voluntary sector is often inflexibility, immobility, and a lack of creativity. For new interests to be heard and new ideas to be expressed, therefore, it has been necessary for alternative movements to arise and engage the established public sphere in a kind of counter-discourse.

Of necessity, the most visible of these alternative movements have been the ones that engaged in political dialogue—criticizing both the state and the voluntary sector's role in supporting the state. The peace movement, the feminist movement, and various environmental movements stand as chief examples. Though organized sometimes as political parties themselves, these movements have tried to challenge the assumptions on which established political discussion is based. For example, they have questioned the meanings of taken-for-granted words, engaged in street theater and other iconoclastic activities, and parodied the rituals of established political parties. Yet to the extent that political objectives have been their primary focus, many of these movements have themselves succumbed to the imperatives of political debate.

A somewhat broader array of alternative social movements has sought to infuse new values into the public sphere without focusing primarily on the state. Self-help movements, therapy and meditation groups, quasi-religious or spiritually-oriented movements, communes, and even leisure associations oriented toward special interests constitute the bulk of these movements. Few would argue that these alternatives have been effective in fundamentally revamping the character of public discourse. But effectiveness itself is sometimes a value that these groups seek to delegitimate.

Societies with multiparty systems and with proportional representation at the district level (Italy being perhaps the clearest example) are more likely to generate alternative social movements oriented toward realizing their values through the political process, whereas societies with two-party systems and single-member district representation (such as the United States) appear more likely to develop social movements that remain more autonomous from the political sector. In the former much of the grass-roots activity involved in mobilizing support for voluntary associations is likely to be channeled into the formation of political parties, while in the latter the same efforts may result in religious movements, service organizations, and lobbying groups.

Among many of the social movements that have appeared since the 1960s among youth, or as protests against dominant social institutions, there has also been a new effort to blend questions of power with broader questions of values and personal identity. Feminist groups, for example, have recognized the extent to which gender is not only a fundamental dimension of personal identity but also a basis for political oppression and exclusion. "New Age" religious movements have sometimes argued for withdrawal from politics and yet found themselves drawn into the political arena by lawsuits brought against them. Even self-help movements concerned primarily with personal addictions have increasingly recognized the relevance of tax laws governing medical claims for mental-health treatment to their objectives, or the value of lobbying for substance-abuse laws, or the necessity of giving legal testimony as expert witnesses. The blending of political and apolitical concerns within these movements is thus further evidence of the growing importance of the state to the voluntary sector and, in turn, to the structuring of public discourse.

In all this the role of the intellectual remains worthy of special consideration. Neither the primary work of intellectuals nor their primary places of work lie squarely within the voluntary sector, yet their voices in the public sphere are subject to the same constraints as those of the voluntary sector, even if the intellectuals are sometimes heard more distinctly. In countries like France and Italy, where grass-roots participation in voluntary organizations is relatively limited, the intellectual plays a more prominent role in shaping public discourse. Shielded from norms of efficiency and profitability in much the same way nonprofit organizations are, the intellectual is able to consider a wide range of individual and collective values. The restrictions imposed by the state and the marketplace, though, are increasingly felt by these elites as well. In some societies—England, for example—government policy has led to wholesale emigration of intellectuals in the nontechnical fields, while in others, such as France and Italy, intellectuals have often been drawn into the narrow debates of political parties. The audience for their ruminations, moreover, may be severely limited compared with that of informal voluntary associations or formal organizations such as the church.

THE ROLE OF RELIGION WITHIN THE VOLUNTARY SECTOR

Among all organizations in the voluntary sector, religious organizations continue to be most explicitly concerned with debating fundamental human values. Questions of meaning, human worth, morality, and direction in life, as well as more collective values such as community, peace, equality, and justice, frequent the discussions of theologians and grass-roots religious leaders alike. In countries like Israel and the United States, religious values often become the focus of controversies about more specific political programs as well. But two developments in advanced industrial societies appear to be limiting the contribution of formal religious bodies to the public sphere.

One of these developments is the sheer erosion of religious commitment itself in advanced industrial societies. Although the United States continues to manifest high levels of religious involvement, this level of involvement is the exception rather than the rule. Among other advanced industrial societies, level of religious involvement is negatively associated with level of industrialization (Wald 1987). Numerous theories have been put forward to account for this pattern, but empirical studies, although limited, suggest that rising levels of education are the major factor, as compared with changes in other social conditions, such as urbanization and industrialization (Christiano 1987). The effects of education, in turn, can be attributed partly to the disruption of geographic and kin networks that often accompanies the pursuit of higher education, and partly to the subculture of scientific rationalism and cultural relativism that pervades many institutions of higher learning. Even in societies like the United States, where organized religion remains strong, significant declines in literal, orthodox beliefs have taken place over the past half century in conjunction with rising levels of education (Wuthnow 1988).

The other development of importance is the gradual exclusion of religious conviction from public life. According to most interpretations, the so-called privatization of modern religion has taken place over a relatively long period of time and has been accomplished both by pressures from without and by adjustments from within the religious establishment (Luckmann 1967; Martin 1978). The external pressures have come primarily from the state. In its efforts to regulate religious conflicts historically, and in its more recent attempts to provide services formerly administered by religious bodies, the state has made it increasingly difficult for religious groups to play significant roles in the public sphere. Religious leaders have in turn accommodated the state's demands by focusing more of their efforts on matters of personal spirituality. Sometimes their timidity has stemmed from direct legal requirements preventing charitable organizations from engaging in political activity. In other instances, they have simply found themselves at a competitive disadvantage relative to secular voluntary associations that were permitted to receive government support.

THE QUALITY OF PUBLIC DISCOURSE ABOUT COLLECTIVE VALUES

Although certain values such as individual freedom, economic growth, and religious tolerance pervade all advanced industrial societies, the most notable feature of public discourse about these core values remains its diversity. Different ways of expressing generalized values and different ways of putting these values into practice in individual lives and in social programs are the subject of continuing debate. These debates, moreover, are institutionalized in ways that ensure their continuing diversity. Political parties succeed by registering the diverse opinions built into the social infrastructure—its class divisions, its regional and ethnic variations, and increasingly its cleavages that are rooted in gender differences, age differences, and educational levels. Educational institutions themselves institutionalize the articulation of diverse points of view, particularly at the higher ends of the educational spectrum where creativity and innovation are the formal bases on which rewards are allocated. Religious pluralism adds to this diversity, as does the multitude of special interests represented within the voluntary sector.

The quality of public discourse in advanced industrial societies does not suffer, therefore, from a narrowing of the substantive topics that can be articulated as much as it does from the social and cultural forces that limit the manner in which these topics are expressed. Questions of efficiency, practicality, cost-effectiveness, instrumental rationality, and expedience appear to dominate much of the public discourse that focuses on collective values (Phillips 1986).

The increasing penetration of the voluntary sector by government appears to be one of the most important of these limiting forces. Although an infusion of government money has generally augmented the programs of voluntary associations in those societies where such funds have been provided, the typical result has been greater competition among voluntary associations for scarce public funds and more explicit contractual relations requiring voluntary associations to pursue narrowly defined objectives. The norms legitimating these contractual relations derive from long-standing assumptions about "public accountability." If the public's money is to be given to voluntary associations, then these associations must make the best possible use of the resources entrusted to them. All this is well and good, particularly in light of recurrent scandals about funds being misused by religious organizations and other voluntary associations less constrained by public scrutiny—and yet the cultural results are not always positive.

When accountability becomes the dominant operating norm, voluntary associations become less clearly distinguishable from government agencies and for-profit firms (Weisbrod 1988). In all three sectors specialization that focused on delimited objectives triumphs, measurable results take precedence over less well defined outcomes, and competitive pressures to gain the most tangible results with the most efficient expenditure of resources rise to preeminence. The work of a voluntary association may still be oriented toward broad societal values such as health, equality, or psychological well-being. But governmental pressures to keep costs down in the interests of not having to raise taxes or because of foreign economic competition are likely to redefine the very meaning of these values. Thus, a nonprofit hospital that implements a more-efficient accounting system may be more likely to receive government funding than one that actually contributes to the recuperation of its patients. In the process, keeping down the high cost of health care becomes defined as a societal goal in place of providing the best possible system of health care itself.

One significant consequence of the voluntary sector's subjugation by norms of bureaucratic and economic efficiency is the tendency for an increasing proportion of the people to retreat from these voluntary associations, just as they have retreated from the political realm, into the more private recesses of their lives (Sennett 1976; Bellah et al. 1985). Working for a nonprofit hospital is no better than working for a for-profit hospital. The activities of large, national bureaucracies in the voluntary sector are viewed much like the work of large corporations and large government agencies. They are cold and impersonal and, despite concerns about efficiency, are viewed as inefficient and cumbersome. In contrast, the places in which warmth and genuine caring abound are restricted to the private sphere. This does not mean individuals care only for themselves; it means the informal caring that takes place among friends and neighbors is increasingly separated from the more formal and public aspects of the voluntary sector.

There is of course a certain irony in all this. As the larger agencies that dominate the voluntary sector have turned to the government for support, they have inadvertently made a pact, as it were, with the devil. Their programs have benefited but their image has suffered, and with their loss of image, they are no longer regarded as bastions of caring and human kindness. They are simply other manifestations of cold rationality. Their souls have been traded for a mess of pottage. The values of intimacy, caring, and community that people in modern societies so much long for have retreated into the networks of informal association, such as family and kin relationships, circles of friends, self-help groups, religious fellowships, neighborhood associations, clubs, gatherings of hobbyists, and therapeutic support groups.

The dominant response to this line of criticism has, of course, been to say that the bureaucratized part of the voluntary sector at least gets the job done. If poverty and homelessness and disease threaten the very fabric of modern society, then surely it is more important to get the job done than to worry about intimacy and caring and community. Those, after all, should be relegated to the private realm rather than being a part of the public sphere.

Perhaps. But if the public sphere loses its human face, have we not lost something of exceptional value? It is little wonder that people disdain public rhetoric and prefer to spend their spare time with family and friends. What Tocqueville saw as the mediating role of voluntary associations (Gamwell 1984) has been lost. Instead of the local community organization that mediates between individual families and the wider society, we now have privatized individuals, on the one hand, and national nonprofit bureaucracies, on the other hand, that try to drum up support from an uninterested public through telethons and mass mailings.

What tempers this otherwise dismal picture is the fact that many local, small-scale voluntary associations continue to function. To be sure, many of these associations function only for the benefit of their own members. Bowling leagues and church suppers abound. To the eye of the social scientist, always

on the lookout for political payoffs, these local associations seem only to remove their members from participating in the vital public debates about large-
scale social issues. But such groups do not exhaust the range of informal voluntary associations that flourish in modern societies. Others take care of the
sick and the elderly, help people with addictions function more effectively,
and champion a wide variety of community causes. Many are linked in larger
federations that do in fact espouse political agendas. And many more facilitate
informal discussion of public issues.

ANOTHER LOOK AT THE VOLUNTARY SECTOR IN THE UNITED STATES

Although differences from country to country in the definition of voluntary
associations make cross-national comparisons difficult, it should be evident
from the foregoing chapters that the voluntary sector in the United States is
indeed one of the largest in the developed world (Oleck 1980; Kramer 1984).
Certainly this is the case in absolute terms: because of its size, economically
and demographically, in comparison with other advanced industrial democracies, the United States is able to pour more money and person-hours into the
work of voluntary associations than any other single society. Taking account
of these differences in size, the relative strength of the voluntary sector—in
comparison with the role played by government and business—is also quite
strong. Voluntarism is simply more valued, more a part of the culture, and
more important to the nation's way of addressing its priorities than it is in
many other societies.

The differences, however, should not be exaggerated. One of the stereotypes that the comparisons in this volume have, we hope, put to rest is the
view that the United States is simply in a league by itself with respect to voluntarism. The evidence on the United Kingdom and Israel shows that voluntarism is also terribly important in those societies. And even in societies like
Sweden and Germany, where a reputation of corporatism and centralized welfare has prevailed, the indications are that something at least similar to voluntary associations in the United States has a long history and has been encouraged in recent years by the state itself.

What is perhaps as distinctive about the United States as the actual services
provided by the voluntary sector is the *ideology* that surrounds voluntarism in
American society. We not only give time and money to voluntary associations
as a way of supplementing the work of government and business; we believe
strongly that voluntarism is the best way of doing things. We cherish the
traditions and values it stands for. We want it to be an autonomous sector. And
we view it as an alternative to the other main sectors of our society. In contrast
with France, for example, where voluntarism is often described as a second-
best way of doing things that the state should really be taking care of, Americans are likely to champion the voluntary sector as a way of keeping govern-

ment in its place. Unlike Sweden, where it is simply expected that voluntary associations will be orchestrated by the government, we feel nervous about too close an alliance between the nonprofit realm and government.

Some results from recent national surveys in the United States will help underscore the ideological convictions we attach to the voluntary sector. Ninety-two percent of a representative sample of the American public in one study, for example, agreed that "charities play a very significant role in our society." In the same study, 82 percent thought the need for charities was increasing (Hodgkinson 1988:61–62). Although people vary in the degree of confidence they are willing to place in any public institution, voluntary organizations also tend to receive more favorable reactions than most other sectors of American society. For example, 46 percent of the public said they had a great deal or a lot of confidence in "charities providing health or social services," compared with only 21 percent who said the same for business, 28 percent who said this about the United States Congress, and 22 percent who felt as much confidence in organized labor. At the other extreme, fewer than one person in twelve registered "very little" confidence in charities, compared with as many as one person in three for these other institutions (Hodgkinson 1988:60). When asked specifically about various ways to make America a better society, the public's faith in volunteer activities is particularly apparent. One person in two (47 percent) believed that "getting everyone who could to donate five hours a week to volunteer organizations" would help a lot, another 38 percent felt this would help a little, and only 14 percent believed it would not help. By comparison, the public had much less confidence in the ability of government programs to improve society. For example, only one person in five (21 percent) thought that "spending more money on government welfare programs" would help a lot, while 42 percent of the public thought it would not help at all. Faced directly with the comparison between voluntary organizations and government programs, moreover, 72 percent of the public said they agreed with the statement "Private charities are generally more effective than government programs" (Wuthnow 1991).[1]

Symptomatic of the faith most Americans place in the voluntary sector is the fact that many people not only look to it to provide services to the needy but also want it to play a larger role in shaping our nation's goals and values. Only one person in ten, for example, thinks the nonprofit sector has too much influence in shaping our goals and values, whereas one person in three thinks it has too little influence. In other words, those who would like to see nonprofit organizations exercising greater influence outnumber those who would like to see this influence curtailed by a ratio of three to one. By comparison, our views of the influence of politicians and business leaders are quite different.

[1] These figures and those in the next paragraph in the text are from a nationally representative survey of 2,110 adults that I conducted in 1989.

302 · Robert Wuthnow

Seven people in ten think politicians have too much influence; only one person in ten thinks they have too little influence. For business leaders, one person in two says they have too much influence, while one person in seven thinks they have too little.

From one perspective, then, the voluntary sector appears to play a unifying symbolic role within the public sphere in the United States. Its importance is something about which most of us agree. Indeed, to speak about its vitality is to speak about the limitations we feel are inherent within the state and the marketplace. For many Americans, the voluntary sector symbolizes personal freedom, individualism, and the capacity to choose and to make a difference as an individual, despite the growing role of large-scale institutions in our society. It also symbolizes the more communal ethic in our culture: camaraderie, warmth, intimacy, personal caring, as opposed to the more impersonal facade of big government or the utilitarian mentality of big business. At a deeper level, the voluntary sector also casts an aura of optimism and hope on the public sphere by conjuring up images of the good people we have known personally, or the public figures, like Mother Teresa or Martin Luther King, Jr., who have made compassion a public virtue (Wuthnow 1991).

What might be termed the mythic dimensions of the voluntary sector are thus of considerable significance to the public sphere in the United States. Voluntarism symbolizes the antithesis of impersonality, bureaucracy, materialism, utilitarianism, and many of the other dominant cultural trends we worry about in our society. And yet, as David Harrington Watt has emphasized in his chapter on the United States, these are also real trends to which the voluntary sector is increasingly subject. We may cherish heroic images of lowly volunteers who, like the Lone Ranger, ride into town and whip the bad guys. But an increasing share of the volunteer work that actually takes place in our society is carefully orchestrated by paid administrators, promoted with the help of Madison Avenue advertising agencies, and carried out by staffs of overburdened specialists and technicians. In this sense, the voluntary sector does not so much bring alternative values into the public sphere as it reinforces the values that are already there. The advertisements that tell us to support a soup kitchen because it will make us feel good, or the scandals we read about concerning priests and preachers in the public eye, simply reinforce the somewhat cynical vision we already have of the public sphere.

With its high level of overall involvement in religious organizations and a long tradition of infusing moral issues into the political realm, the United States has also been particularly subject to a polarization of the public sphere in recent years (Wuthnow 1988). The sources of this polarization are not entirely dissimilar from structural changes in other advanced industrial societies. The restructuring of the economy that has taken place since World War II has created a new elite of college-educated professionals, middle managers, and media elites, on the one hand, and a large underclass of unskilled service workers and semiskilled technicians, on the other hand. Owing much of their elevated social position to cultural skills, the former have become a vocal segment of the public sphere, often advancing claims for tolerance and expressive individualism at the expense of more traditional values. The latter have often been more narrowly constrained by economic interests, but have increasingly found spokespersons willing to advance a cultural perspective different from that of the more-established elite. The main result of this polarization has been an intense struggle within the religious sphere over such issues as biblical interpretation, gender roles, and sexual standards. During the 1980s this conflict also became politicized, as groups such as the Moral Majority and Christian Voice sought to influence the nation's political leaders on issues such as abortion and homosexuality. For the voluntary sector more broadly, this polarization has been evident in an increasing number of special-purpose groups—both religious and secular—concerned with questions of public ethics and morality. In this respect, the sectional, regional, and class interests that observers see dominating the public sphere in other societies are scarcely absent from the United States. The evidence that suggests this polarization is increasing—and perhaps even overshadowing the more traditional image of religious and cultural pluralism in some quarters—is nevertheless disturbing, especially in light of the observations that derive from the Italian case about the negative consequences of such polarization for the voluntary sector. In the short run, a dominant cleavage in the public sphere is likely to increase the number of special-purpose groups vying to make their voices heard. But should such divisions prevail over a longer period of time, the claims of these groups are likely to be focused increasingly on narrow political objectives, and in the process, particularistic claims of various constituencies may overshadow universalistic values—or, more likely, the values espoused by minority groups and by voluntary associations not aligned with either of the major factions will find their role in the public sphere diminished.

THE CHALLENGES THAT LIE AHEAD

Despite the historic differences that make the voluntary sector relatively more or relatively less important to the functioning of various societies, the larger forces to which all advanced industrial societies are subject seem likely to perpetuate the work of voluntary associations at some significant level. Within these societies themselves, economic development has not done much to reduce extreme disparities between the rich and the poor. Fiscal limitations have made central governing agencies reluctant to do as much as some would like them to do to solve the problems of homelessness, schooling and medical needs, the special requirements of an aging population, or the side effects of urban decay. If these domestic problems are not enough to warrant the continuing role of voluntary associations, the interdependence of the developed and the underdeveloped world adds vastly greater challenges.

To meet these challenges, increasing attention will have to be devoted by all concerned—government officials, business leaders, and the administrators of nonprofit associations alike—to questions of funding, solicitation, motivation, the identification of solvable needs and efficient solutions, and the coordination of complex efforts on a national and an international scale. Although legal distinctions will continue to separate the voluntary sector from other parts of society, it also seems likely that closer cooperation will be needed between this sector and government, on the one hand, and this sector and the for-profit sector, on the other hand. Especially where there are secular and religious voluntary associations that already have experience in addressing particular needs, government agencies will probably find it more efficient to channel resources to these associations than to start totally new initiatives under direct government supervision. Governments may also have some success in enlisting the assistance of the business community, especially in societies where social service is sufficiently valued to render public-relations payoffs for such assistance.

Perhaps an even greater challenge than the provision of services by the voluntary sector, however, is that of contributing to a dynamic and creative public sphere. What is already evident in most advanced industrial societies will probably continue: a distinct tension between the instrumental and the expressive dimensions of the voluntary sector. On one side, political and economic concerns will encourage voluntary associations to pursue specific objectives with criteria of efficiency and accountability at the forefront. On the other side, critics will raise their voices against the sacrifices required by such instrumentalities. The questions being raised about the quality of caring within the health professions—at the same time that politicians are pressing the health-care system for greater efficiency—is one example. In religion, a similar debate exists between those who advocate aggressive growth campaigns and more cost-efficiency in administering programs, and those who worry whether spirituality is somehow being sacrificed in the process. Much the same is evident in more politicized realms, where one side finds ways of winning at any cost, while the opposition tries to search for broader ways of thinking about basic societal values.

As long as democratic structures exist to protect and encourage this diversity of opinion, the greatest threat is unlikely to come from big government, big business, or even big nonprofit organizations that somehow find better ways of solving society's problems, and squeeze out their smaller competitors. The danger is not so much the totalitarianism from above that Tocqueville wrote about, but the other threat that was of equal concern to him: the retreat of individuals into their private lives. Should that happen, public discourse would indeed be left to the demagogues, the elites, the captains of industry, the specialists capable of manipulating the mass media.

In the end, the voluntary sector in advanced industrial societies still faces the same paradox that Tocqueville identified a century and a half ago.[2] To combat totalitarianism from above, voluntary associations must achieve some success in solving societal problems, even if this means large bureaucracies and instrumental programs. But to combat the withdrawal of individuals from public life itself, voluntary associations need to remain small, informal, personal, and diverse (Durkheim [1911] 1957). Only in this way can the individual be drawn into a community of others who reflect together about their fundamental values and engage the public sphere in discourse about those values.

---

[2] I am grateful to Jane Mansbridge for presenting a paper at the first symposium held at Princeton University in 1987 during the planning phase of our project—a paper that focused on Tocqueville's paradox.

References

Adams, James Luther. 1986. *Voluntary Associations*. Chicago: Exploration Press.

Alford, Robert R., and Roger Friedland. 1985. *Powers of Theory*. Cambridge: Cambridge University Press.

Anheier, Helmut K., and Wolfgang Seibel. 1990. *The Third Sector: Comparative Studies of Non-Profit Organizations*. Berlin: De Gruyter.

Bell, Daniel. 1973. *The Coming of Post-Industrial Society*. New York: Basic Books.

———. *The Cultural Contradictions of Capitalism*. New York: Basic Books.

Bellah, Robert N., et al. 1985. *Habits of the Heart: Individualism and Commitment in American Life*. Berkeley and Los Angeles: University of California Press.

Bendix, Reinhard. 1977. *Nation-Building and Citizenship*. Berkeley and Los Angeles: University of California Press.

———. 1978. *Kings or People: Power and the Mandate to Rule*. Berkeley and Los Angeles: University of California Press.

Billington, James H. 1980. *Fire in the Minds of Men: Origins of the Revolutionary Faith*. New York: Basic Books.

Boli, John. 1980. "Global Integration and the Universal Increase of State Dominance, 1910–1970." In *Studies of the Modern World-System*, edited by Albert Bergesen, pp. 77–108. New York: Academic Press.

Bremner, Robert. 1983. "Doing Good in the New World." In *America's Voluntary Spirit*, edited by Brian O'Connell, pp. 35–44. New York: Foundation Center.

Carnoy, Martin. 1984. *The State and Political Theory*. Princeton: Princeton University Press.

Christiano, Kevin J. 1987. *Religious Diversity and Social Change: American Cities, 1890–1906*. Cambridge: Cambridge University Press.

Durkheim, Emile. [1911] 1957. *Professional Ethics and Civic Morals*. London: Routledge and Kegan Paul.

Gamwell, Franklin I. 1984. *Beyond Preference: Liberal Theories of Independent Association*. Chicago: University of Chicago Press.

Gilbert, Neil. 1983. *Capitalism and the Welfare State: Dilemmas of Social Benevolence*. New Haven: Yale University Press.

Habermas, Jürgen. 1976. *Legitimation Crisis*. Boston: Beacon Press.

———. 1985. *The Theory of Communicative Action*. 2 vols. Boston: Beacon Press.

Hodgkinson, Virginia A. 1988. *Giving and Volunteering in the United States*. Washington, D.C.: Independent Sector.

James, Estelle. 1987. "The Nonprofit Sector in Comparative Perspective." In *The Nonprofit Sector: A Research Handbook*, edited by Walter W. Powell, pp. 397–415. New Haven: Yale University Press.

———, ed. 1989. *The Nonprofit Sector in International Perspective: Studies in Comparative Culture and Policy*. Oxford: Oxford University Press.

Kramer, Ralph M. 1984. *Voluntary Agencies in the Welfare State*. Berkeley and Los Angeles: University of California Press.

Lindblom, Charles E. 1977. *Politics and Markets: The World's Political-Economic Systems*. New York: Basic Books.

Lipset, Seymour Martin. 1968. "Party Systems and the Representation of Social Groups." In *State and Society*, edited by Reinhard Bendix, pp. 276–94. Berkeley and Los Angeles: University of California Press.

Luckmann, Thomas. 1967. *The Invisible Religion: The Transformation of Symbols in Industrial Society*. London: Macmillan.

Martin, David. 1978. *A General Theory of Secularization*. New York: Harper and Row.

Meyer, John W. 1980. "The World Polity and the Authority of the Nation-State." In *Studies of the Modern World-System*, edited by Albert Bergesen, pp. 109–38. New York: Academic Press.

Michels, Robert. [1915] 1962. *Political Parties: A Sociological Study of the Oligarchical Tendencies of Modern Democracy*. New York: Free Press.

Murray, Charles. 1984. *Losing Ground: American Social Policy, 1950–1980*. New York: Basic Books.

Odendahl, Teresa. 1987a. "Independent Foundations and Wealthy Donors: An Overview." In *America's Wealthy and the Future of Foundations*, edited by Teresa Odendahl, pp. 1–26. New York: Foundation Center.

———. 1987b. "Wealthy Donors and Their Charitable Attitudes." In *America's Wealthy and the Future of Foundations*, edited by Teresa Odendahl, pp. 223–46. New York: Foundation Center.

Oleck, Howard L. 1980. *Nonprofit Corporations, Organizations, and Associations*, 3d ed. Englewood Cliffs, N.J.: Prentice-Hall.

Phillips, Derek L. 1986. *Toward a Just Social Order*. Princeton: Princeton University Press.

Poggi, Gianfranco. 1978. *The Development of the Modern State: A Sociological Introduction*. Stanford: Stanford University Press.

Powell, Walter, ed. 1987. *The Nonprofit Sector: A Research Handbook*. New Haven: Yale University Press.

Salamon, Lester M. 1987. "Partners in Public Service: The Scope and Theory of Government-Nonprofit Relations." In *The Nonprofit Sector: A Research Handbook*, edited by Walter W. Powell, pp. 99–117. New Haven: Yale University Press.

Sennett, Richard. 1976. *The Fall of Public Man: On the Social Psychology of Capitalism*. New York: Vintage.

Tocqueville, Alexis de. [1835] 1945. *Democracy in America*. 2 vols. New York: Vintage.

Wald, Kenneth D. 1987. *Religion and Politics in the United States*. New York: St. Martin's Press.

Weisbrod, Burton A. 1988. *The Nonprofit Economy*. Cambridge, Mass.: Harvard University Press.

Wolch, Jennifer R. 1990. *The Shadow State: Government and Voluntary Sector in Transition*. New York: Foundation Center.

Wuthnow, Robert. 1988. *The Restructuring of American Religion: Society and Faith since World War II*. Princeton: Princeton University Press.

Wuthnow, Robert. 1989. *Communities of Discourse: Ideology and Social Structure in the Reformation, the Enlightenment, and European Socialism.* Cambridge, Mass.: Harvard University Press.

——. 1991. *Acts of Compassion: Caring for Others and Helping Ourselves.* Princeton: Princeton University Press.

Notes on Contributors

HELMUT K. ANHEIER is assistant professor of sociology at Rutgers University. He has also been a research fellow at Johns Hopkins University and for the United Nations in Austria. The author of numerous articles on nonprofit organizations, he is the editor (with Wolfgang Seibel) of *The Third Sector: Comparative Studies of Non-Profit Organizations*.

JAMES A. BECKFORD is professor of sociology at the University of Warwick in England. A prominent contributor to the literature on the sociology of religion, his most recent book is *Religion and Advanced Industrial Society*.

JOHN BOLI is a visiting scholar at Lund University in Sweden. He has also been a visiting professor in the Department of Sociology at Stanford University. He has written widely on the state in advanced industrial societies. His most recent book is *New Citizens for a New Society: The Institutional Origins of Mass Schooling in Sweden*.

HELEN HARDACRE is professor of Japanese studies at Griffith University in Australia. She formerly taught in the religion department at Princeton University. The author of numerous publications on Japan, her most recent books include *Shinto and the State: 1868–1988* and *Kurozumikyō and the New Religions of Japan*.

ELIEZER D. JAFFE is professor of social work at the Hebrew University of Jerusalem. He is a consultant to several foundations and has served on the social policy committees of three Israeli prime ministers. His recent books include *Unequal by Chance* and *Givers and Spenders: The Politics of Charity in Israel*.

MICHÈLE LAMONT is assistant professor of sociology at Princeton University. The author of numerous articles on the sociology of culture and sociological theory, she is currently completing a book entitled *Money, Manners, and Morals: Exploring Symbolic Boundaries in the French and American Upper-Middle-Class Cultures*.

TED PERLMUTTER is assistant professor of political science at New York University. Since completing his dissertation at Harvard University on intellectuals and urban protest in Turin, he has been writing a book on the development of party structures in Italy.

JACK VEUGELERS is currently a doctoral candidate in the department of sociology at Princeton University. He is writing a dissertation on the rise of right-wing political parties in France, Italy, and Great Britain since 1968.

DAVID HARRINGTON WATT is assistant professor of religion at Temple University. The author of *A Transforming Faith: Explorations in Twentieth-Century American Evangelicalism*, he is currently writing a book on religion and the public sphere.

ROBERT WUTHNOW is professor of sociology and director of the Center for the Study of American Religion at Princeton University. He is the author of a companion volume on voluntarism in the United States: *Acts of Compassion: Caring for Others and Helping Ourselves*. His recent books also include *Communities of Discourse: Ideology and Social Structure in the Reformation, the Enlightenment, and European Socialism* and *The Restructuring of American Religion*.

Index

accountability, 49, 298
Adams, James Luther, 275
adult education, 82, 106, 113
Aid to Families with Dependent Children (AFDC), 249
Amutot, 198
Ashkenazi Jews, 202, 211
associational system, 71. *See also* peak associations; voluntary sector
atheism, 134n
authority, of state, 6, 95

Bagdikian, Ben, 256
Balibar, Etienne, 149
banking system, of U.S., 252
Baptist church, 54, 114
Begin, Menachem, 192
Ben-Gurion, David, 192
Berger, Peter, 254–55
Berlinguer, Enrico, 164
Berrigan, Daniel, 265–66
Bismarck, Otto von, 69
Booth, Charles, 35
brain death, Japanese ethical problem of, 217, 231, 234–36, 239
British Mandate in Palestine, 190–91, 196
Buddhism, 226–27, 229, 233
Bundesverband der Deutschen Industrie (BDI), 77–78
bureaucracy: British social policy and, 59; dynamics of, 13; Italian, party dominance of, 159, 161; politicization of, in France, 127; voluntary sector norms and, 298–99. *See also* welfare state
business. *See* market sector
business associations, West German, 76–78

capitalism: American attitudes towards, 255–56; changing dynamics of, 13, 16–17; modernization and, 254–55; public sphere erosion and, 246–47; U.S. religion and, 268–69
Caritas, 84, 85, 86
Catholic Action, 169, 170

Catholic church: Bismarck and, 69; British social welfare and, 34; French public sphere and, 132–35; in Italy, 158–59, 163, 168–71, 177, 179, 181; in U.K., 54; in West Germany, 84, 85, 86, 71–72
charities: in British voluntary sector, 41, 46–52; in Sweden, 96. *See also* social welfare; voluntary sector
Charities Aid Foundation (CAF), 49–50
Charity Commission, 41, 47, 48, 49, 50
child welfare, Jewish philosophy of, 203
Chirac, Jacques, 145–46, 148, 149
Christadelphians, 54
Christian Democratic party (Italy), 161–65
Christian Democratic Union (CDU), 75n
Christian Science church, 54
Christian Social Union (CSU), 75n
church. *See* religion
Church of England, 53–54
Church of Scotland, 53
citizens' initiative movement, in West Germany, 87–88. *See also* social movements
class. *See* socioeconomic class
Clientelism of Italian welfare state, 173
collective bargaining, and Swedish labor court, 108–9
collective values, 22–24, 288–89; Habermas on, 14; Japanese religions and, 230; sectoral model of, 9; state roles regarding, 14. *See also* public discourse
common good, 14
communicative rationality, 14
Communione e Liberazione, 170
Communist party: in France, 131, 144–45; in Italy, 160, 161–64, 166–67, 177, 181; Japanese religious organizations and, 228; social movements and, 166–67; third sector and, 177, 181
community organization, in Britain, 38
community trusts, 50
comparative methodology: countries chosen for, 26–27; three-sector model and, 5–12, 25–26
constitution, Japanese, 223

anese tradition of, 227; Jewish philosophy of, 201–4
planning: French bureaucracy and, 127; West German economic, 79
Poland, 26n
political action: British charitable organizations and, 50, 51–52; British churches and, 55–56; German nonprofit organizations and, 75; in France, 137; Swedish pressure groups and, 104; Swedish trends and, 116–19; voluntary associations and, 3. *See also* interest groups; political parties; social movements
political parties: in Britain, 30, 37; elite control of, 159; expanding roles of, 16; in France, 126–28, 139, 144–46; in Israel, 192–93, 194, 204–6, 208; in Italy, 157, 159, 161–68, 181–82; in Japan, 222, 228–31; public sphere and, 126–28, 139, 157, 181–82; Swedish local governments and, 94, 103–6, 117; U.S. citizen participation in, 250–51; in West Germany, 74–76; youth organizations and, 83. *See also specific parties*
politicization, 16; French bureaucracy and, 127; French press and, 130; Israeli religion and, 204–6; public sphere and, 65–66; state expansion and, 291; Swedish churches, 115–16; Swedish local governments, 103–4. *See also* political parties
Poor Law, 34, 35
Postman, Neil, 256
poverty, British social welfare and, 35
Presbyterian church, 54
press: French public sphere and, 129–30; Swedish, political autonomy of, 118. *See also* media
pressure groups. *See* interest groups
private activities, 8–9, 39. *See also* market sector
privatization: of French education, 133n; in Israel, 195; of Italian health care, 179n; of religion, 261–64, 266, 297; in Sweden, 119–20; in Thatcher's Britain, 31; and U.S. voluntary sector, 279
Protestant churches, 54–55, 72
public activities, 8–10. *See also* voluntary sector
public discourse: American conceptions of, 244; in Britain, 30, 53–54, 59–60; defined, 22; diversity vs. quality of, 297–98; French

bureaucracy and, 127; French religious organizations and, 132; Habermas on, 14; Japanese problems, 227, 231–38; rationality in, 264–66; religion and, 53–54, 132, 227, 244, 266–67; Swedish *föreningar* and, 119; U.S. commodification of, 256; U.S. state expansion and, 251; voluntary sector and, 22–24. *See also* public sphere
public sphere: bourgeois roots of, 65, 67–68; British society and, 59–61; capitalist threat to, 246–47; church-state conflict and, 69; citizens' initiative movements, 87–88; counterpublic sphere vs., 66–67, 86–88; defined, 244; French case, Habermas contradicted, 125, 139, 151; French institutions and, 126–40; functional ambiguities and, 65–66; future challenges to, 304; Habermas on, 14; historical development of, 67–70, 289–90; intellectuals in, 65, 130–32, 139, 149, 296; Israeli problems of, 209–12; in Italy, 157–60, 181–82; in Japan, 217, 239; media in, 64–65; pluralist conception, 244–45; politicization of, 65–66; private interests in, 218; rationality in, 14; religious rationality and, 264–66; social movements and, 182, 295–96; state-sanctioned religion and, 58, 60; state/market expansion and, 15; Swedish voluntary sector and, 107–10; U.S. independence of, 276–78; U.S. voluntary sector and, 279–80; in West Germany, 64–70, 79–80. *See also* public discourse; *specific institutions*
Pyle, Kenneth, 224

racism, French problems with, 144, 146–47
Radical party (Italian), 167
radio, 128
rationality: in public discourse, 14, 264–66; religion and, 264–66
reading societies, 68
Reagan, Ronald, 250
Red Cross: in Japan, 228; in Sweden, 106; in West Germany, 85, 86
Reichley, A. James, 269
religion, 8, 19–22; common good and, 266–67; in France, 132–35, 148–49; free-church movement, 112; in Great Britain, 34–35, 52–58, 60; heterogeneity of, 257, 260–61, 267; in Israel, 200–206; in Italy, 158–59, 168–71, 179; in Japan, 220, 221–23, 225–31, 233, 239–40; political action and, 55–

tions of, 270–71; West German churches and, 71

technology: government support of, 15–16; media and, 130n

television: French public sphere and, 128; German organization of, 83; U.S. religion and, 262–64. *See also* media

temperance movements, 95, 112

tenants' unions, 110

Thatcher, Margaret, 58

Thatcher administration, 31–32, 53

Third Reich, 70

third sector. *See* voluntary sector

three-sector model: collective values in, 9; definitions of, 5–6, 8; generalizability problems and, 25–26; overlapping boundaries in, 10–12; public-private distinctions in, 8–10

Titmuss, R., 173

Tocqueville, Alexis de, 3–5, 12, 15, 245–47, 274–75

Touraine, Alain, 149

Tracy, David, 264

Unification Church, 50

unions: in France, 136–37; in Israel, 192; Swedish political parties and, 94; U.S., strength of, 253; in West Germany, 78–79, 86

unitary trade unions, 78–79

United Jewish appeal, 207

United Kingdom. *See* Great Britain

United Reform church, 54

United States: church-state relations in, 267–70; economic sector of, 251–56; government expansion in, 247–51; historiographical themes in, 243; religion in, 257–70; Tocqueville on, 3–5, 245–47, 274–75; voluntary sector in, 270–79, 300–303; welfare programs in, 249

universities, state control of, 82

urban movements, in Italy, 166

Vatican, 159, 169

voluntary sector: boundaries of, 10–12; bureaucratic norms vs., 298–99; class and participation in, 294; classical theory, 12–13; cross-national comparisons, 274–75; defined, 7, 38–39; in East Germany, 88–90; economic growth and, 291–94; future challenges, 303–5; historical development

of, 289–90; intellectuals and, 296; in Italy, 157, 177–81; Japanese religions and, 226–31; market expansion and, 14–19; market threats to, 17; in the Netherlands, 273–74; religion and, 19–22, 296–97; state competition with, 99–100; state creation of, 111–14, 199; state expansion and, 14–19, 291–92; subsidiarity principle, 72; support for democracy, 288; three-sector model, 5–12; welfare state threats to, 17

voluntary sector, in Britain: charities in, 41; churches and, 57–58; definitions, 38–39; funding, 42–46; membership data, 41–42; political activity of, 50, 51–52; registered charities in, 46–52; Thatcher administration and, 32; welfare state and, 37–52

voluntary sector, in France: antiracist groups, 146–47; legal status of, 143n; market forces and, 142; membership of, 127n; public sphere and, 135–40; state promotion of, 142–43n; state relations with, 140–42

voluntary sector, in Israel, 196–97; foreign Jewish support of, 206–8; future challenges, 212–13; non-Jewish religions, 208–9; state creation of, 199; state relationships with, 197–200

voluntary sector, in Sweden, 94–95; autonomy of, 118–20; terminology problems, 100–102. See also *föreningar*

voluntary sector, in U.S.: heterogeneity of, 271–72; historical significance, 275; independence of, 276–78; privatization of, 279; public attitudes, 300–303; public sphere and, 279–80; religious organizations and, 259–60; service economy and, 274; statistical analysis, 272–73; tax status definitions, 270–71; Tocqueville on, 3–5, 245–47, 274–75

voluntary sector, in West Germany: corporatism and, 77; development of, 67–71; public sphere and, 64, 79–82; state control of, 68. *See also* peak associations

voting behavior: in Italian subculture, 162–63; in Sweden, 104–5, 117; in U.S., 117n, 250

wealth, redistribution of, 253

Weber, Max, 12

Weimar republic, 69

Weitzman, M. S., 271

welfare pluralism, 36